Changing Lanes in China

Foreign Direct Investment, Local Governments,
and Auto Sector Development

This book addresses two of the most important trends in political economy during the last two decades – globalization and decentralization –
in the context of the world's most rapidly growing economic power.
The development of the Chinese auto industry is a classic example
of China's efforts to re-make inefficient and technologically backward
Chinese firms into powerful national champions, and it is an industry on
which many of the world's most powerful multinationals have staked
their future.

The intent of the book is to provide a better understanding of how
local political and economic institutions affect the ability of Chinese
state-owned firms to effectively utilize foreign direct investment, and
how these institutions shape the prospects for development. In a global
economy, the author argues, local governments are increasingly the
agents of industrial transformation at the level of the firm. Local institutions are durable over time, and they have important economic consequences. Through an analysis of five Chinese regions, the book seeks to
specify the opportunities and constraints that alternative institutional
structures create, how they change over time, and ultimately, how they
prepare Chinese firms for the challenge of global competition.

Eric Thun is the Peter Moores University Lecturer in Chinese Business
Studies at the Saïd Business School and a Fellow of Brasenose College
at Oxford University. He formerly served as Assistant Professor of
Politics and International Affairs at Princeton University's Woodrow
Wilson School. Dr. Thun has held grants from the International Motor
Vehicle Program, the Social Science Research Council, and the Mellon
Foundation. He holds a Ph.D. from Harvard University and was a post-
doctoral Fellow at the M.I.T. Industrial Performance Center.

Changing Lanes in China

Foreign Direct Investment, Local Governments, and Auto Sector Development

ERIC THUN

Saïd Business School and Brasenose College
University of Oxford

CAMBRIDGE
UNIVERSITY PRESS

CAMBRIDGE UNIVERSITY PRESS
Cambridge, New York, Melbourne, Madrid, Cape Town, Singapore, São Paulo

Cambridge University Press
40 West 20th Street, New York, NY 10011-4211, USA

www.cambridge.org
Information on this title: www.cambridge.org/9780521843829

© Eric Thun 2006

First published 2006

Printed in the United States of America

A catalog record for this publication is available from the British Library.

Library of Congress Cataloging in Publication Data

Thun, Eric, 1968–
Changing lanes in China : foreign direct investment, local government, and auto sector
development / Eric Thun.
p.   cm.
Includes bibliographical references and index.
ISBN-13: 987-0-521-84382-9 (hardback)
ISBN-10: 0-521-84382-0 (hardback)
1. Automobile industry and trade – Government policy – China.   2. Investments,
Foreign – Government policy – China.   3. Industrial policy – China.
4. Regional planning – China.   I. Title.
HD9710.C528T48   2006
332.67'30951 – dc22   2005030030

ISBN-13   978-0-521-84382-9 hardback
ISBN-10   0-521-84382-0 hardback

For my parents

Contents

List of Figures and Tables

FIGURES

TABLES

List of Abbreviations

BAIC:	Beijing Automobile Industry Corporation
BJ:	Beijing
BJC:	Beijing Jeep Company
CAD:	computer assisted design
CCP:	Chinese Communist Party
CKD:	Complete-knocked down (kit)
CNAIC:	China National Automotive Industry Corporation
DCAC:	Dongfeng Citroen Automobile Company
FAW:	First Auto Works (Changchun)
FAW-VW:	First Auto Works-Volkswagen
FDI:	foreign direct investment
GM:	General Motors
GPAC:	Guangzhou Peugeot Automobile Company
GZ:	Guangzhou
HK:	Hong Kong
JV:	joint venture
MIT:	Massachusetts Institute of Technology
MMI:	Ministry of Machinery Industry
MNC:	multinational corporation
MOFTEC:	Ministry of Foreign Trade and Economic Cooperation
MOU:	memorandum of understanding
R&D:	research and design
RMB:	renminbi (Chinese currency)
SAIC:	Shanghai Automobile Industry Corporation
SAW:	Second Auto Works (Wuhan)
SEC:	Shanghai Economic Commission

SGM: Shanghai General Motors
SLC: Santana Localization Community
SOE: state-owned enterprise
SPC: State Planning Commission
SVW: Shanghai Volkswagen
VW: Volkswagen
WTO: World Trade Organization

Preface

As my taxi made its way through the streets of Guangzhou, a city in southern China, the evidence of two decades of unprecedented economic growth flashed by the window. The darkened windows of a Mercedes-Benz sped by on the left; a family of four on a motorbike puttered along on the right; kamikaze taxi drivers veered in and out; a minibus trolled for passengers. My driver, at the wheel of a Chinese-made Volkswagen Jetta, was oblivious to the surrounding chaos, and as he maneuvered for position, I asked him how his car stacked up against the competition. "Better than most Chinese cars," he replied. "It's made in China, but under the hood it's almost all foreign." He proceeded to rank the quality of the cars on the road based on their percentage of foreign content: imports at the top, joint venture cars in the middle, pure local at the bottom. Although hardly a charitable assessment – the quality of domestically manufactured cars was improving rapidly – it was nevertheless truthful. It was 1997, my first year of field research for this project, and although China had come a long way from the lumbering two-ton "Liberation" truck in the breakdown lane, it was still a long way from the sleek Mercedes in the passing lane. The gap has been narrowing quickly.

In the eight years since I began the research for this book, the Chinese auto industry has gone from being something of a curiosity to being one of the most important automotive markets in the world. In the fall of 1996, when I arrived in China to begin field research, there were four multinational auto firms with major assembly joint ventures (and two more that were in the final stages of negotiations) and there was the usual talk about the future potential of the Chinese market. Most of this was just talk. Sales of passenger vehicles for China as a whole hovered around a half million cars, and more than three-quarters of these were institutional purchases (the government, state-owned firms, and state-owned taxi companies). Technology in the industry was decades behind global levels, but given the protection of high tariff barriers, firms had little incentive to introduce new technology or cut costs. A joint venture between Volkswagen and the Shanghai Auto Industry Corporation (SAIC) controlled more than half of the domestic market for sedans with a model that was based on technology from the 1970s.

In the span of eight years the Chinese auto industry has been transformed. A combination of massive investment on the part of both foreign and domestic firms, a rapidly growing private market, and accession to the WTO have created an intensely competitive market and rapidly increasing capabilities. Both the opportunities and the risks have been abundantly clear in recent years. In 2002 and 2003, annual growth rates were well in excess of 50%, and the primary concern among multinational auto firms was not being able to increase capacity fast enough to meet demand – not even the most optimistic of auto executives would have dared predict such astronomical growth rates. Only a year later, however, the domestic market cooled quickly, after the government began to tighten access to financing, and executives who had worried about missing the boat in China were suddenly concerned about overcapacity and an industry shake-out. Optimism about the long-term potential of the market remained, but it was becoming clear that the near-term survival of individual firms could not be taken for granted. In the spring of 2005, Volkswagen and General Motors were fighting for market share with more recently created Korean and Japanese joint ventures, and independent Chinese firms were rapidly increasing the production of models that often looked suspiciously similar to the models of their foreign competitors.

The road forward will certainly not be smooth – the fragilities of the Chinese economic system, continued dependence on foreign technology, and looming overcapacity in the auto sector insure this – but there can be little doubt as to whether China will have a large and powerful auto industry. Even at relatively modest annual growth rates of 10%, the Chinese market continues to provide far greater prospects for growth than the stagnant markets of the developed world. Chinese firms are also rapidly becoming major exporters of automotive components, and the export of cars has only just begun. What remains to be seen is whether the Chinese auto industry will be one that is controlled by the large multinationals – under the hood all foreign, as the taxi driver described it – or whether it will eventually lead to the development of large and powerful Chinese firms.

This book uses the dramatic context of the Chinese auto industry as a means of understanding the rise of China as an industrial power and its integration with the global economy. The book is first and foremost a work of comparative political economy. It seeks to understand how local institutional structures, and in particular local governments and business groups, shape and influence the process of industrial development and the prospects for Chinese firms. Although the framework is academic, the story of the Chinese auto sector is of interest to more general readers as well, and to an extent, it can be read independently. The theoretical context and argument are presented in general terms in Chapter 1, and a roadmap for the book as a whole is provided at the close of this chapter. Readers who are less interested in the theoretical argument of the book, but are interested in the rise and development of the Chinese auto industry, might prefer to skim through this first chapter, begin reading Chapter 2, which provides the context and background on auto sector development efforts, and then proceed to the case studies. The early development efforts of each region (prior to WTO accession) are the subject of Chapters 4, 5, and 6. Chapters 7 and 8 analyze the more recent challenges of technical upgrading and governance in the post-WTO era.

As might be expected, I was helped by many while researching and writing this book, although I alone remain responsible for the final product. Ironically, the people who were most critical to this process are those that I cannot thank – the factory managers and government officials in China who graciously took the time to explain to me the inner workings of the Chinese auto sector, but wished to remain anonymous due to the subject of the information they shared with me. It was always humbling to realize the extent to which the success of my research depended on the kindness and patience of others.

There are many, of course, whom I can thank. The book began its life as a dissertation in the Government Department of Harvard University, where I was fortunate to be under the guidance of Roderick Mac-Farquhar, Iain Johnston, and Dwight Perkins. Their comments, suggestions, and encouragement were invaluable at every stage of the project. While at Harvard I benefited from the advice and encouragement of many, but in addition to my advisors, I would particularly like to thank Lawrence Broz, Peter Hall, Yuen Foong Khong, Jean Oi, Elizabeth Perry, Ezra Vogel, and Yasheng Huang. At every step of the graduate school process I was surrounded by friends and fellow graduate students, who were always there to push, prod, encourage, and commiserate in both Cambridge and China. They include: Allen Carlson, Chen Bozhong, Fu Jun, Juliet Gainsborough, Mary Gallagher, Sini Gandhi, Jinxin Huang, Patrick Joyce, Andy Kennedy, Liang Jie, Liang Jing, Lü Naicheng, Ben Read, Elizabeth Remick, Adam Segal, Ed Steinfeld, Lily Tsai, Kellee Tsai, Alan Tung, and Yang Danhe. I am very much in their debt. Grants from the Mellon Foundation, the Social Science Research Council, and the International Motor Vehicle Program provided critical financial support during this period.

Although my tenure as postdoctoral Fellow at the Industrial Performance Center (IPC) at M.I.T. was relatively brief, the members of the IPC research teach had a profound influence on the way I viewed the process of globalization. The IPC also introduced me to the pleasure of interdisciplinary team-based research. I am particularly indebted to Suzanne Berger for her advice and comments on the manuscript.

The final stage of this project was done at Princeton University, where I was blessed with another set of wonderful friends and colleagues. For reading and commenting on different parts of the manuscript, I would particularly like to thank Nancy Bermeo, Eun Kyong Choi, Kent Eaton, Jeff Herbst, Bevan Jones, Atul Kohli, Evan Lieberman, Illan Nam, Kate McNamara, Lynn White, and Robert Willig. Rita Alpaugh provided assistance of every sort, and invariably did so with good humor and efficiency. I am also grateful to the Center of International Studies (now the Princeton Institute for International and Regional Studies), the Woodrow Wilson School, and the Class of 1934 Preceptorship for financial support during the final rounds of research and revisions.

At Cambridge University Press, I am most appreciative of Mary Child's initial interest in this project and the help of Scott Parris in bringing it to fruition. Scott proved to be a gracious and capable editor. Maggie Meitzler at TechBooks skillfully shepherded the book through the production process and patiently dealt with my many requests. I also greatly appreciated the detailed comments and suggestions of Greg Noble, John Ravenhill, and the anonymous readers solicited by Cambridge University Press.

Portions of Chapter 2 are based on my article "Industrial Policy, Chinese-Style: FDI, Regulation, and Dreams of National Champions in the Auto Sector," in *Journal of East Asian Studies*, vol. 4, no. 3, September–December 2004 (copyright 2004 by the East Asia Institute). These parts are used with permission of Lynne Rienner Publishers.

Finally, I would like to thank my family for their love and support during what surely must have seemed to be an endless process. I was fortunate to have my brother, Chris, living close by at several different stages of the project; my sister, Kirsten, and the entire Dunn family provided a welcome refuge in Vermont on many occasions. My wife, Jennie, has endured my lengthy absences, while I was in both Princeton and China, with little complaint and with unfailing support, and I could not be more grateful for all the happiness that she has brought to my life.

I dedicate this book to my parents. At every stage of my education they provided encouragement and support (even when there was good reason to be skeptical), and from very early on, they demonstrated the importance of asking questions and seeking answers.

Eric Thun
Princeton, New Jersey

PART I

INTRODUCTION

ONE

Local Governments, Foreign Direct Investment, and Industrial Development

The challenge for Chinese leaders during the first two decades of reform and development – much like in Japan in the 1960s or Korea in the 1970s – was to choose a development path that would lead to the creation of competitive industries. Like its neighbors in previous decades, China faced the classic problems of late development. Rather than accept the division of labor dictated by comparative advantage, China sought to develop industrial sectors that would create a "multidimensional conspiracy"[1] in favor of development: sectors and firms that would foster entrepreneurial activity and create positive spillovers in the economy as a whole. For reasons that had as much to do with national security and pride as economics, China's leaders were not content to build yet another workshop for the developed world, manufacturing whatever products required cheap labor and low skill levels. They wanted to fly airplanes made in Shanghai, use computers built in Beijing, and drive automobiles manufactured in Guangzhou. China was a poor country at the beginning of the reform era, but it was not lacking in ambition.

Although the ability of China to realize these ambitions rested on many factors, none was more important than its capacity to effectively utilize foreign direct investment (FDI) as a means of developing its own industrial base. By definition, a "late" developing nation confronts the challenge of creating strong and independent firms in a context of intense competition from the industrialized world. However, as Alexander Gerschenkron pointed out in the 1960s, there are also distinct economic advantages to being a late developing country. Industrialization has the potential to be

---

[1] The term is Albert Hirschman's, cited in Evans (1995: 7).

more rapid when a society, rather than moving forward through a tedious process of trial and error, can borrow the most recent technology and techniques from more advanced nations.[2] In some cases, it may even be possible to jump past established firms that are burdened with outdated technology and ideas. The challenge is to maximize the advantages of "backwardness" by drawing on the knowledge, technology, and capital that is available in advanced industrial economies, while taking care to prevent firms in nascent industries from being either inundated or co-opted by the more established foreign competitors.

China's neighbors excelled at this process of leapfrogging forward in the development process. Indeed, the success of Japan, Korea, and Taiwan in managing the industrialization process led to the rise of a new development paradigm. Rather than being condemned to positions of dependency in the global economic system due to structural factors beyond their control, some observers of rapid growth in East Asia concluded, states could control their own destiny.[3] Autonomous and well-trained state officials could facilitate the accumulation of capital, carefully control interaction with the global economy, and through a process of selective intervention, promote the development of sectors that were deemed to be of strategic importance. Although this account of rapid economic growth was certainly not without its critics,[4] the "developmental" state model was extremely influential, particularly among states that hoped to emulate the rapid success of the East Asian miracle. China was no exception, and there were many early indications that Chinese policymakers sought to emulate the example of its neighbors: from plans for "pillar industries" beginning in the mid-1980s to formal industrial policies in the mid-1990s.

The international context within which China was confronting the challenges of economic development, however, was very different from that faced by its neighbors in the 1950s and 1960s. The Cold War provided an unusually benign context within which American allies could focus on economic development. As part of its effort to contain the Soviet Union, the United States donated extensive foreign aid to its allies in East Asia, unilaterally opened its markets to their goods, and embraced

---

[2] Gerschenkron (1966).

[3] On the "developmental state" in East Asia, see Johnson (1982), Amsden (1989), Wade (1990), Woo-Cumings (1999). These views were subject to considerable revision in the aftermath of the Asian financial crisis. See Pempel (1999), Haggard (2000), Prakash and Hart (2000). The problem of institutional change in East Asia is explored at greater length in Chapter 9.

[4] See, for instance, Saxonhouse (1983), World Bank (1993), Krugman (1994).

them under its security umbrella. The rapid rise of Japan, Korea, and Taiwan, far from being perceived by the United States as a threat to its economic supremacy, was the explicit objective of U.S. strategy in the decades following World War II. In the current era of the World Trade Organization (WTO), developing countries are granted concessions, but they are carefully limited. In the case of China, the United States was not willing to grant even the normal concessions, due to the demographic and economic size of the country, and in some areas, Chinese obligations actually exceeded WTO standards.[5]

In addition to the altered international context, the Chinese were integrating into a global economy that had changed tremendously in the decades since Japan, Korea, and Taiwan had begun the development process. Accession to the WTO represented not only a dramatic change in the formal rules of the game, but also recognition on the part of (at least) some Chinese leaders that the very nature of the game itself was changing. Although the globalization of manufacturing in itself was nothing new – multinational firms have been relocating manufacturing facilities to the developing world for centuries – what was new was the degree to which production chains had become globalized. Rapid advances in transportation and telecommunications were making it possible to divide production chains, and firms were increasingly outsourcing components based on comparative advantage rather than geographic convenience.[6] The result was a bifurcation of the manufacturing process in some sectors. The research and design of technology-intensive products such as computers, cars, and planes continued to be performed in relatively few locations, as did the final assembly in some cases, but for components that did not require co-location with an assembler or other major suppliers, sourcing could be done from wherever costs were lowest. Improvements in transportation and communications technology, along with an improved ability to codify complex information through digitization, increased the ability of multinational companies to widely disperse the production of components even when design and development remained geographically concentrated. Boeing, for example, continued to design and manufacture planes in Seattle, but outsourced parts and components from more than 70 countries.[7] Not joining the WTO would both prevent China from fully participating in global production networks – and the country clearly had

---

[5] Lardy (2002: 2 and 10).
[6] For work on international production networks, see Borrus, Ernst, and Haggard (2000).
[7] Lardy (2002: 21). Even design work is beginning to be more widely dispersed as firms seek to take advantage of inexpensive and high quality engineering talent in countries such as India and China.

a great deal to gain – and make it more difficult for Chinese firms to develop the competitive ability that would allow them to carve out high-value–added pieces of such networks. For reasons of prestige and power, Chinese leaders did not want domestic companies to be temporary cogs in production networks controlled by foreigners.

By the late 1990s, according to Joseph Fewsmith, "China's leadership had determined that globalization was unstoppable and that China could either join the trend or be left behind."[8] WTO accession, it was hoped, would provide the final pressure necessary to restructure the state-owned sector and create a new breed of internationally competitive Chinese firms. As Premier Zhu Rongji explained at a joint Washington press conference with President Clinton in April 1999, "The competition arising [from WTO membership] will also promote a more rapid and more healthy development of China's national economy."[9] And there was certainly reason for optimism. Since the start of the reform period in 1978, the gross domestic product of China had expanded at an average of 9% a year and foreign trade had grown at an average of 15% a year. After 25 years of reform, China's trade surplus with the United States was twice that of Japan's, it was attracting over $1 billion of FDI every week (on average), and depending on the measure, it was either the second largest economy in the world (using purchasing power parity) or the sixth (using market prices).[10] Integration with the global economy had transformed the Chinese economy, and it was a force to be reckoned with. The gradual decline of tariff barriers would create new challenges, but these challenges would, in the long run, only increase the global competitiveness of Chinese firms.

The less sanguine view, however, and one that was not uncommon in Beijing in the late 1990s, was that WTO accession represented the final capitulation. Zhu Rongji's compromises in Washington were seen as the "new 21 demands selling out the country" – a reference to Japan's infamous attempt to colonize China in 1915.[11] Chinese firms that had benefited from high tariff walls, despite two decades of reform and development, would not be able to meet the challenge of international

---

[8] Fewsmith (2001: 206).

[9] "Joint Press Conference of the President and Premier Zhu Rongji of the People's Republic of China," Office of the Press Secretary, The White House, April 8, 1999. Accessed from www.usconsulate.org.hk/uscn/wh/1999/0408b.htm

[10] Figures are from "Behind the mask: A survey of business in China," *The Economist*, March 20, 2004, p. 3.

[11] Fewsmith (2001: 211).

competition. Skeptics in China and abroad pointed not only to the profound weaknesses in the Chinese economy, such as the crippling burden of non-performing loans in the financial sector and the rapidly growing income inequalities between coastal regions and the interior, but the extent of Chinese dependence on foreign firms.[12] While it was true that the country's exports were rising rapidly, as much as 50% of these exports were from foreign-invested firms. As Yasheng Huang argued in his provocatively titled book, *Selling China*, even prior to China's accession to the WTO accession, an institutional bias against truly private firms (a result of favoritism toward state-owned enterprises and economic fragmentation) created an unnecessary dependence on foreign firms.[13] Further lowering the restrictions on foreign investment, one might reasonably expect, would only increase the dominance of foreign firms in the Chinese industrial landscape.

This book seeks to understand how two decades of reform, development, and foreign investment have prepared state-owned Chinese auto firms for the challenge of global integration. Why the auto industry? First, the auto industry exemplifies the aspirations of Chinese leaders to cultivate powerful new business groups (*jituan gongsi* or *jituan qiye*) that can represent the country in the global economy. This effort began in the 1980s, long before similar efforts in other industries, when the automotive sector was chosen as a "pillar" industry and became a primary target of government industrial policy. The industry is not one in which government officials simply threw up their hands and hoped for the best. There has been a conscious effort to shape development in the sector, and the industry has emerged as one of the key drivers of growth in China. Sales of passenger vehicles increased nearly five-fold between 1998 and 2004, from 484,000 cars to 2.3 million. Foreign firms, lured by projections that the Chinese auto market would be the second largest in the world by 2015, invested approximately $12 billion in China between 1994 and 2003.[14] How has a country that is moving away from state planning – the core of the reform process – used the state to promote development in a critical industry?

Second, foreign investment has been central to auto sector development in China. It is the only industry in which each of the core projects is a

---

[12] Chang (2001); Wolf et al. (2003).

[13] Huang (2003).

[14] Automotive News (2004: 3). By the beginning of 2004, foreign firms had already committed to investing an additional $10 billion by 2007. Sales volume for 2004 is from "China's auto output and sales exceed 5 million in 2004," *Asia Pulse*, January 18, 2005.

joint venture (JV) with a foreign firm, and as such is emblematic of China's efforts to leverage foreign firm's access to the domestic marketplace for their technology and managerial skills. As explained later in this chapter, the prevalence of joint ventures, and the variation in both regional strategies and outcomes, makes it possible to choose multiple cases within a single industry. There are auto business groups in China that are healthy, if still dependent on foreign technology, but are indeed being spurred on by increased foreign competition. There are also business groups that have essentially collapsed in the face of increased competition, and have sold out to foreign firms. When the overall objectives have been the same – using foreign joint ventures as a catalyst for local development – why have results varied so widely?

Third, the development challenges within the auto sector are appropriate. At the local level, the supply network is critical to success. My interest is not in the success of individual firms, but in networks of firms, and the auto industry is unusual in the intensity of backward linkages – it is not uncommon for 60% of the value of a car to be purchased from outside suppliers. While success at a single assembly plant is heavily reliant on individual firms (both the Chinese and foreign partner), the successful development of a regional supply network requires the dissemination of technology, capital, and management skills to hundreds of firms. At the global level, the industry is an ideal example of the new development challenges that are posed by globalization. Multinational firms no longer relocate to a developing country and recreate a supply network with local firms, as was the norm when China began the process of reform and development in the 1980s. It has become a truly global industry characterized increasingly by common global platforms, rapidly changing technology, and consolidation in increasingly fewer firms. Will Chinese firms be able to carve out their own niche on this global stage?

The Argument in Brief

The core argument of the book revolves around local institutions in China, both political and economic, and how they shape industrial development and integration into the global economy. The starting premise is that firms are at the heart of the industrial development process. Many actors are involved in the process, but at some level, all of them – international institutions, governments, unions, or industry associations – revolve around individual firms, and their ability to compete in the global marketplace.[15] The development needs of firms vary systematically by sector, however. All firms must deal with the challenges of human capital (training workers, bargaining with labor), access to financial capital and governance of its utilization, and inter-firm relations (relationships with suppliers of both inputs and technology, customers, and other members of a supply network), but the specific nature of these challenges will vary by sector.[16] The ability of firms within a sector to meet these needs is central to the process of industrial development, and success is fundamentally shaped by the context of institutions and organizations in which the firms operate. There are three central points.

First, local governments are increasingly the agents of industrial transformation at the level of the firm. The extent to which this is true will vary by country, but in an era in which decentralization has been the dominant political and economic trend, it is often local political and economic institutions that must help firms meet their day-to-day development needs, and this is particularly true in the case of China. It is, of course, not unusual or new to focus on the developmental role of local governments. It is less common to focus on systematic patterns of institutional *differences* between localities.[17] There is no single dominant approach to development at the local level, whether it be market-led growth or local state corporatism, but rather multiple patterns. By focusing on the internal structure of local bureaucracies and economic organizations it is possible to characterize distinct institutional patterns – even in a country that was for decades centrally planned – and these differences have important economic consequences. Because different institutional arrangements vary in their ability to meet the development needs of different industrial sectors, it becomes possible to speak of a locality's comparative institutional advantage. There is no one-size-fits-all development approach, but a mosaic of local patterns within the national framework.

Second, the institutional differences that distinguish localities, while not unchanging, are durable over time. This is particularly important in

---

[15] On theories of business in political economy, see Stephan Haggard, Sylvia Maxfield, and Ben Ross Schneider, "Theories of Business and Business-State Relations," in Maxfield and Schneider (1997).

[16] This characterization of a firm-centered view of development follows Hall and Soskice, although they characterize firm needs somewhat differently. Hall and Soskice (2001: 6–7).

[17] I will at times interchange the term "region" for "locality," and I use both terms to refer to a subnational jurisdiction of either the provincial or municipal (city) level.

the case of industrial development because the needs of industrial sectors tend to change quite rapidly. Not only do industries evolve as they grow and mature, but the external context of development can change rapidly (e.g., moving from a closed to open economy). An institutional pattern that is conducive to the development of a sector in one stage of growth might not be appropriate in the next stage, and it is difficult to transform institutions rapidly enough to meet evolving economic needs. This is especially true when economic and political institutions are closely intertwined because the latter will respond to a broad range of noneconomic incentives. As a result, it is both unrealistic to expect states to be able to easily imitate more successful development "models" and, in that success might be short-lived, probably unwise. It is more important to understand the historical roots of a particular set of local institutions, and the opportunities and constraints they create; analysis must be across time as well as space.

Third, while localities are the basic building block of industrial development, they must fit into the broader framework of national policies. Local states are not nation-states. The central government creates the framework of rules within which local governments operate (e.g., taxation policy, environmental policy, corporate law, etc.) and the form of interaction with the global economy (e.g., tariff policy, participation in international organizations, etc.). Throughout the reform period in China, local governments have exploited the inattention of the center to experiment with new policy approaches, but this does not negate the fact that the stamp of the central government is inevitably sought as these experiments develop and expand. The dynamics of local-center relations are important in the present and in the past. In the past, the relationship with the center is a key determinant of the structure of local institutions. In the present, the national economic framework – for instance, the degree of openness to international competition – creates the opportunities and constraints within which local states must operate, and a local policy that is highly effective in one national framework will not necessarily be as effective in another. As a result, analysis must be multi-tiered, and examine the interaction of the central and local state.

The remainder of this chapter develops each of these central points. The first section explains how decentralization has created new opportunities for local states. The second section argues that the political and economic structures of local states will vary, and this variation gives each an institutional comparative advantage with respect to different economic sectors. The third section explains how analysis of the local state fits into a broader national and international framework. The final section provides a roadmap for the book as a whole.

I. THE NATION-STATE: PRESSURED FROM ABOVE AND BELOW

The relationship between institutions and economic performance has always been central to the study of comparative political economy, of course, but traditionally the unit of analysis has been the nation-state.[18] Economic outcomes are explained by analyzing the relationship between domestic state institutions, patterns of industrial policy, and social actors.[19] Successive generations of this approach have analyzed how national institutional structures have responded to the challenges of economic adjustment in the advanced capitalist world. Early variants of this approach focused on the varied capacity of "strong" and "weak" states to carry out industrial intervention[20]; later approaches used the concept of neo-corporatism to explain the ability of governments to forge cooperative relationships with producer groups in an open economy.[21] Recently, the focus has been on the varieties of capitalism in the developed world, and whether the increasing integration of the global economy will ultimately lead to the convergence of different national models.[22] As Peter Hall and David Soskice write in the introduction to their work on varieties of capitalism, "comparative political economy revolves around the conceptual frameworks used to understand institutional variation across nations." In continuing in this tradition, they make the case that "the most important institutional structures – notably systems of labor market regulation, of education and training, and of corporate governance – depend on the preserve of regulatory regimes that are the preserve of the nation-state."[23]

Studies of late-development and transitional economies have generally followed from this traditional focus on the nation-state in that successful economic development is thought to be contingent upon getting national political and economic institutions right. Lessons are drawn from

---

[18] On the problem of "whole nation bias" in political science, see Rokkan (1970: Chapter 2); Snyder (2001). This juxtaposition of a traditional national approach to political economy and a local approach builds on Segal and Thun (2001: 558–560).
[19] The classic work in this tradition is Shonfield (1965).
[20] See Katzenstein (1978); Zysman (1984).
[21] See Schmitter and Lehbruch (1979); Berger (1981); Katzenstein (1985).
[22] See Berger and Dore (1996); Hall and Soskice (2001).
[23] Hall and Soskice (2001: 1 and 4).

analyzing the national institutional arrangements of successful cases of development, and prescriptions are drawn for less successful cases. Advocates of the developmental state approach, for instance, argue that an activist government and strong institutions were responsible for rapid growth in countries such as Japan, Korea, and Taiwan. Although the details of each case varied, the state was able to direct capital into targeted sectors, and large multidivisional enterprises structured the economy and served as the agent of expansion and development – these are the nation-states that sometimes gain an Inc after their name.[24] Those from a more neoclassical tradition, of course, make the opposite argument. Success was the result not of an activist government, but a government that allowed markets to operate freely. Protection was minimized, exports were promoted, and a stable macroeconomic environment was maintained.[25] The approaches clearly differ (and often bitterly) over what the "right" policies are, but they agree that the study of economic development should be focused on the national level.

Although this traditional focus on the nation-state as the primary unit of analysis in political economy endures, there is increasing recognition that the influence of national governments is coming under increasing pressure from both above and below.[26] As Anwar Shah and Theresa Thompson of the World Bank comment, "it is increasingly apparent that nation-states are too small to tackle large things in life and too large to address small things."[27]

From above, the question involves the extent to which globalization impinges upon the autonomy of national governments. The extreme view is that the liberalization of trade, finance, and investment across national borders has dramatically decreased the capacity of national governments to adhere to national "models" of social and economic relationships. Global markets, competition for trade and investment, and technological diffusion in a "borderless world" serve as a "golden straitjacket" on national governments that, if it were not for the demands of the global economy, might prefer to pursue more distinctive paths.[28] Others, of

---

[24] For the most prominent examples of this approach, see Johnson (1982), Amsden (1989), Wade (1990). These accounts are not without their critics. The conventional depiction of Japan as a developmental state, for instance, is challenged in the work of Kent Calder (1993).

[25] World Bank (1993) is a fairly moderate example of this viewpoint.

[26] Doner and Hershberg (1999: 48).

[27] Shah and Thompson (2002: 5).

[28] Ohmae (1990) refers to the "borderless world"; Friedman (1999) the "golden straitjacket."

course, argue that the claims of a borderless world are vastly overstated, and that national systems of economic activity remain intact.[29] While the resilience of national institutions might be debated, few would question that international constraints have increased. National governments that do not consider international capital markets and foreign investors before making policy changes, do so at their own peril. National governments that consistently flout the influence of supranational institutions – whether in the form of the European Community, the World Trade Organization, the World Bank, or the International Monetary Fund – risk finding themselves on the outside of the world trading system. Indeed it is because national governments have had no choice but to relinquish control over a wide range of issues to supranational institutions, that there have been cries of a democratic deficit; citizens find that important issues that were once controlled by their elected governments are now controlled by supranational institutions over which they have only an indirect influence at best.[30]

China is no exception to this global trend. While the national government loses no opportunity to reiterate its very traditional conception of national sovereignty,[31] it nevertheless continues to commit itself to a development path that is dependent on trade and foreign investment, and submit itself to the authority of ever more supranational institutions. The most dramatic manifestation of this trend was membership in the WTO, a commitment that entailed not only opening Chinese markets to foreign competition, but also broad changes in the most sensitive of areas of the domestic economy, including financial services, basic telecommunications services, and information technology. On a wide variety of economic issues (e.g., intellectual property rights), Chinese law is being shaped not according to a consensus among national leaders, but according to the need to be in accordance with WTO standards. One year after joining the WTO, the national government had amended 2,300 laws and regulations and abolished 830 in an effort to comply with the accession agreement.[32] While formal changes do not guarantee actual implementation, they are an indication of the extent to which the formation of national policy is influenced by supranational institutions.

From below, the traditional focus on the nation-state is being challenged for at least two reasons. First, although the extent of heterogeneity

---

[29] Hirst and Thompson (1996); Garrett (1998).
[30] On the democratic deficit, see Thompson (1999) and Berman and McNamara (1999).
[31] On Chinese conceptions of sovereignty, see Carlson (2000).
[32] "China's WTO Implementation Efforts," *China Business Review*, vol. 29, no. 4, July–August 2002.

may vary, national economic systems are in fact composed of disparate regional economies. Richard Locke, for instance, makes the case for viewing the Italian economy not as "a coherent national system but rather as an incoherent composite of diverse subnational patterns that coexist (often uneasily) within the same national territory."[33] By focusing on how divergent sociopolitical networks – the patterns of associationalism, intergroup relations, political representation, and economic governance – create different constraints and resources for economic actors, Locke argues, it is possible to understand how industrial decline and entrepreneurial dynamism coexist in the same national economy. That these differences exist should not be surprising, writes Gary Herrigel with respect to Germany, in that "different groups of industrial actors...will invariably conceptualize, organize, and enact industrial activity in ways that reflect their own pasts...."[34] Studies that focus either broadly on national macroeconomic planning, or narrowly at the level of the firm, miss the heterogeneity of regional development efforts.

Second, there is good reason to believe that the importance of subnational regions is increasing around the world; decentralization has been one of the dominant economic and political trends of the last two decades.[35] This move toward decentralization, Richard Snyder argues, started in advanced industrial nations in which free-market policy reforms were accompanied by a "devolution revolution" that transferred authority and resources from central to local governments, and the revolution was transferred to the developing world by the World Bank and development NGOs under the guise of fiscal federalism.[36] In Latin America, the wave of neoliberal reforms in the 1980s and 1990s gave rise to multiple patterns of decentralization; in the former Soviet Union, the move away from central planning created new roles for local actors.[37] Between 1986 and 2001, the World Bank had programs in support of decentralization in 74 countries.[38] Decentralization, it was believed, improved policy making not only because local officials had better information on local problems

---

[33] Locke (1995: x).

[34] Herrigel (1996: 26).

[35] Decentralization can be defined as the process of devolving political, fiscal, and administrative powers to subnational units of government. Burki, Perry, and Dillinger (1999).

[36] Snyder (2001: 93).

[37] On differing patterns of decentralization in Latin America, see Willis, Garman, and Haggard (1999); on new roles for local actors in Russia, see Stoner-Weiss (1997); on the evolving center-local fiscal relationships in Russia, see Treisman (1996).

[38] Shah and Thompson (2002).

and preferences, but also because they were more directly affected by the negative consequences of failed policies.[39] When decentralizing reforms are enacted, of course, the capacity of the central government to coordinate economic activity decreases, and governance of the economy becomes increasingly multi-tiered. While the degree of decentralization varies, it is the general trend for many states.[40]

China has been at the fore of the movement toward decentralization; decentralization has been the central feature of the reform process.[41] The decision-making authority of local governments and enterprises has increased to an unprecedented degree, and this expanded autonomy has been complemented by increased incentives.[42] Under the policy of fiscal decentralization, begun in 1980, the fiscal responsibilities of each province were formalized in a contract signed with the center; revenues above this amount could be retained at the local level.[43] This system was duplicated (albeit with great variation) at each level: between provinces and prefectures, prefectures and counties, and between counties and townships.[44] The result was that localities had great incentives to promote local development, sometimes by implementing a local industrial policy that ignored national objectives, but maximized local revenue.[45] Even on issues officially controlled by the center, a local government's interpretation and/or the degree of compliance to the dictates of the

---

[39] For a good review and evaluation of the decentralization and fiscal federalism literature, see Rodden and Wibbels (2002). In 2001, there were 24 federal countries (with 25.4% of the world's population) and 20 decentralized unitary countries (with 35% of the world's population), Shah and Thompson (2002: 1).

[40] Fiscal decentralization generally involves three components: autonomy in revenue raising, autonomy in expenditures, and autonomy in borrowing privileges. Shah and Thompson (2002) detail the range of variation across countries.

[41] William Skinner pointed out the importance of regional economic variation in China in the 1960s. See G. W. Skinner, "Marketing and Social Structure in China," *Journal of Asian Studies*, Nov. 1964, Feb. 1965, May 1965. In more recent work, see Remick (2002), Tsai (2002), Segal (2003).

[42] See Fu (1992: 72–76). Decentralization is not a new concept in China, see Donnithorne (1972), but as Fu points out, during the Maoist periods of decentralization the localities were still expected to implement the decisions of the center; under Deng this was no longer the case. As I will explain, decentralization is also a concept central to the work of Montinola, Qian, and Weingast (1995).

[43] Shirk (1993: 149). See also Oksenberg and Tong (1991); and Tong (1989).

[44] Oi (1992: 103).

[45] The degree of autonomy varied both regionally (some cities had more autonomy than others) and over time (the central government would periodically reassert control). On varying degrees of autonomy, see Kleinberg (1990: 183); for the cyclical nature of the Beijing's policy, see Howell (1993).

central government were often the more important determinant of actual policy.[46] As Christine Wong, among others, has argued, the reform process increased local control over key means of influencing economic activity – allocation of workers and materials, appointment of managers, access to investment finance,[47] even the formulation of social welfare policies – and in key measures of fiscal decentralization, China was consistently among the most decentralized.[48]

It is generally assumed, of course, that decentralization is a good thing.[49] This is partly because political decentralization is associated with a deepening of democracy and increased political stability.[50] The devolution of political power away from a centralized state creates the opportunity for opposition parties to be incorporated into the political process. Even in cases that do not involve democratization, however, decentralization is believed to increase the quality and flexibility of government policy. Quality improves because local officials are thought to be more aware of local needs, better situated to respond to these needs, and more accountable to local constituents for the results.[51] Flexibility improves because decentralization creates the opportunity for local governments to experiment with a variety of economic approaches to a particular problem, and then the incentive to imitate those policies that are most successful.

Economic decentralization in China, according to this perspective, creates the opportunity for local governments to experiment with a variety of policies aimed at attracting foreign investment, and fiscal decentralization gives local governments the incentive to choose the policy that appears to be the most successful. Within a national context it is expected

---

[46] Kleinberg (1992: 197).

[47] Wong (1987: 391). Because capital markets are underdeveloped, banks are the most important source of finance for large industrial firms. These banks are controlled by the government, and lending decisions are heavily politicized.

[48] In 1997, for instance, subnational governments in China raised 52% of public sector revenues compared to an average of 18.4% for other transitional economies and 16.6% for other developing countries. Similarly, subnational expenditures in China as a percentage of total public expenditures were 56%, compared to 22.3% for other transitional economies and 19.6% for other developing countries. Shah and Thompson (2002: 9 and 11).

[49] As I will explain at greater length, exceptions to this generally positive view are those scholars that point to the problems that emerge when subnational units do not have sufficiently hard budget constraints. See, for instance, Burki, Perry, Dillinger (1999: Chapter 3) and Rodden (2001).

[50] For examples of political decentralization, see Burki, Perry, Dillinger (1999: Chapter 1). On the relationship between political and economic decentralization, see Doner and Hershberg (1999).

[51] Ostrom, Schroeder, and Wynne (1993).

that localities with different interests, expectations, and capabilities will make a variety of policy choices, and then as outcomes become known, there will be gradual policy convergence among localities with similar policy objectives. Jean Oi, for example, speaks of the local state bureaucracy as "an information grid where government officials are the primary nodes in the network that provides information to local enterprises."[52] She depicts the manner in which local governments hold meetings, hire outside experts, and organize study tours with the objective of duplicating development strategies from afar. Although Oi does not assume these efforts will be successful, this expectation is explicit in theories of market-preserving federalism. "As the results of [regional] experiments and policies become known," write Montinola, Qian, and Weingast, "individuals and policymakers will update their expectations about the effects of various policies.... Competition among jurisdictions provides incentives to replace poorly chosen strategies with variants of strategies that appear to succeed elsewhere."[53] When authority over economy policymaking is decentralized, local governments are expected to act as rational, utility-maximizing unitary actors.

While taking the importance of decentralization as a starting point, this book does not assume that the result is improved economic policymaking. Local governments are not utility-maximizing unitary actors that simply respond to the incentives created by a central government, they are political jurisdictions that have long political and economic histories and distinct institutional structures. Decentralization may increase the incentive to rapidly adapt economic models that are perceived to be the most successful, but as explained in the next section, the internal characteristics of the localities upon which successful implementation depend (both bureaucratic and the structure of economic organizations) are not easily changed. When a locality implements a policy for which it does not have the appropriate institutional infrastructure, the result is suboptimal economic performance, and often, local protectionism. Rather than assume that, given the proper incentives, localities can easily adapt new development models, it is necessary to understand the development needs of different industrial sectors and the ability of different local institutional configurations to meet these needs. Decentralization increases

---

[52] Oi (1999: 123).

[53] Montinola, Qian, and Weingast (1995: 59). Complete uniformity, however, is not expected by these authors because different regions will have differing preferences and need for public goods.

the capacity of local governments to meet different economic challenges in ways that are appropriate to local characteristics.

II. THE COMPARATIVE INSTITUTIONAL ADVANTAGE OF LOCALITIES

Economic institutions do not do all things equally well. "A market," wrote Charles Lindblom, "is like a tool: designed to do certain jobs but unsuited for others. Not wholly familiar with what it can do, people often leave it lying in the drawer when they could use it. But then they also use it when they should not, like an amateur craftsmen who carelessly uses his chisel as a screwdriver."[54] Although perhaps an obvious point, it is one that is often overlooked.

In the case of transitional economies, the tendency is to assume the market is suitable for all jobs. Because it is abundantly clear that bureaucrats in the central planning system did a poor job of allocating resources and motivating workers and managers, the natural reaction is to assume that market forces are the solution. Although this viewpoint is obvious in the case of those who argue in favor of a big bang approach to economic reform, it is also true in the case of those who point out the merits of an incremental approach to reform. An incremental approach allows for a certain degree of experimentation and it grants time for the creation of new institutions as old ones are torn down, but it is always the market that is focused on as the primary engine of growth.[55] As the economy grows, the portion of the economy controlled by the state remains fixed, and consequently, becomes less important relative to market forces. This emphasis on the market as a coordinating mechanism is not surprising given that transitional economies are moving away from disastrous experiences with central planning. But making the transition from a planned economy to a market economy does not necessarily mean that the market must be the only means of coordinating economic activity. Similarly, arguing in favor of state intervention in cases of "late" development does not mean that state intervention is the answer in all cases. Even within capitalist

---

[54] Lindblom (1977: 76).

[55] See, for example, McMillan and Naughton (1992). Not only is it the non-state sector in which growth is most rapid, but even in the state sector, improved performance is seen as the result of gradually increased exposure to market forces. This was partly because the non-state sector put increasing competitive pressure on state-owned firms, and partly because under a dual-track system (*shuangguizhi*) state-owned firms could sell production above a fixed amount on open markets. (Byrd: 1991; Naughton: 1992, 1995).

economies there are multiple ways of organizing economic activity; there is variation between countries, and between sectors within a single economy.[56] To extend Lindblom's analogy, the key challenge is to understand both the nature of the job at hand and the tools with which you have to work.

Development Needs: Sectors

The requirements of the development process vary according to the type of industrial sector targeted. Sectors are those subsets of the economy that involve a combination of highly complementary activities (tasks, services, goods, etc.) that must operate in coordination to produce a certain end product.[57] Firms within the same sector address similar questions of development and control both inside and outside the enterprise; these firms are more likely to adopt the same production processes, to allocate resources and information in a similar way, and to create equivalent property rights structures.

There is more than one means of distinguishing between different sectors. One approach is to focus on the nature of transactions within the sector. According to Oliver Williamson, transaction costs will vary according to the degree of asset specificity, uncertainty, and the frequency of interaction between economic actors. When the investments of a firm are not highly specific (to a particular customer, location, or production process), the degree of uncertainty is not high, and the frequency of interaction is not intense, the arms-length market relations of the neoclassical model will suffice.[58] But in complex and frequent interactions with high degrees of asset specificity, there is abundant opportunity for opportunistic behavior on the part of less than scrupulous actors. The solution is to "make" within the hierarchical safety of the firm rather than "buy" from an uncertain market. At the very core of the new institutional economics is the idea that different governance structures will be more or less appropriate for different types of economic activity, and this logic can be extended to sectoral analysis. When transaction costs are low, there is little reason not to rely on market interactions, but as transaction costs rise, the value of non-market forms of coordination also increases.

---

[56] Berger and Dore (1997); Locke (1995); Herrigel (1996); Soskice (1997).
[57] Definition is from Hollingsworth, Schmitter, and Streeck (1994: 8). Sectoral analysis has a long lineage in political economy, but for recent examples, see Frieden (1991), Kitschelt (1991), Milner (1988), and Shafer (1994).
[58] Williamson (1985) as cited in Kitschelt (1991: 464).

Herbert Kitschelt supplements Williamson's emphasis on the cost of a transaction with the idea that sectors will also vary in the form of techno-logical systems they employ. Within a sector, Kitschelt argues, a common technological system is used to deal with the environmental uncertainties of the production process, and this system shapes governance structures.[59] He distinguishes between sectors based on the tightness of technological coupling and the level of complexity in the technological system. The former refers to the degree to which each step of the production pro-cess is separated from every other step in space and time; it is a measure of the degree to which the pieces of the production process are inter-linked. The latter refers to the extent of causal interaction between steps in the production process. Low complexity, for instance, will be a linear process – A causes B but B has no impact on A – whereas high com-plexity involves feedback and learning between the different steps of the production process.[60] By understanding the basic characteristics of the sector, Kitschelt argues, it is possible to make predictions about gover-nance structures: Tightly interlinked production processes and complex causal interaction may increase the need for nonmarket coordination in the same way that high asset specificity and contractual uncertainty do.[61]

In addition to making distinctions between industrial sectors, it is nec-essary to make distinctions across time – the needs of an industrial sector are not a constant. In a classic statement of industrial change, Michael Piore and Charles Sabel argue that industrial societies have "rare break-throughs in the use of labor and machines," what they call industrial divides.[62] The choice of an industrial system is not pre-ordained by tech-nology, but is closely linked to regulatory institutions and patterns of consumer demand. The mass production, or Fordist system, for exam-ple, with its emphasis on specialized machinery, low-skilled labor, and high fixed costs, made sense in an environment with large, stable markets and slowly changing technologies, and in industries that produced a rel-atively standardized product at high volumes. As Doner and Hershberg

---

[59] Kitschelt (1991: 460). In constructing his theory, Kitschelt builds upon the work of Charles Perrow.

[60] Kitschelt (1991: 461).

[61] Kitschelt diagrams the potential combinations of technological systems, governance structures, and property rights on p. 465. His assumption (1991: 468) is that "over time, learning and evolutionary selection should yield identical governance structures in iden-tical sectors, regardless of their embeddedness in broader domestic or international insti-tutional environments."

[62] Piore and Sabel (1984: 4).

comment, the mixture of public policies that supported the mass production system were well-known – Keynesian demand management, support for general infrastructure, macroeconomic stability, protection of domestic industry, etc. – but became increasingly difficult to sustain as increasing globalization made it difficult to sustain these policies. The shift to floating exchange rate led to more volatile financial markets; oil shocks increased uncertainty for mass producers; mass markets for standardized products began to break up.[63] The response to this complicated set of circumstances in some product areas was the move toward flexible specialization, or post-Fordist manufacturing, a pattern that Piore and Sabel describe in the context of small firms within Italian industrial districts. Firms within a post-Fordist system are characterized by their ability to shorten lead times and lower inventories, continuously improve the quality of a product, and keep costs low.[64] The clusters within which these firms are located, usually characterized by dense horizontal and vertical inter-firm ties, facilitate specialization and a collective response to shared problems.[65] The dramatically different context, of course, creates very different development requirements for firms.

Given the number of industrial sectors, and their differences, a multi-industry study is inevitably complex, and conclusions often will say more about the differences between sectors than the role of development policy and institutions. Focusing on one sector, by contrast, insures that comparisons are between like units, and as long as the characteristics of the sector are well defined, a single industry becomes a potential building block for cross-sector comparisons.[66]

The case studies in this book analyze one sector in two different stages of development. In the first stage, from the early 1980s to the late 1990s, firms were operating in a highly protected market and employed classic mass production manufacturing techniques. The sector had several dominant characteristics. First, capital requirements were intense due to the importance of economies of scale and the need for complementary investment. The massive investment in an auto assembly plant, usually in the hundreds of millions of dollars, had to be rapid (so that it would be able to quickly increase production volumes and capture economies

---

[63] Doner and Hershberg (1999: 49).
[64] Doner and Hershberg (1999: 49).
[65] Nadvi and Schmitz (1998: 62).
[66] For examples of other single-industry studies, see Evans (1995) and Segal (2003). For an example of single-industry research paving the way for cross-sector comparisons, see Segal and Thun (2001).

of scale), and in the context of nationally mandated localization require-ments, it had to be matched with a coordinated investment program in supply firms. When the auto sector was first targeted for development in China, there were few pre-existing suppliers the joint venture assem-bly plants could rely upon, yet national regulation required that the joint ventures either increase local content according to a strict schedule, or pay severe penalties. Because a typical automotive supply base consisted of hundreds of firms, even though the capital requirements of individual firms were not necessarily large, the need for simultaneous development in the initial stage of development translated into high capital require-ments for the sector as a whole. If a locality could overcome the collective action problem among suppliers and increase local content, it would be freed of foreign exchange restrictions, and thus able to raise volumes.

Second, a high degree of asset specificity was common at this stage. Supply firms were often reluctant to invest in the new technologies and equipment necessary to form linkages with an assembly plant not only because the assembly plant initially had very low volumes (and a very uncertain future), but also because they would be dependent on one pri-mary customer after they had undergone the process of technical upgrad-ing (a problem that was exacerbated by local protectionism). Again, the fate of any individual supplier was closely linked to the fate of the net-work as whole; if all invested at the same time, the assembly plant would be able to lower its dependence on imported components, lower costs, and raise production volumes.[67] As volumes went up, economies of scale would be captured, and in a virtuous cycle, all the members of the supply network would begin to prosper.

Finally, the learning that took place between firms was linear but feed-back was critical; managers of supply firms were instructed in established manufacturing procedures much the way a student is taught mathemati-cal formulas by a teacher. Although the objective at this stage was not for the supplier to be innovative, it had to be able to consistently manufac-ture components to the specifications requested by the assembly plant.[68]

---

[67] In China it was impossible at this time to raise production volumes using imported com-ponents not only because of localization requirements, but because access to foreign exchange was strictly controlled.

[68] Amsden (2001: 4) distinguishes between three different forms of technical capability: production capability (the skills necessary to transform inputs into outputs), project execution capability (the skills necessary to expand capacity), and innovation capability (the skills necessary to design entirely new products and processes). During the 1980s and 1990s, Chinese auto firms were squarely concentrating on production and project execution capabilities.

The dominant product in the Chinese marketplace during the 1990s (the Santana), for instance, was based on 1970s technology, and it remained virtually unchanged for over a decade after its introduction in China. In the mid-1980s, when the joint venture (JV) assembly plants were first establishing their operations, there were few local suppliers capable of meeting the technical and quality standards of the JVs. As with the challenge of complementary investments and asset specificity, learning was a relational problem: Successful resolution depended on the form of the relationships that a firm formed with customers, other firms within a supply network, and government bodies. In Kitschelt's terms, the importance of learning and feedback in the different steps of the production process created high complexity.

The second stage of development began at the end of the 1990s, and dramatically altered the demands of the sector. This was partly because the overall sector was more mature. For example, the problems that resulted from the tight coupling in the auto sector during the initial stage of development – asset specificity and the need for complementary investment – were not necessarily as severe at more advanced stages. In a developed context, the assembly plant and the supply firms had a broader range of pre-existing customers and suppliers, and the existence of these firms was more stable. Consequently, there was not the same need for complementary investment, nor the same degree of vulnerability in the relationship between supplier and assembler; high asset specificity would still exist in some cases, but when the very existence of the assembly plant was not in question, this problem could now be dealt with through long-term contracts.

The most important change was the rapid convergence with global standards of efficiency and quality. Many new joint venture projects were created and after accession to the WTO it became clear that only those that were able to raise quality and lower costs would be able to compete. At the level of the supply firm there was a bifurcation of expectations that mirrored the global structure of the industry. In the lower tiers, where the manufacturing of relatively unsophisticated components took place, price increasingly determined supply relationships. Nurturing these suppliers was no longer possible. If supply firms did not lower costs, they would not get the business and because the domestic industry was far more developed (and imports more feasible), the assembly plants had choices that previously had not been available. In the upper tiers, however, the technical demands placed on suppliers increased, as the nature of learning shifted from a linear process, to one in which the suppliers were expected to participate in the design of rapidly changing models.

Rather than being students learning basic manufacturing processes, the suppliers were expected to be equal partners with the assemblers. In the span of 15 years, the challenges of supplier development in China were transformed, and it was not at all clear that Chinese firms would have the capabilities necessary to survive in the upper tiers of the industry.

Development Tools: Local Institutions

An understanding of the characteristics of a given industrial sector gives insight into the nature of the development challenge, but little ability to predict whether these challenges will be able to be overcome in any given setting. For this we need to know what "tools" there are at our disposal. Institutional and organizational structures, while not determinant of economic outcomes, create opportunities and constraints for different sectors. Following Douglass North, institutions are defined as the rules, formal or informal, that actors within a society generally follow. An institution may be as formal as a national constitution or legal code, or it may be as informal as a code of conduct or social convention. An organization is created to take advantage of the opportunities created by the institutional framework, and consists of groups of individuals bound by common purpose: a political body such as a political party or a bureaucratic agency; an economic body such as a corporation or firm; a social body such as a club or association.[69] "The key [to a comparative institutional approach to political economy]," writes Peter Evans, "is to identify differences in the way states are organized and then connect these differences to variations in developmental outcomes."[70] Typically, as I have argued, the states that have been the traditional focus of political science are *nation*-states.

Despite the focus on nation-states, when we think of vibrant (or decaying) industrial sectors it is more often with respect to a region: Silicon Valleys and Auto Cities. Within the European Union, according to the geography literature, "local differences in economic structure and economic growth rates within member countries are much larger than the disparities between countries."[71] Why do industries cluster in particular regions of any given nation, particularly given that political scientists say national institutions are the key variables that explain development?

---

[69] North (1990: 3–5). Although the distinction between institutions and organizations is important, I will at times use the two interchangeably.

[70] Evans (1995: 40–41).

[71] Martin and Sunley (1996: 278).

There are straightforward explanations for industrial clusters. In the field of industrial geography, for example, scholars emphasize the transition from mass production to flexible specialization among small firms. These firms cluster together to minimize transaction costs and maximize their share of specialized labor markets. The technological and knowledge spillovers that occur within the clusters are a benefit to all.[72] In economics, the rise of "new trade theory" has led to a focus on increasing returns to scale, and how this may explain why one region has an advantage over another despite similar factor endowments. The advantage of any particular region is derived from falling production costs as output rises, and this advantage is accentuated as firms try to minimize transportation costs and develop forward and backward linkages in the locations that were the first to develop. Large-scale regions, argues Paul Krugman, are more significant as economic units than nation-states.[73] While economic geography is useful for explaining why clusters of economic activity grow and prosper, it is less useful in explaining the origins of these clusters. The emphasis is usually on historical accident, not only an explanation that is of little use to policy-makers in the developing world, but also one that fails to explain why there would be a variation in outcomes when different localities at similar starting points seek to develop the same industry. A comparative institutional approach is necessary, but at the local level.

The literature on Chinese political economy has certainly not neglected the role of local institutions, but rarely has the focus been on institutional *differences* between *like* units. Jean Oi, for instance, describes a new form of state-led growth in rural China, what she calls local state corporatism: a system in which local governments "treat enterprises within their administrative purview as one component of a larger corporate whole."[74] Jane Duckett speaks of the entrepreneurial state in Tianjin.[75] Victor Nee, focusing on the increased market pressure to which rural firms are exposed and their need to form alliances with local governments as protection against a highly uncertain environment, depicts a form of corporatism based on coalitions between local governments, marketized firms, and private enterprise.[76] Andrew Walder points to the organizational differences

---

[72] Martin and Sunley (1996); Nadvi and Schmitz (1998); Doner and Hershberg (1999).

[73] This discussion of "new trade theory" is based on Martin and Sunley (1996).

[74] Oi (1995: 1132; 1992). Blecher and Shue (1996) also analyze the close relationships between county officials and production units, and the manner in which they have evolved over two decades.

[75] Duckett (1998).

[76] Nee (1992: 3).

Table 1.1: *Variation of the Explanatory Variables*

		Bureaucratic Organization	
		Unified	Fragmented
Dominant Form of Inter-Firm Relations	Hierarchical Coordination	Shanghai	Changchun, Wuhan
	Market Coordination	Japan (quasi-market ties)	Beijing, Guangzhou

between state-owned firms operating in rural and urban areas as a key reason for variation in performance.[77] The approach of this study draws inspiration from these earlier studies – the case of Shanghai, for example, looks very much like Oi's local state corporatism – but the emphasis is on a diversity of development approaches. There is no single correct model that dominates in any given type of jurisdiction (i.e., urban or rural), there are multiple patterns, each determined by the industrial history and politics of a region.[78] In this respect, my approach is very similar to Adam Segal's work on information technology firms in China.[79]

If the development needs of firms vary by sector, and the institutions that are critical for meeting these needs vary at the subnational level, it makes sense to categorize local jurisdictions according to their institutional characteristics. When the internal institutions of localities differ, development outcomes will vary.

I use two primary dimensions to categorize localities in the Chinese auto sector (see Table 1.1).[80] The first is the structure of the bureaucracy that is overseeing development efforts in the locality. Although local governments may appear to be similar in structure, the manner in which they function varies widely; bureaucracies are the product of the political and economic history of the region, and in particular their relationship to

[77] In particular, the size and degree of internal diversification of a government jurisdiction (e.g., small township vs. large municipality) affect the intensity of financial incentives and budget constraints on firms and the ability of the government to monitor performance and enforce financial discipline. Firms owned by the lower levels of the government hierarchy are monitored more closely, less affected by nonfinancial objectives, and generally far more efficient. Walder (1995).

[78] Susan Whiting looks explicitly at the variation in local institutional structures in her study of rural industry, but rather than relate these differences to development outcomes, her primary purpose is to explain why property rights arrangements evolve in different ways and how this variation affects the extractive capacity of the state. Whiting (2001).

[79] Segal (2003).

[80] Each of these dimensions is explained in greater detail in Chapter 3.

the central government. Using one of the primary developmental roles of the state as a measure – capital accumulation and investment – I distinguish between bureaucratic structures that are unified and those that are fragmented. A unified bureaucratic structure uses the allocation of capital in a coordinated fashion to advance the process of industrial transformation. Resources are concentrated in targeted firms. A fragmented bureaucratic structure is unable to coordinate the allocation of resources, and is characterized by individual government ministries each pursuing its own developmental objectives with little or no coordination. The form (and source) of fragmentation may vary. In some cases it may be fragmentation within the bureaucratic structure of a locality; in other cases, it may be a result of a sector being supervised partially at the central level and partially at the local level. No matter what the source of fragmentation, the result is the same: There is not a coordinated and focused effort to concentrate resources in local firms.

The second dimension is the dominant form of inter-firm relationships within the region. Because firms in the Chinese auto sector are organized by business groups, this book in effect, focuses on the differences within emerging business groups in China. Again, although it is often assumed that these economic organizations with the same name – *jituan qiye* – are structured in similar fashions, I found that internal structures varied widely in different localities.[81] The pattern of inter-firm relations within a business group can be placed along a spectrum that has pure market relations at one end and pure hierarchical relations at the other. In most contexts, of course, there is a wide range of combinations in between these two endpoints. In the first stage of auto sector development in China, however, virtually all of the auto firms were state-owned, and hence the range of possible forms of inter-firm relations was more circumscribed (e.g., quasi-market network relationships between firms were rare). As I will explain, the ownership of firms was a key determinant of inter-firm relations. In cases where all of the firms were owned by a single business group, the dominant form of inter-firm relationship was hierarchical; in cases where ownership of firms was divided between business groups, there were market relations between the firms that did not share the

---

[81] Lisa Keister provides the most comprehensive account of Chinese business groups, and she depicts a common organizational structure for the *qiye jituan*, consisting primarily of large SOEs. See Keister (2000: Chapter 4). Peter Nolan (2001) also analyzes the development of large business groups, but does not distinguish between their structural characteristics.

same owner.[82] It was only in the second stage of development, when private firms began to play a larger role and local bureaucracies (i.e., the owners) became more flexible toward firms, that more complex patterns of inter-firm relations became possible.

By categorizing localities according to these two dimensions, three patterns of institutional arrangements emerge in the Chinese auto sector (see Figure 1.1). The first pattern is that of a *local developmental state* (unified bureaucracy and hierarchical relations between firms). It is a developmental state in that government officials, albeit at the local level, compensate for underdeveloped capital markets by taking charge of the process of capital accumulation and playing the role of investment banker. The bureaucratic institutions of the local state are unified and cohesive in their mission to cultivate and develop local firms. By adapting an activist role with respect to investment, the local government eases the collective action problems that hinder early development efforts; individual firms are confident that individual investment and commitment to the success of the assembly plant will be complemented with a broad-based development effort. The efforts of the local state are complemented by a local business group that organizes relations among firms according to a hierarchy rather than the market. The head office of the group allocates resources within the group, assists in the development of new technical and managerial skills in firms, and monitors firm development – the classic multi-divisional hierarchy. Because the head office of the group fully owns and controls firms within the group, it has the necessary incentives to invest in supplier development; strong support from the municipal bureaucracy (and top-level linkages) gives it the power to be effective. Even small firms with limited resources are capable of importing technology and learning new manufacturing techniques, and the result is a coordinated "big push" approach to development. The municipality of

---

[82] In some respects it might appear that there is really a single independent variable doing most of the work in this argument: bureaucratic structure. Not only does bureaucratic structure determine the pattern of resource allocation, it also determines the pattern of ownership. For example, when bureaucratic structures are fragmented, ownership of firms will be split between the different parts of the bureaucracy, and when it is unified, firms will be within a single business group. The pattern of ownership in turn determines the inter-firm relationships: hierarchical relationships will dominate within a group that is under common ownership and market relations will dominated if firms have different owners. But this will only be the case when all firms are state-owned and the state is playing a key role in determining purchasing patterns. In other words, although under certain circumstances the structure of the bureaucracy may shape the form of inter-firm relations this is not inevitable, and the two variables are analytically distinct.

Alternative Patterns of Development

Pattern 1: Local Developmental State – Shanghai

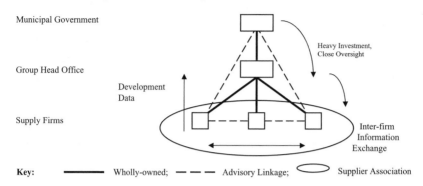

Pattern 2: Laissez-faire Local State – Beijing and Guangzhou

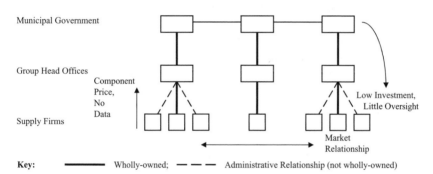

Pattern 3: Centrally-controlled SOE – Changchun and Wuhan

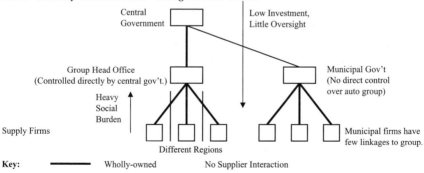

Figure 1.1: Alternative Patterns of Development.

Shanghai, in the first stage of auto sector development, was a local developmental state.

The second pattern is the *laissez-faire local state* (fragmented bureaucracy and market relations between firms). The state in such a locality is laissez-faire in that it is not excessively interfering (or, to put it another way, assisting) with development efforts. This is because the bureaucratic structures that oversee a given sector are divided, and competing bureaucracies fail to coordinate whatever development efforts they might make. Investment is dispersed, and firms suffer from a shortage of capital. Relationships between firms are also laissez-faire in that, within the business groups, firms have little more than market relations with each other. Because individual supply firms are not always wholly owned by the head office of the corporate group that they are in, the head office has little incentive to invest in their development; assembly plants use multiple suppliers for each component so as to be able to use competition as a means of forcing suppliers to lower their prices. Although an effective, and often used, strategy in established supply networks, in a nascent network it prevents firms from increasing production volumes or receiving any return on the large investments required by technical upgrading. The long-term contracts and confidence-building measures that are often used in "networks" of firms that are linked by neither hierarchy nor pure market relations are also not present. The municipalities of Beijing and Guangzhou were examples of laissez-faire local states.[83]

The third pattern is that of a *firm-dominated locality* (fragmented bureaucracy and hierarchical relations between firms). Although fragmented bureaucratic structures may result from multiple causes, in these cases it is the result of the primary business group being controlled from the central (rather than local) government, while it is the local government that is primarily concerned with local development. In these cases, the municipal officials have few financial resources of their own, and they can neither guarantee a market for the product of a local supply firm, nor improve their financial situation by influencing the pricing policy of the assembly plants. The business groups are hierarchically organized in these cases, and their orientation is national rather than local. In the Chinese auto sector, the municipalities of Changchun and Wuhan were both examples of firm-dominated localities.

---

[83] It is important to note that these characterizations are not necessarily general. The label of laissez-faire local state applies to the auto supply network, and in particular the form of relationships between an assembler and its supply firms, rather than the locality as a whole.

The fourth combination of the two dimensions (unified bureaucracy and market relations between firms) was not present in the case of the Chinese auto industry during the first 15 years of development. When a unified bureaucracy directed auto sector development efforts, it invariably owned the firms that it sought to develop, and due to the complexity of the ties between the state and firms, these linkages were not easily altered. The result was hierarchy. In regions where market competition existed due to either an abundance of private firms or competition between state-owned firms controlled by competing bureaucratic actors, there was no unified bureaucratic support. In the following section, which details the outcomes for each of these alternative institutional arrangements, international comparisons are used to compensate for this missing combination.

Institutions and Outcomes in the Chinese Auto Sector

How did these alternative patterns of institutional arrangements relate to outcomes? As explained in the next chapter, the local developmental state in Shanghai was more successful during the first stage of development by virtually every measure. The primary challenges of Chinese suppliers at this stage were not too different from those faced by Henry Ford or Alfred Sloan. The focus was not on rapidly driving down costs or increasing innovation, but on increasing basic manufacturing skills and quality standards. The institutional framework of the local developmental state was suited to this purpose in two primary respects. First, the municipal government collected 5 billion RMB between 1988 and 1994 by means of an "auto component tax," and managed the disbursement of these funds to municipal firms. This allowed for coordinated development. The unified approach within the municipality eased the fears of opportunism, and made it possible for individual supply firms to make large investments in activities that were often highly asset-specific. Second, the hierarchical structure of the business group (and the municipal government) guided supply firms through a process of incremental upgrading. Rather than abandon a supply firm that was having problems, the ownership links within the municipality created a commitment to working through any problems that emerged, and this process was supported by municipal organizations specifically created to facilitate supplier development. The result was a virtuous cycle. Rapidly increasing local content (not to be confused with domestic content) allowed the Shanghai assembly plant to increase production volumes because it was no longer reliant on government-controlled foreign exchange for imports; rising production volumes made it possible to capture economies of scale, lower costs, and capture market share; high profits at both the level of the assembly and supply plants was then re-invested in the sector. During most of the 1990s, Shanghai firms controlled over 50% of the Chinese market for sedans.

There was nothing virtuous about the development process for firms in localities with laissez-faire local states. The fragmented local bureaucracies were unable to concentrate resources in key firms, and thus did little to ameliorate the collective action problem within the network of local suppliers. Although the local business groups might have attempted to compensate for these shortcomings, they also made little effort to support firms, primarily because divided ownership would prevent them from reaping the full rewards of their investment. Rather than guarantee a market to firms that had not yet achieved economies of scale, the local business groups forced them to compete against each other, and under such conditions, local supply firms quickly withered on the vine. Neither locality could source more than 30% of their components from local supply firms, and eventually the effort to support local supplier development was abandoned. In Guangzhou the (initial) foreign partner withdrew and most of the local suppliers to the joint venture went bankrupt. Towards the end of this first stage of development, both Beijing and Guangzhou became increasingly reliant on Shanghai suppliers and foreign partners.

The outcome was not much better for the firm-dominated localities of Changchun and Wuhan during this early stage. Although the fragmentation had a different source in these cases – the split was between centrally controlled business groups and the locality – the result was the same: Domestic firms at the local level did not have the financial resources that development required. Due to the national orientation of the business groups, they were just as likely to invest in far-flung provinces as they were in the local network. Supply firms were not forced to compete with each other, as was the case in the laissez-faire local states, but they also received relatively little support. Without a local impetus for the development effort, the local firms had little means of upgrading their technical capabilities, and the centrally controlled business groups turned their focus to more promising regions.

What might have happened if a locality had combined a unified bureaucratic approach with market relationships between firms? In some respects this is the pattern that might come closest to characterizing the highly successful Japanese auto industry. Because Japanese assemblers did not have the resources to pursue strategies of vertical integration in the early stages of development, they continued to rely on independent supply firms with which they had market relationships, usually organized in the shape of a tiered pyramid.[84] But there is a critical caveat to this story: Because market relationships were thought to work counter to long-term, cooperative relationships, the arms-length ties were supplemented with careful monitoring and confidence-building exercises.[85] Buyers were able to exert pressure on suppliers (the benefit of market relations) at the same time that a long-term relationship, and the trust that it fostered, facilitated the open flow of information within the network of firms and served to reduce transaction costs (the benefit of hierarchical coordination).[86] While pure market relationships maximized bargaining power at the expense of a collaborative technical approach, the quasi-market ties in the Japanese system facilitated the dissemination of the tacit knowledge that was so critical to technical and managerial upgrading.[87] In China, however, there was little evidence of these intermediate forms of coordination in the 1980s and 1990s – firms that are just beginning to master market relationships perhaps cannot be expected to adapt sophisticated variations of quasi-market relations – and consequently there was little effort to compensate for the shortcomings of market relationships.[88] If there had been a combination of unified bureaucracy and market relations between firms in the universe of Chinese cases, strong bureaucratic support might have provided supply firms with the financial resources to buy new technologies, but would have done little to facilitate the inter-firm sharing of information and tacit knowledge that pure arms-length market relations so often precluded. It is unlikely that this hypothetical case would have matched the success of the local developmental state.

---

[84] As explained in Chapter 3, the Japanese assemblers also believed a pure hierarchical approach to supplier development would stifle supplier development. See Womack, Jones, and Roos (1990).

[85] See Smitka (1991) and Sako (1992).

[86] This form of relationship is particularly successful in promoting the dissemination of the sorts of tacit knowledge that are not easily codified and bought, but can be critical to the successful adaptation of new technical and managerial skills.

[87] As Helper (1991: 808) argues, the U.S. auto industry prior to the 1980s was a classic example of how pure market relationships may hinder a collaborative approach within a supply network. On the importance of tacit knowledge in the upgrading process, see Amsden (2001: 5).

[88] One indication of the sophisticated relationships between firms in a Japanese-style network, and how far Chinese networks are from this standard, is the efficiency of inter-firm delivery systems. In 2004, transportation costs for Chinese automakers on average accounted for 15% of revenues, much higher than the comparable figure in Japan (5%) or Western countries (8%). "Auto industry logistics in China: Automakers tackle high cost and inefficiency," *Fourin China Auto Weekly*, October 12, 2004, p. 1.

Does the success of Shanghai mean that the local developmental state is a general model? In sectors with different developmental characteristics outcomes varied. In the information technology (IT) sector, for instance, many firms (i.e., software design) have relatively low capital requirements (in comparison to auto assembly firms), fewer linkages to other firms, and high rates of innovation – ideal characteristics for a laissez-faire state. The role of the state is important, but as Segal argues, it is less intrusive. Rather than playing the role of investment bank and key coordinator of the development effort, the state must define property rights and allow horizontal networks of innovation to flourish. The municipality of Beijing was highly successful at playing this more modest, yet critical role, while the municipality of Shanghai essentially smothered innovation with its heavy-handed attempts at planning.[89] What worked very well for autos, did not work as well for small, innovative technology firms. The point is important, particularly given the temptation to believe that Shanghai's leaders simply had a better understanding of the auto sector than their competitors; Shanghai's leaders did not transform the municipality into a local developmental state because they had a deeper understanding of auto sector development; they were doing what they always did, and it worked for sectors with the appropriate characteristics.[90] As is argued in the next section, the success of Shanghai was also challenged by change over time.

III. NESTED INSTITUTIONS: LOCAL, NATIONAL, GLOBAL

Although this book emphasizes the importance of local states in China, this should not be interpreted to mean that local states act alone. Decentralization increases the importance of local states, but it does not make them nation-states. This is an important point in two respects. First, the history of the interaction of national and local levels is a key determinant of the structure of local institutions. A local government does not have complete autonomy within its jurisdictions. It must act in accordance with a federal constitution, or in the case of unitary states, through a process of negotiation with the center. Second, a local government cannot control its interaction with the international economy. Trade and investment

---

[89] Segal (2003). I explore the complementarities between Segal's work and my own in Chapter 9.

[90] It is also telling that the high-tech firms that have tended to thrive in the Shanghai area tend to be either capital-intensive projects such as semiconductor manufacturing and/or foreign investments.

policy, even in the most decentralized of countries, are set by the central government. Local institutions may define a range of capabilities in a particular context, but the central government defines this broader context. The center has the capacity to force a locality to move from one stage of development to the next.

Institutional Origins

Although the autonomy of Chinese local governments during the reform period is a common theme in the China literature, and it is sometimes argued that fiscal decentralization has created a quasi-federal structure, it is important not to obscure the enduring influence of the central government over local policy. The center, in both the past and the present, plays a primary role in determining the amount of tax revenue that the municipality retains, the degree of contact that the municipality has with the international economy, the role that the municipality plays in the national economy, and the career paths of local officials.[91] Unlike in a true federal structure, provincial autonomy is at the bequest of the central government rather than a legal right. The framework of local-center relations creates the opportunities and constraints that, over time, shape the organizations that form a distinctive local political economy.

Each of the case studies of this book examines the historical roots of the local institutional structures, and in particular, how they have been shaped by local-center relations. Guangzhou, for instance, has historically enjoyed far more autonomy from the central government than Shanghai, particularly with respect to the amount of revenue retained at the local level and the authority over local economic policy.[92] Shanghai, by contrast, was the industrial core of the planned economy, and the central government was unwilling to risk experimentation – the municipality remained tightly planned well into the reform era.[93] These contrasting relationships with the central government created different incentive systems for political officials and firm managers in the two cities, and not surprisingly the economic institutions in the two cities – both government bureaucracies

---

[91] On the evolution of center-local relations in China, see Jia and Lin (1994); on localities' fiscal dependence on the center, see Wedeman (1999); on contact with the international economy, see Zweig (2002); on central control over the nomenklatura system, see Burns (1994).

[92] This contrast is explained in detail in Chapters 4 and 5.

[93] On the extensive reach of the state in Shanghai, see White (1989, 1998a).

Regional Paths to Auto Sector Development

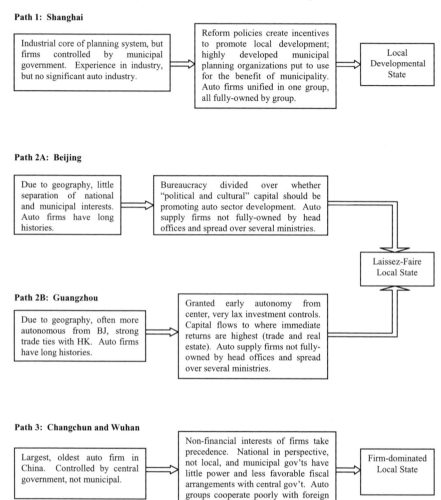

Figure 1.2: Regional Paths to Auto Sector Development.

charged with the oversight of the economy and actual firm structures – evolved in very different ways (see Figure 1.2).

Why is this history important even after these differences have long since been smoothed over? The impact of the institutional context of local-center relations is cumulative; a locality may gain more autonomy at a particular point in time, but institutions are shaped over time and change only slowly.[94] Just as a particular technology will not be abandoned even after a more effective replacement has been discovered – there may be replacement costs, learning costs, and/or coordination effects – political and economic institutions will endure even after they are no longer efficient responses to the policy challenge for which they were originally formed.[95] The path-dependent nature of institutional change is not new, but it has important implications for development policy. If a region has an institutional advantage (or disadvantage), it is the product of decades of political and economic history, and in the absence of strong external pressure it is unlikely that policymakers will be able to easily change this advantage, either to conform to the whims of policy fashions, or to satisfy the needs of an evolving economic sector. This makes it all the more important to understand and capitalize on the existing institutions of a region.

Evolving Context

The institutional framework created by the center is not only a key determinant of how local institutions evolve over time; it also determines the broader policy framework within which local economies must operate in the present. The next chapter considers in detail the manner in which central government policy affects auto sector development, but the point here is more general: The center determines – or to be more accurate, tries to determine – both the domestic and the global context of development efforts.

At the national level, it is the central government that must ensure that local governments are operating with hard budget constraints and in a competitive environment. Decentralization increases the autonomy of local governments and gives them the incentive to promote economic growth, but just as important are the hard budget constraints that will ensure that local governments are accountable for their decisions. Transfers between levels of government must be rule-based, expenditure responsibilities must be clearly allocated, and the ability of local governments to borrow funds must be limited.[96] Similarly, the national

---

[94] For good reviews of the broad tradition of historical institutionalism, see Hall and Taylor (1996) and Thelen (1999). Whiting (2001) gives a sophisticated account of institutional change in China.

[95] See Pierson (2000a).

[96] See Burki, Perry, and Dillinger (1999: Chapter 3).

government must be able to preserve a common domestic market; local governments must not be able to protect local enterprises from domestic competition. Unfortunately, in a developing country such as China, where decentralization is often a result of central government weakness, it is far easier to delegate authority to local governments than it is to impose the necessary framework of constraints.[97] Local governments in China at many points in time have been notorious for flouting the will of the central government, and their ability to do so often enabled them to protect inefficient firms.

Even in cases when a central government is unable to completely impose the necessary constraints on localities, it is able to control the broad framework of their interactions with the global economy, and the trade and investment regime is another key determinant of the opportunities and constraints acting on local governments. In the auto sector it was the primary determinant. As I have explained, the development of the Chinese auto industry corresponded with a process of deepening global integration. Local governments were not passive in this process – as David Zweig argues, they lobbied the central government constantly – but the broad trend of moving from a closed economy to an open economy was made at the central level.[98] This is important, of course, because the broad framework of national policy (i.e., whether it is an open or closed economy) is a critical determinant of whether a local policy will be effective. Even when the authority of local governments is broad, comments Fred Pyke, "where political authority is located at higher levels, at the very least decisions, rules, and regulation should not be hostile to the industrial sector strategy carried out at the local level."[99] The import substitution that Shanghai used with such great effect in the context of a protected domestic market, for example, would hardly have been possible if the center had decided to lower tariff barriers a decade earlier.

The path-dependent nature of local institutional change and the limited ability of local governments to control the broader context of their development efforts create something of a dilemma: the former hinders the capacity for change and the latter may well demand it. Even in the absence of a change in the broader context, the very success of a development effort will result in an economic environment that is different

---

[97] This is a point developed by Tsai (2000: 35–36).
[98] Zweig (2002) provides the best account of the process of global integration in China, and the interaction between local governments and the center.
[99] Cited in Doner and Hershberg (1999: 75).

Stages of Development in the Chinese Auto Sector

Stage 1: Development as a Coordination Problem	Stage 2: The Race for Competitiveness
• Need for coordinated development of a supply network creates *high level of capital intensity* for sector as a whole.	• Broader range of pre-existing customers and suppliers leads to a *decreasing need for investment coordination* for the sector as a whole.
• The small number of potential customers (due to low levels of development and local protectionism) leads to *high levels of asset specificity* for many key supply firms.	• An *urgent need for cutting costs* is created by rapidly increasing levels of competition. Effective governance of firms becomes critical.
• Urgent need to master manufacturing and project execution skills makes *learning and feedback critical,* particularly in forms conducive to the dissemination of tacit knowledge.	• For firms that aspire to belong to the upper tiers of the supply chain and compete with global suppliers, the *development of technical and design skills* are of paramount importance and the key to future competitiveness.

Figure 1.3: Stages of Development in the Chinese Auto Sector.

from the one in which the initial policy was formulated. The question is not whether change will occur, but whether states will have adequate capacity to respond, and the Chinese auto sector was no exception.[100]

In the course of a decade the development context was transformed (see Figure 1.3). During the first stage of development (1980s to late 1990s) firms were far less efficient than global firms and products were greatly inferior, but high tariff barriers provided the opportunity for the local state to coordinate and nurture firm development. In the second stage (beginning in the late 1990s), the rise of a private market for autos, a dramatic increase in the level of competition and the prospect of an increasing level of global integration led to rapidly falling prices and rising technical demands on supply firms.[101] The need for coordinated investment was lessened as the sector matured, the need to cut costs increased, and technical upgrading became imperative. The key challenge in this

---

[100] The idea that "the institutions favorable for one stage of economic growth are less suitable for a subsequent stage" has been labeled "growing into trouble" by Doner and Ramsay (2004). This is yet another reason that attempts to re-make the state for relatively narrow developmental pursuits should be approached with caution.

[101] According to the analysis of McKinsey & Company in 2001, the cost of manufacturing auto components in China continued to be 20% higher than in western economies. Goldman Sachs (2003: 30).

second stage of development, and a return to the start of this chapter, is the extent to which local firms will be able to carve out competitive and high value-added niches in a global industry.

Firms in the *laissez-faire local states* of Beijing and Guangzhou should have had an advantage in the new context of intense competition – a ruthless emphasis on price is exactly what is needed to drive down prices – but failure in the first stage substantially altered the prospects for local supplier development in the second stage. Because local supply firms did not have the benefit of going through a step-by-step development process, they had limited capacity to meet the needs of the new joint venture partners, and as a result, they were largely abandoned as the competitive environment increased. This does not necessarily mean that these regions will lack an auto sector, however. Chastened by early failure, the local governments shifted strategies and allowed new foreign partners greater autonomy to organize local supply networks as they pleased. In practice, this meant bypassing the local firms that had been the focus of earlier development efforts in favor of suppliers from other regions and the home-country suppliers of the foreign partner. This is particularly true of Guangzhou, for instance, which is emerging as a major base of operations for Japanese firms. The new approach might very well lead to vibrant regional auto networks – particularly if the new reliance on foreign firms leads to the creation of Japanese-style networks – but there may also be very little that is Chinese about these networks. In fact, it might be argued that the locality is essentially benefiting from the institutional characteristic of its foreign partners' home country; the Japanese networks that might emerge in Guangzhou are the result of a Japanese context and the primary local input was the Guangzhou government's decision to grant its foreign partners the autonomy to replicate their standard supply networks. In the absence of strong state support in the initial stage of development for local Chinese firms, these firms will find it difficult to meet the technical demands of the higher value-added parts of the supply network in the second stage.

The fortunes of the *firm-dominated localities*, Changchun and Wuhan, improved considerably – to a certain extent a dramatic increase in demand solved the problems that had been caused by weak support at the local level during the lean years – but it is also possible the improvement might be too little too late: not enough failure to provide the motivation for a completely new strategy and too little early success to provide a strong local base. Perhaps not surprisingly, in the second stage of development, the centrally controlled business groups that had their bases in these regions began to increasingly focus their efforts on projects in new regions and greenfield sites. As in the laissez-faire local states, the advantage of relying on firms from outside the home locality was that the weaknesses of the local institutional structure could be avoided. It is much easier to utilize outside resources than it is to make the institutional changes required to cultivate similar resources at home.

The *local developmental state* had a considerable advantage over its regional competitors because success in the first stage of development gave it a strong base to build upon. In a highly competitive industry, the major assembly firms have neither the time nor inclination to put local firms through a lengthy apprenticeship – it is much easier to source from global suppliers. Local resources become critical, and Shanghai firms had the advantage of two decades of nurturing and incremental upgrading. But Shanghai, while highly effective at coordinating investment, lowering risk for individual firms, and promoting learning, was far less effective at driving down manufacturing costs. Much to the contrary, the local bureaucracy and business group did everything possible to shield individual firms from competitive market pressures, and as might be expected, there was resistance to changing long-accepted approaches. The local developmental state, if it was to survive, had to introduce a greater degree of competition into the supply network.[102]

The Shanghai municipal government, like governments the world over, was beset by competing objectives and imperfect measures of success and accountability, and withdrawing the warm blanket of support from local firms proved almost as difficult as figuring out how to effectively provide it. The impetus for change came from beyond municipal borders, and consisted of a combination of increased foreign investment and fear of the impact of WTO accession. The creation of a new joint venture project in Shanghai brought a foreign partner that was committed to establishing operations that would be competitive in a post-WTO context, and using the global benchmarks for individual component prices as evidence of local weakness, the new partner exerted strong pressure for introducing competition within the local supply network and allowing purchases from low-cost suppliers outside of Shanghai (particularly in neighboring Jiangsu and Zhejiang provinces). The influence of the

---

[102] In other words, Shanghai had to move from the upper-left quadrant of Table 1.1 toward the lower-left quadrant.

hierarchical business group in Shanghai did not immediately dissolve, but it was increasingly supplemented (and constrained) by market forces and costs began to decline.

The effectiveness of the internal governance of the Shanghai business group is still very much in question – it remains a state-owned enterprise with many of the classic problems of its breed – but the early success of the local developmental state has given it a wealth of resources and a potential trajectory that is quite different from its domestic competitors.[103] Globalization and the rapidly shifting needs of an industrial sector necessitate a more nuanced role for the state, but the importance of this role is as vital as ever.

IV. CASE SELECTION AND STRUCTURE OF THE BOOK

Although the primary focus of this book is a single industry in a single country, the research methodology is explicitly comparative.[104] My intent is to understand how alternative political and economic institutional structures affect the ability of a developing country to promote the development of networks of supply firms around a core foreign-invested project. The focus on a single country makes it possible to hold constant the macroeconomic environment and the policy framework set by the central government – such as localization requirements, foreign exchange restrictions, and tariff levels – while having variation at the subnational level.

Within the single country, the population of potential cases might have included all local governments that utilize FDI. As explained in this chapter, a focus on a single industry makes it possible to hold constant the characteristics of the sector – the capital intensity, the degree of asset specificity, and the nature of learning within a supply network.[105] The auto industry was appropriate because of the extent of FDI in the sector, the heavy emphasis the government placed on the sector and its importance to the overall economy, and the extent to which development success

---

[103] As I will discuss in Part III, in 2004, the Shanghai business group began a process of global acquisitions aimed at complementing the capabilities that it had gained from its foreign partners, and perhaps more to the point, compensating for those that it had not.

[104] As Gerring (2004: 342) comments, a "country may function as a case, a unit, a population, or a case study. It all depends upon what one is arguing."

[105] As I will explain at greater length in the conclusion, when drawing conclusions for other sectors, the motivations driving foreign investment in a sector, and in particular whether it is market-seeking or cost-cutting, are also of critical importance.

depends on broad networks of firms. Again, the dependent variable of the study is *not* the success of particular joint venture assembly plants, but rather the development of the networks of supply firms that support these assembly plants.

Within the potential population of localities that have been supporting the development of the local auto industry, five cases were selected: Beijing, Guangzhou, Changchun, Shanghai, and Wuhan. The automotive industry covers a diverse set of activities, of course, and this book focuses only on municipalities with joint venture projects for passenger vehicles. The purpose of limiting the sample to cities with JVs was to control for the long-term objectives and quality standards of the enterprise. Most auto enterprises in China are extremely small scale. Believing high profits are to be had, every town and province wants to manufacture their own mini-van, small bus, or truck.[106] Firms use the protection of the local government to supply a captured market, and when quality is not a concern, locating – as opposed to *developing* – local suppliers is not a problem. The municipalities with JV assembly projects, by contrast, must receive the approval of the central government and they have the common objective of mass-producing sedans in high volumes and marketing them nationally.

In contrast to the vast majority of these local operations, the objectives of both the political and economic actors in the five selected case studies were similar. From the perspective of these local governments, the objective was not simply to manufacture cars, but to develop basic manufacturing capabilities in a wide variety of industries. Extensive forward and backward linkages created the potential for a tremendous positive spillover effect. At the hub of an integrated industrial structure would be the joint ventures. Linkages with foreign firms would increase the technical knowledge and management skills of the joint venture assembly plants, and this knowledge would then disseminate to the hundreds of supply firms that would be required to support the core assembly plant. The assumption was that Chinese firms would rely on foreign partners in the short-term, but over time, networks of Chinese firms organized in business groups would increase their own manufacturing and development capabilities, and evolve into strong and independent economic actors. From the perspective of the firms, the objective was to compete nationally with each other, and in the same market niche:

---

[106] In 1996, for instance, 22 out of 30 provinces and municipalities designated the local auto industry as a key area for economic growth.

All were producing cars that by Chinese standards would be considered mid-to upper-range cars. The quality standards of the foreign partners and the degree of competition made it important to maintain high quality standards, and these standards made the localization process a critical challenge. The enterprises invariably began by importing complete knocked-down kits (CKDs), but had to quickly develop a domestic supply base that was capable of manufacturing parts of the same standard as the car that the foreign company was producing at the assembly plant. Foreign partners did not want to produce a car under their brand name that would fall apart as soon as it hit the Chinese roads (which are not known for being smooth). In short, the opportunities and constraints of these firms were roughly similar.

I excluded cases that did not have a track record of at least one decade from formal analysis (although they will be considered in a peripheral fashion). This was partly because municipalities with more recent JV projects did not have a significant track record to analyze, but even more importantly, the challenges of localization have substantially changed. There is a strong pre-existing base of supply firms on which new JVs can rely, and it is easier to import components.[107] The primary cases of this study were all starting at a low level of development and each was initially attempting to build its own network of suppliers. A sixth municipality, Tianjin, also developed a significant base for the manufacturing of sedans during the same period, but it did not have a joint venture project until 2002. Until the formation of the joint venture, Tianjin licensed technology, and produced a lower end vehicle (the Xiali). The lower quality standards made the localization process fundamentally different.

Finally, within these five cases, the variation was also appropriate (see Table 1.1). The one limitation was the absence of one combination of the explanatory variables (unified bureaucratic structures and market-based firm relations), but this combination did not exist in the universe of

---

[107] Foreign investment in the passenger vehicle sector can be broadly grouped into three waves. The initial wave of investment occurred in the mid-1980s, when the central government approved the formation of three joint venture assembly projects: Beijing Jeep, Guangzhou Peugeot, and Shanghai Volkswagen. These were the early pioneers. The second wave came in the early 1990s, when the central government approved a second VW project, this time with FAW in Changchun, and then a partnership between Dongfeng and Citroen in Wuhan. The third wave began in the late 1990s, when General Motors formed a second JV in Shanghai and Honda took over the Peugeot operation in Guangzhou. These more recent entrants were followed by Toyota, Hyundai, Nissan, and Ford.

possible cases. As explained in Chapter 2, there was also wide variation on the dependent variable. Data was systematically collected across the five cases for each of these variables by means of a "structured, focused comparison."[108] As explained in more detail in the appendix on research methods, a series of structured interviews was conducted in each case study. Interviews with the full range of actors within each locality (local government officials, Chinese and foreign managers at the assembly plants, and managers at the supply firms), and multiple visits with many of these actors over a span of seven years, allowed confirmation and reconfirmation of the data. Between 1996 and 2004, 187 interviews were conducted in China.

This is not the first book that has used the Chinese auto industry as a case study. Eric Harwit, in particular, uses the early history of the joint venture projects to analyze the bureaucratic policy-making process, and his book provides an excellent account of the JVs in Beijing, Guangzhou, and Shanghai up until 1993. Its emphasis, however, is on the bureaucratic decision-making behind the joint venture assembly plants, and utilizes a decision-making framework in the tradition of Graham Allison. It is an "analysis of bureaucratic politics, government bargaining, and political misperception."[109] Jim Mann, a journalist with the *LA Times*, uses Beijing Jeep in the 1980s as an example of the perils of doing business in China. This classic book on the perils of doing business in China is rich in detail and anecdote with respect to the joint venture, but it is not a systematic account of development efforts and there is little discussion of the broader sector. Xiaohua Yang does focus on supply firms, and the linkages between Chinese and foreign firms, although primarily with respect to the truck industry in the late 1980s.[110] Yang's conclusions are also the opposite of my own. She saw few obstacles to supplier development, and believed that different regions would easily converge on the most effective approach.[111]

This book's approach, in contrast to these earlier works, is to focus on how political and economic institutions affect the ability of supply firms to meet certain development challenges. Rather than focusing on decision making at a JV assembly plant, like Harwit and Mann, this

---

[108] See King, Keohane, and Verba (1994: 45).
[109] Harwit (1995: 4). Harwit provides a partial update on his work in Harwit (2001).
[110] Yang (1995: Chapter 4).
[111] Yang (1995: 176).

book emphasizes the varying means of organizing a broad economic sector, and the economic consequences. The focus is on networks of firms in a given locality, not individual joint venture projects. Rather than assume that supplier development will follow easily from foreign linkages, like Yang, this book analyzes how alternative institutional structures shape the ability of supply firms to meet the challenges of development. The research for this book benefited greatly from these pioneering works, but in analyzing the relationship between local institutional patterns and supplier development it takes a significantly different tack. Not of least importance, the most recent of these previous works was published more than a decade ago, and the industrial landscape of China has, needless to say, changed dramatically in that time.

A Road Map

Local development efforts in the Chinese auto sector have varied widely, and this book seeks to understand why. Chapter 2 establishes the broader context for these local development efforts. It analyzes the role of the central government: its objectives with respect to auto sector development, the means at its disposal to realize these objectives, and the obstacles in its path. The center has the ability to broadly shape the structure of the industry, I argue, but central government policy cannot explain the dramatic regional variation within the industry. Using a variety of measures (the most important being the purchasing patterns of the actual JV assembly plants), I provide evidence of Shanghai's dominance in the protected market. As the market became increasingly competitive due to deepening global integration, Shanghai firms began to expand outward to other localities. JV assembly plants in Beijing, Guangzhou, and Changchun became increasingly competitive during this period, but the local supply bases in these localities were less successful. The chapter also introduces alternative explanations of this variation.

Part II of the book examines auto sector development during the first stage of development – within a protected domestic market. Chapter 3 explains the dimensions along which local development patterns varied (bureaucratic structures as they relate to investment and inter-firm relations), and the case study chapters – Chapters 4, 5, and 6 – are then organized according to the various combinations of these two dimensions. The primary intent is to understand outcomes: How did different institutional patterns lead to dramatically different development outcomes? A secondary purpose is to explain the choice of development strategy: Why did municipalities with the same objective take such different approaches? Each of the case studies explores the historical and political roots of each municipality's approach to auto sector development.

Successful development within a highly protected domestic market is hopefully only an interim objective, of course, and only a useful step in the long run if it leads to the development of internationally competitive firms. Part III examines development in the context of a more competitive environment. As integration with the global auto industry deepened in the late 1990s, firms faced two key challenges: increasing efficiency and raising the quality of vehicles. The focus of Chapter 7 is technical upgrading, and the challenges that Chinese firms faced as they integrated with a post-Fordist global auto industry. Although assembly plants with strong foreign partners had little problem increasing their quality levels in this new era of competition, the fate of the supply networks hinged on their level of development in the previous stage of growth – they had to learn to crawl before they could run. Chapter 8 focuses on the challenge of corporate governance. The primary focus of this chapter is Shanghai, simply because that was the only region that had capable suppliers at the start of the second stage, albeit ones that were highly inefficient. The dilemma for Shanghai was that the institutional structures that had proven so useful in the early stages of growth, made it extremely difficult to cut costs in the second stage of growth. Deepening integration was a key source of pressure for change, although it is still not clear whether it will prove to have been a sufficient source of change. The concluding chapter returns to the central themes of the book, and considers the implications of the argument.

TWO

The View from the Center

Long after the start of the reform period – and well after the proven success of the private sector – the fate of the state-owned sector in China continues to disturb the sleep of policymakers in the Chinese central government.

During much of the 1990s, the problem was nightmares, largely because of the government's dependence on an ever-weakening state sector. Unlike in rural areas, where the non-state sector transformed the labor force, in the politically sensitive urban areas, the state sector continued to employ a relatively stable share of the workforce until 1995.[1] At the beginning of the reform period, SOEs employed 78% of urban workers; in 1995, despite a dramatic decrease in output, they continued to employ 65%.[2] In urban areas the state sector accounted for half of the new jobs created between 1978 and 1995.[3] Similarly, the SOEs, despite their declining share of output, continued to contribute 71% of the Chinese government's revenue.[4] This dependence on state-owned firms would not have been a problem if these firms were healthy, of course, but unfortunately this was far from being the case. In 1996, the number of loss-making enterprises began to exceed the number making a profit, and the ratio of liabilities to assets for the sector as a whole was at an all-time high of 85%.[5] Fortunately, the locus of job creation moved away from the

---

[1] The problems of the state sector in the 1990s have received extensive attention. See, for instance, Lardy (1998) and Steinfeld (1998).

[2] Lardy (1998: 26).

[3] Lardy (1998: 28).

[4] Steinfeld (1998: 17).

[5] Lardy (1998: 40).

state sector after 1995, and toward private and foreign-invested firms. It became increasingly common for SOEs to lay off or furlough (*xiagang*) workers. Nevertheless, 78.8 million workers continued to be employed in the state sector in 2000, an amount virtually unchanged from two decades earlier, and the nonfinancial SOEs produced approximately one third of China's GDP.[6] Despite the hope that dependence on the state sector will continue to decrease in the future, in the present, there continues to be a great dependence on a sector that is, to an increasing extent, bankrupt.

Strangely, when policymakers were not having nightmares about the state sector during the 1990s, they were indulging in dreams of grandeur. The fate of the largest SOEs was an issue that tied into how policymakers viewed the China of the future, and these visions were not modest. The non-state firms that grew so rapidly during the first 20 years of the reform period were usually small- and medium-sized firms. Often township and village enterprises in rural areas, these firms increased the competitive pressure on small SOEs in urban areas, and the share of industrial output of the former rose at the expense of the latter.[7] These small non-state firms operated the factories that stock the shelves of the Wal-Marts of the world. They produced shoes, clothing, toys, tools, lighting fixtures, and picture frames – as most consumers in advanced industrial countries are well aware, almost anything that is relatively low-tech and inexpensive is made in China.

But while these flexible, market-oriented firms fueled an export boom in China, they were not viewed as replacements for large SOEs. Partly this is a statement of fact – the share of industrial output of large SOEs declined less rapidly than small- and medium-sized SOEs grew[8] – but even more importantly, it is about the future trajectory of the economy and Chinese firms. Small nonstate firms, while dynamic and nimble competitors, were not likely to provide the primary inputs of the Chinese economy, nor would they develop into the powerful, technologically advanced companies that Chinese leaders hoped would be both the backbone of a modern economy and the nation's representatives in the global economy. A small toy factory might very well generate a great deal of foreign

[6] Employment figure is from Rawski (2002: Table 4); share of GDP is from Mako and Zhang (2002: 3).

[7] Naughton (1995: 164).

[8] Naughton (1995: 164). As of 2000, large enterprise groups as a whole (defined as private and state-owned firms whose sales revenue and total assets were in excess of RMB 500 million) accounted for 22% of exports and 57% of total assets in the industrial sector, and of these, SOEs accounted for 92% of assets and 87% of sales. Mako and Zhang (2002: 1).

exchange, but even given time it would not become a General Motors, Boeing, or Microsoft. Chinese firms, while tremendously successful at competing on the basis of costs, had tremendous difficulty in moving away from commodity production and into the higher value-added, nonsubstitutable activities of the globally branded multinational corporations.[9]

Chinese leaders depended on the country's small and competitive firms, but were enthralled with the concept of building modern business (or enterprise) groups (*jituan qiye*).[10] Such groups were defined by Chinese regulation as "a combination of legally independent enterprises" consisting of a parent company, subsidiary companies in which the parent had majority ownership, member companies in which the parent had minority ownership, and other member enterprises or institutions.[11] These groups of firms were believed by many to be the cornerstone of a modern economy. To a certain degree this was because large firms were thought to be a solution to many of the key problems of Chinese industry: fragmented production (and a consequent inability to capture economies of scale), uncoordinated technology transfer (and consequently redundant investment), low research and development capability, weak brands, and poor overall quality.[12] As important, however, was the power of example. Rightly or wrongly, large firms were seen as a foundation of U.S. economic power, as well as the key element in the economic "miracles" of neighboring Korea and Japan, whose success China hoped to imitate.[13] As vice-premier Wu Banguo explained in 1998:

> In reality, international economic confrontations show that if a country has large companies or groups it will be assured of maintaining a certain market share and a position in the international economic order. America, for example, relies on General Motors, Boeing, Dupont and a batch of other multinational companies. Japan relies on six large enterprise groups and Korea relies on ten commercial groupings. In the same way now and in the next century our nation's position

---

[9] This is not to say that large private firms such as Midea and Galanz, both of which produce home appliances in Guangdong Province, are not trying to upgrade their technical capabilities, but thus far their progress has been limited. Steinfeld provides excellent analysis of why Chinese firms have difficulty moving into the higher value-added parts of global production chains in "Chinese enterprise development and the challenge of global integration," in Yusuf, Altaf, and Nabeshima, eds. (2004: Chapter 6).

[10] Both Peter Nolan (2001) and Lisa Keister (2000) provide accounts of the Chinese desire to build strong business groups.

[11] Mako and Zhang (2002: 1).

[12] See Industrial Group Division of the National Economic and Trade Commission (1995).

[13] For representative articles on the "lessons" of the Korean and Japanese experiences, see Chen Bingcai (1996), Huan (1996).

in the international economic order will be to a large extent determined by the position of our nation's large enterprises and groups.[14]

The Asian Financial Crisis and the continued difficulties of state-owned firms influenced debates over *how* to support the development of large firms, but there was little change in the objective. Support for large SOEs was given official sanction as a core of the reform program at the 15th Party Congress in 1997. According to the principle of "grasp the large and release the small" (*zhuada fangxiao*), the vast majority of small- and medium-sized SOEs were to go bankrupt or to change their ownership through corporatization, shareholding, or leasing. Large enterprises, however, were targeted for further reform and support.[15] Many interpreted the creation of the State-owned Assets Supervision and Administration Commission (SASAC) in the spring of 2003 as the new instrument for controlling these firms, and its hands-on style of management in subsequent years has lent credence to this view.[16] Only the number of firms that will be actively managed by the state has varied. In 1996, reference was made to 1,000–2,000 firms; in 1997, reference was made to 500 firms; in 2003, the number of firms controlled by the SASAC was set at 196, and the intent was to include the top 3 companies in each major economic sector, and 30–50 of these were to be globally competitive "national champions" by 2010.[17] The industrial policy statement issued for the auto industry in 2004 reiterated the government's objective of creating internationally competitive Chinese auto firms by the end of the decade.[18] These large, state-owned enterprises were the firms that would challenge the dominance of foreign multinationals, explained the chairman of SASAC in

[14] Cited in Nolan (2001: 17).

[15] Through "preferential policies" and "government financial support" the government's intent was to "to increase the competitiveness of Chinese industry in the globalized market," commented one observer. Fu Jing, "Colossal SOEs to Advance WTO Role," *China Daily*, December 8–9, 2001, p. 1, cited in Rawski (2002: 23).

[16] In its first two years of existence, it became increasingly apparent that SASAC would play an active role in controlling the activities of China's largest firms. "Its influence over policy has expanded, its direct, top-down control of the more sizable companies strengthened and it's at the center of many major decisions," commented the director of research at a consulting group that has advised SASAC. Chris Buckley, "In China, power to the center: State firms' agency still calls the shots," *International Herald Tribune*, June 1, 2005.

[17] Dwight H. Perkins, "Industrial and financial policy in China and Vietnam: A new model or a replay of the East Asian experience?" in Stiglitz and Yusuf (2001: 256). Fu Jing, "Colossal SOEs to Advance WTO Role," *China Daily*, December 8–9, 2001, p. 1, cited in Rawski (2002: 23). *China Economic Quarterly*, vol. 7, no. 3, 2003, p. 20.

[18] State Development and Reform Commission (2004).

the fall of 2004.[19] As one observer wryly commented, while foreigners preferred to focus on the "release the small" part of the new approach, Chinese policymakers focused on "grasping the large."[20]

This chapter focuses on the central government efforts to develop strong business groups in the auto industry. The center created a framework for industrial development, but was limited in its ability to determine outcomes in individual cases. The first section of the chapter describes the efforts in the early reform period to transform traditional state-owned factories into "pillars" of a modern economy, and the difficulty the center had directing development efforts. The central government could not direct and monitor the allocation of state capital in a manner that would avoid the problems of moral hazard, and it could not constrain local governments from pursuing their own objectives, even when they were in direct contradiction of central government policies.

This is not to say that the central government was helpless. The second section points to the primary levers of central government control, and in particular, its ability to regulate the entry of foreign investment and force firms to merge into corporate groups. By controlling and regulating foreign investment in the sector, the central government has been able to leverage the desire of foreign companies to access the domestic market in China, and concentrate the benefits in chosen projects. In the context of rapidly growing market demand, and the expectation that China would become one of the top three global automotive markets by 2010, the strategy has had a certain amount of success. The policies of the central government do not, however, explain why some localities utilize FDI as a means of promoting local development far more effectively than others. The final section of the chapter describes the regional variation that cannot be explained at the central level, and this paves the way for the local level analysis that follows in Part II of the book.

I. THE LIMITS OF CENTRAL POWER

At the start of the reform era, the Chinese auto industry had all the problems of Chinese industry in general: out-dated technology, dispersed

---

[19] "To accelerate the strategic adjustment of China's economic structure," Li argued, "we must vigorously pursue a strategy of creating major corporate conglomerates." Chris Buckley, "In China, power to the center: State firms' agency still calls the shots," *International Herald Tribune*, June 1, 2005.

[20] *China Economic Quarterly*, vol. 7, no. 3, 2003, p. 20.

The Chinese Auto Market (Passenger/Commercial)

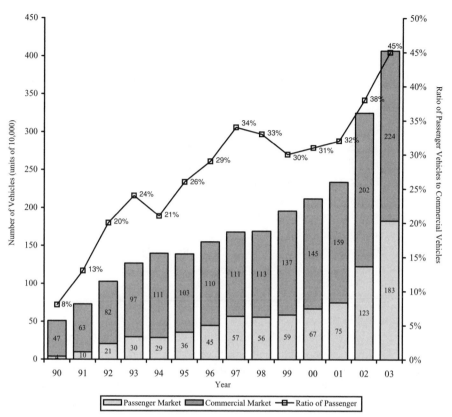

Figure 2.1: The Chinese Auto Market (Passenger/Commercial). *Source*: Honda Motor Company.

production, and consistently low quality. Three decades of intermittent development had resulted in very little progress.

Historically, the primary focus of the industry has been truck manufacturing (see Figure 2.1). Plans for the development of the First Auto Works (FAW) in Changchun began only six months after the formal establishment of the People's Republic, and it was one of the first projects to benefit from the Chinese alliance with the Soviet Union. The Chinese relied almost completely on the technical knowledge of Soviet advisors to construct the massive manufacturing facility.[21] It would be more accurate

---

[21] On the early history of the Chinese auto industry, see Harwit (1995: Chapter 2).

to call the factory a production unit rather than a firm in the micro-economic sense, because raw materials were allocated by central planning and output was swallowed by the same plan. All the manufacturing operations, from production of the most rudimentary components to final vehicle assembly, were carried out in one cavernous enterprise.[22] Although hardly an efficient approach to manufacturing, in the context of a weak industrial base, extensive vertical integration precluded the need for the coordinated development of a supply base – a much more difficult task. Needless to say, with the government as the sole customer, there was little need to consider production costs or worry about profitability.[23]

In 1956, the first "Liberation" truck rolled off of the FAW assembly line, and two years later the "Red Flag" limousine, a luxury model based on the Daimler-Benz 200 sedan, followed. The manufacturing system certainly was far from productive, but when the first car was delivered to the leadership compound in Beijing, Mao Zedong reportedly expressed his great happiness at finally riding in a domestically manufactured car.[24] The Shanghai Automotive Plant also began producing a passenger car, the "Phoenix," in 1958, but conditions did not allow for the mass production of sedans; production volumes were limited both by lack of demand and lack of a supply base.[25]

Over the next two decades, although the number of truck manufacturing facilities increased, production was extremely dispersed. Strategic concerns worked against rational production patterns. Rather than develop large-scale manufacturing facilities in industrial centers, Mao relocated factories to remote regions of the country where they would be safe from invading forces. The number of manufacturing operations increased, but production volumes and technical capabilities did not.

In 1978, at the start of the reform period, China had 56 auto assembly plants that produced 149,062 vehicles of all types, and 2,640 sedans.[26] Vehicles continued to be based on Eastern Europe designs from the 1950s. Americans auto experts visiting Chinese assembly and component factories shortly after the beginning of the reform program reported that "most [auto factories] operate at only about 20 percent of capacity, either because they produce only for their locality, lack some critical raw material input, or are simply unfamiliar with the potential economies

---

[22] Hiraoka (2001: 499); Marukawa (1995: 330).
[23] Zhang and Taylor (2001: 263).
[24] Cao Zheng Hou, "Yaolan de Huihuang" [Glory of the Cradle], in Sun (1995: 102).
[25] Shanghai Auto Industry History Editorial Committee (1992: 40).
[26] Ministry of Machinery Industry (1994: 63 and 73).

of scale."[27] In 1981, the Chinese auto industry employed 904,000 workers and produced 176,000 four-wheeled vehicles. In 1980, by contrast, 683,000 Japanese autoworkers produced 11,043,000 four-wheeled vehicles.[28]

In 1984, Premier Zhao Ziyang announced that China sought to produce automobiles up to world standards (i.e., exportable) by 1990, double production volumes, and switch from an "all-under-one-roof mentality of small-scale development" to a "cooperative industrial complex system, centered around large-scale factories based on modern technology...."[29] The effort to develop the auto industry began in earnest in 1986, when the central government designated the sector as a "pillar industry." The objectives of government policy were clearly defined: first, production was to be consolidated and there was to be no independent producers under provincial control; second, the development of passenger car production would take priority and become the core of the industry; third, the technological capabilities of the industry were to be upgraded through linkages to international auto companies; fourth, local content was to be steadily increased; and, finally, production levels were to be increased to 600,000 units a year.[30] These objectives were reiterated and formalized in 1994, when the State Planning Commission issued a formal industrial policy for the auto industry, the objective of which was to change "the current situation of dispersion in investment, small production scale and backwardness of auto products... [and to] build China's automobile industry into a pillar industry of the national economy."[31] In a series of meetings sponsored by the Ministry of Machinery in the same year, the examples of Korea and Japan were put forth as cases in which governments had successfully promoted industrial development, and thus should be imitated.[32] The desire for a state-led industrial policy peaked during this period. As Chen Yuan, son of the party elder Chen Yun and an influential economic policy specialist in Beijing, forcefully argued in a 1991 article, China could not take the path of a small country; it needed a complete and advanced industrial system, and market forces

---

[27] Weil (1986: 29).
[28] Marukawa (1995: 333).
[29] Iwagaki (1986: 11).
[30] Takayama (1991: 17–19) and Iwagaki (1986: 11). For a detailed account of the central government political structures overseeing auto sector development during this period, see Harwit (1995: Chapter 3).
[31] "Industrial Policy of China's Automobile Industry," State Planning Commission, February 19, 1994, reprinted in Hu and He (1995: 183).
[32] For a summary of these meetings, see "Yantaohui Zongshu," [Symposium Summary], Ministry of Machinery Industry (1994b: 11).

alone could not be relied upon to direct scarce resources to strategic industries.[33]

Despite the central government's apparent desire to direct the development of the auto sector and other "pillar" industries, its ability to do so was limited. The first problem was financial. As I will explain at greater length in the next chapter, finance was a key element of the developmental state in Japan and Korea. Under the direction of an industrial bureaucracy that was to a certain extent isolated from societal pressures, the government-controlled financial system channeled investment capital to what were perceived to be strategic sectors. Individuals, with no choice but to make their deposits in the closed financial system, ended up subsidizing the large firms that received subsidized credit. The state was thought to be more reliable than the market.

In keeping with this model of a developmental state, Beijing policymakers such as Chen Yuan viewed the market as an unreliable means of directing scarce resources to strategic industries. In China, however, the central government was even *more* unreliable, assuming strategic is meant to refer to sectors and firms that would increase the country's long-run competitiveness. The country was not short of capital during this period – Chinese saving rates were among the highest in the world. Between 1986 and 1992, the savings rate was approximately 36% and between 1994 and 1997, it increased to 42%.[34] The problem was that the central government usually defined "strategic" according to political rather than economic criteria, and as a result, directed the resources of the financial system to those places and firms that were least competitive, either out of a desire to preserve the dominant economic role of the state or a fear of the political consequence of massive failure in the state sector. Efforts in the 1990s to curtail policy loans had only a limited impact: bankrupt SOEs continued to receive the predominance of lending, sometimes necessary simply to pay their workers, and the government increased its effort to transfer resources from the rapidly growing coastal areas to the less competitive – and vastly poorer – hinterland.[35] While few would argue with the goal of paying workers and lessening the vast regional inequalities within China,

---

[33] Fewsmith (2001: 86).
[34] Huang (2003: 45). As Huang notes, only Singapore had a higher savings rate. Savings rate is defined as the difference between GDP and final consumption divided by GDP and his data is from the Chinese State Statistical Bureau.
[35] On the relationship between SOEs and the financial sector, see Steinfeld (1998). On the financial sectors systematic discrimination against competitive private sector firms, see Huang (2003).

the result of doing so through the financial system was highly problematic. Capital was allocated to those sectors and regions that were least likely to utilize it productively, while those that were most productive were unable to secure bank financing. Not only was the state unable to direct capital to economically strategic sectors in the manner of a developmental state, the market could not either.[36]

The finances of the central government itself were in ever worsening shape during this period. At exactly the same time that the central government was speaking of the need for a centrally controlled industrial policy – the early 1990s – the economic resources of the central government were reaching an all-time low: in 1978, fiscal revenue in China was 31.2% of GNP, but by 1992 the ratio had dropped to 14.2%.[37] Scholars warned of a crisis in China's state capacity and, unless the trend was reversed, the potential disintegration of the Chinese state.[38] A major overhaul of the tax system in 1994 improved the situation, but nevertheless, resources at the center were limited.

The second key problem limiting the central government's ability to direct auto sector development was its inability to properly constrain local governments. The demands on local governments were heavy; the increased incentives that flowed from fiscal decentralization were matched with increased responsibilities, and to a great extent localities were forced to rely on their own resources to meet these responsibilities. The situation was exacerbated by the tax reforms of 1994 – the objective of which was to solidify the central government revenue – because the share of official budgetary revenue retained by the localities declined, but local expenditures did not.[39] Fiscal decentralization in the 1980s had initially

---

[36] Even if the central government had been able to direct resources at selected sectors, this would have been problematic given that the overall purpose of reforms was to move away from government planning and toward a market economy. As an official in the State Planning Commission's Department of Long-term Planning and Industrial Policy commented with respect to the 1994 industrial policy plans, "Not only did the central government not have the financial resources, but the general desire to move towards a market-based system, made an old-style industrial policy very difficult." After much debate, he commented, the central government (despite the dissension of many line ministries) began in 1995 to move away from an industry-specific approach and toward a functional approach. Interview, no. B12, April 25, 1997.

[37] Wang and Hu (2001: 53).

[38] In the worst case scenarios, Wang and Hu (2001: 61) warned, "the state's financial extractive capacity would decline steadily and, in not too many years – perhaps in just a few – we could go from economic disintegration to political fragmentation, and, in the end, fall into national disintegration."

[39] Zhang (1999: 134–5).

created the incentives for local governments to place local developmental objectives over national; because the 1994 reforms often coincided with economic difficulties that were created by overproduction and shrinking demand, these incentives were only accentuated.[40] The combination of continued social burdens in locally controlled firms and fewer resources to meet these needs meant that local governments did everything possible to keep local firms afloat both as a source of revenue and employment – often in direct opposition to the directives of the central government.

While in an ideal system, the center would create incentives for localities to promote growth and all levels of government would cooperate to maintain a unified domestic marketplace, in reality, the latter half of this equation was missing.[41] As with individual firms, the center had difficulty imposing hard budget constraints on local governments. First, even after the central government's attempts to reign in local investment after 1994, creative local officials could always find sources of capital for favored projects: foreign investment, extra-budgetary funds, control over local banks, even local curb markets.[42] In fact, according to some scholars, the quantity of nonbudgetary funds available to local government in China during the 1990s was often considerably more than twice the quantity of the official budget.[43] Second, and in the event that a local project was not competitive, local officials would resort to protectionism. In the late 1980s and early 1990s, for instance, reports of regional blockades were commonplace. For any product for which production capability was relatively evenly distributed across regions – televisions, refrigerators, washing machines, liquor, cement, farm machinery, cars, and so on – local governments would openly prohibit the purchasing of products from outside their jurisdiction, use technical restrictions to restrict their sale, or levy extra sales taxes so as to decrease their sales.[44] At times the protectionist measures could be quite subtle, and very difficult for the central

---

[40] Li (1993: 41).

[41] This idealized version is described in the concept of market-preserving federalism. See Montinola, Qian, and Weingast (1995).

[42] Tsai (2000: 4).

[43] For careful explanation of the how non-budgetary funds are defined, collected, and utilized, see Zhang (1999: 126).

[44] Li (1993: 38). To give one indication of how internal trade barriers affect the domestic market, inter-provincial trade fell from 37% of national retail trade in 1985 to about 25% in 2000. Tenev and Zhang with Brefort (2002: 21). Yasheng Huang (2003) similarly points to institutional barriers to interprovincial investment. Because of such barriers, he argues, the demand for FDI is artificially increased. Wedeman (2003) provides excellent analysis of the dynamics behind local protectionism.

government to combat. Because state-owned enterprise were the dominant market for vehicles, for example, a local government could protect
the local market for automobiles simply by directing enterprises under
its control to purchase from a particular manufacturer, or by attaching
higher fees to cars manufactured in other localities.[45]

The central government could prevent a local auto manufacturer from
expanding beyond its home jurisdiction – it used the security bureau
to deny licenses to cars that were not manufactured by an approved
plant – but if a firm was content to stay within the home locality, the local
government could provide it with the necessary approvals.[46] The result
was predictable: local authorities promoted enterprises within their geographic jurisdiction without regard to quality or efficiency, and protected
the local market. Despite the importance of economies of scale in the auto
industry – it is typically believed that 250,000 units of a given model is a
minimum efficient scale – there were 115 vehicle assembly plants in China
in 1998. Out of 31 provinces, only five did not have their own assembly
plant.[47] Although few of these factories were able to capture economies
of scale, with the benefit of local protectionism they were able to siphon
off the markets of the larger firms that had central government support.

Failure to consolidate the auto industry is not necessarily a sign of
government incompetence. It is a task that has frustrated governments
that are usually credited with otherwise being quite adroit at industrial
planning. The Ministry of International Trade and Industry (MITI) in
Japan, for instance, grew increasingly concerned in the early 1960s that
over-investment in the auto sector would prevent manufacturers from
achieving economies of scale. It sought to restrict the number of new
entrants and reorganize existing producers into three mass production
"groups" – a familiar goal – but had only limited success.[48] As in China,

---

[45] In 1998, even after significant growth of the private market, private sales accounted for
only 30.2% of overall sales of passenger vehicles. Government purchases accounted for
17.1%, taxi companies (almost always state-owned) accounted for 34.7%, and business
sales accounted for 18%. Zhongguo Qiche Jishu Yanjiu Zhongxin (2000: 136).

[46] Dongfeng (SAW), for instance, had a great deal of trouble entering the bus market,
according to Marukawa, "because most of the purchasers of buses are the local civil
engineering bureaus and transportation offices which buy buses produced by firms under
their control; they do not purchases buses from other firms." Many produced just a few
dozen vehicles a year. Marukawa (1995: 344).

[47] Huang (2003: 115). The average production volume for the industry as whole was about
14,165 units.

[48] Machiko Watanabe, "Japan – Industrial Policy and the Development of the Automotive
Industry," in Inoue, Kohama, and Urata (1993: 202–3). Capital investment in the industry
increased from 4 billion yen in FY 1955 to 52.6 billion yen in FY 1960 to 112.8 billion yen

new firms continued to enter the market for passenger vehicles.[49] But
the central government in Japan was able to preserve the constraint of
domestic competition, and despite the protected national marketplace,
firms had to survive withering domestic competition in order to survive.

In China, by contrast, it was not unusual in the 1990s to see Chinese
newspapers reporting on the unusual phenomena of "trade" negotiations
being conducted by municipal governments, and the central government
readily acknowledged the severity of the problem.[50] A growing number
of intellectuals, concerned about the broader trend that this represented,
began to argue that a more powerful, authoritarian central government
was necessary to overcome the vested interests of local governments and
push forward economic reform and full marketization.[51]

II. THE SOURCES OF CENTRAL POWER: INDUSTRIAL POLICY, CHINESE-STYLE

Despite the limited nature of its power, the central government has not
been helpless. In fact, when the 1986 objectives for the auto sector – consolidation, passenger vehicles as the core, increased technical capabilities,
high local content, and high production volumes – are compared to the
current state of the industry, it is not unreasonable to say that Beijing has,
in some respects, achieved its objectives. Although the overall number of
vehicle assemblers continues to be high, the number of major producers

in FY 1965 as Toyota, Nissan, Isuzu, Prince, Hino, Fuji, and Honda all began building
passenger vehicle manufacturing facilities. The government was successful in arranging
the Nissan merger with Prince and the Toyota tie-up with Hino in 1966.

[49] The Korean government, although largely successful in consolidation efforts, sometimes
found it had limited capacity to overcome determined private interests. For a description of Korean efforts to rationalize the auto industry in the 1970s and 1980s, see John
Ravenhill, "From National Champions to Global Partners: Crisis, Globalization, and the
Korean Auto Industry," in Keller and Samuels (2003: 116–119).

[50] On the "trade" negotiations of local governments, see *Zhonghua Gongshang Shibao*
(China Business Times), December 17, 2002, as reported in "China Hubei official urges
talks with Shanghai on removing protectionist auto laws," ChinaOnline, December 23,
1999 (accessed September 23, 2002). On the concerns of the central government, see
"Zhongyang caizheng lingdao xiaozu dui qiche gongye fazhan de zhibiao" [Targets of the
Finance Leading Small Group for the Auto Industry] in *Guojia Qiche Gongye Zhengce
Xinbian* [Collection of New Auto Industry Policies] (1994: 72); see also the series of
research reports written for the Development Research Centre of the State Council,
Long (1996, 1996b). The importance of local protectionism in the auto sector lessened
as the private market began to expand in 2002 and 2003.

[51] This refers to the rise of "neoconservatism" in the 1990s. Fewsmith (2001: 77).

Share of Sedan Market by Manufacturer, 2002

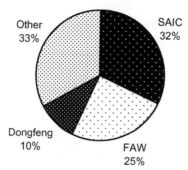

Figure 2.2: Share of sedan market by manufacturer in 2002. *Note*: SAIC percentage includes Shanghai Volkswagen, Shanghai General Motors; FAW percentage includes FAW-VW, FAW-Xiali; Dongfeng percentage includes Dongfeng-Citroen, Dongfeng-Fengshen. *Source*: KPMG, "China automotive and component parts market."

is much smaller. The three dominant corporate groups in the industry – FAW, Dongfeng, and SAIC – accounted for 67% of sedan manufacturing in 2002 (see Figure 2.2), and their combined production in 2003 was 1.38 million sedans.[52] This dominance declined in 2004 and 2005, as competition increased, but the challengers were also mass producing on a large scale. The major producers are still not at international levels with respect to costs, but they are close to world-class standards in terms of quality and technology. Local content rates for most models are high, and exports of components are increasing rapidly. How did a seemingly hapless central government, in at least several respects, make significant progress towards achieving its initial objectives?

Merger and Acquisitions

Despite its limited ability to prevent the emergence of local production facilities, the center has used merger and acquisitions to push the development of the targeted large corporate groups, part of a larger effort to develop what Peter Nolan has called a "national team" of enterprise

[52] The production volume figure is from "China emerges as the world's fourth-largest auto maker," *Taiwan Economic News*, April 16, 2004.

groups in sectors that are considered to be of strategic importance.[53] FAW, for instance, evolved from a loose affiliation of ten member enterprises in the early 1980s to a corporate group that included 155 automakers, components firms, trading firms, and research organizations in 1992.[54] In 2002, it acquired a controlling stake in Tianjin Auto, a giant in the Chinese auto industry in its own right.[55] Similar strategies were behind the acquisitions of Dongfeng and SAIC, which, along with FAW, had clearly been designated by the central government as the core corporate groups in the auto industry.[56] Often what happens is a process of co-option: a locally controlled firm increases in size and the center uses its regulatory power to force it under the umbrella of one of the major groups.[57] As in many industries, the central government has shown a clear preference for controlled competition between a limited number of large firms.[58]

Although such mergers increase the size of a member of the "national team" in the auto sector, it cannot be assumed that, from an economic perspective, the results are positive. It is tempting to see parallels between the mergers in the Chinese auto industry and the global auto industry – in an industry characterized by overcapacity the strong take over the weak

---

[53] Other sectors included electricity generation, coal mining, electronics, iron and steel, machinery, chemicals, construction, transport, aerospace, and pharmaceuticals. Nolan (2001: 18).

[54] Tomoo Marukawa, "WTO, Industrial Policy and China's Industrial Development," in Yamazawa and Imai (2001: 36–7).

[55] "Toyota inks tie-up with FAW group," *The Nikkei Weekly*, September 2, 2002.

[56] Wu Xiaohua, director of the State Bureau of Machine Building Industry, announced in December 2000 that no new sedan manufacturing facilities would be established during the 10th Five Year Plan. Instead, emphasis would be placed on developing FAW, SAW, and Shanghai. "China to accelerate the restructuring, concentration of its auto industry," ChinaOnline, January 4, 2000 (accessed September 22, 2002). In that plans for the major expansion of the Beijing and Guangzhou automotive groups were announced only 2 years later, it is clear that the central government continued to have difficulty focusing support on only three corporate groups.

[57] When the Chery Automotive Company of Anhui Province emerged as a rapidly growing player in 2000, the center would not grant it a license to sell outside of Anhui until SAIC bought a 20% stake in the firm. "Chery sedan ready to drive in Chinese New Year," ChinaOnline, January 22, 2001 (accessed April 4, 2003). Similarly, after Honda formed a JV with the local government in Guangzhou, the center directed Honda to create an engine JV with Dongfeng. The ties between Chery and SAIC were severed in 2004 after the Anhui firm was accused of pirating GM designs, but in light of Chery's success, it enjoyed significant state support of its own at this point.

[58] As Margaret Pearson (2003) argues, in its desire for controlled competition, the central government has used its regulatory power to both break up monopolies (telecom, electric power, and insurance) and, as in autos, avoid excessive fragmentation (airlines). In each case the preferred outcome seems to be competition between 3 or 4 dominant firms.

and cut costs by eliminating overlapping capabilities, merging complementary capabilities (both in terms of products and geographic reach), and pooling development costs. In many (if not most) cases, however, the Chinese mergers are not made after careful due diligence by the firms involved, but are made at the bequest of the government. In fact, in many instances, the acquiring firm opposes the merger because it is acquiring nonperforming assets that will only add to the burden of existing assets.[59] Although the policy of mergers may look impressive because it appears to be leading to the creation of powerful corporate groups, it can also be a convenient way for the government to avoid the trauma of allowing firms that are not economically viable from failing. The government's attitude, according to Jia Xinguang, a researcher at the China Institute of Auto Industry Development, is that the healthy can carry the sick, but in that the problems of the sick are often so severe, "the living are getting tired to death from carrying the dead."[60]

Foreign Direct Investment

The most important source of leverage for the central government is its ability to regulate and control foreign investment in the auto sector. In essence, it is industrial policy on the cheap. Rather than pay for foreign technology through licensing – as was more the norm for Japan and Korea – it has paid for technology and managerial skills by trading access to the domestic market. Reliance on foreign investment, of course, is in many respects the defining feature of China's development path.[61] Over the last decade, China has consistently been one of the world's most popular destinations for foreign investment; in 2002, in part due to a stagnant American economy, it gained the number one ranking.[62] From 1992 to 1997 China attracted US $196.8 billion in FDI, and

---

[59] As I will explain in Chapter 6, this is particularly true in the case of FAW, but far from unusual elsewhere. In 1997, for instance, SAIC took over two local television manufacturers in Shanghai. At the time, "analysts said the decision to bring [SAIC] into the picture was part of a radical play by the municipal government to get powerful unlisted state-owned enterprises to rescue badly-run companies from bankruptcy." Foo Choy Peng, "SAIC joins bailout group," *South China Morning Post*, March 14, 1997, p. 5.

[60] "First Auto Works unhappy, unwilling to absorb Tianjin Auto," ChinaOnline, April 15, 2002 (accessed September 22, 2002). This problem is examined in detail in later chapters.

[61] For an excellent study of early FDI policy and joint ventures in China, see Pearson (1991).

[62] China attracted US $52.7 billion in FDI in 2002. Simon Cartledge, "The other side of China's success," *The Financial Times*, January 20, 2003, p. 11.

since 1997 it has attracted over $45 billion annually.[63] Since 1995, over half of China's manufacturing exports have been from foreign-invested enterprises.[64]

It is important to distinguish between the motivations of FDI, however. Much of it is cost-cutting investment from firms in neighboring countries that are trying to escape rising costs at home. Firms relocate manufacturing operations to China in order to take advantage of low-cost labor and less stringent regulation, and the products are then exported. Between 1990 and 1997, for example, 53.1% of FDI in China was from Hong Kong and 8.5% was from Taiwan.[65] The vast majority of this investment is in labor intensive, low-tech industries – the top three industries for HK investment in 1993 were electronics (23.37%), plastic products (12.14%), and textiles (11.22%) – and the final products are exported.[66] Foreign-invested enterprises dominate Chinese exports in a wide swath of industries: food processing (57.5%), garments (60.5%), furniture (75.1%), plastic products (77.2%), and electronics and telecommunication (94.5%), to name a few.[67] Because such investment is driven by a desire to lower costs, it is sensitive to any attempt at regulation and control, and investment-hungry local governments end up competing for investment. The central government does little to control the inflow. In fact, according to Yasheng Huang, the dominance of foreign-invested enterprises in such industries is an indication of institutional weakness in China, a sign that competitive firms in China – that is, private firms – face systematic discrimination and market fragmentation prevents interprovincial

[63] These figures are for realized FDI. Cassidy (2002: 42).

[64] Huang (2003: 16). For details on China's extraordinary dependence on FDI, see Huang (2003: Chapter 1).

[65] Cassidy (2002: 53). The Hong Kong percentage is inflated both because companies from other Asian countries invest through Hong Kong (including Taiwanese companies seeking to avoid political complications) and companies from mainland China invest via Hong Kong subsidiaries so as to take advantage of preferential policies for FDI – what is called round-trip FDI. Even an accurate accounting for these forces – Huang (2002) estimates round tripping to account for 32% of Hong Kong FDI – would be unlikely to dramatically decrease the overall importance of Hong Kong FDI.

[66] Huang (2003: 22–23). For a careful study on the manner in which Hong Kong firms have relocated to China, see Berger and Lester (1997).

[67] These percentages are for the exports of foreign-invested enterprises as a share of total exports for that industry in 1995. Huang (2003: 24). In 2004, according to the Customs General Administration of the PRC, foreign-invested firms exported US$338.61 billion worth of goods, and this accounted for 57.1% of China's total exports. 78.7% of the exports from foreign-invested firms was accounted for by the processing trade. Zhang et al. (2005: 13).

investment.[68] If the central government were more effective, in other words, FDI would not be so high.

Investment in the Chinese auto sector represents an entirely different breed of FDI in China – market-seeking investment.[69] Companies such as Motorola, Nokia, Otis, Schindler, Proctor & Gamble, Nabisco, Coke, and Kodak, like the big auto companies, invest in China not because they want to cut costs – although this can certainly be an added benefit – but because they want access to the 1.3 billion consumers.[70] As Joe Studwell argues, the sales pitch for companies such as these has been the same for centuries: "the prospect of adding one quarter of the world's population to a corporation's list of potential clients in a single move, the prospect of a market with the statistical potential to become the biggest in the world."[71] The difficulty of realizing this potential, of course, has frustrated many a foreign firm, and for two decades the Chinese auto market was put forth as a classic case of how "the China dream" can blur the vision of even the most hard-headed of CEOs: billions of dollars were invested in a market that could barely support one assembly plant.

But the auto sector also provides tantalizing glimpses of how this potential can be realized. After a decade of painfully slow growth, sales of passenger vehicles exploded after 2001, increasing by more than 50% in 2002 and 2003 (see Figure 2.1), and the multinationals that dominated the market enjoyed record profits.[72] Driven by a nascent middle class

---

[68] Huang (2003).

[69] While it is difficult to determine exactly what percentage of Chinese FDI is market seeking, it is generally assumed that at the least, investment from advanced capitalist economies tends to be market seeking. Between 1990 and 1997, 7.4% of Chinese FDI was from the United States, 2.3% was from the UK, and 1.2% was from Germany. Cassidy (2002: 53). As Sun (1998: 27) notes, the average size of these investments is also larger: US $1.26 million for U.S. projects, US $5.43 million for UK projects, and US $5.43 million for German projects.

[70] Until 2002, when Honda announced plans for an export factory in Guangzhou, every JV assembly plant in China was focused primarily on the domestic market.

[71] Studwell (2002: xi).

[72] The profits of multinationals operating in China are notoriously difficult to pin down, but given the rapid growth in 2002 and 2003 and the continued benefits of a protected market, anecdotal evidence indicated that China was the most profitable market for many firms. Peugeot-Citroen, one of the few firms to publish profit data for its China operations, reported an operating profit margin of 12.2% for 2002: three times as high as its profits in Europe. James Mackintosh and Richard McGregor, "A leap over the cliff," *The Financial Times*, August 25, 2003, p. 15. According to another report, the profits of Shanghai GM in 2000 were 16% (compared to 6% for GM globally), the profits for Shanghai VW were 15% (compared to 2% for VW globally), and the profits for Guangzhou Honda were 22% (compared to 3% for Honda globally). Gao (2003: 5).

of 100 million people with an average annual income of US $4,000, expanding access to credit, and price cuts, the Chinese market was poised to overtake Germany as the third largest in the world.[73] From the perspective of the multinationals there were still considerable risks in China – looming overcapacity, fierce price wars, and a highly fragile financial system being the most prominent – and indeed, in 2004 a combination of intense price competition and a significant slowdown in demand quickly brought auto firms back to earth, but their long-term view remained unchanged. In 2000, China had 10 passenger cars on the road for every 1,000 people, as compared with 250 in Taiwan and more than 500 in Germany and the United States.[74] When faced with the prospect of stagnant growth at home, the risks in China were deemed to be acceptable. The multinationals may have been lemmings headed over a cliff, but few believed they could afford not to have a presence in China.

It is exactly this attitude that creates leverage for the Chinese government. Firms that are motivated by a desire to access the Chinese marketplace, rather than a general desire to cut costs, are more vulnerable to host government pressure in initial negotiations, and the Chinese government takes advantage of this leverage at every opportunity: the national investment regime in China, although open in comparison to its neighbors, has been far from liberal.[75] In the 1980s, not only did the ambiguity of the Joint Venture Law provide the government with a great deal of leeway for interpretation, but the specific terms regulating managerial control, access to the domestic market, taxation, and foreign exchange were highly restrictive. In fact, these restrictions, and the conflicts they inevitably gave rise to at Beijing Jeep, led Jim Mann to conclude that there was little hope for foreign firms that wanted to do business in China.[76] Only in specially designated areas – initially in the 4 special economic zones and then the expanded 14 open coastal cities – was there room for experimentation and special regulations.

In the 1990s, particularly after Deng Xiaoping's southern tour in 1992, the investment environment improved considerably. Foreign investors

---

[73] James Mackintosh and Richard McGregor, "A leap over the cliff," *The Financial Times*, August 25, 2003, p. 15.

[74] Gao (2002: 1).

[75] Although Bennett and Sharpe (1985) argue that market size and growth was a source of host country bargaining leverage in Latin America, Doner did not find a correlation between market size and the intensity of inter-MNC competition in SE Asia (Doner 1991: 92). The size of the Chinese economy may make it an exception.

[76] Mann (1989).

were granted greater access to the domestic market and greater control over management boards, tariffs on imports were lowered, the Chinese currency became convertible for transactions in the current account, and the development of a Company Law in 1994 increased the transparency of the FDI process.[77] The government was always careful to maintain control, however.[78] In response to concerns that foreign firms were being allowed to purchase key state assets in 1998, for instance, the central government issued the Industrial Catalogue for Guiding Foreign Investment, which divided FDI into four categories: encouraged, permitted, restricted, and prohibited. The intent was to insure that foreign investment was compatible with government industrial policies, and that the Chinese state would retain control in the "pillar" industries. In "restricted" categories, for instance, limits were placed on the equity stake of the foreign partner; in "prohibited" categories, foreign participation was barred completely.[79]

While a small firm with relatively low capital investment could always fly below the radar screen and, with the assistance of an investment-hungry local government, evade national regulations, an auto assembly joint venture could not. The central government had to approve the creation of a new assembly joint venture, the partners involved, the terms of the deal, and the model that would be produced.[80] This regulatory power gave the central government an unusual amount of leverage over both foreign and domestic firms. The result was an industrial policy of sorts. With respect to the foreign side, the central government played the multinationals off of each other. It would announce that it was going to approve one final assembly joint venture, and foreign firms, desperate not to be locked out of one of the last great auto markets, would claw over one another to get the contract.

---

[77] Sun (1998: 13–17) describes different phases of FDI regulation in detail. For impact on auto industry, see "State Trade Policies and their Impacts on Car Industry," *China Auto*, vol. 4, no. 1 (January–February 1994), p. 8–11.

[78] As Rosen notes, even after the central government published the "Provisional Guidelines for Guiding the Direction of Foreign Investment," in 1995 the center continued to have enormous arbitrary power: "vague language in the restricted category permits central authorities (who automatically review some projects and have final say on all) to arbitrarily reject projects they object to; ventures in encouraged sectors can also be blocked." Rosen (1999: 23).

[79] See Patrick M. Norton and Howard Chao, "Mergers and Acquisitions in China," *The China Business Review*, September–October (2001). The Catalogue is updated on a regular basis and has become increasingly liberal.

[80] For a general discussion of the governmental role in the choice of JV partners and the formulation of performance, local content, and technology transfer requirements, see Rosen (1999: Chapter 2).

The second assembly joint venture in Shanghai was a classic example. Two years were spent negotiating with four prospective partners – GM, Toyota, Nissan, and Ford – and then, once GM was chosen from these four, another year and half was taken to negotiate the joint venture agreement.[81] Even after they were engaged in exclusive negotiations, the GM side spoke of the "Ford Shadow," a reference to the fear that if GM did not give the Chinese what they wanted, the Chinese would renew negotiations with Ford.[82] At the top of the list of demands was technology. The Chinese partner wanted not only the general spec drawings of the models that would be produced in Shanghai, it wanted online access to the databases of GM's technology development center in the United States, and it wanted Computer Assisted Design (CAD) capability in a new technical development center in Shanghai. Although people involved in the negotiations were not specific with respect to the final terms of technology transfer, they would comment that GM "could not have gone much further." It wanted to build cars in China, and it was willing to pay in order to do so.[83]

The central government has also attempted to use its regulatory control over FDI to promote the development of centrally sanctioned domestic firms. It was one of the few means by which the central government could give a tangible positive benefit to a particular firm, and as such, could complement the merger and acquisition strategy. In theory, the "chosen" groups were able to obtain central government approvals for joint ventures with foreign firms and thus gain access to the technology and managerial skills that come with these partnerships. As the domestic automotive market develops and opens up to international competition, according to this line of thinking, the only firms that will be viable players will be those that have linkages to foreign partners. This is not (completely) the result of Chinese firms' weakness, so much as it is an indication of the costs of research and development in the auto sector, the rapid rate of change, and the needs for global economies of scale to cover these costs. Indeed, few firms from any country can go it alone anymore. By controlling the entry of foreign firms into China, leveraging the

---

[81] On the Chinese side, the chief negotiating party was the Shanghai Auto Industry, but it had to get multiple approvals at the central level (in particular, MMI, SPC, and MOFTEC). Often, according to negotiators on the GM side, the local government would play "good cop" to the central government's "bad cop." Interview, no. S11, May 31, 1997.

[82] Interview, no. S11, May 31, 1997.

[83] Interview, no. S11, May 31, 1997.

foreign firm's desire for market access into technology transfer, and then partnering these foreign firms with centrally sanctioned domestic firms, the central government gives dramatic advantage to a chosen few. It is no accident that the three firms that the central government would like to be the core of the Chinese auto industry – First Auto, Dongfeng, and Shanghai – each have two foreign partners.[84] As the central government is well aware, one partner is good, but when there are two, they can very effectively be played off of each other.

In practice, of course, even the central government has had difficulty focusing its support on particular firms. Following the 1986 designation of the "three big and three small" producers, for example, two additional firms were quickly added to the list of centrally sanctioned projects – Changan Automobile Corporation and Guizhou Aviation Industry Corporation. Both were owned by the military, and their high-level patrons in Beijing could easily lobby those in charge of the auto industry industrial policy.[85] At the end of the 1990s, the central government stated its attention to focus on the development of three corporate groups – First Auto, Second Auto, and Shanghai Auto – yet despite this declaration, major new auto projects continued to emerge.[86] The Beijing Automobile Industry Corporation announced in 2002 that it would be capitalizing upon new joint ventures with Hyundai and DaimlerChrysler to build an "auto city" in the suburbs of Beijing.[87] Guangzhou Automobile Industry Corporation has been using its partnerships with Honda and Toyota to develop a major automotive base in southern China. But even though the center has been scattered in its focus, it has attempted to roughly mold the shape of the industry – by denying licenses to small producers, by forcing mergers, and by controlling access to foreign partners.

Although the support of the central government may at times be useful, it is clearly an insufficient explanation for success in the Chinese auto sector. If it were a sufficient explanation, we would expect to see all regions

---

[84] First Auto is partnered with VW and Toyota (in Tianjin); Dongfeng is partnered with Citroen and Nissan (in Guangdong); Shanghai is partnered with VW and GM.

[85] Interview, no. B31, March 19, 1997.

[86] See, for instance, the comments of Wu Xiaohua, director of the State Bureau of Machine Building Industry in *Zhongguo Xinxi Bao* [China Information], December 28, 1999. "China to accelerate the restructuring, concentration of its auto industry," ChinaOnline, January 4, 2000 (accessed September 22, 2002).

[87] "Renault partners with Beijing auto to produce the scenic in China," ChinaOnline, January 21, 1999 (accessed September 23, 2002); "Hyundai Motor commits US$250 million to JV in Beijing," ChinaOnline, February 8, 2002 (accessed September 22, 2002).

that received foreign partners and central support to succeed.[88] This has not happened. As I explain in the next section, there is significant variation within the industry that cannot be explained at the central level.

III. BELOW THE CENTER: MEASURING THE SUCCESS OF LOCAL AUTO SECTOR DEVELOPMENT

How can the success of local auto sector development be measured? Two points are important to note. First, and as I pointed out in the previous chapter, my primary focus is not the success of a joint venture assembly plant, but the success of the local auto sector as a whole. While a successful assembly plant is certainly a necessary ingredient of broader success, it is not sufficient; it would be possible to have a very successful assembly plant that had few linkages to the local firms, and this would *not* be viewed as a successful example of local auto sector development. Second, it is necessary to distinguish between domestic success and international success. As of 2004, it is possible to come to relatively firm conclusions about the former (the subject of Part II), but assessment of the latter must be preliminary (the subject of Part III). Of course, localities that cannot succeed within a protected domestic market are unlikely to succeed once these tariff barriers have been removed.

Measuring the relative health of local auto sectors within China is straightforward: the sourcing patterns of the different joint venture assembly projects are used. Because the joint ventures are obviously intent on finding high-quality parts for the lowest possible price, their sourcing policies are a good indication of where the most competitive supply firms are located. It is a particularly good measure because each joint venture should have a strong preference for local supply firms. First, the Chinese partner has a strong financial interest in giving business to parts enterprises within its own business group – it can make profits at each step of the production process. In those cases where the Chinese partner is a division of the local government (Beijing, Guangzhou, and Shanghai), fiscal decentralization further strengthens the incentive for the Chinese side to favor local firms (with local defined as being within municipal borders). Second, as with auto companies everywhere, supply links with

---

[88] In fact, the official 1994 industrial policy for the auto industry did not specify which projects would receive support, but simply stated that the central government would support those projects that had achieved specified economies of scale by the end of 1995. State Planning Commission, "Industrial Policy of the Motor Industry," *China Auto*, vol. 4, no. 4, July–August 1994.

Table 2.1: *Percentage of Components Sourced Locally by JV[a]*

Joint Venture	1985	1997	2003
Beijing Jeep	0%	20–30%	5–10%
Shanghai VW	0%	88–90%	88–90%[b]
Guangzhou Peugeot	0%	20%	–
First Auto-VW	–	15%	20%
Dongfeng-Citroen	–	not available	10%[c]
Shanghai GM	–	0%	60%+[d]
Guangzhou Honda	–	–	22%[e]

[a] The percentages are by component (not value), and are from interviews with the supply division of each JV. A locally sourced part is defined as being manufactured within the municipality within which the JV is located. The percentages are for the following models: Jeep Cherokee (Beijing Jeep), Santana (SVW), all Peugeot models (GZ Peugeot), Jetta (FAW-VW), Fukang (DCAC), Accord (GZ Honda), Buick Regal (SGM). The designation "–" indicates that a JV was not yet in existence. JVs are ranked from earliest to most recent.

[b] This number is unchanged since 1997 because it is at the highest possible level.

[c] It should be noted that this percentage is low in part because DCAC has a second factory in Xiangfan (approx. 400 km from Wuhan) that does all of the machining for the Wuhan assembly plant.

[d] This is the percentage by value of components sourced from SAIC first tier suppliers, all of which are within Shanghai municipality. The percentage from all Shanghai firms is higher.

[e] This percentage is for the number of suppliers in Guangdong. Consequently, the percentage for Guangzhou alone is probably lower. To give some indication of this, Honda is only using 4 former Peugeot suppliers.

Source: Firm Interviews

firms that are of close geographic proximity are easier to manage. This is especially true in China due to the poor transportation network. Given the overwhelming preference for using local supply firms, if a particular joint venture assembly plant *does* rely heavily on outside suppliers, this is strong evidence that the local supply base is extremely weak.

When each joint venture assembly project was created, the foreign partner initially imported 100% of the components for the assembly plant – the joint ventures at this stage had 0% local content.[89] For the Chinese partner, the objective was to gradually increase the percentage of parts that were sourced locally. As Table 2.1 indicates, the only

[89] It is important to note that this measure of "local content" is very different from the more commonly used "domestic content" (even though this latter is often referred to as local content). Domestic content is a measure of components sources within *all* of China, and a certain level is required by the central government. Consequently, published reports will invariably be in accordance with requirements.

Table 2.2: *Percentage of Components (by value) Sourced from Shanghai in 2002[a]*

Beijing Jeep	50%+[b]
Shanghai VW	90%+
First Auto-VW	20%
Dongfeng-Citroen	50%+
Shanghai GM	60%+[c]
Guangzhou Honda	8%[d]

[a] Percentages are from interviews with the supply division of each JV.

[b] The supply managers at both Beijing Jeep and Dongfeng Citroen reported that 50% of their components by quantity came from Shanghai, and a far higher amount by value.

[c] This is the percentage by value of components sources from SAIC suppliers, all of which are within Shanghai municipality. The percentage from all Shanghai firms is higher.

[d] Because engines are considered to be outsourced in Guangzhou (they are made by the Dongfeng Honda JV), the percentage by value sourced from Shanghai is quite low. 32% of the total number of suppliers, however, are located in Shanghai.

Source: Firm Interviews

municipality that has been able to rely heavily on the local auto sector was Shanghai – approximately 90% of the components for the Shanghai Volkswagen (SVW) Santana and well over 60% of the components for the Shanghai General Motors (SGM) Buick are manufactured within the municipal borders of Shanghai. No other municipality has reached even 25%.

While this is certainly strong evidence of weakness in the supply bases of areas outside of Shanghai, it is not necessarily a sign of Shanghai's strength – Shanghai might simply be more unyielding in its refusal to use outside suppliers. Given the tendency of other joint ventures to lean on Shanghai firms, however, this seems unlikely. First, as Table 2.2 indicates, given the weaknesses of their own supply bases, the other localities have increasingly been forced to rely on Shanghai suppliers. Not only do Shanghai joint ventures use Shanghai suppliers, everybody else does too. Second, it became quite common for foreign partners at assembly plants outside of Shanghai to urge their global suppliers to form linkages with Shanghai firms. In 1997, for instance, as many Citroen suppliers had signed agreements with Shanghai firms as with local Hubei firms (23), only 5 were signed in Beijing, and 7 in Guangdong (many of which have since failed).[90]

[90] Interview DCAC, 15 May 1997.

Similarly, in order to support the FAW-VW operation in Changchun, 17 auto part joint ventures were formed in the local province of Jilin, 28 in Shanghai, 4 in Beijing, and none in Guangzhou. These newer operations clearly gravitated to Shanghai when building a supply network.

Heavy utilization of the Shanghai auto sector is a strong indication that it is more capable than its rivals, but not necessarily an indication of financial soundness. It is difficult to provide data on the financial health of the different supply networks for several reasons. First, statistical information is available for either a corporate group or an assembly joint venture, but not distinct supply networks. For FAW or Dongfeng, in particular, it is impossible to assess the health of supply firms without including all of the truck operations, and these are the bulk of their operations. Second, information on the profitability of firms operating in an environment that is not completely marketized must be treated with caution. Firm profits can in some cases be heavily dependent on forces external to the firm, such as subsidized inputs or "policy" loans, and these factors are not readily apparent on a balance sheet.[91] There is reason to believe, however, that these problems might be less severe in joint ventures, as opposed to SOEs.[92] Finally, in the auto sector, profit levels of an individual firm within a corporate group depend on the pricing relationships between assemblers and parts suppliers, and these may vary between groups. Assembly operations may exert their significant leverage to force suppliers to lower prices, and in so doing they concentrate the sector's profits in the primary enterprise. Alternatively, the assembler may bolster the health of suppliers by allowing them to retain a higher degree of profit.[93]

I try to get around these problems by providing a range of data. Table 2.3 provides data on local auto sectors in their entirety – the degree of supplier investment in the component firms and the return on

---

[91] See Steinfeld (1996: 50).

[92] In auto JVs, for instance, inputs are purchased at market prices, and although prices on output were regulated by the state until recent years, enterprises were affected in a uniform manner. Subsidies may be granted, but this is probably less common and more transparent because local governments are usually more interested in drawing capital from the foreign partner; if capital is increased, both sides have an incentive to insure that it is done by both sides in equal proportions.

[93] When these two alternatives are taken into account, however, they most likely would only increase the gap between the JVs that were profitable and those that were losing money: the enterprises that were struggling would squeeze their suppliers, and those that were doing well could afford to be more generous.

Table 2.3: *Shanghai, Beijing, and Guangzhou Auto Groups Compared*

	Component Production as Share of Output Value[a]		Component Production as Share of New Fixed Asset Investments in 1997	Return on Assets[b]	
	1992	1997		1992	1998
SAIC	17.8%	27.0%	81.1%	27.2%	14.9%
BAIC	21.0%	17.4%	4.5%	15.1%	−2.99%
GAIC[c]	0.0%	5.6%	10.0%	10.4%	−3.64%

[a] Components include engines, but not chassis.
[b] Returns on assets are given by: pre-tax profit divided by the sum of net fixed assets and current assets. Pre-tax profits are used because tax rates often differ among firms.
[c] Data on GAIC are not available, so the data is for the municipality of Guangzhou.
Source: Huang 2003: 283.

assets – but only for Beijing, Guangzhou, and Shanghai. Because the corporate groups in these municipalities consist of primarily the assembly joint venture and the supply firms, it is possible to make such a comparison. Figure 2.3 provides profitability data for all five cases, but only for the joint venture assembly plant (not the local auto sector as a whole). It gives an indication of the general health of the assembly operation at the core of each region's auto sector. Figure 2.4 provides information on the sales volumes of each joint venture. A virtuous circle linked production volumes to the health of a supply network: local suppliers made it possible to raise volumes (due to restrictions on foreign exchange) and high volumes created the economies of scale that made a components business viable.

The pattern that emerges from this data – even making allowances for possible problems with the data – is quite clear. The Shanghai auto sector is in a league of its own, as measured by the sourcing policies of the joint ventures, the return on assets in the corporate group as a whole, joint venture profitability, and production volumes. By the same measure it is equally evident that the Beijing supply sector (prior to the arrival of Hyundai) and the Guangzhou Peugeot project had failed. In acknowledgement of this fact, Peugeot pulled out of the latter joint venture in 1997; Beijing Jeep continued to flounder. The cases of Changchun, Wuhan, and Guangzhou Honda are more complicated. Profitability and production volumes at the joint venture assembly plants have been steadily rising. In fact, according

Relative Profit Levels of Auto Joint Ventures 1985–2003

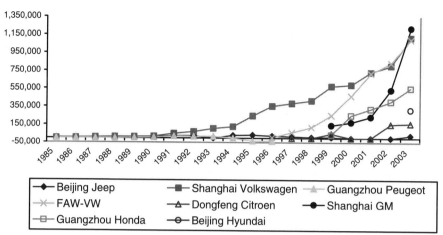

Figure 2.3: Relative profit levels of auto Joint Ventures, 1985–2003 (in units of 10,000 RMB). *Note*: Because of slight inconsistencies in the form of the data in different years, this figure is meant to indicate relative profit levels. Data from 1985 to 1996 is *lirun zong e* (total profits), and the source does not indicate whether the data has been adjusted for inflation. Data for 1997 to 2003 is *lishui zong e* (total profits plus minor taxes that are levied on sales but not including VAT or corporate income tax). *Source*: Data for 1985 to 1996 is from *Qiche Gongye Guihua Cankao Ziliao* (1997: 80–81); data for 1997 to 2003 is from *China Automotive Technology Center* (various years).

to VW managers, the volumes at FAW-VW will eclipse SVW by 2007.[94] Guangzhou will soon be a production base not only for Honda, but also for Toyota and Nissan. On the other hand, the local supply networks in these municipalities are weaker than those in Shanghai. As Tables 2.1 and 2.2 indicate, there continues to be a great reliance on outside suppliers in each of these localities, despite the high incentives to use local suppliers, and most of these outside suppliers are in Shanghai. Wuhan, however, is more dependent on Shanghai than either Changchun or Guangzhou Honda. In short, it is necessary to explain not only the overwhelming relative success of Shanghai and early failures in Beijing and Guangzhou, but the mixed outcomes in the other cases and the potential of late resurgences in localities that experience early failure.

[94] VW has introduced its Audi luxury models at FAW-VW. Production of the Audi A6 began in 1999; the Audi A4 was introduced in 2004. "Audi strives to be market leader," *Business Daily Update*, May 18, 2004.

Changing Lanes in China

Auto Joint Venture Sales Volume (in number of vehicles)

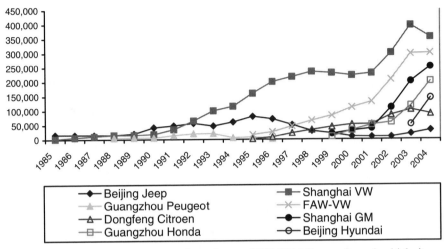

Figure 2.4: Auto joint venture sales volumes, 1985–2004 (in number of vehicles). *Note*: Data for 1985 to 1997 is for production rather than sales volume, but during this period the two statistics are virtually identical. The two statistics began to diverge only when competition intensified in recent years. I use production volumes for the early period because it is available as time-series data. *Source*: Data for 1985 to 1996 is from *Qiche Gongye Guihua Cankao Ziliao* (1997: 27–28); data for 1997 is from Interview, no. W13, May 15, 1997 and Interview, no. C7, July 25, 1997; data for 1998 to 2003 is from "Passenger Car Sales by Maker and Model, 1998–2003, *Four in China Auto Weekly*, July 1, 2004; data for 2004 is from "Shanghai VW, FAW-VW, Shanghai GM dominate China sedan," Xinhua Financial Network News, January 31, 2005; "Beijing sees fastest growth in auto sector," Xinhua Economic News Service, January 20, 2005.

IV. CONCLUSION

Are there perhaps some relatively straightforward explanations of these varied outcomes – ones that might preclude lengthy analysis of local political economies? While some alternative explanations can be dismissed quickly, others will have to be considered throughout the analysis and returned to in the conclusion.

With respect to the former category, one possibility is that SVW simply had a far superior product than its competitors. This would be particularly important in the late 1980s, because if the Shanghai product were superior to that being manufactured in Beijing or Guangzhou, this would allow it to quickly capture market share and achieve economies of scale. There is little evidence that this was the case, however. All of the products were based on designs from the 1970s, and thus inferior by international standards, but were roughly similar to each other in terms of quality.[95] It is possible to make arguments about consumer preferences, but this is always possible with hindsight. Not only is consumer preference malleable, but none of the arguments are so persuasive as to explain the vast discrepancy in outcomes.[96] Perhaps most importantly, demand was high until 1993 and all of the joint ventures – no matter what the product – sold everything that rolled off of the assembly lines.[97] This was the period during which Shanghai pulled ahead, and while its product gained a loyal following over the years, it is difficult to argue that its initial success was solely based on product superiority.

A second possibility is that Shanghai itself was somehow better suited to auto sector development. One form of this argument would be that Shanghai had a much larger local market, and with the help of local protectionism, was able to provide a captive market for local industry. This simply was not the case. Because of severe traffic restrictions and high registration fees within the municipality of Shanghai, the local market for sedans was smaller than both Beijing and Guangzhou, and the rate of private vehicle ownership was well below the national average.[98] Another form of the argument would be that Shanghai had a history of auto sector production, and thus, once SVW was formed, it was significantly easier to develop a supply base in Shanghai than in Beijing. But there is little support for this hypothesis either. Prior to the initial localization drive that took place in the late 1980s, there was no significant auto industry in Shanghai – the primary product of the local partner had been tractors. As late as 1990, Shanghai's share of the national total of automotive components output value was only 7% as compared to 11.2% in Beijing.

[95] In fact, comprehensive quality tests conducted in 1988 found that the product of the Shanghai Auto Industry Corporation to be inferior to that of Guangzhou and Beijing. Quality was measured as miles traveled before failure. Huang (2003: 263).

[96] The Peugeot 504 was heavier than the SVW Santana, for instance, and the higher fuel consumption made it unpopular with taxi drivers. The weight, however, was from a heavier chassis, and this gave it added strength on rough roads. Similarly, the Beijing Jeep Cherokee was an SUV, and this might have been an unpopular model type. But SUVs certainly have become popular elsewhere, and they might have been advertised as the ideal choice for Chinese roads. In recent years, Great Wall Auto, a private auto firm located in Hebei Province, has done extremely well in the SUV segment.

[97] In fact, demand for the Jeep Cherokee in the late 1980s was strong enough to support a black market: dummy corporations would buy the jeeps in dollars at government set price and then sell them in *renminbi* for a huge mark up. Mann (1989: 285).

[98] On the demand for autos in various cities, see Guojia Xinxi Zhongxin (1999: 387). Guangdong has the largest vehicle market in China, and is a particularly important market for mid-range sedans. See "China's 2003 Vehicle PARC," *Fourin China Auto Weekly*, January 11, 2004 and "Faltering sales reveal growth factor insights," *Fourin China Auto Weekly*, January 17, 2005.

Six years later, once the results of the localization drive were fully realized, it accounted for 20% as compared to 4.3% in Beijing.[99] Similarly, it did not seem as if the Shanghai workforce had any inherent advantage over Beijing. As measured by share of technicians in the workforce of each city's auto business group, the ratio for Beijing in 1990 was 25.9% as compared to 14.7% in Shanghai.[100]

It is true, of course, that Shanghai had a history as the strongest industrial base in China, and this is an important part of my explanation, but it does not provide an easy explanation. As I will explain, Shanghai did not have a history of auto sector production. If industrial history is a primary determinant of success, the First and Second Auto Works (Changchun and Wuhan) should be the most successful, because they had by far the most developed auto bases in the 1980s. The key importance of Shanghai's industrial history was not in actual production figures, but in its knowledge of how to structure large-scale industrial organizations. It was the software of institutions that proved to be critical, rather than the hardware of actual factories.

Finally, there is the possibility of central government favoritism. This argument might take several forms. One version would be that a central government dominated by former Shanghai municipal officials, as it was for all of the 1990s, insured that the auto sector succeeded. While the center bestowed all manner of preferential policies on Shanghai in the 1990s, with respect to the auto sector the timing is wrong: the preferential policies did not begin until 1992, and as will be explained in Chapter 4, this was after the most significant developments in the auto sector had taken place. In fact, central government policy put Shanghai at a disadvantage in the late 1980s, particularly when compared to Guangzhou. A more plausible version of the central favoritism argument would be that the center intended First Auto, Dongfeng, and Shanghai to be the core auto bases from the outset, and thus insured that they would succeed. There are problems with this argument too. Not only has Dongfeng-Citroen not succeeded by any measure, but Guangzhou Honda has rapidly turned Guangzhou into a success. As argued in this chapter, central government support is a necessary, but not sufficient, condition for success. The stated government policy was that the central government would support any project that reached the specified production volumes, no matter what the location.

---

[99] Huang (2003: 264–5).
[100] Huang (2003: 263). It might also be argued that Shanghai had superior universities, and consequently a better educated population, but try making this argument in Beijing.

There is one alternative explanation that does have considerable merit and is one that I will return to often – the identity, role, and strength of the foreign partner. Volkswagen, for instance, despite its difficulties as competition has increased in recent years, had a long run of great success. This might have been due to structural differences in the joint venture assembly projects (as I will explain, Peugeot had a much smaller stake in its Guangzhou joint venture, than VW in Shanghai), but it is also a testament to VW's skill. In addition to its early success in Shanghai, VW did well at the Changchun assembly plant, where it had a minority share. General Motors, I will argue, brought a management approach that was very different from that of VW. Hyundai and Honda have enjoyed rapid growth in localities where other firms failed.

The role of the foreign partner, however, is more important at the assembly plant than the supply network. The foreign partner plays the key role in transferring technology to the joint venture and teaching their Chinese counterparts how to run a modern assembly plant. But the role of the foreign partner is necessarily focused on the operation of the joint venture itself, rather than the development of an entire supply network. The example of Volkswagen's operations in Shanghai is indicative. The number of expatriate managers was not large (in 1997 VW had 14 German managers at SVW), and their primary attention was necessarily focused on the joint venture. It was also a question of responsibility. As one German manager explained, VW is a car manufacturer not a tire manufacturer.[101] There were enough problems to deal with in the assembly plant without having to run the operations of over 200 suppliers. VW gave technical support to suppliers, pinpointed problems, provided guidance, and helped form linkages between Chinese and German suppliers, but ultimately the local supply base was not its responsibility. VW was very dependent on local suppliers (although it would have often preferred to use competitive firms from other regions), and it could play a very constructive role in building a network of firms, but it did not determine success or failure.

A strong foreign partner is certainly a great help in the construction of a local supply base, but the primary responsibility remains on the Chinese side. Evidence of this can be found in the contrast between Changchun and Shanghai: the results at the FAW-VW assembly plant are comparable to SVW – impressive profit levels and rapidly rising production volumes – but the Changchun supply network is not in the same league as

---

[101] Interview no. S25, June 17, 1998.

Shanghai: after a decade of production, FAW-VW can only source 20% of its components locally. Similarly, the local linkages in the supply networks of Beijing and Guangzhou, despite the recent success of the Hyundai and Honda joint venture assembly plants, are far shallower than in the supply base of Shanghai.

In summary, the role of the Chinese central government is an important explanation of the framework for auto sector development: it pushed the development of large business groups, it shaped key regulations, and it controlled the entrance of foreign firms. In the first stage of development, this framework consisted of high tariff barriers and limited competition within the domestic marketplace. The role of the central government is an insufficient explanation, however, for the wide variation in outcomes at the local level. In the four chapters that follow, I argue that within the protected market created by the central government, local political and economic institutions were a critical determinant of a locality's ability to develop a strong network of supply firms.

PART II

DEVELOPMENT IN A PROTECTED MARKET

THREE

Coordinating Development in the Auto Sector

For a developing country intent on transforming moribund state-owned firms into proud national champions, the auto sector is an obvious target. "As in the highly industrialized countries, the automotive industry ... is becoming and will be without doubt the leading sector of the entire economy, by force of its magnitude, complexity, and dynamism."[1] Although these words were spoken by a forward-looking official in Brazil in the 1930s, they very well might have been uttered by an official in Tokyo in the 1950s, Mexico City in the 1960s, Seoul in the 1970s, or Beijing in the 1980s. The automobile industry has an enduring appeal for developing countries because the broad supply network creates extensive linkages and because it is often seen as a symbol of a modern industrialized country.[2] Sheer numbers are in part responsible for its importance – currently nearly 50 million new vehicles are produced a year – but given the scope and complexity of the manufacturing processes in the auto industry, it has also been an important testing ground for new ways of organizing economic activity.

China has also used the auto sector as a testing ground, but as I explained in the previous chapter, rather than the central government dictating the development approach, it has been local governments that have experimented with new forms of organizing economic activity. The challenge for each local government during the first stage of development was the same: through the localization process of the joint venture

---

[1] Shapiro (1994: 38).

[2] In a study of the U.S. auto industry, for instance, it was calculated that "backward" linkage industries contributed nearly 60% of the value of the vehicle produced. Harwit (1995: 36).

assembly project, they hoped to promote the development of local state-owned firms. In the protected domestic market, the joint venture assembly projects sought to produce a product that, while far short of international standards, was of a quality and technical level that was consistently higher than the standards of most local supply firms, but they could not do this alone: barriers to importing components, local content requirements, and foreign exchange restrictions created a need for local suppliers. If the local firms were to become suppliers for a joint venture assembler, however, they would have to increase their manufacturing and technical skills so as to meet the joint venture standards.[3] Success, in other words, depended not on the operations of a single joint venture assembly plant, but the coordinated development of an entire sector.

The previous chapter provided evidence that localities varied in their ability to meet this challenge. In providing an explanation for this variation, the case studies that follow characterize the organization of each locality's auto sector according to two primary dimensions: the bureaucratic structure of the local governments and the form of interfirm relationships. The purpose of this chapter is to introduce each of these variables, and explain how they relate to auto sector development.

I. COORDINATING INVESTMENT: THE ROLE OF THE STATE

The literature on industrial policy often focuses on the role of the state in overcoming collective action problems, situations in which there is "an interdependency among the participants, so that the contributions or efforts of one individual influence the contributions or efforts of other individuals."[4] In political economy, the forms a collective action problem may take are numerous. Gregory Noble, for instance, in his study of industrial policy in East Asia, focuses on R&D consortia and production cartels (in which firms or nations have the incentive to free-ride on the actions of others) and the setting of standards (in which firms or nations would like their own approach to become a standard, but the need for coordination necessitates compromise).[5] A third type of coordination problem involves investment in manufacturing activities that depend on the coordinated development of other firms within a

---

[3] Two years after SVW started production, for instance, the only local parts that met VW specification, and hence were locally sourced, were the tires, radio, and antennae. Li (1997: 116).

[4] Todd Sandler as cited in Noble (1998: 2).

[5] Noble (1998).

production network. If investment in the manufacturing capability of one firm will only reap a return if other firms invest at the same time, there is the start of a coordination problem; it is intensified when the manufacturing capability of one firm, without the benefit of investment in complementary activities, has few alternative uses (i.e., it is relatively asset specific).

The auto industry is a classic case of an industry with intense coordination problems in the initial stages of development. Typically 60–80% of the value of a car will be produced by outside suppliers, and the supply network is often composed of hundreds of firms. As explained in Chapter 1, the heavy investment in an auto assembly plant must be rapid (so that it will be able to quickly increase production and capture economies of scale) and it must be matched with a coordinated investment program in the supply network. Although not all firms within the sector are capital intensive – many suppliers are small- and medium-sized enterprises – the need for complementary linkages means that the overall capital needs of the sector are high. Similarly, firms within the supply sector will vary in the degree to which their knowledge and manufacturing capabilities are specific to a given buyer.[6]

This complementary investment is particularly difficult in a development context. Inadequacies in the financial sector are an initial problem – primarily underdeveloped financial institutions – but even more important, the risk for each individual supply firm, in the absence of coordination, is extremely high. If the manager of a supply firm decides to invest in the new technology and equipment that is necessary to upgrade the firm's manufacturing capability, a process that will potentially disrupt existing production, the manager will usually feel more comfortable knowing that there will be a reliable customer for the new product after this process is completed.[7] If an assembly plant can guarantee it will purchase millions of brake systems, for instance, the investment in new manufacturing equipment at the supply firm will be guaranteed a good return. The assembly plant can only increase volumes, however, if it can quickly replace expensive imported parts for the entire car with less expensive components that are manufactured locally. Without coordinated development, costs will remain high, volumes low, and success unlikely. This was particularly true in China during the 1980s, the initial stage of auto sector development, because tariffs on imported components were high and

---

[6] On asset specificity in the auto industry, see Monteverde and Teece (1982).
[7] This logic is accentuated depending on the degree of asset specificity.

foreign exchange was limited.[8] Without a strong network of firms supplying locally manufactured components, it was impossible to raise production volumes.

How can this coordination be achieved? Alexander Gerschenkron, in his classic study of late nineteenth-century industrial development in Germany, argued that the requirements of large-scale economic activity and the shortcomings of the private economic networks necessitated an active state role. In order to compete with established industrial states in sectors that are technology and capital intensive, the state must assist industry in its efforts to acquire the most advanced technology and construct a financial system to insure that firms have the means to quickly reach economies of scale.[9] The advantage of industrialized countries, in other words, is in part a result of their superior ability to channel capital into large firms. Developing countries that have underdeveloped capital markets, insufficient skills, and little capital cannot depend upon the market alone to compete against the large industrial enterprises of advanced industrial nations.

East Asia has been a receptive audience for such arguments. Japan was seen as an early model. It was neither a capitalist free-market economy nor a Soviet-style command economy, according to Chalmers Johnson, but an entirely different breed: the "capitalist developmental state."[10] State bureaucrats, insulated from societal pressures, had the tools and capability to direct scarce resources to those economic sectors that they believed to be critical to national economic development. Other scholars pointed to a similar investment role of government in later cases. In South Korea, argues Amsden, "the allocation of subsidies has rendered the government not merely a banker, as Gerschenkron conceived it, but an entrepreneur, using the subsidy to decide what, when and how much to produce."[11] In Taiwan, according to Robert Wade, corporatist and authoritarian political arrangements have provided the basis for market guidance, "augmenting the supply of investible resources, spreading

---

[8] In 1994, China reduced many tariffs, but for developmental reasons, they remained high in the auto sector. Tariffs on vehicles, which ranged from 200–240% prior to 1994, were reduced to 110–150% after 1994. Huang (1998: 45).

[9] Gerschenkron (1962: 20) used Russia at the end of the nineteenth century as an example of a country in which private economic networks were incapable of funding the massive investment required by large-scale enterprises. "Supply of capital for the needs of industrialization required the compulsory machinery of the government, which, through its taxation policies, succeeded in directing incomes from consumption to investment."

[10] Johnson (1982).

[11] Amsden (1989: 143).

or 'socializing' the risks attached to long-term investment, and steering the allocation of investment by methods which combine government and entrepreneurial preferences."[12] The specific role of the central government may vary between cases, but according to the advocates of the developmental state approach, it always plays a critical role in mediating the role of the market in allocating capital.[13]

The development of the auto industry in East Asia has been no exception. In Japan, the auto industry might not have survived the enforced austerity program of the U.S. occupation if it were not for the financial assistance of the government-run Reconstruction Finance Bank and the Japan Development Bank (JDB). Toyota and Isuzu, for instance, unable to secure financing from commercial banks, received financing from the Reconstruction Finance Bank.[14] The auto assembly sector as a whole, from 1951 to 1956, received 4% of total capital investment (about one billion yen) from the JDB.[15] Beginning in 1956, with the enactment of the Machinery Industries Promotion Law, automotive components firms also began to receive preferential access to government financing. Between 1956 and 1964, the JDB gave loans to 63 auto parts firms, all of which manufactured relatively important components.[16] By the early 1960s the financing situation was less dire: large component firms could borrow more readily from commercial banks, they could raise equity on the stock market (18 parts firms listed during 1961–1962), and smaller firms could turn to credit unions and small business banks.[17]

In Korea, a similar progression began with the promulgation of the Automotive Industry Promotion Law in 1962. Imported vehicles were banned, and the Ministry of Trade and Industry was given the discretion to determine which companies could begin manufacturing cars. The firms that were chosen received the benefit of full government support: subsidized loans and tax incentives for investments, and export subsidies including export promotion loans that made it possible for Korean firms to sell vehicles in foreign markets for less than half of the domestic market

[12] Wade (1990: 27).
[13] On variations between these cases, see Noble (1998). As noted in Chapter 1, there are other potential explanations for the success of these cases.
[14] Smitka (1991: 53).
[15] Machiko Watanabe, "Japan – Industrial Policy and the Development of the Automotive Industry," in Inoue, Kohama, and Urata (1993: 210).
[16] Smitka (1991: 72). These components firms also benefited from a law that required auto firms that licensed foreign technology to achieve 100% local content.
[17] Smitka (1991: 72).

price.[18] An industrial policy for the auto sector was the centerpiece of the Korean government's "Big Push" into the capital-intensive industries in the early 1970s; renewed attention in the early 1980s focused began the export drive of Korean manufacturers.[19]

In short, the early development and subsequent export success of Japan and Korea was complemented by coordinated and coherent investment policy on the part of the state. The East Asian cases, argues Dani Rodrik, suggest that investment is causal where economic growth is concerned: "an increase in investment, for whatever reasons, tends to spur growth." In the short term, the relationship is erratic, but over a span of decades cross-national studies have shown that investment is one of the few robust correlates of economic growth across countries.[20] The challenge is in creating a coherent investment policy, and the institutional structures that such a policy requires.

II. COORDINATING INTERFIRM RELATIONS: MARKETS, HIERARCHY, AND NETWORKS

Investment is only the beginning of the coordination challenges involved in auto sector development. In addition to gaining access to investment capital, manufacturers must be able to procure inputs and distribute output, they must have access to the appropriate manufacturing technology, and they need detailed information about the preferences of customers. Firms within an industrial sector must be linked, and resources must be allocated by a coordinating mechanism, whether this is a market, informal network of associations, a hierarchical structure, or the state. The auto sector is only unusual in the number and intensity of these linkages.

What is the most effective way to coordinate auto sector development? In considering alternative methods of organizing an auto sector it is useful to think of coordinating mechanisms as a spectrum with pure market coordination at one end and pure bureaucratic coordination at the other.

---

[18] This description is from John Ravenhill, "From National Champions to Global Partners: Crisis, Globalization, and the Korean Auto Industry," in Keller and Samuels (2003).

[19] Ronald Rogers, "Industrial Relations in the Korean Auto Industry," in Deyo (1996: 91).

[20] Rodrik (1999: 15–16). Rodrik (1999: Chapter 3) also examines the institutional foundations of effective investment in the East Asian cases. The extent of investment in Asia, as opposed to its effectiveness, was what led Paul Krugman (1994) to famously conclude that there was nothing special about the Asian Miracle: long-term growth would require productivity gains as opposed to high investment.

A country that is moving away from an economic system based on state planning is moving across this spectrum toward a market-based system. The two ends of this spectrum are ideal types, of course, and all economies contain a mixture of coordinating mechanisms. In between these two ends one may find self-enforcing modes of coordination such as associations and networks.[21]

Markets

Pure market coordination involves economic actors of equal power, in horizontal relationships to each other, conducting transactions based upon freely fluctuating prices. In its ideal type, a market would consist entirely of arms-length transactions between individuals; there could be no firms because the internal structure of a firm is based on a hierarchy rather than a market. The advantages of a market are well known.

Freely fluctuating market prices are advantageous first, because they are a highly efficient means of transmitting information. "In an ideally functioning system of markets," Milgrom and Roberts write, "all that anyone needs to know is his or her own capabilities and tastes and the prevailing prices. There is no need to transmit detailed information about preferences, technological possibilities, resource availability, and the like that would be needed to achieve a centralized solution because the prices summarize all the relevant information."[22] Second, markets preclude the need to threaten or persuade actors to behave in a certain manner: when markets are functioning properly, people are motivated by their own self-interest to "achieve an efficient, coordinated pattern of choices."[23] Manufacturing companies that are interested solely in increasing private profits will produce the goods and services that consumers value most highly with as little cost as possible. Similarly, investors and financial institutions will invest capital where they believe the returns will be highest. Coordination is seemingly effortless.

In the early stages of auto sector development it is not uncommon for relationships within the sector to be coordinated by the market: production volumes are low and operations are decentralized. When components are purchased from outside suppliers, the relationship is governed

---

[21] See Campbell, Hollingsworth, and Lindberg (1991); Hollingsworth, Schmitter, and Streeck (1994).

[22] Milgrom and Roberts (1992: 27).

[23] This discussion of markets draws from Milgrom and Roberts (1992: 27).

by price, and there is no assumption of a long-term relationship. The transition from small-scale manufacturing to mass production transforms not only the operations within an assembly plant – a shift from craft production to mass production on an assembly line, or Fordism – but also the relationship with suppliers. Given the high proportion of a car (by value) that comes from outside suppliers, an assembly plant is only as good as its suppliers, and one-time market relationships with suppliers can become increasingly unsatisfactory.

Specialization, the heart of mass production, creates two sets of problems for an auto manufacturer.[24] First, because the process revolves around a system of interchangeable parts, it becomes increasingly important to insure that parts are produced to exact specifications, and that deliveries are reliable. When the sector is organized by markets, and assembly plants play suppliers off of each other in an effort to lower prices, price became the exclusive focus of assembler-supplier relations, to the detriment of the broader relationship. Because prices and contracts are continually being negotiated, relationships are characterized not by cooperation, but mistrust. Although contracts are short term, suppliers are aware that it becomes more difficult for an assembler to switch suppliers after production has started, hence an initial contract can lead to a long stream of business. Consequently, suppliers make a low initial bid, and then raise their prices in later years by hiding actual costs during the annual cost adjustment for follow-on contracts.[25] Rather than fostering a relationship that emphasizes sharing information in an effort to lower costs and raise quality, each side tries to hide any information that might be taken advantage of by the other in pricing negotiations.

The assumption on both sides in such a relationship, according to Richard Lamming, is "that the supplier and customer exist in two separate but related industries that come together only to trade. The preoccupation of the buyer with short-term advantage from finding a cheaper price creates this assumption. The natural response of the supplier – to gain as much from the business as possible while it has the chance – reinforces it."[26] The trading relationship, in effect, precludes a strategic, cooperative relationship. The result is that manufacturing innovations in the supply firms lag behind the assembly plant, and imprecise quality standards and deliveries from suppliers disrupt the smooth functioning of assembly lines.

---

[24] See Womack, Jones, and Roos (1990) and Lamming (1993).
[25] Womack, Jones, and Roos (1990: 141).
[26] Lamming (1993: 155).

A full return on an investment made in an assembly plant can only be realized if parallel investment is made in supply firms; an entire sector has to be developed rather than a single firm.

The second set of problems revolves around transaction costs. As Ronald Coase pointed out in the 1930s, even from a neoclassical perspective it is clear that there are costs associated with using a market; even in the simplest transaction a buyer or seller must be found, a product or service evaluated, and a price negotiated. In the 1980s, Oliver Williamson argued that the problem of coordination was exacerbated because of human nature.[27] The problem of bounded rationality makes it impossible for actors to foresee every contingency that might affect an agreement between two actors, hence contracts can never be complete; the problem of opportunism means that each actor has to expect the other to act not only out of self-interest, but potentially with deceit and guile.[28] In light of these assumptions, it is apparent that the costs of some market transactions are higher than others. It is necessary to identify and analyze the key dimensions along which transactions vary: the frequency with which transactions recur, the degree of complexity and uncertainty to which transactions are subject, and the degree of asset specificity.[29]

In the auto industry, transaction costs are particularly high. This is partly because of the number of components that must be purchased and the high production volumes, but as important are the vulnerabilities created by specialization and a high degree of asset specificity. The division of the production process necessarily creates dependencies between firms; not only for an assembler dependent on a timely supply of quality parts, but also for a supplier that has few alternate customers for specialized parts. Once the supplier makes an investment, the buyer and seller become locked into a situation of bilateral monopoly due to physical, technological, and/or skill-based specificity. It is exactly the sort of mutual dependence that according to Williamson, creates potential for opportunism and mistrust, and it makes parallel investment throughout the supply network highly problematic. Although the assembly plant depends on the development of supply firms, from the perspective of a small supply

---

[27] Williamson (1981: 1545); Milgrom and Roberts (1992: 28–33, 129).
[28] Williamson (1981: 1545).
[29] This discussion is drawn from Williamson (1975) and Williamson (1981). Milgrom and Roberts add two additional dimensions: the difficulty of measuring performance in a transaction and the connectedness of the transaction to other transactions between the same actors, Milgrom and Roberts (1992: 30).

firm with no commitment from the assembly plant, investment is a risky endeavor. The degree of asset specificity varies between firms within a sector (for some products there will be alternate customers) and over time, but it is particularly acute in the early stages of development.

Hierarchy

When transaction costs are high – whether due to the frequency, complexity, uncertainty, or degree of asset specificity of the transaction – a hierarchical relationship between actors may be more efficient than market relations because common ownership reduces the incentives of the actors to be opportunistic. In the event of a dispute, the organization will have ready access to the relevant information, and the matter can be settled internally by fiat.[30] A multidivisional hierarchy will only be effective, however, if effectively organized. After a period of rapid expansion between its founding in 1908 and the early 1920s, for instance, Alfred Sloan complained of the complete chaos within General Motors: "there was a lack of control and of any means of control in operations and finance, and a lack of adequate information about anything."[31] The task he set out to accomplish was to create an organizational structure that would allow the operating divisions to maintain their autonomy, but at the same time be coordinated and controlled by executives in a general office.[32] As in any large industrial firm, the organizational structure has to be able to effectively coordinate internal activity, properly structure internal incentives, and effectively monitor performance.

Effective coordination depends on the quality of the information available to a head office. The intent is to develop data and procedures that insure that a head office, while aloof from the day-to-day operations of the separate profit centers, can assess the performance of these divisions, coordinate the flow of resources them, and anticipate future needs.[33] Effective utilization of this information depends on the internal incentive system.

[30] Williamson (1981: 1549).
[31] Sloan (1964: 42).
[32] The general office would have the necessary expertise to provide divisional managers with advice when necessary, and its advice would have to be heeded because it controlled the purse strings. Incoming receipts at the divisional level went into central banks, and the allocation of capital resources above a set amount required approvals from the general office. Chandler (1962: 146–7).
[33] Chandler (1962: 145).

When Sloan was restructuring GM, for instance, he sought to make managers of in-house divisions operationally autonomous so as to preserve individual initiative and prevent complacency.[34] When a particular component was being sourced, in-house divisions were required to proffer a bid just as if they were external to the corporation. Managers who performed well were rewarded with bonuses in the form of stock options (to insure that managers always retained a broad corporate perspective), and consistently good performance would lead to a vice-president position in the general office.[35] The intent was to create an internal structure that mimicked the functioning of external capital markets to as great a degree as possible; based on extensive information flows, managers would direct resources to where they would yield the highest return.[36]

It is important to note that the incentive structures within corporate structures that are outwardly quite similar, may in fact be quite different. It is necessary to examine the ownership relationships between parts of an organization and the manner in which profits are distributed within the organization. The head office of a corporate group, for instance, might be far more eager to invest in the development of an individual firm (both financially and technically) if it fully owns the firm and will reap the full benefits of the increased productivity that follows from such investment. Alternatively, if a head office manages a particular firm, but does not have rights to actual profits, heavy investment is unlikely. These prove to be critical differences between Chinese corporate groups.

---

[34] As the 1942 GM annual report formally stated, the management policy "evolved from the belief that the most effective results and the maximum progress and stability of the business are achieved by placing its executives in the same relative position, so far as possible, as they would occupy if they were conducting a business on their own account." Sloan (1964: 407).

[35] Sloan (1964: Chapter 22).

[36] In some respects, the Korean chaebols were quite similar to the General Motors model of the modern industrial enterprise: firms within the group manufactured key components and a head office directed overall operations. Firms such as Hyundai Motor Company and Daewoo Motor Corporation used subcontractors to a degree that GM did not, however, both because they had relatively limited financial resources and because the government pressured it to support the development of small and medium-sized firms. Within both groups, a Parts Development Department was established to assess and raise the technical standards of subcontractors. Although the government blocked the groups from purchasing the subcontractors outright, the relationships were long term and each supplier had a monopoly on the component that it manufactured. In that the success of the assembly plant depended on its ability to raise the standards of suppliers, the relationship was a partnership, although inevitably one in which the assembler had the upper hand. Amsden (1989: 180–189).

Networks

In between markets and hierarchy, and drawing from the advantages of both, are relationships based on networks of firms. When Japan began rebuilding its auto industry in the 1950s, engineers considered the conventional manners of organizing supply networks, but concluded that they were insufficiently nurturing. Horizontal market relations, although adequate in a context where large independent component makers were already well established, such as Europe, were quickly dismissed because they did not provide enough support in a developmental context. A strict contractual relationship between component firm and assembly plant was not thought to be conducive to a long-term cooperative relationship.[37] Vertical integration, on the other hand, provided the assembler with a great deal of control, but stifled supplier development. Japanese assemblers did not have the capacity to undertake all aspects of product development, and they consequently hoped to develop well-rounded supply firms that could participate in the development of components.[38]

The result is a supply chain that is neither vertical nor horizontal, but a dense network of ties in the shape of a pyramid. Relationships between suppliers and assembly plants are arranged in tiers. An assembly plant is supplied by a relatively small number of first tier suppliers; the first tier in turn organizes the second tier of suppliers. This structure serves both to combine supply firms with complementary assets in the same tier, so as to enable them to help each other, and makes it possible for each level of the structure to create stronger relationships with the firms in the level below.[39] In some cases, shared capital and financial ties between firms within a group insure that there is a focus on mutual benefit and cooperation (an advantage of vertical integration), but in other cases, relationships between separate firms are solidified simply through long-term interaction and elaborate monitoring and confidence-building exercises.[40]

---

[37] Shimokawa (1985: 11).

[38] Shimokawa (1985: 10). For an account of how Japanese firms transformed automobile production techniques, see Womack, Jones, and Roos (1990).

[39] Lamming (1993: 170). When the assembly plant itself deals with each supplier, as was often done in Europe and the U.S., relations were inevitably impersonal due to the huge number of suppliers the assembler must coordinate.

[40] Much of the work on Japanese supply networks emphasizes the role of mutual trust in purchasing relationships, and the manner in which trust serves to reduce transaction costs (Smitka: 1991; Sako: 1992), but trust is cultivated by very specific mechanisms (Lincoln 2001: 32). Because of long-standing relationships, firms are not as concerned about the

Although a major supplier will usually have a relationship with only one assembler – necessary due to the shared design work – the assembler will use multiple suppliers to preserve a sense of competition within the group (an advantage of horizontal market relations).[41] If supplier A falls short of expectations based on a system of ratings by the customer (the assembly plant or first tier supply firm), the customer gives the supplier a detailed accounting of its shortcomings, and begins to source a larger percentage from supplier B until supplier A improves its performance.[42] Accurate and complete information concerning costs and prices greatly enhances the ability to analyze and improve production techniques; the long-term contract arrangements for sharing profits provide the incentive to do so. New production techniques flow down the pyramid of suppliers in what has been called a process of technological cascading: "new technological learning taking place first at the parent plant, next at the subsidiary plants, and then down at the smaller subcontracting factories, which helps to narrow the operational gaps between gradational entities."[43] It is the long-term relationship and the consequent development of trust that reduces transaction costs and allow for a cooperative form of coordination.

The vertical ties within the Japanese automobile supply chain are supplemented with a network of horizontal linkages. Supplier cooperation associations (*kyoryoku kai*) in Japan were an outgrowth of the government's efforts to organize suppliers into *keiretsu* groups. Toyota's association (*Kyohokai*), for instance, was established at a roundtable conference of Toyota suppliers in November 1939, and was designed to promote good relations between assembler and suppliers on a nonhierarchical basis.[44] Interfactory inspection tours and technical subcommittees served to diffuse best practice in manufacturing techniques and management between firms, and social events provided a forum for sharing information on

danger of hold-up that stems from asset specificity. A cost reduction curve is agreed upon in advance for the life of a product, and the supplier retains savings beyond this fixed amount. Because the supplier's base level of profit is set in advance, the assembler need not worry about sharing proprietary information concerning costs and production techniques with the assembler, and the two work together in an effort to lower costs. Womack, Jones, and Roos (1990: 148–9).

[41] Lamming (1993: 169); Shimokawa (1985: 6).
[42] Asanuma (1989: 5). Suppliers receive grades based on the number of defective parts delivered, the percentage of on-time deliveries in the proper sequence and quantity, and performance in reducing costs.
[43] Nishiguchi and Ikeda (1996: 222).
[44] Nishiguchi (1994: 39 and 47).

business trends and plans.[45] Given the mutual interdependence of a supply group, improving the performance of the entire group works to the advantage of each individual firm.

As I will explain in more detail, although differences endure, there has been a great deal of convergence between the traditional models of interfirm relationships within the auto industry. On the one hand, many of the core elements of the Japanese approach to interfirm relations (which some call the Toyota model) have become the global dominant model. It is now commonplace for suppliers to be organized in tiers, for top tier suppliers to play a critical role in the design process, and for these suppliers to support individual assemblers on a global base.[46] Contracts with suppliers are for the life of a particular model, and strict performance clauses are built in. On the other hand, some of the Japanese *keiretsu* ties have begun to weaken, particularly in those cases where controlling stakes have been bought by foreign firms (Nissan and Mitsubishi).[47] Differing means of coordination each have their advantages, and as the ties between formerly distinct production bases become closer, the challenge has been to draw from the advantages of each.

III. CONCLUSION

Policy makers and researchers in the Chinese central government were well aware of these alternative approaches to auto sector development, and there were distinct preferences. With respect to finance, both planning documents[48] and academic articles[49] in the early 1990s, focused on the role of the Japanese and Korean state during the process of industrial development: the importance of using tax and tariff policies to shape the structure of the industry (by influencing what is produced and where), the need for tax credits and preferential loans to facilitate the process of

---

[45] Smitka (1991: 6). The associations played an instrumental role in disseminating new concepts such as statistical process control and total quality control in the late 1950s and early 1960s, value analysis and value engineering in the late 1960s, and computer-aided design in the 1980s. Womack, Jones, and Roos (1990: 153). In other context, industry associations have been found to play a similarly beneficial role for small firms. Lamming points to the West German foundry industry as an example. Lamming (1993: 65).

[46] See Entienne de Banville and Jean-Jacques Chanaron, "Inter-firm Relationships and Industrial Models," in Lung et al. (1999).

[47] Noble (2002: 46). For an argument on why *keiretsu* ties endure, despite competitive pressures, see Lincoln (2001: 139–143).

[48] See Ministry of Machinery Industry (1994b: 11).

[49] Zhang (1994: 33); Huan (1996: 65).

technology transfer, and the need for subsidies to allow for rapid expansion. With respect to industrial organization, there was a general emphasis on the role of large business groups.[50] Business groups, noted one Chinese scholar, are seen in modern Western economic theory as an intermediate organization between the market and enterprises. Larger firms desire closer relationships with small firms so as to take advantage of their cheaper costs and the benefits of specialization; "by joining the production system of large enterprises the smaller ones were sure to secure orders from them for their own survival, along with guidance and support from large enterprises in technology, equipment, personnel, funds, and management."[51] As I have argued, however, the central government's ability to implement its ideas at the level of the firm was limited.

Limitations at the center translated into opportunities for the localities. Local governments had strong incentives to promote the development of local firms and the autonomy to choose what they believed to be the most effective means of doing so.[52] In the case studies that follow, I characterize each locality according to the structure of the local bureaucracy (unified or fragmented) and the form of interfirm relations (hierarchy or market) within the local business groups (see Table 1.1).

The extent to which a local bureaucratic structure is unified or fragmented is characterized according to the ability of the local bureaucracy to concentrate investment capital in targeted firms. Only one locality accumulated relatively large amounts of capital, and played an active role with respect to investing this capital in firm development: Shanghai. Between 1988 and 1994, the Shanghai municipal government collected over 5 billion RMB by means of a localization tax on local auto sales, and as I will explain, it carefully focused the investment of this capital.[53] In the remaining cases, the investment role of the local government was hindered by fragmentation. Guangzhou accumulated a sizeable amount of investment capital by means of a localization tax – close to 3 billion RMB[54] – but, as I will argue, this money was not actually invested in auto

---

[50] See Nolan (2002) on the central government's desire to develop powerful business groups.
[51] Sun Xiuping in Gao and Chi (1997: 116); see also Chen (1996).
[52] Tax revenue and profits from local firms both made the jobs of local political leaders easier (by creating revenue for new programs, employing workers, and providing social services) and strengthened their prospects for career advancement.
[53] Interview, no. S12, May 26, 1997. The political maneuvering with the central government that allowed Shanghai to retain the bulk of this capital is discussed in the next chapter.
[54] Yan Yue, "Guangbiao" [Guangzhou Peugeot], *Shanghai Qiche Bao* [Shanghai Auto Industry News], May 31, 1998, p. 11.

firms: different ministries pursued different objectives. In Beijing, the municipal government collected and dispersed virtually no capital for the auto sector. Table 2.3 gives an indication of the contrasting approaches toward supplier development of Shanghai, Guangzhou, and Beijing: in 1997, 81.1% of new fixed asset investment in SAIC was in components firms as compared to 15.1% in Beijing and 10.4% in Guangzhou.[55] Wuhan and Changchun were hindered by the fragmentation between the centrally controlled business groups (that were national in orientation) and the local governments that sought to promote local firms but had few resources. In Wuhan the municipal government allocated only RMB 140 million for auto sector development[56]; in Changchun there was no capital. Although sources of fragmentation varied, the result in all cases was insufficient resources for firm development.

The form of interfirm relations is used to characterize the structure of the business groups in the five localities. Although the term describing the business group in each city – *jituan gongsi* or *jituan qiye* – was the same, these had become catch-all phrases that were so common as to be nearly meaningless. The challenge is to distinguish between these structures in order to understand how they operated and how the structures affected development and performance. Key indicators of the internal structure of each group include: sourcing policy of the assembly plant (multiple or single suppliers for each component), pricing policy (hard bargaining or fixed price), nature of ties between head office and divisions (promotion patterns, information flows, degree of decision-making autonomy, etc.). A sector in which multiple suppliers were used, prices were bargained over, and firms had a great deal of autonomy from the head office are characterized primarily by market relations. This description characterizes Beijing and Guangzhou. If an assembly plant used a single supplier for a component, the head office set the price, and firm managers had very little autonomy, the sector is characterized primarily by hierarchical relations. This is true in Shanghai, Changchun, and Wuhan. The hope, of course, was that at least one of these auto groups would emerge as a national champion in the manner of a Toyota or Hyundai.

By characterizing the localities according to these two dimensions it is possible to group them into three different institutional patterns: the

---

[55] As explained in Chapter 2, comparable figures are not available for Changchun and Wuhan.

[56] Interview, no. W1, July 23, 1998. This amount is approximately U.S. $17 million (using the 1997 exchange rate of RMB 8.2 = U.S. $1).

local developmental state (Shanghai), the laissez-faire state (Beijing and Guangzhou), and the firm-dominated locality (Wuhan and Changchun). At this stage, network relationships played a relatively small role. In each of the case study chapters that follow, I explain why a particular locality took the approach that it did, and how the approach led to a particular development outcome in the period when the objective was increasing the manufacturing capability of local firms – they did not yet face competition from international firms. I start with Shanghai, the local developmental state.

FOUR

Shanghai

A Local Developmental State

Despite the dramatic twists and turns that have typified China's economic history during the last century, the city of Shanghai has more often than not symbolized each particular era. In 1987, writing in the party mouthpiece *Hongqi*, Mayor Jiang Zemin put forth the official CCP view of Shanghai history: "Before Liberation it was a microcosm of old China. It reflected in a concentrated form the major contradictions and various pathologies of the colonial, semi-colonial, and semi-feudal society. After Liberation, as the important economic centre and industrial base of our nation, its development fully manifested the vitality and superiority of the socialist system."[1] Three decades of rigid socialist planning removed many of the outward signs of bourgeois capitalism, but – despite official pronouncements to the contrary – also removed much of the city's former economic vitality. Losses in the state sector, which dominated industrial output and urban employment in the city, continued to rise during the 1980s; the symbol of socialist development became the symbol of socialist stagnation.[2] Shanghai's leaders sought once again to transform the city, this time through reform and development.

Shanghai municipal leaders, like leaders in other cities, chose the auto sector as a prime candidate for development because the extensive linkages of the industry created the potential for a broad impact. These same

---

[1] Cited in Wong Siu-Lin, "The Entrepreneurial Spirit: Shanghai and Hong Kong Compared," in Yeung and Sung (1996: 36–37).

[2] As late as 1994, the state sector was contributing over 42% of Shanghai's industrial output, and accounting for over 72% of urban employment. One third of large and medium-sized SOEs in 1994 were suffering losses. Peter T. Y. Cheung, "The Political Context of Shanghai's Economic Development," in Yeung and Sung (1996: 54).

linkages, however, increased the challenge of coordinating development in the sector. In the first section of this chapter, I argue that the unified bureaucratic structure of Shanghai was particularly well suited to auto sector development in the context of a protected and stable market: the local government played a pivotal role with respect to capital accumulation and investment; a hierarchically organized business group provided a structure that facilitated learning, coordination, and development among small firms; and a supplier association promoted horizontal ties between firms. In addition to nurturing firm development, these organizations allowed for the monitoring of firm development. The hierarchical business group monitored the performance of each firm, and the bureaucratic structure of the local government insured that top leaders were both informed and accessible. These nonmarket structures provided a halfway house of sorts for firms that were struggling to adjust in a transitional economy; Shanghai became a local developmental state.

Why was Shanghai able to so effectively create an institutional framework for auto sector development? The second section of the chapter traces the origins of the institutions that shaped development in Shanghai. Institutional change was not impossible, but it was distinctly path-dependent. As David Stark argues, "actors who seek to move in new directions find that their choices are constrained by the existing set of institutional resources. Institutions limit the field of action, they preclude some directions, they constrain certain courses. But institutions also favor the perception and selection of some strategies over others."[3] Institutional resources in Shanghai heavily favored a developmental approach that emphasized government planning largely due to the history of its relationship with the central government. Because the municipality had been the core of the central planning system, the local economy had been carefully controlled during the pre-reform period, and Shanghai was a planned economy to an extent far greater than in any other municipality. Local leaders and bureaucracies were accustomed to active participation in the local economy; local firms were accustomed to having many services provided to them by the comprehensive planning system. It was hardly surprising that movement toward a market economy was not rapid. The importance of path dependence means that complete transformations are halting at best, and as I argue in Chapter 8, this meant that institutional advantages in Shanghai lessened as the needs of the local auto sector began to rapidly evolve at the end of the 1990s.

---

[3] Stark (1992: 17).

I. THE LOCAL DEVELOPMENTAL STATE IN SHANGHAI

When Shanghai Volkswagen (SVW) was formed as a joint venture between Volkswagen (VW) and the Shanghai Automobile Industry Corporation (SAIC) in October 1984, the German partner had little incentive to speed up the localization process.[4] Over the long term, localization would be an important means of lowering costs, but VW's immediate concern in the initial stage was quality. "Automobiles are the most expensive of industrial products, and if consumers are to spend their hard earned money, they should receive a product that is safe, of high quality, and consistent with foreign standards," was the stated position of the Germans.[5] The car produced by the joint venture – the Santana – carried the VW name, and for reasons of reputation the Germans wanted to make sure that no part was localized before quality could be insured. VW also, of course, had a financial interest in doing business with pre-existing suppliers outside of China. International supply firms operating at high volumes could offer lower prices than Chinese suppliers, and this increased VW's profitability both in China and internationally.[6] This motivation, while hardly surprising, was not publicly stated.[7]

The Chinese perspective was quite different. The intent of the Shanghai municipal government was to make the automobile industry a "pillar" of the local economy, and to play a leading role in the city's efforts to restructure and upgrade its industrial infrastructure. Localizing the production of Santana parts held obvious benefits for SAIC. Unlike VW, which

---

[4] 50% of the investment in the JV came from VW, 35% from the Shanghai Tractor and Automobile Company (which would soon become SAIC), and 15% from the Bank of China.

[5] Li (1997: 117).

[6] VW would profit internationally from using non-China suppliers if: one, the supply firm had financial ties to the VW Group; or two, based on the higher volumes being ordered from a certain supply firm, VW could negotiate a lower price for all the Santana manufacturing bases using that supplier. In 1985, when SVW began manufacturing the Santana in Shanghai, VW was operating Santana manufacturing facilities in Germany, Brazil, Argentina, and Nigeria.

[7] As one VW manager explained, in the mid-1980s there was a great deal of uncertainty as to whether an auto assembly JV in China would make any money; consequently the foreign partner was motivated to earn a profit where one could be guaranteed: in the components business. A high price was charged for the CKD kit, and this price was simply passed on to the customer. In light of these incentives, during the SVW contract negotiations, the German side insisted that imported CKD kits be used in the initial stage of assembly operations. The contract took into account the need to eventually localize the Santana, wrote Eric Harwit (1995: 97) in his study of the industry, but "responsibility for providing quality parts made in China rested squarely with the Chinese; VW had no obligation to hasten the process."

profited in China only from the manufacturing operations of the joint venture itself, SAIC had three sources of revenue: its share of the joint venture profits, the huge mark up between the factory price of the automobile and the distribution price,[8] and the revenue from the supply firms that were part of the SAIC group. SAIC naturally wanted to increase the use of its own supply firms for it was these firms – not the assembly plant joint venture – that formed the core of its revenue base.

The interests of SAIC and the Shanghai Municipal government were identical because SAIC was essentially a division of the municipal government. Seventy-five percent was owned by the municipal government, and 25% was owned by the Shanghai International Trust and Investment Company (SitiCo), the financial arm of the municipal government.[9] SAIC's leading unit (*lingdao danwei*) was the Shanghai Economic Commission (*Shanghai jingji weiyuanhui*), and its president reported directly to Shanghai's mayor.[10] The municipal government, of course, hoped that the auto sector would drive growth in related industries as well, including steel and iron, nonferrous metals, plastics, rubber, petrochemicals, textiles, light industry, and construction. According to the calculations of Hu Runsong, vice-president of Shanghai's Planned Economy Institute, "if the city reached an annual capacity of 300,000 cars by the end of the century, it would gain 20 billion yuan ($4.2 billion) worth of industrial output, accounting for one tenth of the city's total."[11] Charlie Wilson, a president of General Motors and Secretary of Defense during the Eisenhower Administration, was widely reported to have claimed, "what's good for General Motors is good for the country."[12] Whether this was indeed the case in the United States is debatable, but an analogous statement was clearly believed to be true in Shanghai: what was good for Shanghai Volkswagen was good for Shanghai.

---

[8] VW did not have the distribution rights to SVW's product. While demand was high, SAIC was able to charge a huge mark-up for Santana's. In 1988, for instance, SVW sold each Santana to SAIC for 70,000 RMB ($18,800 US), and SAIC then resold the cars to authorized distributors for 140,000 RMB ($37,600 US). Harwit (1995: 102). The central government's State Price Bureau set guidelines for the retail prices of cars.

[9] Interview, no. S11, 31 May 31, 1997.

[10] Interview, no. S17, May 27, 1997; and Interview, no. S14, May 20, 1997.

[11] Cao Yang, "Car makers must take a lead role," *China Daily*, April 29, 1990. According to one factory manager, the municipal government was not concerned whether the assembly plant had losses or not, as long as the supply firms were profitable. Interview, no. S10, May 22, 1997.

[12] Wilson's actual statement was, "We at General Motors have always felt that what was good for the country was good for General Motors as well." Maynard (1995: 28).

Initial localization efforts were not successful, however. There were reports during the first year of the project that banks were slow in providing funding to the assembly plant and supply firms, construction authorities delayed projects, and city officials were not pushing the localization process.[13] In 1986, incentives were given to encourage investment in the supply sector, primarily in the form of low-interest loans and tax holidays, but the impact was minimal.[14] According to Wang Rongjun, the Managing Director of Shanghai Volkswagen in 1986, the Shanghai supply base was simply too weak:

> The technical standards of Chinese automobile component suppliers in 1986 were nearly 30 years behind component manufacturers of Europe, Japan, and the United States. . . . We needed a fundamental shift, not only in parts design (as cars are a little different from trucks) but also in the technology. In the beginning there wasn't a single local parts supplier which could produce a part we could assemble into the Santana.[15]

Upgrading local supply firms to a level that would enable them to form linkages with the more advanced Santana manufacturing processes was an expensive proposition; technology had to be licensed from foreign companies, equipment needed to be imported, and workers had to be trained. Funds for investment in the industry were insufficient, and tax-free status for the industry had little impact when there was not a good foundation. Pressuring VW to use local parts was futile if local suppliers could not provide the quality parts required.[16] As of early 1987, two years after the start of production at SVW, only 2.7% of the value of a Santana consisted of parts manufactured in China: the tires, the radio, and the antennae.[17] The Shanghai supply base, still at the level of the 1950s according to Wang Rongjun, was simply too weak to support localization.[18]

Despite the slow start, the manufacturing capability of the Shanghai automobile industry increased sharply over the course of the next decade. Although the term "local content rate" officially refers to the percentage of a product that is manufactured within all of China, in the case of SVW

---

[13] Harwit (1995: 98).

[14] Shanghai Auto Industry History Editorial Committee (1992: 128).

[15] Upton and Seet (1995: 19). See also interview with Wang Rongjun in Zhang Han Shou, "Santana zai jiakuai guochanhua" [Santana speeds up localization], *Zhongguo Qiche Bao* [China Auto News], June 9, 1988, p. 1.

[16] No matter how great the pressure from the Chinese side, VW could refuse to use parts that did not meet its quality standards. A German laboratory was transferred to Shanghai for the purpose of testing the quality of locally sourced parts.

[17] Li (1997: 116).

[18] Wang Rongjun, "Chenggong zhi lu" [The road of success], in Sun (1995: 140).

Development of Active Suppliers at Shanghai Volkswagen

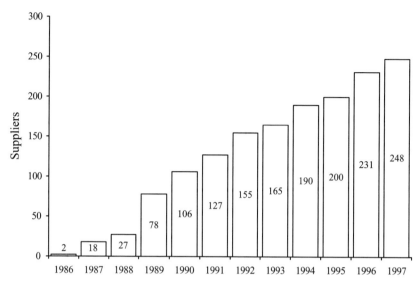

Figure 4.1: Development of active suppliers at Shanghai Volkswagen. *Source*: Shanghai Volkswagen.

it was truly local: the SVW supply network was almost exclusively within Shanghai. The domestic content rate of the Santana increased from 2.7% in 1987 to 92.9% in 1997 (see Figure 4.1 for the growth in active suppliers), and 88–90% by value of this amount was produced within the municipality of Shanghai (Figure 4.2), 50% by the 40 suppliers within the SAIC group.[19] An initial indication of the strength of these supply firms can be found in VW's internal quality audits, the criteria for which remained constant: the number of "A" suppliers increased from 1 in 1990 to 27 in 1997; the number of "B" suppliers increased from 30 in 1990 to 203 in 1997; the number of "C" suppliers decreased from 34 in 1990 to 5 in 1997 (Figure 4.3).[20] The most persuasive indicator, and the one that I provided details of in

[19] Interview no. S25, June 17, 1998. The local content rate would not rise above this percentage because the remaining 7% consisted of parts that were used in volumes too small to be economically produced in China.

[20] Suppliers that were given an "A" ranking were capable of guaranteeing VW's quality standards and providing parts according to this standard on a consistent basis. "B" level suppliers would conform with VW standards under most circumstances but not with complete consistency; when defects emerged they had to be assisted in correcting the problems. "C" level suppliers did not have the capability to maintain quality levels, and had to receive continual technical and managerial assistance from SVW. Wang Rongjun,

Shanghai Volkswagen Purchasing Volume by Province, 1997

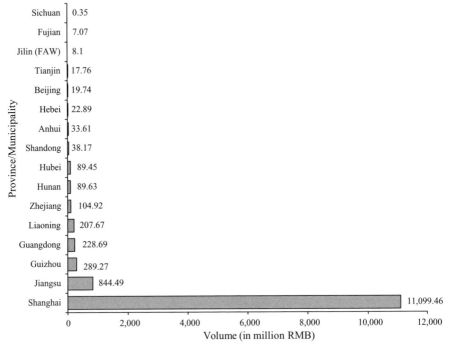

Figure 4.2: Shanghai Volkswagen purchasing volume by province, 1997. *Source*: Shanghai Volkswagen.

Chapter 2, is the extent to which assembly projects in other municipalities, despite strong incentives to use their own suppliers, increasingly relied on Shanghai suppliers.

There is little doubt that Shanghai had the strongest supply network in China, and rapidly rising local content rate was a key factor in the success of SVW during the pre-WTO period of development. When local content was low in the mid-1980s, production levels at SVW were limited by restrictions on foreign exchange (which were necessary to import CKDs), as local content increased, however, production volumes could increase dramatically.[21] When the central government increased restrictions on

---

"Chenggong zhi lu" [The road of success], in Sun (1995: 145). The numbers of firms in each category are from an SVW internal audit of local suppliers.

[21] As I will elaborate later, the relationship between rising local content and increased production was a virtuous circle: rising production at SVW allowed the suppliers to achieve economies of scale and lower costs.

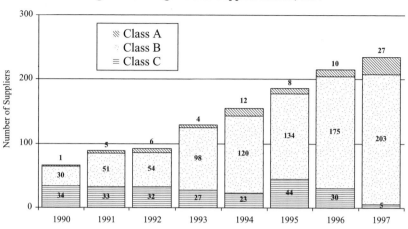

Figure 4.3: Shanghai Volkswagen local supplier audits, 1997. *Source*: Shanghai Volkswagen.

foreign exchange, the exposure of SVW was significantly reduced and it could continue to increase production volumes (see Figure 2.4). Similarly, when market demand softened, because SVW was not dependent on expensive CKDs, it was more resilient than its competitors and could continue to expand. Rising production volumes during the early 1990s allowed SVW to obtain the economies of scale that are so critical in the automobile industry, and to capture market share. In 1996, 52% of the sedan cars sold in China were produced by SVW.[22] The Ministry of Foreign Trade and Economic Cooperation consistently ranked SVW number one among the top 500 overseas-invested enterprises in China based on annual sales during this period.[23]

A. Shanghai Municipal Government as Key Investor

The broad development of the Shanghai supply base between 1986 and 1996 was the result of local government policy. In 1986, one year after the creation of SVW, the Shanghai municipal government began to take on many of the characteristics of a local developmental state: it fine-tuned

[22] Craig Smith, "Shanghai Volkswagen Says Price Cuts Hurt Industry," *Asian Wall Street Journal*, February 6, 1997.
[23] Sun Hong, "Shanghai Volkswagen: No. 1 of overseas funded," *China Daily*, November 2, 1996.

the bureaucratic structure so as to be able to effectively coordinate and monitor developmental efforts, it played the primary role with respect to capital accumulation and investment, and it directed the overall development process. How was a local government able to take on such an active role?

The central government, incapable of directing industrial development itself, created the opportunity. At the same time that the Shanghai municipal government began to focus on possible means of invigorating the city's stagnant industrial base, the central government was loosening its control over industrial firms. In 1986, writes Joseph Fewsmith, Premier Zhao Ziyang began to abandon a top-down approach to reform in favor of a bottom-up approach: "both the desire to minimize political and economic risks and the need to find a way around the planning apparatus led Zhao to focus on the reform of the microeconomy."[24] If the planning system was responsible for weakening the incentives of factory managers, the logical solution was to grant enterprises a greater degree of autonomy.

The impact on the auto industry was not long in coming. In the summer of 1986, Zhao summoned the top leaders of the China National Automobile Industry Corporation (CNAIC), Rao Bin and Li Gang, to the summer resort of Beidaihe.[25] He believed that CNAIC, the central government body charged with oversight of the auto industry, was gaining too much control over the industry, and was beginning to stifle reform, he told them.[26] It would have to be weakened. "Your fate has been settled (*zai jie nan tao*)," Zhao told the two auto industry leaders, and refused to listen to their protests. The Premier cared little about the auto industry itself, a top CNAIC official later explained, but his conception of reform had a big impact on the industry; his desire to give power to enterprises weakened the center with respect to the localities, for it was to the localities that most of the auto enterprises belonged. In May of 1987, State Document No. 5 (1987), issued by the State Council, downgraded the status of CNAIC to that of a federation (*lianhehui*).[27] As a federation, the organization would

---

[24] Fewsmith (1994: 176).
[25] This account of these events was given by a former top CNAIC official. Interview, no. B39, June 8, 1998.
[26] Zhao told the leaders they could not have a monopoly over the domestic auto industry. They replied that they didn't, but Zhao retorted that they would soon.
[27] "Zhongguo Qiche Gongye Lianhehui Chengli" [The China National Auto Federation is Created], *Zhongguo Qiche Bao* [China Auto News], June 29, 1987, p. 1; "The History of Administration System & Organization of China Auto Industry," *China Auto*, vol. 2, no. 3, June 20, 1992, p. 7.

serve as a consultant to firms and a liaison between firms, but "just like the UN," a former CNAIC official commented ruefully, "it had no power of enforcement."[28]

The weakening of central control coincided with a growing realization in Shanghai that localization efforts were making no progress. Although Shanghai had been trying for a year to pressure SVW to use only local suppliers, the municipal leaders realized that a tactical retreat was necessary while the municipality prepared an institutional framework to support the development of the local auto sector. The retreat consisted of a decision by Mayor Jiang Zemin's office to allow sourcing to take place on a nationwide basis.[29] The primary motivation for sourcing nationwide was the preservation of foreign exchange.[30] In order to lower costs and capture market share, SVW had to increase production volumes, but this was impossible as long as production required imported CKDs – foreign exchange restrictions were too tight and too subject to fluctuation. Only by replacing imported parts with domestically sourced parts could SVW begin the critical step of expanding production. Rather than beat a dead horse in Shanghai, SVW was allowed to utilize army and aerospace factories in Guizhou and Xian that had slightly higher technical levels (and were becoming increasingly interested in defense conversion), and the First and Second Auto Works (FAW and SAW) which had already begun to import foreign technology. The problem of domestic content was by no means solved – the technical levels at these factories were not particularly high either – but the strategy gave Shanghai some much needed maneuvering room. With production volumes beginning to rise (Figure 2.4) the municipal government could begin laying the groundwork for constructing a local automobile supply base.

Stage One: Institutional Changes. The first prerequisite for a successful localization drive in Shanghai was a slight reorganization of the municipal bureaucracy responsible for auto sector oversight. As I argued in Chapter 2, the size of China's market gave the Chinese an unusual degree of leverage over foreign auto companies. The challenge from the Chinese perspective was knowing what demands to make, and being able to take advantage of the opportunities that were created.[31] To capitalize

---

[28] Interview, no. B39, June 8, 1998.
[29] Interview, no. S12, May 26, 1997.
[30] Interview, no. HK1, July 4, 1997.
[31] As Stephan Haggard (1990: 20) has written in another context, "the conduct and performance of multinational firms is only an intervening variable between policy choices

on the opportunities presented by the presence of SVW, the Shanghai municipal government needed to strengthen and centralize the institutional structure that managed the local auto industry.

Given the manner in which many governmental structures in China are fragmented vertically along functional lines (each in its own system, or *xitong*), coordination can be achieved across separate ministries only if a coordinating office has sufficient power. Bureaucratic structures of equal rank bargain continually and intensely – any resource that is scarce will be the subject of bargaining – but in many cases are only able to reach a decision and ensure compliance by appealing to higher authorities.[32] In the auto industry, this problem of fragmented authority was particularly vexing because investment capital was extremely scarce and the widespread linkages of the industry drew a large number of governmental offices into the policymaking process. Bureaucratic infighting was more common than coordinated development. Institutional power, consequently, had to be centralized not as a means of increasing leverage over foreign investors, but as a means of controlling local actors. Without this bureaucratic reorganization, it would not be possible to coordinate development in the sector.

In September 1986, the same time that nationwide sourcing began, the Shanghai Municipal government formed a Santana Localization Small Group (*Santana jiaoche guochanhua xietiao xiaozu*) under the leadership of the Shanghai Economic Commission, but it soon became apparent that the political power of this group was insufficient.[33] When the Santana Localization Small Group was situated under the Economic Commission, it was in many instances, only equal in bureaucratic strength to the offices that it was supposed to be coordinating.[34] The result was a poorly coordinated initial localization effort. The solution, carried out in July of 1987, was to create the Automobile Industry Leading Small Group (formally entitled *zhiyuan dazhong jianshe lingdao xiaozu*) directly underneath the mayor's office, and composed of the directors of every government office that might potentially affect development of the city's automobile industry.[35] The Santana Localization Small Group was transformed into

---

and economic outcomes. Dependency [on foreign actors] is as much an effect of national policies as their cause."

[32] See Lieberthal and Oksenberg (1988); Lieberthal and Lampton (1992).

[33] Shanghai Auto Industry History Editorial Committee (1992: 128).

[34] Lack of a full-time staff increased the institutional weakness of the small group; it most likely consisted of representatives of offices and ministries relevant to the auto industry.

[35] The Leading Small Group was composed of 22 members: two vice mayors, the directors of Shanghai's Economic Commission, Planning Commission, Science Commission, and

Shanghai Municipal Government and Auto Sector until mid-1990s

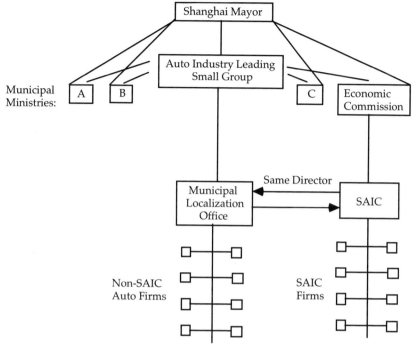

Figure 4.4: Shanghai municipal government and auto sector until mid-1990s.

an office (*bangongshi*) with a full-time staff, and placed under the leadership of the new Leading Small Group (see Figure 4.4).[36]

The importance of these new offices was indicated by the officials chosen as leaders. The Leading Small Group was deemed worthy of two vice-Mayors: Huang Ju was the director (he would succeed Zhu Rongji as Mayor in 1991) and Li Jiaoji was the vice-director. The Localization Office was to be directed by Lu Jian, vice-chairman of the Shanghai Economic Commission (SEC). According to the official history of the Shanghai auto industry, these institutional changes made it clear that the municipal

Construction Commission, the directors of the Customs Department, Personnel Department, and Finance Department, the directors of three banks (Bank of China, Construction Bank, and Communications Bank), the directors of the Personnel Ministry, Finance Ministry, and every industrial ministry (Electric, Light, Second Light, Chemicals, and Textiles), the president of SAIC, general manager of SVW, and the head of Anting County (in which the SVW plant is located). Based on internal government reports (the author of which wished to remain anonymous).

[36] Shanghai Auto Industry History Editorial Committee (1992: 128).

government was intent on making the local auto industry one of the three primary bases of sedan production in China and one of the six pillars of the Shanghai economy.[37]

The bureaucratic apparatus that emerged from this reshuffling was at every level unified and coordinated in its view of how industrial development in the auto sector should proceed. The Localization Office dealt with the auto industry on a daily basis – it was in a sense the head office for the local industry. A problem that was particularly intractable, however, would lead to a meeting of the Leading Small Group. Intractable problems were more often than not issues relating to coordination between various government agencies, hence a meeting involving the directors of every related agency usually had the power to arrive promptly at a solution. Finally, at the very top bureaucratic layer, it was clear that the industry would receive political support when necessary. Mayor Jiang Zemin called the top leaders of the auto industry into his office explicitly to emphasize the importance of their role in modernizing Shanghai's industrial infrastructure. "When you have problems," he told them, "come find me. We must maintain a hot line between us."[38]

Stage Two: Capital Accumulation. With a coherent institutional structure for managing the industry established, the municipal government started focusing on the need for investment capital, and it became an investment bank in the Gerschenkronian sense. In 1988, the Shanghai government began the process of capital accumulation by creating what it called an "auto component tax" (*qiche lingbujian shui*). For every Santana automobile sold, a tax of 28,000 RMB would be levied (in June 1990 the amount was decreased to 23,000 RMB), and the proceeds would form a localization fund controlled by the municipal government's automobile localization office. From 1988 to 1994 (the tax was abolished in 1994 when the VAT tax was created) the city of Shanghai collected over 5 billion RMB, an amount that was not subject to central government taxation.[39] Working together with SAIC and SVW, the localization office could use this sizable war chest to assist the local supply firms that required investment capital to import foreign technology and equipment.

---

[37] Shanghai Auto Industry History Editorial Committee (1992: 127–128).

[38] "*You kunnan, ni jiu lai zhao wo, women baochi rexian lianxi.*" Quoted in Li (1997: 116).

[39] Interview, no. S12, May 26, 1997. The political maneuvering with the central government that allowed Shanghai to retain the bulk of this capital is discussed in the final section of this chapter.

Stage Three: Development. After the necessary investment capital had been collected, the challenge shifted to utilizing it in an effective localization drive. The Localization Office was extremely effective, although the objective was limited: at this stage the goal was not to create a capability to manufacture components at globally competitive prices, but simply to manufacture components that met SVW standards. Toward this end, the Localization Office carried out a very straightforward import substitution policy, with import defined as any component purchased outside of the Shanghai municipality. The Localization Office examined the list of components that SVW was either importing from abroad or elsewhere in China, and determined which could most successfully be produced by Shanghai factories. Potential factories were considered, meetings were held with factory managers to discuss a particular factory's needs and capabilities, and an evaluation made. Based on the evaluation, a decision would be made as to whether a particular factory had the capability to manufacture a given component.

The Localization Office, although small – it consisted of approximately 10 officials – was well suited for working with the managers of supply firms who hoped to upgrade their technical capabilities and form linkages to SVW.[40] Each official in the office was responsible for 10–20 factories in a particular subsector of the auto industry, and in most cases the official had extensive background in his or her particular jurisdiction (light industry, textiles, machine tools, electronics, etc.).[41] The person responsible for light industrial firms, for instance, most likely was formerly an employee at either a light industry enterprise or the Shanghai Light Industry Corporation, the municipal office governing this sector. Consequently, the officials at the Localization Office were familiar not only with the technical characteristics and needs of the firms they dealt with, but also with the bureaucratic politics of the related ministries and municipal offices.

Based upon the initial evaluation of the supply firms' capabilities, the Localization Office gave specific advice concerning the equipment and technology that had to be imported. Even more importantly, however, it provided the necessary financial backing. Managers of supply firms faced a dilemma at this stage. When the Santana assembly plant first began operations in 1985, volumes were low and consisted entirely of

---

[40] The description of the Localization Office that follows is based on interviews with managers of supply firm whom had had extensive interaction with the office. Officials at the Localization Office itself repeatedly refused requests for interviews.

[41] Interview, no. S6, June 6, 1997; Interview, no. S13, May 30, 1997.

imported CKDs.[42] SVW wanted to develop the local supply base, but had no money of its own to invest in supply firms. From the perspective of a supply firm, making the financial commitment necessary to forge a linkage with SVW was extremely risky. A great deal of capital was required in order to upgrade technical capabilities, current production would be disrupted, and the low volumes at SVW did not necessarily guarantee a sufficient return on the required investment. At this stage there was no guarantee that SVW would successfully increase production volumes, and if it did not, the supply firm would not be able to attain the economies of scale that would bring profitability (and repay its loans). As one SAIC manager later commented, in the initial years of the joint venture, most supply firms were unwilling to bear the risk of linking to SVW.[43] If all the supply firms upgraded their technical capacities in a coordinated manner, the increase in domestic content would allow SVW to rapidly raise production volumes, and both SVW and the suppliers would prosper. Acting individually, however, each individual supply firm had no guarantee that coordinated investment would occur, and the risk of investing alone was high. The problem was exacerbated by the high degree of asset specificity inherent in the relationship between an auto supply firm and an assembly plant: given the small number of potential customers for a particular auto component (particularly at this very early stage of development) the supplier was vulnerable to opportunism on the part of an assembly plant that was continually struggling to lower costs. There either had to be coordinated development of the whole sector, or very little development at all.

The Localization Office served to ease the risk of individual supply firms by providing access to investment capital at preferential rates, and managing relations with the assembly plant. Throughout Shanghai, managers of supply firms tell a familiar story. Factory A, for instance, which manufactures automobile accessories, began working with the Localization Office in 1988. After the factory was evaluated and decisions were made with respect to what technology needed to be licensed and what equipment needed to be imported, the factory began receiving loans arranged by the Localization Office. From 1989 to 1994 the enterprise received a total of 22,500,000 RMB in three parts (2,200,000 RMB; 4,800,000 RMB; and, 15,500,000 RMB), 30% of which were preferential

---

[42] 1,733 Santanas were produced in 1985, 8,500 in 1986, and 10,538 in 1987. *Shanghai Dazhong Nianbao 1997* [SVW Annual Report 1997], p. 40.
[43] Interview, no. S28, June 19, 1998.

loans directly from the localization office, and 70% of which were bank loans with an extended repayment period. The loans were used to fund three new projects, and enabled the factory to rapidly raise production volumes.[44] At Factory B, the pattern is almost identical. Between 1986 and 1990 the Localization Office provided loans totaling 2,000,000 RMB, and between 1990 and 1995 the total was 5,000,000 (between 1996 and 2000 a projected 9,000,000 in loans were expected). The corresponding increase in production volumes was dramatic: from 10,000 in 1990 to 250,000 in 1996.[45] A third enterprise used a combination of capital sources to fund an expansion program in 1991–1992: the Localization Office provided 45% of the investment capital at 5% interest, banks provided 45% at 14% interest, and enterprise profits were relied upon for 10%.[46] Two of these firms later became joint ventures, but during the years of heaviest expansion they were SOEs relying on licensed technology.

As the manufacturing capability of Shanghai enterprises improved, SVW gradually began to shift its sourcing patterns. Whereas initially it may have been sourcing 80% of a particular component outside of Shanghai, this percentage decreased as the technical level of local factories improved.[47] Both SAIC and the municipal government – in the form of the Localization Office – carefully monitored SVW's sourcing practices to insure that local firms were being utilized as fully as possible. Once there was local capability to manufacture a particular part, SVW had no choice but to use the Shanghai supplier. Domestic content began to rise very quickly, with the sharpest increase between 1987 and 1990 (from 5.7% to 60.1%).[48]

The objective of the Shanghai municipal government was to create a well-rounded local automobile sector, and this was the guiding purpose of the Localization Office. This not only involved monitoring SVW's sourcing patterns (i.e., making sure that Shanghai parts firms were being properly utilized), but also insuring that the city did not develop excess capacity in one particular area (e.g., textiles). If an enterprise was proposing to develop a manufacturing capability that the Localization Office did not view as necessary, the enterprise would be warned. In a completely

[44] Interview, no. S13, May 30, 1997.
[45] Interview, no. S8, May 28, 1997.
[46] Interview, no. S14, May 20, 1997.
[47] Because production volumes at SVW were increasing dramatically actual numbers may not have changed much – outside suppliers got a smaller slice of a bigger pie. Consequently, SVW could keep everybody happy. Interview, no. S12, May 26, 1997.
[48] Harwit (1995: 100).

marketized economy, of course, price fluctuations would have provided a firm with a great deal of the necessary market information, but within the Shanghai auto sector, prices were not determined by the market. In most instances, enterprises would heed the advice of the Localization Office because it was thought to have a broad perspective on the sector, and its market information was viewed as unequivocal.[49] If necessary, however, the Localization Office had powerful means of control at its disposal. Given its ties to the Shanghai Economic Commission, it could prevent a project from getting the proper approvals, and because it controlled the massive Localization Fund, it could also deny a project access to capital. Without the support of the Localization Office a new project was simply not possible.

However, the Localization Office was not solely an enforcer; it also played an important role as an advocate and advisor to local supply firms. Two primary coordinating functions can be identified. First, just as it helped the government control the supply firms, it helped the supply firms manage government relations. This was particularly important during periods of development, because development required an endless series of approvals, and dealing with the byzantine Chinese bureaucracy was notoriously difficult. SAIC, of course, could always draw upon both its size and its high-level linkages to the municipal government to assist firms within its group, but the problems of smaller non-SAIC supply firms were seldom important enough to warrant high-level government attention.[50] The Localization Office consequently, served as their "head office," providing a vertical linkage into the government hierarchy. When a supply firm needed an import license for new equipment, for instance, the Localization Office would have the necessary connections, and it could utilize them to smooth the way with the necessary agencies.[51]

---

[49] As the manager of one local supply firm commented with respect to the market information of the Localization Office, "they knew what was needed and how much. If they didn't provide us with this sort of information we wouldn't know." Interview, no. S15, May 23, 1997.

[50] A striking example of preferential treatment for SAIC enterprises during this period, according to the western manager of one JV, could be found in the Shanghai Customs Bureau. The bureau used three different designations to distinguish between Shanghai firms: most trusted, trusted, and not trusted. Most trusted firms did not have to file a customs claim when importing, trusted firms could file the claim themselves, not trusted firms had to file with the Customs Bureau and imports would be held for a minimum of one week. All SAIC firms had the "most trusted" designation; no western firm did. Interview, no. S21, June 18, 1998.

[51] Interview, no. S13, May 30, 1997.

The second coordination function was creating and facilitating horizontal relations between firms. When a supply firm was trying to upgrade its technical capability and improve its management techniques, it inevitably encountered problems. When it did, the manager contacted the relevant person within the coordination office. The Localization Office official probably would not have the answer itself, particularly if it was a technical problem, but usually would know who would have an answer. The supply firm manager would be put in contact with a supply firm that previously faced a similar obstacle, and from them, learn how to best deal with it. When a particular problem was quite common, the Localization Office often organized study trips to "A" level enterprises. Managers of supply firms were able not only to get a first-hand view of successful production techniques, but also an opportunity to discuss the relative merits of various approaches.[52] Development within a particular auto supply firm was not a unique process. Much to the contrary, each firm was traveling the same road, and the ability to share and compare notes was extremely valuable.

B. The Local Business Group: Shanghai Automobile Industry Corporation

The bureaucracy of the Shanghai municipal government had tremendous power over local firms, but it was not completely intrusive either. In other words, while the Localization Office had the capability to influence firm behavior – primarily through access to investment capital – its function did not necessarily preclude an important role for market coordination. Within the sector there could have been vigorous market competition between firms, and the local developmental state could have made investment decisions based on performance. This was not the case, however, because state influence was extended by means of a hierarchically organized business group, a coordinating mechanism that effectively precluded the use of a market within the Shanghai auto sector. The structure of SAIC extended the reach of the local government into every aspect of enterprise behavior.

Within SAIC, internal coherence was provided by an organizational structure strikingly similar to Alfred Chandler's conception of a modern industrial enterprise.[53] The coordination center was the SAIC head office,

---

[52] Interview, no. S13, May 30, 1997.
[53] "Each unit within the modern multiunit enterprise has its own administrative office," writes Chandler. "Each is administered by a full-time salaried manager. Each has its own

Shanghai Automobile Industry Corporation's Auto Operations, 1997

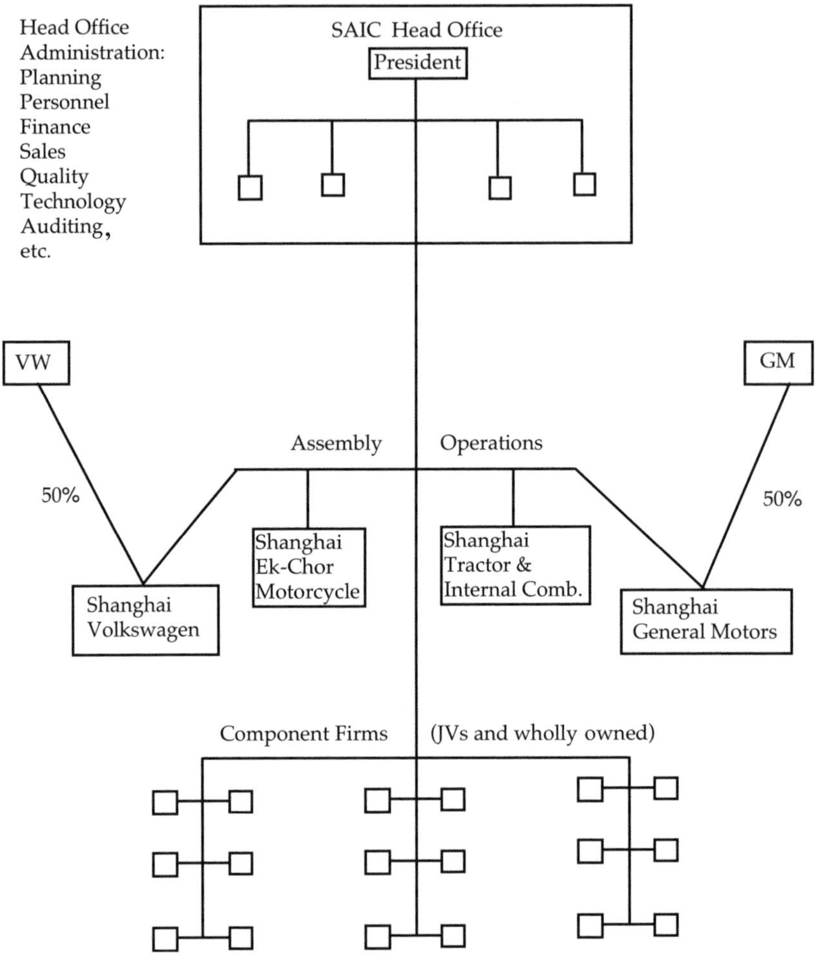

Head Office
Administration:
Planning
Personnel
Finance
Sales
Quality
Technology
Auditing,
etc.

SAIC Head Office
President

VW   50%

GM   50%

Assembly   Operations

Shanghai
Ek-Chor
Motorcycle

Shanghai
Tractor &
Internal Comb.

Shanghai
Volkswagen

Shanghai
General Motors

Component Firms   (JVs and wholly owned)

Figure 4.5: SAIC's Auto Operations in 1997.

occupied by the president and the five vice-presidents (see Figure 4.5). Beneath this top tier were the administrative divisions that collected and provided the information necessary to run the conglomerate: planning, personnel, cadre, finance, quality control, auditing, technology, foreign

set of books and accounts that can be audited separately from those of a large enterprise. Each could theoretically operate as an independent business enterprise." Transactions between units become routine, the cost for information on new markets, sources of supply, and manufacturing techniques are reduced, and the hierarchy allows for smooth administration of the flow of goods from one unit to another. Chandler (1977: 2–7).

exchange, and the president's office. In the next tier were a series of companies that were independent legal entities (*duli faren*). Some of these were closely related to the core business of automobiles (an auto sales company, an auto technology center), others had a broader scope (a real estate development company, a finance company). Finally, laid out below this central hierarchy were the manufacturing operations. There were five primary assembly operations (Shanghai Tractor and Internal Combustion Engine, Shanghai Ek Chor Motorcycle, Shanghai Bus and Coach Company, Shanghai Volkswagen, and Shanghai General Motors) and 32 auto supply firms, 18 of which were joint ventures in the mid-1990s.[54] Each of these was legally independent, and had an internal hierarchical structure that mirrored the structure of the head office. A person in the planning department of a components factory, for instance, communicated not only with the manager of the enterprise, but with the planning department of the head office.[55] Relationships that could have been coordinated by a market were organized according to a strict hierarchy. In the initial stage of development, when the primary concern was developing manufacturing capability, the SAIC hierarchy served three critical functions: it allowed for internal control, facilitated development and coordinated planning, and promoted learning.

Internal Control. The head office of SAIC was kept extremely well informed concerning enterprise operations. In most cases, detailed reports were sent once a month from the operating divisions to the head office.[56] Based on this information, the head office was able to direct operations in the individual divisions by means of its control over finance and personnel.

Finance was a powerful lever of control simply because the capital and assets of all enterprises within the group belonged to SAIC.[57] At the beginning of each year (January or February) the managers of an enterprise and representatives from the head office, using financial records from the previous year as a guide, determined the percentage of the year's

---

[54] This description is based on Interview, no. S17, May 27, 1997; and the Shanghai Automobile Industry Corporation (Group) Annual Report 1996. As I explain in Chapter 7, this structure began to change in the late 1990s.

[55] In this sense, the SAIC structure was very similar to governmental structures in China: each level duplicated the one above. Relationships had to be managed horizontally within a particular level, and vertically within a certain *xitong*. Interview, no. S27, June 22, 1998.

[56] These reports included both technical and financial information (budgets, materials flowing in, materials flowing out, production figures, etc.). Interview, no. S19, June 16, 1998.

[57] The only difference in a joint venture within the SAIC group was that the SAIC portion of capital and assets varied according its equity stake in the JV.

profits that would be turned over to SAIC, and the percentage that would be retained by the enterprise. Generally speaking, approximately 80% of enterprise revenue went to the head office.[58] As I will explain, there were reasons why it was difficult to accurately assess a firm's performance (profitability, etc.), but this was not viewed as a critical problem; no matter where the profits ended up they were within the SAIC group. At the end of each year an annual review of each firm assessed improvements in quality and technical level, and the degree to which profit objectives were filled. If a firm exceeded its annual plan, each employee of the firm received a salary bonus.[59] When an enterprise required investment capital (for a new project or the upgrading of equipment) it had to apply to SAIC for capital. A feasibility study was performed by the Planning Department, an evaluation made, and a decision made accordingly. Planning for investment was done at the same time that profit distribution was determined.[60]

Personnel decisions were a second means of control within the SAIC hierarchy. The top management of each SAIC enterprise was appointed by the head office: the general manager, deputy general managers, and the directors in charge of personnel, sales and marketing, technical and quality control, and development and planning.[61] Twice each year a head office team of two or three people arrived at the enterprise to review the work of the preceding six months. Interviews were conducted with a range of enterprise employees, finances were reviewed, and the work of each manager was evaluated. Based on the reports that were written, decisions were made concerning who should be promoted or demoted, and who should be transferred to other SAIC firms.[62] At some supply firms, even mid-level managers reported pressure to defend their position by

---

[58] At the supply firms visited, the percentage of profits submitted to SAIC varied from 80% to 100%. Some supply firms pointed out that if their profits were unexpectedly large they would voluntarily submit more to SAIC. It was all within SAIC, so it was not seen to be important. Interview, no. S14, May 20, 1997. The incentive structure, of course, encourages firms to sandbag the budget so that investment figures are high, and profits – the vast majority of which are not retained by the enterprise itself – are low. Interview, no. S1, May 28, 1997.

[59] Interview, no. S28, June 19, 1998. According to some accounts bonuses can be as high as 30% of an employee's salary. Salaries do not decrease when performance is poor.

[60] Even if an enterprise does not require capital for a new project, approvals must be given by the head office before the project is launched.

[61] Interview, no. S15, May 23, 1997; Interview, no. S14, May 20, 1997.

[62] I received conflicting reports as to whether managers could be fired. Some said that if a manager performed poorly and it was judged to be his/her fault, the manager could be fired. Others said this never happened; being demoted was far more likely.

learning new skills – computers, languages, new technologies – either in their spare time or by attending company-sponsored night school.[63] Each level of staff was evaluated regularly by the level above, and in contrast to financial decisions concerning the whole firm, personnel decisions provided a highly credible threat.

The tight control that SAIC exerted over its managers gave it powerful leverage not only within its wholly owned enterprises, but also within the joint ventures. The Chinese management, according to one foreign general manager of a joint venture, "knew exactly where they have latitude and where they don't."[64] Rather than being members of a cooperative joint venture, SAIC managers viewed themselves as representatives of the parent company, and in many cases the Chinese managers were effectively positioned so that they could control the joint venture operations. In one supply firm, for instance, the Chinese general manager was responsible for purchasing and sales, the front and the end of the company, and the Chinese deputy general manager was responsible for personnel, the middle of the company. The foreign managers, frustrated because the Chinese "hold all the strategic points in the joint venture," controlled finance, quality, and technical issues. The result, according to one foreign manager, was that "we couldn't make a move without SAIC."[65]

Development and Planning. SAIC served as a planning base for the enterprises within the group, complementing the role of the Municipal Localization Office during the development process, making adjustments when a supply firm was struggling, and providing overall coordination for the automobile sector. During the development process, in addition to having a great deal of influence within the Localization Office concerning capital disbursements (after all, until 1995 the president of SAIC also served as the director of the Localization Office), SAIC had an independent capability to fund new projects. The mark up between the factory price of the Santana and the final sales price (see footnote 8) provided SAIC with a tremendous amount of capital that was then reinvested in the parts industry. Because this investment was in wholly owned enterprises, it was in many instances not considered to be a loan. When it was on a loan

[63] Interview, no. S14, May 20, 1997.
[64] Interview, no. S1, May 28, 1997.
[65] Interview, no. S2, May 30, 1997. "To give an example," the foreign manager continued, "we can't decide to raise our worker's salaries by 1 RMB without consulting SAIC. Their control is very tight."

basis, the terms were always more favorable than those offered by the Localization Office or the banks.

Even more important than financial assistance, however, was SAIC's comprehensive view – and control – of the automobile industry. Funding expansionary efforts was futile if there was no market for the products being manufactured, and the market information available to supply firms was often limited, particularly given the vagaries of a transitional economy. Because local protectionism was the norm in the Chinese automobile industry, the potential customers for any particular supply firm was extremely limited at this stage. The SAIC head office, however, knew exactly what SVW required and it transmitted this information to the supply firms. When the initial investment decisions were being made at a supply firm, the managers knew that they would have a market after the investments were made because SAIC had the ability to guarantee a market. Controlling the product mix of supply firms allowed SAIC not only to balance the growth of firms, but also insured that there was no repetition. Within SAIC there was no competition: each firm had a monopoly on the component that it manufactured.

In the event that a certain supply firm was struggling, SAIC had several recourses, depending on the nature of the problem. In situations where there seemed to be little demand for a particular product, SAIC assigned the supply firm with a new product to manufacture, one that had greater demand. In some cases, rather than switching products, SAIC combined a weaker factory with a stronger. Good management techniques, it was hoped, would be diffused across the combined operations, and economies of scale would be maximized. Although it is not clear whether the stronger firms actually had a positive influence on the weaker – it probably would have been more effective to allow the weak firms to fail – it is clear that SAIC was willing to inject the large amounts of capital in the newly combined operations that was necessary to make them successful. A clutch supplier, for example, was formed through the combination of three factories in 1991, 30 million RMB was invested in 1992, and this amount was increased by 10 million RMB in each of the following four years (with the exception of 1995).[66] In 1993, the enterprise began licensing and importing technology from a German supplier, and in 1995 a joint venture was formed. From 1992 to 1996, sales figures rose dramatically, and it emerged

---

[66] Interview, no. S14, May 20, 1997. The new firm was formed through the combination of an injection molding factory, a screw, bolt, and chain factory, and a clutch factory.

as the strongest clutch factory in China. It was the sole supplier for SVW, FAW-VW, and Beijing Jeep.[67]

Learning. The structure of SAIC also facilitated learning during the development process. The hierarchical structure of management insured that head office directives were heeded at the lower levels of the conglomerate. Managers at supply firms reported a steady stream of "new thinking" flowing down from SVW and the head office. Information on management and manufacturing techniques was transmitted through workshops (on techniques such as just-in-time delivery and quality assurance), by means of trips that were organized to take managers to get a first-hand view of foreign auto operations (Toyota and VW), and by annual sessions at the SAIC Automobile Industry Training Center. Employees at all levels made an annual trip to the training center, typically for two weeks.[68]

Technical advice was provided by a program developed by SAIC and VW that brought retired German engineers to Shanghai to serve as short-term consultants. When a supply firm was in the process of learning how to operate newly imported equipment, for instance, an engineer from the Senior Expert Service in Germany served as a consultant to the firm until the new technology was mastered.[69] Supply firm managers uniformly praised the results of this program: the costs to SAIC were not high (living expenses/small stipend for the engineer), and the impact on the supply firm was often tremendous.[70] New technology was of little use until the firm knew how to properly utilize it, and because it was often tacit knowledge that was critical, hands-on instruction was by far the most effective means of learning. SVW monitored the progress of each supply firm in an annual review. The operations of a supply firm were audited, and suggestions were made on how to improve its operations.[71]

Horizontal ties were as important to supply firm development as vertical, and the common ownership of firms within the SAIC group facilitated the sharing of information. Unlike in some vertically integrated companies in the West, manufacturing units did not compete against each other,

---

[67] Interview, no. S14, May 20, 1997.
[68] Interview, no. S28, June 22, 1998.
[69] As one manager pointed out, because the technologies being brought to China were still relatively dated, the retired engineers were a perfect match; their understanding of the technologies was superior even to younger engineers. Interview, no. S25, June 17, 1998.
[70] Interview, no. S12, May 26, 1997; Interview, no. S8, May 28, 1997.
[71] Interview, no. S14, May 20, 1997.

and consequently there was no incentive to hide information that might be beneficial to other firms within the group. The rotation of top management was one means of disseminating information throughout the group – effective managers were often transferred from successful firms to ones that were struggling – overlapping memberships on each firm's board of directors was another.

One foreign joint venture manager explained the method by which financial analysis techniques spread between firms. At his joint venture, he had been shocked to discover that the accounting department did not know how to conduct basic financial analysis, and there was no attempt to develop a basic business plan. The foreign managers began to teach their Chinese counterparts how to define the enterprise's core businesses (capable of sustaining the firm), identify strategic markets (where should investment be made, and how), and how to raise a return on an investment. In other words, the Chinese managers were being taught basic business techniques. The students quickly turned into teachers as the joint venture managers began to share their newfound knowledge through their role as board members at other firms within the SAIC group. The chief financial officer of the firm, for example, gave 10 to 15 seminars at other supply firms on how to raise a return on an investment.[72] This is exactly the sort of cross-fertilization that could be extremely helpful to firms during the initial stage of development.[73]

III. THE ORIGINS OF A LOCAL DEVELOPMENTAL STATE

Given the skill with which Shanghai coordinated auto sector development, it might seem as if municipal officials had a nuanced understanding of the industry and the obstacles to its development. This would be a mistake. When Shanghai municipal leaders set out to develop the auto industry in 1986, they pursued a development path that was shaped by

---

[72] Interview, no. S1, May 28, 1997.

[73] The Santana Localization Community (*Santana jiaoche guochanhua gongtongti*), which included all the members of the Shanghai automobile sector – assembly plant, supply firms, university research centers, and relevant government agencies – also fostered horizontal ties within the Shanghai auto sector. When Mayor Zhu Rongji created the Community in 1988 it consisted of 105 supply firms and 16 research centers; it currently has 150 supply firms. It functioned very much like the Japanese supplier associations upon which it was modeled. The meetings of the Community provided a forum within which members (in and outside of SAIC) could raise problems and discuss potential solutions. See Ye Ping, *Zai Santana gongtongti di jiu ci chuanti huiyi shang de jianghua* [Minutes of the Ninth Meeting of the Santana Localization Community], November 6, 1996.

the resources and constraints of the locality. There were no dramatic transformations; there were no grand blueprints that were imposed from the outside. The developmental approach that was chosen was very much a direct descendant of the municipal planning system of the command economy. Organizational and leadership skills that previously had been used to implement a state planning system that exploited Shanghai for the benefit of the nation, now directed developmental efforts for the benefit of the municipality. Understanding the role that the local government assumed with respect to the auto sector requires an understanding of the city's industrial history and its relationship to the central government. The former determined the capabilities of the local government and the needs of local firms, and the latter explained the range of opportunities that were available to the locality.

Shanghai Industrial History

Although the dominance of Shanghai industry has remained relatively constant in China for much of the last century, the means by which the local economy has been organized have undergone dramatic changes. The development pattern that emerged in the 1980s has historical roots that can be traced to elements from both before and after the 1949 victory of the Chinese Communist Party.

Pre-1949 Shanghai. Unlike cities such as Guangzhou and Wuhan, which were dominated by trading firms and light industry, Shanghai had a history of large industrial enterprises. The key legacy that Shanghai retained from pre-revolutionary China was the experience of running large industrial enterprises and a strong industrial base. Prior to 1937, large-scale modern industrial production in the city accounted for approximately half of the total for all of China. In 1932–1933 there were 2,435 modern factories in China, and 1,200 of these were in Shanghai.[74] The city had nine large-scale shipyards (which were able to compete with American, European, and Japanese yards) and was an international textile manufacturing center.[75] In many respects, even at this early date, Shanghai was developing skills

---

[74] The factories in Shanghai dominated the national production of textiles, machinery, vehicles (including boats), chemicals, metal working, etc. Murphey (1953: 166). Murphey is citing the figures of Liu Ta-chun, *The Growth and Industrialization of Shanghai* (1936), and explains that a "modern" factory is defined as one that employs 30 or more people and uses power-driven machinery.

[75] Murphey (1953: 175).

that would serve it well when it began focusing on auto sector develop in the 1980s.

In pre-revolutionary Shanghai, as in the 1980s, cooperation with foreign firms was the primary means of developing the skills to run new business organizations. Foreign investment in the late 1800s was used in the same manner that joint venture auto projects were used during the reform era: as a conduit for foreign technology and managerial skills. The comprador, a local manager who served as the middleman in a company's interactions with the Chinese, became the critical repository of modern business skills. Much like a Chinese manager in a contemporary joint venture, compradors in the late nineteenth century recruited and managed the Chinese staff of a foreign firm, served as treasurer of the firm, supplied market information, dealt with local banks, and generally assisted the foreign general manager in all dealings with the Chinese. The firms in which they worked had the most modern, equipment, technology, and ideas, and the compradors became skilled managers of modern businesses.[76] As these Chinese managers began to amass considerable fortunes of their own, they became key investors in supplying capital to new industrial projects. It was out of the comprador class, according to Parks Coble, that much of the community of modern Shanghai capitalists grew during the twentieth century.[77]

In stark contrast to later periods, Shanghai capitalists enjoyed a great deal of autonomy from the state in the 1920s and 1930s. The international settlements, in which all the banks and many enterprises were located, were beyond the reach of local authorities, and the central government during the 1920s was at its weakest. The Shanghai capitalists relied upon themselves, argues Coble, and formed "a variety of organizations designed to represent themselves politically, to provide self-regulation in the absence of government control, and to facilitate personal connections which were essential to Chinese business."[78] Business

---

[76] Hao (1970: 2–3 and 146). There were many Chinese officials and gentry members who were interested in economic development during this period, Yen-P'ing Hao argues, but they "proved incompetent when confronted with what were essentially management problems of an enterprise, such as making advance plans and calculations, determining the cost structure, pricing the product, and predicting the profitability of the enterprise." The compradors, by contrast, were "equipped with the knowledge of handling modern business." Hao (1970: 138 and 146).

[77] Coble (1980: 15).

[78] Coble (1980: 18–21). Attempts at self-regulation, for instance, occurred in the early 1930s when many Shanghai associations tried to limit production among member firms. Coble (1980: 151).

associations were formed along industry lines (bankers, cotton-mill owners, shipping-company owners, etc.) in guild-like organizations, as well as across industrial sectors.[79] Leaders of commerce in the city often served in multiple business associations and interlocking board of directors served to reinforce the cross-cutting ties across industries.[80] The cross-cutting associations such as the Shanghai General Chamber of Commerce and the Chinese Rate-payers Association of the International Settlement, in addition to providing an additional mechanism for greasing the wheels of commerce in the city, also gave the key economic actors in the city significant political clout.[81] The Shanghai capitalists directed the most advanced economy in China, and set the stage for the unique place Shanghai would occupy under the central planning system that would follow.

Post-1949 Shanghai. After the communist victory in 1949, the new leaders of China sought to harness the Shanghai industrial base for the benefit of the entire nation. Primarily because of the city's importance as an industrial base, but also no doubt because of the city's bourgeois pre-Liberation reputation, the new regime systematically subjected Shanghai business to political control. Although the city retained its prominence in the national economy, there was a price: in exchange for the protection from the central government, Shanghai industry lost its former autonomy. The central government allowed the jurisdiction of the city to expand almost tenfold in land, gave the city provincial status, and made sure that local industry enjoyed a favored position in the central planning system (a stable supply of low-priced raw materials and a guaranteed market share), but in return, Shanghai was closely supervised by Beijing and forced to contribute far more to the national treasury than any other region.

In terms of financial resources, the city became the cash cow for the entire country. Between 1949 and 1980, approximately one sixth of overall government revenue came from Shanghai, and the city was allowed to retain less than 13% of this amount.[82] Although some of the money remitted to the central government was eventually returned, the amount was small, and the city had little money to invest in infrastructure or

---

[79] Guilds were also commonly formed according to the native-place origins of the members. Perry (1993).

[80] Coble (1980: 25).

[81] In 1905, for instance, the Chamber of Commerce played an active role in the creation of an elected city council in the Chinese section of Shanghai, the first such body in China. Coble (1980: 21–22).

[82] Lin, "Shanghai's Big Turnaround since 1985," in Cheung, Chung, and Lin (1998: 51).

local industry. Not content with just money, the central government also siphoned off the human and physical resources of the city. Technical talent and machines were systematically moved out of Shanghai to the provinces. When the First Auto Works was created in Changchun in 1953, for instance, over 10,000 Shanghai engineers and workers traveled to Manchuria build it.[83] Shanghai may not have had auto sector experience, but its background in industry was far superior to any other region, and the central government intended to exploit these skills.

Over the course of three decades, the relationship between Shanghai and the central government, and in particular the key role that the municipality played in the central planning system, fundamentally changed the nature of Shanghai enterprises. The reach of state planning within China varied considerably, and as Lynn White has argued, in Shanghai the planning system was at its most extensive. Factory managers were hemmed in not only by more rules and regulations than existed in other regions, but more attentive supervising agencies (*zhuguan*).[84] In the case of most firms, according to White, a municipal agency (*ju*) or a state holding company (*gongsi*) would supervise – they were commonly referred to as "mother-in-laws" (*popo*) – a group of factories or stores that were spread out across the city. To a far greater extent than in other municipalities, these supervising agencies took the primary responsibility for arranging both upstream and downstream product flows for the factories.[85] Well into the reform period the economy continued to be dominated by SOEs: in 1987, state-owned firms accounted for 98% of Shanghai's industrial output. The development of private firms was constrained both by the high rates of taxation – private firms had to pay an 84% accumulation tax (*leijin shui*) – and excessive fees.[86]

Shanghai in the Reform Era. In the 1920s, the Shanghai economy had been dominated by networks of vibrant and autonomous capitalists; in

---

[83] In one year alone, 196 factories were moved out of Shanghai. White (1989: 23).

[84] This section draws heavily from White (1989: 23–24). See also Tian (1996: 46–47).

[85] As late as 1988, according to White, many SOEs in Shanghai still relied on the state plan to provide over 90% of their raw materials. As the comprehensiveness of the state plan weakened during the reform era this caused problems when there were shortages because the sources of the raw materials preferred to sell to those place where they could command higher prices. Shanghai often found itself without the necessary inputs. White (1989: 24 and 64–66); White (1998a: 170–174).

[86] According to the manager of a metal-punching factory quoted by White, his profits would increase by RMB 50,000–60,000 if he relocated a few kilometers to the west in Jiangsu Province where there was a combined tax burden of 25% on private enterprises (opposed to 84% in Shanghai municipality). White (1989: 25–26).

the 1980s, local enterprises were heavily dependent on the state. The relationship between the state and local firms was one of codependence: because the central government depended so heavily on Shanghai firms for revenue, firms were able to demand preferential treatment from the state, and the firms consequently became increasingly unable to fend for themselves. The tightly planned structure of the local economy invited complacency on the part of firm managers. First, it was easier to depend on government subsidies and bailouts than it was to improve the efficiency of firms. Firm managers had strong incentives to hide actual resources so as to increase their bargaining position with the state.[87] Second, as White argues, because state control over firm operations was so extensive, firm managers also had strong incentives to forswear responsibility for any problems with upstream suppliers or downstream markets – these became the responsibility of higher level officials who could withstand criticism when the system did not operate smoothly.[88] "Shanghai was the 'golden-milk cow' of the planned economy," wrote an editor of the *World Economic Herald*. "As long as the state fed and protected it, Shanghai continued to give the most milk. But in the process, the city learned to rely on the state and lost its ability to organize its own markets and sources of raw materials."[89]

The planning system, according to White, largely destroyed Shanghai's once-fabled entrepreneurialism.[90] Even when Shanghai managers did come up with innovative business techniques, it often could not act on them due to the restrictive nature of government control. It was left to other cities to experiment with new tax rates, stock systems, bankruptcy laws, and short-term money markets during the early reform period – industrial production in Shanghai could not be risked. The municipality began to gain a reputation as being a "house that follows the law." Even Mayor Zhu Rongji commented on how "very law abiding" the Shanghai people were. If a directive was not on an official document with red letterhead it was not a directive that could be followed.[91] Given the bottom-up

---

[87] See Kornai (1980, 1990).

[88] White (1989: 25); As of early 1988, 92% of Shanghai's state-owned firms still had "guaranteed management contracts" with their supervising corporations. The guarantees were threefold: remit a certain amount of profit, maintain technical quality, and (sometimes) guarantee certain amounts of foreign exchange from export sales. White (1998a: 278).

[89] Cited in White (1989: 23).

[90] White (1989: 25). Similarly, Gang Tian writes: "after being controlled by the central planning system, Shanghai lost its ability to explore its potential advantages and existing opportunities." Tian (1996: 82).

[91] White (1989: 29). Zhu's comment, cited by White, was made in September 1988. As White comments, it is not clear whether the comment is a compliment or a snicker.

nature of innovation during the reform period, Shanghai's adherence to regulations imposed from above often served as a disadvantage. In other localities, firm managers and local officials exploited the latitude they were granted to experiment; successful experimentation was usually followed with approvals from upper governmental levels (see the discussion of Guangzhou in the next chapter). Shanghai did not experiment, and the pace of change was consequently slower. People in the city believed that they should be protected by the state because such a large percentage of their revenue was swallowed up by the state, two reporters for a Beijing journal wrote critically. Shanghai enterprises became like flowers in a hothouse, they argued, unable to stand the winds of competition.[92]

Path-Dependent Development in the Auto Sector

In light of the manner in which Shanghai's relationship with the central government created a local economy that was subject to close government oversight, the path that auto sector development in Shanghai followed is not surprising. In the late 1980s, when the central government was giving more power to the localities, the Shanghai municipal government simply adapted planning functions that formerly had been controlled at the central level. Although Zhao Ziyang had weakened the power of the central government in the hope that the autonomy of individual enterprises would increase, in Shanghai, the municipal government began the process of tightening its control over local firms immediately after the power of CNAIC was weakened – when the central government gave it an opening, the municipal government seized it.[93] The central government was not explicitly favoring Shanghai over other localities; much to the contrary, in the late 1980s Shanghai was only just beginning to receive the preferential policies that Guangdong had been receiving since 1980.[94] In fact, the advantages that Shanghai had over other localities with respect to auto sector development were derived partially from the disadvantages of its relationship with the central government.

First, the municipal leadership, led by Mayor Jiang Zemin, was desperate to alleviate the pressure of the stagnant state sector by focusing on

---

[92] White (1989: 99).

[93] This is not to imply that CNAIC would inevitably have opposed the Shanghai strategy (according to several sources, Rao Bin was in full support of the Shanghai strategy, see Li 1998: 87–88), but because of the weakening of CNAIC this did not become an issue.

[94] Zhimin Lin, "Shanghai's Big Turnaround since 1985" in Cheung, Chung, and Lin (1998: 69–70).

the development of new, pillar industries. Because tight regulation in the city did not allow for experimentation in the manner that occurred in a city such as Guangzhou (see Chapter 5), the sectors that were chosen for development benefited from leadership attention that was both unified and focused. Shanghai, until the early 1990s, did not have the vast array of opportunities that were common in other coastal cities. Second, the same planning apparatus that was so detrimental to the entrepreneurial spirit of local firms, proved to be quite conducive to the development of manufacturing capability in the auto sector. The development of auto supply firms was not a process of innovation, but as Amsden emphasizes in her work on late development in Korea, a process of learning and imitation, and small supply firms benefited from the overlapping organizational ties that guided them through this process.[95] The city's aptitude for planning could be put to good use.

The influence of the state plan endures long after the era of the state plan has ended. As Dorothy Solinger writes, the existence of the state plan "is manifest in its old offices (even if they now hang out a new nameplate), in the habits it shaped, the patterns of association that it fostered, and the *guanxi* developed between those who have lived by those habits and patterns."[96] After the decision was made to promote the auto sector as a pillar industry in Shanghai, municipal leaders did what they were accustomed to and what they were best at: developed an institutional structure that would make it possible to carefully plan and monitor the development of the local auto sector. The Localization Office became the supervising agency, or "mother-in-law," directing and organizing the development of firms that were accustomed to being cultivated and nurtured like hot-house flowers. Rather than being subject immediately to the harshness of market forces, firms would have a transition period during which they would hopefully reacquire the skills that they had lost during the era of central planning.

An institutional structure that allowed leaders to closely monitor firm development would have been of little use if the leaders at the top of this structure did not have the ability to enact the appropriate policies. During the critical years of auto sector development in Shanghai, the municipality was led by men whose experience mirrored that of the city – all had extensive backgrounds in industry and industrial planning. Jiang Zemin, the Shanghai mayor from 1986–1988, graduated from the Department

---

[95] Amsden (1989).
[96] Solinger (1993: 197).

of Electric Motors of Jiaotong University in Shanghai, served in the Shanghai Ministry of Machine-Building Industry in the early 1950s, as a trainee at the Moscow Stalin Automobile Plant in 1955, and as director of the First Auto Works power plant from 1956–1962.[97] When he returned to Shanghai in the 1960s he once again was posted within the Ministry of Machine-Building Industry. Zhu Rongji, who followed Jiang as Shanghai mayor in 1988, graduated from the Department of Electric Motor Engineering Department of Qinghua University, and his first job was in the Production Planning Section of the Industrial Department of Northeast China. In the years that followed he had positions in industry, academics, on the State Economic Commission, and on the State Planning Commission. Huang Ju, the vice-mayor who was appointed the director the Leading Auto Small Group in 1986, was a graduate of the Department of Electric Motors of Qinghua University, and served as a technician and engineer at various Shanghai industrial factories during the 1960s and 1970s, and he became the secretary of the Shanghai Industrial Committee in 1983. He succeeded Zhu Rongji as mayor of Shanghai in 1991. Even at the top level of the municipal government, the leaders had backgrounds appropriate to industrial development.

Shanghai leaders increasingly used their expertise in industry and knowledge of the bureaucratic bodies governing Chinese industry to serve as advocates for local industry. The protection of the capital collected by means of the Shanghai component localization tax from 1988 to 1994 is a prime example. In 1990, the State Planning Commission (SPC) demanded that Shanghai turn half of the proceeds from the component tax over to Beijing in the interest of "balanced" growth. According to top officials in the industry, Mayor Zhu Rongji played the pivotal role in protecting the localization fund.[98] In effect, he told the SPC officials that their demands were foolish: the primary problem in the auto industry was that investment was too dispersed, and if the localization fund did not remain in Shanghai it, too, would fail to develop a strong supply base. Well-schooled in bureaucratic politics, Zhu began delaying tactics. When the director of the SPC arrived in Shanghai to enforce the central government edict, Zhu met with him, and managed to persuade him of the validity of Shanghai's position. Beijing colleagues, both at the SPC and MMI (which would most likely

---

[97] The biographical information in this paragraph is from *Who's Who in China: Current Leaders* (1994: 228, 260, and 943).

[98] This account is based on an interview with a top Shanghai automobile industry official, no. S12, May 26, 1997, and was confirmed in interviews with both other Shanghai officials and former officials of the Ministry of the Machinery Industry in Beijing.

control the disbursement of the central government's portion of the money) remained firm in their conviction that it was preposterous for Shanghai to retain so much investment capital, however, and a second group of cadres set off for Shanghai. At their first stop, SVW, managers explained that the joint venture played no role in the dispute; the money went to Shanghai supply firms, not SVW, and therefore it was the concern of municipal officials. Continuing on to the municipal government, the Beijing officials were told that the matter had already been settled by their respective bosses. Arguing and tough negotiations ensued, but Shanghai held its ground. In the end, Shanghai agreed to send along a nominal portion to the center, but the vast majority remained in Shanghai. As one participant in these negotiations commented admiringly, "Zhu knew how to deal with this sort of situation."[99]

As I have argued, the auto business group in Shanghai complemented the role of the municipal government. The structure of the group facilitated the monitoring of firm development and the dissemination of knowledge and technology from the joint venture projects within the group, and as in every other case in this study, the organizations that shaped auto sector development in Shanghai were a product of the industrial history of the region. Although compradors played a strikingly similar role at the turn of the century to joint venture projects in the 1980s – both were critical conduits for Western technology and managerial skills – it is impossible to draw direct linkages between such distant periods. By the time SAIC was established, business leaders from the pre-1949 era had long since passed from the scene, and three decades of communism had fundamentally altered local attitudes towards foreigners. What had not changed, however, was the experience of operating large-scale industrial enterprises. While working for foreign firms, compradors developed the skills to run large manufacturing operations in sectors such as textiles and ship-building, these skills were then transferred to the Shanghai capitalists of the 1920s and 1930s. After the communist revolution, the character of these large industrial firms was fundamentally changed, but their mere existence meant that Shanghai continued to be an important industrial base with large-scale enterprises. The increasingly intrusive role of the state dampened all incentives for firm managers to be efficient and productive, but it also reinforced their willingness to heed the directives of their organizational superiors. The comprehensive planning apparatus

---

[99] Interview, no. S12, May 26, 1997. The amount turned over to the central government was said to be several tens of million renminbi (*ji qian wan* RMB).

of the city created firms that were not entrepreneurial, but they were obedient. It was in this mold that SAIC was formed.

IV. CONCLUSION

Shanghai, like Beijing and Guangzhou, did not have extensive experience manufacturing cars, but unlike these other two cities it did know how to build an organizational structure that was conducive to developing the manufacturing capability of a supply network. In the next chapter, which analyzes the cases of Beijing and Guangzhou, it becomes clear that the proper method of building such a structure was not something that was readily apparent. In fact, after failing in its initial efforts to develop the local auto sector, the Guangzhou municipal government sent a study group to Shanghai to study the organizational structures of the Shanghai auto sector. Guangzhou had tried to construct similar organizations – a government auto office and a business group – but the historical legacy of the city led them to function in very different ways (see Chapter 5). Although different localities may have the same policy objective, it cannot be assumed that they have the same starting point: historical legacies perpetuate themselves both in the human capital of the locality and the organizational infrastructure. Differing industrial histories and differing relationships with the central government create varied patterns of regional development.

The pattern that emerged in Shanghai was that of a local developmental state. Although it is tempting to assume that a liberal market economy is the solution to all problems, and particularly those of a planned economy, this would ignore the subtleties of modern capitalism and the requirements of development. The initial stage of auto sector development was a process not of innovation, but of learning and utilizing the technologies and managerial techniques of more advanced countries, and economies of scale were critically important: the first firm to raise production volumes would be able to lower costs and capture market share. A unified municipal bureaucracy in Shanghai assisted in the process of licensing and importing technology, and made a coordinated localization drive possible. The hierarchical structure of the local business group served to extend the reach of the local government into every aspect of firm operations. Control within the group was tight, and firm managers had a great deal of assistance as they struggled to adapt to new technologies and manufacturing techniques. As I will argue in the next chapter, the Beijing and Guangzhou case studies did not do this effectively. When the primary interaction between an assembly plant and a supply firm was negotiations over price, the supply firms did not have the capacity to develop. Small firms did not have the investment capital necessary to upgrade their manufacturing capability; they did not have the knowledge necessary to modernize their manufacturing techniques. Firms do need the discipline of the market, but they also need nurturing, and Shanghai gave it to them.

FIVE

Beijing and Guangzhou

Laissez-Faire Local States

In many respects, the municipalities of Beijing and Guangzhou could not be more different. Beijing is a capital city, and with the exception of a few notable interludes, has been so since the thirteenth century. Although the occupants of Beijing's palaces and government offices periodically change, the city itself has remained the cultural and political epicenter of China. Guangzhou, located 1,887 kilometers to the south of the national capital, is distinctly on the periphery of the national scene. Rather than being a home to culture and politics it has thrived as a city of commerce and a window to the outside world. It has often enjoyed a great deal of independence from central power; at many points in Chinese history it has been utilized as a base for those who have challenged Beijing's rule. In Guangzhou, according to the often-quoted proverb, "the mountains are high and the emperor far away." A city of traitors and traders was the description of one manager.

Despite these differences, the patterns of development in the auto sectors of these two cities have been remarkably similar. Both cities chose to promote the sector as a pillar industry, and in the mid-1980s both created joint venture auto assembly projects with the hope of fostering the development of a network of local supply firms. When the negotiations creating Beijing Jeep, a joint venture linking the Beijing Auto Works (BAW) and American Motor Company (AMC), were completed in April 1983, it was the only automobile joint venture in China (one year before SVW) and the largest manufacturing joint venture. The joint venture was created with equity of US $51 million, with 69% contributed by BAW, a manufacturing division of the Beijing Automobile Industry Corporation (BAIC), and 31% by AMC.[1] The Guangzhou Peugeot Automobile Corporation (GPAC) was the third auto joint venture to be created in China – the deal was signed in March 1985, six months after the signing of the SVW deal. It was a US $58.5 million project of which Guangzhou Automobile Manufacturing held 46%, Peugeot held 22%, China International Trust & Investment Corporation held 28%, and the Banque Nationale de Paris held 4%.[2] The primary Chinese partner, and the parent company of Guangzhou Automobile Manufacturing, was the Guangzhou Junda Auto Enterprises Group.

Beijing and Guangzhou formed these joint ventures for the same reason as Shanghai – the lucrative auto sector was seen as a means of filling municipal coffers and saving languishing state-owned supply firms[3] – but neither municipality succeeded in building a supply base in the first stage of development. In this early period, any car that was produced could be sold, even one consisting of high-cost imported components, but when austerity measures led to a dramatic reduction in 1993, neither Beijing nor Guangzhou could compete with Shanghai. Shanghai was the first to build a local supply base; this lowered costs for SVW and enabled it to raise volumes (because it was not dependent on foreign exchange to buy imported parts).[4] Over the next two years, SVW increased volumes from 100,000 to 160,000, while GPAC sank from 20,817 to 8,052 and BJC continued to rely upon a Chinese-vehicle, the 2020 (see Figure 2.4).[5] Peugeot pulled out of Guangzhou in 1997 and was replaced by Honda and a new network

---

[1] Mann (1989: 83). Of the $35 million BAW contribution, $28.4 was the value of land, buildings, and equipment, the remainder was provided in Chinese currency. Of the AMC $16 million contribution half was in cash and half was in the form of technology. The stake of the foreign side has since increased to 50%.

[2] "Peugeot to Build Cars in China," *International Herald Tribune*, March 14, 1985.

[3] The similarity in motivations was clearly evident in the early plans of each municipality. BAIC, in the JV negotiations, refused to even consider the possibility of importing and assembling CKDs. "What do you take us for?" Beijing officials reportedly asked when the issue of CKDs arose in the negotiations. "You just want us to put things together? You don't want us to be able to manufacture? You really consider us to be a colony." Mann (1989: 157). According to the JV contract for Guangzhou Peugeot, a 98% domestic content rate would be reached within 5 years. Harwit (1995: 119).

[4] In 1991, when the domestic content for the SVW Santana was 70%, the domestic content for the BJC Cherokee was 45%, and the Peugeot 505 was 30%. These rates are *domestic* rather than local content.

[5] The 2020 is a Chinese jeep that was originally going to be phased out of production within 5 years in favor of the Jeep Cherokee. Because it was based on Chinese technology, it used all local suppliers, and thus had a far lower price. Long after it was to be phased out, BJC depended upon it for the bulk of its production volume.

of Japanese suppliers. Beijing Jeep continued to limp along, but eventually abandoned its local suppliers in favor of Shanghai suppliers, and as will be explained in Chapter 7, BAIC abandoned its hope of independent capabilities and turned to Hyundai to improve its fortunes. The contrast in outcomes with Shanghai could not have been more pronounced (see Tables 2.1, 2.2, and 2.3).[6]

There were important differences at the assembly plants that might have affected outcomes in these two cases. Product difference is one possibility, but as I explained in Chapter 2, this argument should not be pushed too far. Demand was high for all joint venture products until 1993, and this included Beijing Jeeps and Peugeot 504 and 505s. In the case of Guangzhou Peugeot, the smaller stake of the foreign partner (22%) is another important possibility. As Eric Harwit argues, this certainly affected its ability to control operations at the joint venture assembly plant.[7] While the influence of this structural difference on the development of a supply network cannot be discounted – particularly if it led to lower volumes (but again, demand was high at this point) – it does not negate the basis of a comparison. First, the foreign partners were not playing the lead role in the localization effort of any of the joint ventures. It would only be appropriate to exclude this case based on the smaller equity share if Peugeot had been pushing for an alternative localization strategy, but was hindered by its small equity share. This was not the case, and in fact, Peugeot-Citroen currently has a 50% share in DCAC, but is not pursuing a fundamentally different localization strategy.[8] Second, it is possible to separate the fate of the assembly plant and the supply sector to a certain extent by examining policy approaches. The Guangzhou Auto Office might have pursued the same policies as Shanghai, but failed due to differing levels of success at the assembly plant (stemming from Peugeot's lack of control), but this also is not the case: Guangzhou pursued a fundamentally different approach to localization from the beginning, long before weaknesses at the assembly plant began to emerge.

The difference in outcomes at the supply level points to the importance of internal incentives within seemingly similar political and economic institutions. Although on the surface it might have appeared that the institutional structures organizing firms in the two cities were the same

---

[6] Details on outcomes are given in Chapter 2. In Chapter 7, I explain the current strategy of each municipality.

[7] Harwit (1995).

[8] It is also worth noting that VW has a minority share in FAW-VW (40%), but is doing very well at the assembly plant.

as in Shanghai – a local auto office and business groups – they operated in a starkly different manner. The local governments did not channel investment capital into supply firms, and the business groups neither nurtured the development of firms nor promoted learning. The municipalities failed to meet the challenge of late development.

In centuries past, the primary development role of the state was to construct an institutional arrangement that created incentives for private actors to undertake the sort of activity that would lead to economic growth. According to North and Thomas, this was in large part a matter of property rights: actors make the investments necessary to promote innovation when they are assured that they will capture the consequent rewards.[9] The logic of this argument is often altered in cases of late development, however. First, there are those who argue that the existence of strong and established competitors in capital-intensive sectors necessitate government support. In the absence of such support, investment capital flows primarily to the sectors in which a comparative advantage already exists, as opposed to the sectors in which the government hopes to create one. Second, because late development in the initial stages is a process of learning rather than innovation, relationships between firms must be conducive to the transfer of intellectual capital as well as financial. Not all forms of economic institutions do so.

In the first section of this chapter, I focus on the structure of the business groups in each city, and their inability to foster investment in supply firms and collaborative relationships between firms. In contrast to Shanghai, many of the state-owned supply firms within these groups were not wholly owned by the group, and consequently the head office of the group had no assurances that it would be able to capture the rewards that would result from investment. Rather than receiving a fixed percent of the profits of supply firms within the group, in many instances the head office received only a nominal management fee, and there was consequently little incentive to invest in the development of firms. There was no attempt to forge, long-term collaborative relationships with supply firms in the style of a Japanese approach, and there was little interest in promoting learning and development; the assembly plants forced suppliers to compete against one another. Purely commercial relationships between firms severely limited the ability of supply firms to develop technical and manufacturing skills because the assembly plant would switch suppliers rather than help them overcome obstacles to development.

[9] North and Thomas (1973).

In the second section, I argue that the local governments in each of these localities were incapable of compensating for the weak business groups because they suffered from both fragmented bureaucratic institutions and fragmented incentives. Obstacles to development at the firm level might have been overcome by a coordinated localization drive led by the municipal governments of each locality – a strong state role. As in Shanghai, the local governments would seek to alter incentives by means of financial and policy support for the auto sector. The cases of Beijing and Guangzhou, however, provide clear evidence that altering incentives, far from being an alternative to the creation of efficient economic institutions, requires particularly strong institutions.[10] When it is the government that is attempting to promote growth, the incentives of bureaucratic institutions must be aligned to conform to developmental objectives. The government itself must become an efficient economic organization. Not only must the state be able to insure that investment capital reaches its intended target – protectionist policies and non-market conforming investment policies create abundant opportunities for rent seeking – it must also be able to insure that the capital is efficiently utilized. Shanghai could do the former, but not the latter. In Guangzhou and Beijing, fragmented institutions and fragmented incentives prevented the municipal governments from doing either. In the absence of government investment and policy support the development of supply firms made very little progress.

Why did Beijing and Guangzhou take an approach so different from Shanghai? In each section I trace the roots of the various policy approaches, and as in Shanghai, the approach of each city is closely linked to its history and relationship to the central government. In Guangzhou, the municipal government took advantage of its relative autonomy from the center to pursue a free-wheeling market-oriented approach to reform. Because the central government gave Guangzhou a great deal of autonomy in the early reform period there was very little central supervision. In Beijing, on the other hand, the municipal government was too tightly tied to the central government. It refused to enact policies that would blatantly favor Beijing firms over non-Beijing firms, and its status as a political and cultural center created divisions over how to promote local industry. Despite the same objective as Shanghai, the institutional contexts in

---

[10] This is also a primary conclusion of the World Bank's examination of sectoral industrial policies in East Asia. World Bank (1993).

Beijing and Guangzhou were not conducive to a unified focus on auto sector development.

I. MARKET-DRIVEN BUSINESS GROUPS: PRICE VERSUS DEVELOPMENT

At the very core of the problem was the relationship between the supply firm and the assembly plant. As in Shanghai, the supply firms in Beijing and Guangzhou were organized in business groups and it was these groups that structured the relationships between firms. In Shanghai, SAIC invested heavily in the development of supply firms, with investment defined in the broadest sense of the term. Simply sinking capital into a supply firm was no guarantee that it would successfully develop a strong manufacturing capability. In addition to financial capital, supply firms at this early stage of development also required investment in intellectual capital. They needed help in improving managerial and manufacturing techniques; help in learning how to use the new technologies that were being imported; help in creating horizontal linkages with other firms in the network. The business group in Shanghai did this very effectively.

In Beijing and Guangzhou the business groups invested very little. The problem was essentially one of property rights. All the firms were state-owned, but the head office of the business groups only invested in the development of supply firms that were fully owned by the group because it was from these firms that it collected profits. In Shanghai, the business group fully owned and controlled all the supply firms within the group (with the exception of joint ventures) and the group was fairly comprehensive in scope. In Beijing and Guangzhou auto firms were not concentrated in a single group, and even within a group, control was not centralized. Some firms within the business groups were wholly owned (*quanzi qiye*), with others it had administrative ties (*xingzheng guanxi*); the firms were originally either independent or under a different ministry, and had been transferred by the municipal government to the group for management.[11] Revenue from these managed firms (*daiguan qiye*) was not controlled by the head office of the group, but either by the supply firm itself or perhaps the ministry or bureau to which the firm originally

---

[11] Many of these *daiguan qiye* would appear in the category of joint venture firms: Junda would arrange to provide a portion of the equity from its HK investment wing in order to obtain preferential JV status.

belonged. From the perspective of the municipal government it made sense for the auto groups to manage auto-related firms that the municipal government controlled even if the group did not own them. The head office of the auto group, it was believed, would be able to manage these firms more effectively than city officials who knew nothing about the industry. Because complete ownership and control was not transferred, however, the internal structures of these groups – unlike Shanghai – were quite loose, and the head offices did not have the same incentives to invest in supplier development.

The contrasting internal organizations of the business groups in these cities were primarily a result of history and path dependence. Unlike Shanghai, which had very few auto firms prior to the creation of SVW, both Guangzhou and Beijing had large existing firms. When the joint venture auto projects were created, unifying control and coordination in the local auto sectors was difficult because these existing firms were already enmeshed in a web of governmental and inter-firm relationships. In Beijing, for instance, the Beijing Internal Combustion Engine Factory began manufacturing engines in the 1950s after importing technology from the Soviet Union. For decades the factory was under the direction of the Agriculture Ministry, and its product line was tied in with suppliers and end-users within this ministry. In the 1970s, it was transferred to the Ministry of Machinery Industry (MMI) and then in the 1980s to BAIC. Despite administrative changes, it remained largely independent because its product line involved it primarily with firms outside the BAIC group.[12] When Beijing Internal Combustion began profiting from high auto-industry demand in the late-1980s, it again became independent of BAIC – it didn't want profits and investment to be channeled through BAIC.[13]

The history of Guangzhou firms was similar. The Yangcheng Auto Company, for example, was created in 1958. It was under the control of the Transportation Bureau of the municipal government, and consequently had very little to do with the Junda Group, which was under the Ministry of Machinery and Electronics (MME). It was even difficult to communicate directly with Junda, one manager commented. When there was a particular problem at Yangcheng, information had to be first relayed to the Transportation Bureau, then to the Auto Office. The Auto Office

---

[12] Interview, no. B9, August 11, 1997; Interview, no. B22, August 7, 1997.
[13] Interview, no. B22, August 7, 1997. In the 1990s there was increasing pressure to unify the Beijing auto sector, but because Beijing Internal Combustion was doing very poorly at this point it was not clear BAIC wanted them back – their burden of debt and retirees was too large.

would the contact other auto firms, but at that point, the information would inevitably be distorted.[14] Auto firms in Guangzhou were spread across six different ministries and bureaus. When the GPAC joint venture was created in 1985, the fragmentation of the local auto sector became the subject of attention, and in 1986 a meeting of auto experts – all from a technical background – recommended that the primary auto firms in Guangzhou should be united under the control of one ministry rather than six. It was a good idea, an official in the municipal auto office later commented, but the heads of each respective ministry were concerned that their power would be diminished if they let large firms slip away.[15] Top leaders were not terribly concerned with the issue, and individual ministerial interests prevailed over municipal interests. Unifying control of a sector composed of firms with long and independent histories was not an easy task: the operations of an organization are shaped by its origins and the incremental changes that follow. Unlike in Shanghai, the Beijing and Guangzhou legacy created loose ownership ties between firms within the auto groups and a consequent disincentive to invest. The result was that most supply firms suffered from shortages of both financial and intellectual capital.

A. Financing Development

Any supply firm that hopes to import technology and increase its manufacturing capability must have investment capital. One possibility is internal funding. In Shanghai, in addition to the investment coming from the Localization Fund, SAIC reinvested its profit in the supply sector. It did this both directly and through the pricing policy of SVW – the prices the assembly plant paid to local supply firms for components were artificially inflated to give the supply firms a financial cushion. The auto groups in Guangzhou and Beijing did just the opposite. Rather than provide supply firms with a financial cushion during the lean years of early development, the assembly plants used multiple suppliers for each component as a means of using competitive pressure to force down the prices. Multiple suppliers were not used in the same manner as in a Japanese network– an element of competitive pressure within a stable relationship. Contracts were short, subject to frequent change, and awarded to the lowest bidder. The market governed relations between firms.

[14] Interview, no. G14, July 6, 1998.
[15] Interview, no. G21, July 20, 1998.

The plight of one joint venture supply project in Beijing typified the strategy.[16] The Beijing Jeep assembly plant awarded the supply firm a one-year "open" contract to supply 50% of the volume of a particular component; the remaining 50% was sourced from a Shanghai supplier. If either supplier increased its prices or began to have quality problems, it received less business. The competing Shanghai supply firm could handle this pressure because it was simultaneously providing 100% of SVW's volumes. It had high volumes and was doing very well. But the Beijing supplier, like most supply firms in Beijing, had a deadly combination of high costs (due to low volumes) and low sales prices. It lost money every year, and had very little ability to alter its fate. For political reasons it would be very difficult for BJC to completely abandon a local firm – the municipal government would not be pleased – but it did not go out of its way to help them either. According to a manager in the BJC supply division, multiple suppliers were used as a matter of policy.[17]

From a short-term financial perspective, utilizing a competitive pricing strategy made sense for both BAIC and the Junda group because not all firms within the groups were fully owned.[18] The fully-owned firms (*quanzi qiye*) were profit centers for the group – the head office decided how to divide their profits – but from the firms that it had management relations (*daiguan qiye*) it received only a nominal management fee.[19] The head office of the auto group was a manager acting on behalf of the municipal government – presumably because it had more experience managing auto firms than other municipal ministries. In that the head office of the group did not control the revenue from these firms, it had little incentive to allow them to accumulate profit (through the pricing policy) and little incentive to invest in supplier development. If the assembly plant found the technical capability of a local firm inadequate for a particular component it could always source outside of the municipality (i.e., Shanghai). Supply firms did not have this luxury: due to the local protectionism of other

---

[16] This account is based on Interviews B25, April 22, 1997 and B34, August 6, 1998.

[17] Interview, no. B40, August 17, 1998.

[18] In the example just described, BAIC owned 65% of the joint venture – a fairly high equity stake. In the JV contract, however, it was specified that any profits from the JV would go not to BAIC, but to a retiree fund: BAIC consequently received no benefit from increasing profits at the supply firm.

[19] Interview, no. G7, July 11, 1997. One firm that was managed by BAIC, for instance, reported giving an annual management fee of 3–4% of profits to the head office. Interview, no. B27, May 5, 1997.

localities they generally found it very difficult to find customers outside the home municipality.

The situation for the firms managed by the municipal auto groups was somewhat ironic in that enterprise reforms designed to increase their power and autonomy only weakened them. Until 1987, one manager of a Beijing supply firm explained, 90% of the enterprise's profits went to the Beijing city government. Sales were good during this period, but there was no new investment; planning still dominated and municipal bureaucrats saw no need to invest money when output was allocated according to the state plan rather than direct marketing.[20] In 1987, however, Zhao Ziyang began experimenting with methods of shifting the locus of power from party secretaries to factory managers, efforts that culminated in experiments with various contract responsibility systems and the promulgation of an "Enterprise Law."[21] The autonomy of factory managers increased, as did their ability to retain profits, but because investment had been neglected for so long they could not compete in the increasingly competitive marketplace. The firms had no profits, and because they were now autonomous, no help from the bureaucratic levels above. "When we were making money they took it all," a manager commented. "Now that we can keep more we have none, and we are too far behind to do anything about our situation."[22]

B. Nurturing Development

The consequences of having primarily commercial relationships between firms were not purely financial. They also inhibited the development of manufacturing and technical skills. The reason is not complicated: when price is the primary criteria for choosing a supplier, an assembler will switch suppliers rather than work with one that has manufacturing or technical problems. The supplier, aware of the precarious nature of the relationship it has with its primary (and perhaps only) customer, is similarly unwilling to make the investment necessary to upgrade its manufacturing capability. Supply firms in Beijing and Guangzhou clearly had very little security and very little outside assistance.

A supply firm operating in Guangzhou and Beijing had neither long- nor short-term security. In the long term, it was aware that the multiple

[20] Interview, no. B10, August 14, 1997.
[21] Fewsmith (1994: 209).
[22] Interview, no. B10, August 14, 1997.

supplier policy always posed a threat; in the short term, the increasing number of difficulties at the assembly plant led to decreasing volumes and extremely erratic ordering. Even within a specified contract period there were wild fluctuations in volume. In Beijing, for instance, Beijing Jeep sent each supplier a production plan in January of every year specifying the volumes that would be required each month.[23] The schedule was quickly abandoned, however. Most suppliers reported making weekly deliveries to the assembly plant, and it was not unusual to get mid-week updates from the assembly plant concerning the week's order. Rather than smooth out volumes so that supply firms could master production processes, the assembly plant did just the opposite. Supply firms were forced to maintain large inventories and it was very difficult to train a work force properly. Some weeks there was more work than could be handled, other weeks there was nothing to be done.

The supply firms also received little outside assistance, and it was not simply a matter of insufficient capital. The manager of a BAIC assembly firm (unrelated to BJC) likened the structure of the local auto sector to a family – the municipal government is the grandmother, the head office of the auto group is the mother, the individual firms are children. The parents, he argue, have a responsibility towards the children that goes beyond the financial: "it is important for a child to eat, but a parent must cultivate and teach as well."[24] When asked what sort of assistance would be helpful, he emphasized the need for technical support and coordination. Beijing firms preferred to cultivate relations with other local firms not only because it was cheaper and more convenient, especially given transportation difficulties within China, but quality was simply inferior. Supply firms did not have the internal resources to overcome problems, and because BAIC made no effort to pool knowledge within the head office, supply firms had nowhere to turn.

In Guangzhou the problem was much the same. Firms that wanted to link with GPAC, but could not meet the technical requirements received no assistance. "Of course we had problems," explained a manager whose request to supply GPAC in 1986 was turned down due to poor quality standards. "But they didn't tell us what was wrong, what their requirements

---

[23] It would be more accurate to call the annual plan a wish list. Because the auto group had no network of dealers it had no mechanism for accurately forecasting demand. Consequently, the annual plan was formulated in a manner not too different from a traditional state plan, and was than inevitably abandoned when it became apparent that demand would not be as high as initially hoped. Interview, no. B35, August 11, 1998.
[24] Interview, no. B27, May 5, 1997.

were, or how to go about making necessary improvements. They simply weren't willing to work with us. Finally we said forget it."[25] GPAC treated the firms that did become suppliers little better. If price or quality began to slip, one manager reported, GPAC would not help us find the source of the technical or production problem, they simply would find a supplier elsewhere.[26] Even when money was invested in a supply firm, according to a manager within the Junda head office, there was very little oversight to prevent it from being squandered.[27] In Shanghai, investment was followed by strict oversight to insure that development proceeded smoothly; in Guangzhou, investment was followed by complete neglect.[28]

C. Limited Developmental Capacity

The development problems that resulted from the loose, market-based relationships between firms within the Beijing and Guangzhou supply networks were hardly unique. In some respects, the United States auto industry was in a similar position two decades ago. Prior to the 1980s, auto assembly plants in the United States used a combination of in-house manufacturing and outside suppliers. When a component was sourced from an outside supplier, the assembly plant maintained short-term contracts (usually one year) with multiple suppliers – arm's-length relationships not too different from those that existed in Beijing and Guangzhou. In the stable market that existed prior to the entry of foreign competitors, the American assembly plants exploited their monopsony power over outside suppliers as a means of maximizing profits.[29] As in Beijing and Guangzhou, there was little reason to pay high prices to suppliers if it was not thought to be necessary.

In the case of the U.S. industry, Susan Helper argues, this strategy was not without its costs. In forming relationships with suppliers, "the buyer faces a trade-off between promoting technical progress in the industry and maintaining buyer bargaining power." Quality and innovative capacity suffered as a result of the arm's-length relationships

[25] Interview, no. G4, July 14, 1998.
[26] Interview, no. G16, July 8, 1998.
[27] Interview, no. G17, July 7, 1998.
[28] Guangzhou firms were further handicapped in that JV partners were often Hong Kong firms with no knowledge of the auto industry.
[29] From 1936–1961, the peacetime rates of return on equity for seven major U.S. assemblers averaged 23.8%. The corresponding figure for supply firms was only 8.2%. Helper (1991: 782 and 805).

with supplier. According to Helper, "intense competition led to supplier industries populated by tiny firms lacking in both organizational and physical capital,"[30] a description that could apply almost equally well to supply firms in Guangzhou and Beijing. When inexpensive, high-quality imports began to inundate the American market, however, U.S. auto manufacturers were forced to abandon arm's-length relationships with suppliers. Rather than increase the degree of vertical integration, assemblers began to sign long-term contracts (5 years not being unusual) with independent suppliers – a move towards the Japanese approach. Often wording about pricing was quite vague (something previously unheard of) and the assemblers inevitably lost a degree of leverage over pricing decisions.[31] The relationships became more collaborative, with strong supply firms increasingly shouldering the burden of design and development from the earliest stages of new projects. As a manufacturing executive at Ford explained, "the thing which is driving us to new relations with our suppliers is the desire for more coordination which will lead to more innovation.... "[32] The American assemblers were not about to beat Toyota at its own game – there were many elements of the Japanese model that were not adapted – but there was a distinct response.[33]

When faced with similar competitive challenges, the assemblers in Beijing and Guangzhou placed only more pressure on supply firms to lower the prices of components. Why did these firms not react in the same manner as U.S. firms? The most basic problem involved level of development; when forced, American firms transformed their relationships with suppliers because they could. U.S. assemblers chose to maximize their leverage over suppliers when market conditions allowed, but when the marketplace began to reward firms with innovative capacity, there were strong suppliers with whom the assemblers could forge highly collaborative relationships. Assembly plants began to drop those suppliers that did not have independent development capability in favor of those that did because with these it could share (or perhaps more accurately, it could transfer) the burden of development costs.

---

[30] Helper (1991: 808).
[31] Helper (1991: 813).
[32] Quoted in Helper (1991: 811).
[33] Susan Helper and Mari Sako (1995) use survey data to document the changing nature of American supplier relations in the 1990s. Customer commitment towards supply firms remained higher in Japan, but there was distinct movement away from short-term, arm's length relationships among American firms.

In Guangzhou and Beijing, however, this was not an option. As a Chrysler manager at Beijing Jeep commented, he would have much preferred to move towards long-term, collaborative relationships with a single supplier for each component – he characterized BJC's supplier relations as similar to supplier relations in the United States twenty-five years ago – but it was the Chinese side that was unwilling to make the shift away from multiple sourcing. The reason, he explained, was that under a multiple sourcing system BJC often used a local supplier and an outside supplier. The local supplier was used for political reasons. Although the structure of the local auto sector did not create incentives for broad investment in supplier development, it would have been politically difficult to completely ignore local firms. If BJC were to shift to using a single supplier for each component, however, it generally would be the local supplier that would have to be dropped. Beijing firms were simply not adequately developed, particularly in comparison to Shanghai firms.[34] From the perspective of the assembly plants in Beijing and Guangzhou it was the worst of all possible worlds: they had little incentive to invest fully in the development of local supply firms themselves, the municipal government would not let them completely abandon local firms, and yet the municipal government itself did very little to promote the development of the local auto sector.

II. MUNICIPAL GOVERNMENT: INVESTMENT FAILURE

In the mid-1980s, when BJC and GPAC were being established, the need for coordinated supplier development created an overall need for investment capital that strained the capacity of existing economic networks. Bank lending was controlled by the state, equity markets were not yet existent, and informal lending sources were insufficient for large-scale industrial projects. Successful development was contingent upon finding an adequate source of capital and creating an institutional structure that insured that the capital was invested where it would be effectively utilized. In Shanghai these functions were carried out by a municipal government that had been reorganized so as to create a unified decision-making body that was politically powerful and a business group that had complete ownership and control over the network of supply firms within the group. The government provided the funds, and then utilized the localization office and the auto business group to channel the capital to firms.

---

[34] Interview, no. B40, August 17, 1998.

Guangzhou and Beijing certainly seemed to understand the need for investment capital. After Shanghai placed a localization tax on the sales of Santanas, Beijing and Guangzhou quickly followed suit, and from 1989 to 1994 collected a fee of RMB 20,000 for every vehicle the joint venture assembly project sold.[35] The money was placed in a localization fund that was earmarked specifically for investment in the supply sector. It is true that SVW volumes were higher (and consequently it probably collected more money from the localization tax), but it should be remembered that all the joint ventures were doing well at this stage – the impact of austerity measure did not hit until 1993–1994. Between 1989 and 1994, for instance, GPAC produced 72,359 cars.[36] Assuming all of these cars were sold and the localization tax was levied on each one, the municipal government should have collected an investment fund of RMB 1,447,180,000 from the proceeds of the tax.[37] In Beijing production volumes were higher so the proceeds of the localization tax should also have been higher,[38] yet officials within the city auto industry report that there was only a very small amount of capital available for supporting localization.[39]

Although there is reason to believe that there should have been a considerable amount of investment capital in both Beijing and Guangzhou, in both cities the most consistently reported impediment to development among supply firms was lack of capital. "We are a big enterprise, yet we get absolutely no help from the Beijing Municipal government – they have invested nothing," complained the manager of one Beijing supply firm. Simply to keep the enterprise running, he continued, it was necessary to take annual bank loans of 10 million renminbi at interest rates of 12%. No preferential policies were given.[40] Other auto firms in Beijing uniformly reported that they had to rely on bank loans for capital, although in some instances the government would help them obtain loans at preferential rates. There was no evidence of effective utilization of the proceeds of

---

[35] Interview, no. G7, July 11, 1997.

[36] *Qiche Gongye Guihua Cankao Ziliao* (1997: 28).

[37] This figure is simply the localization tax multiplied by production volumes. Prior to the market downturn in 1993/4 it is plausible to assume that all cars produced were sold.

[38] It is again difficult to separate production of the Chinese jeeps and the Jeep Cherokee, but as I pointed out in Chapter 2, the demand for the Jeep Cherokee in the late 1980s was strong enough to support a black market. Mann (1989: 285).

[39] Interview, no. B3, August 6, 1997. According to one BAIC official, the localization fund in Beijing was actually created before Shanghai's. Interview, no. B37, August 14, 1998.

[40] Interview, no. B2, April 22, 1997.

a localization tax. According to a top American manager of BJC, the money was simply squandered.[41]

In Guangzhou auto firms there was a similar dearth of investment. During the eighth 5-year plan (1991–1995), when Shanghai investment in the auto sector exceeded 10 billion renminbi, Guangzhou investment did not even reach 3 billion renminbi.[42] The municipal government went through all the motions of putting together an investment campaign – collecting funds, creating an investment office (the Anxun Group), and even designating projects – but nothing happened. When the auto office decided in 1991–1992 to support 36 projects that would supply key components, only 15–20% were actually successfully developed.[43] One firm that went through all the proper procedures of applying for investment was promised 8 million renminbi in 1992 by the municipal auto office. The capital was to be used to increase production capabilities. Despite receiving the necessary approvals the money was never received and when the managers of the firm made inquiries at the office, they were simply told there no longer was any money.[44] What was happening to the investment capital in Guangzhou and Beijing? It was not being directed into the auto supply firms because of fragmented institutions and fragmented incentives.

A. Fragmented Institutions in Beijing and Guangzhou

The municipal bureaucracies overseeing the auto industry in Beijing and Guangzhou were organized in a fundamentally different way than in Shanghai, and this contrast led to very different approaches to investment. Both municipal governments created an automobile office to oversee development, but as in Shanghai prior to the institutional reorganization of 1987, fragmentation hindered the efforts of these offices.

The Guangzhou Municipal Auto Office was established in 1988 with the explicit objective of promoting the localization process at GPAC. Because the office was within the Ministry of Machinery and Electronics, however, it did not have the power necessary to influence the behavior of firms that were under the administrative auspices of other ministries,

---

[41] Interview, no. B24, May 5, 1997.
[42] Yan Yue, "Guangbiao" [Guangzhou Peugeot], *Shanghai Qiche Bao* [Shanghai Auto Industry News], May 31, 1998, p. 11.
[43] Interview, no. G6, May 21, 1997.
[44] Interview, no. G16, July 8, 1998.

Guangzhou Municipal Government and Auto Sector (prior to 1994)

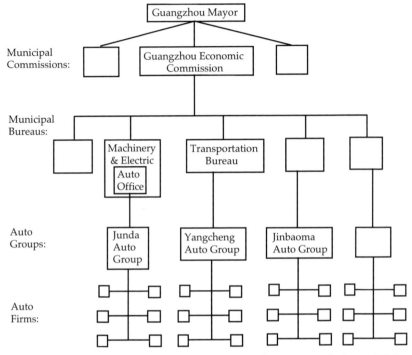

Figure 5.1: Guangzhou municipal government and auto sector (prior to 1994).

and Guangzhou auto firms were spread across ministries to an unusual extent (see Figure 5.1).[45] "We had no power to direct (*lingdao*) enterprises within other ministries," commented an official in the municipal auto office.[46] An important consequence of this lack of control was extremely dispersed investment. Rather than concentrate on key projects, each section of the government that had auto-related industries would support its own. Economies of scale were few and costs high. In Guangdong province as a whole, for instance, 4 different cities were supporting 10 different assembly operations. Total investment was almost twice as high as in Shanghai, but was dispersed across the ten assembly operations and 879 parts firms. Many of these assembly factories manufactured trucks (Yangcheng Auto Group) and buses (Jinbaoma Auto Group), but there

---

[45] On lack of government control see Yan Yue, "Guangbiao" [Guangzhou Peugeot], *Shanghai Qiche Bao* [Shanghai Auto Industry News], May 31, 1998, p. 11.
[46] Interview, no. G9, July 7, 1997.

were also competing sedan projects (Three Star Auto).[47] The production capacity (for vehicles of all types) for the entire province was one half of the capacity at Shanghai Volkswagen, but actual production volumes for the entire province were only a fraction of Shanghai's.[48]

With respect to the Guangzhou localization fund, the problem was not so much the dispersed nature of investment, but the destination of investment. The municipal auto office had the most direct linkage with the Junda Group, because both were under the control of the MME, and consequently the majority of investment flowed into Junda.[49] If SAIC had been the primary conduit for investment funds in Shanghai, the result quite likely would not have been too different from the Shanghai localization office investing directly in supply firms: SAIC was comprehensive in scope and it fully owned the firms under its control (with the exception of the joint ventures, of course). In Guangzhou, however, Junda was not only not as comprehensive in terms of the number of supply firms under its control, but it only fully owned some 17 of the approximately 50 firms that it managed, and again, it was reluctant to invest in firms that it managed, but did not own.[50]

The institutions governing the auto industry in Beijing were similarly fragmented. The auto office was not granted separate status within the municipal government, but was the head office of the Beijing Automobile Industry Corporation (BAIC). This office reported to the Beijing Economic Commission; as in Guangzhou, because the office was nested within a ministerial level organization it did not have sufficient power to coordinate relations between ministries (see Figure 5.2).[51] BAIC was formed in 1973 by pulling together firms from other ministries – primarily

---

[47] Three Star Auto was the competing Guangdong province auto firm. On this enterprise see Su Wu Ying "'San Xing' yu Shichang Jingji" ['Three Star' and the market economy], in Sun (1995). The province also made an aborted attempt at creating an auto JV called Panda Motors, see Harwit (1995).

[48] Total investment in Guangdong according to this authority was 18. 1 billion RMB, and total production capability 100,000 vehicles. Production volume for the province in 1995 was 20,000 vehicles, this number dropped to 13,000 in 1996. Zhang (1997b: 7). On blind investment in Guangdong see Hou Pei Hu, "Guangzhou qiche gongye" [Guangzhou auto industry], *Guangzhou Ribao* [Guangzhou Daily], February 15, 1995.

[49] The director of the Ministry of Machinery and Electronics served as the director of the auto office; one vice-director was from Junda and two were from the ministry. Interview, no. G21, July 20, 1998.

[50] Interview, no. G3, July 15, 1997.

[51] In Shanghai, by contrast, the Auto Industry Leading Small Group was above ministerial status, and hence had the ability to coordinate relations between ministries (see Chapter 4).

Beijing Municipal Government and Auto Sector, 1997

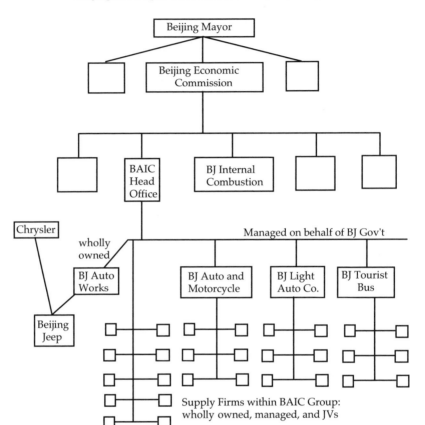

Figure 5.2: Beijing municipal government and auto sector, 1997.

the Ministry of Machinery and Electronics, the Agriculture Ministry, and the Beijing Automobile Company – and like Junda, the disparate origin of the various parts of the auto group created problems of control.[52] By the early 1990s, the group consisted of 31 enterprises and research institutes, but the head office functioned more as a manager than an owner. As I explained in the previous section, the manufacturing operations within the group operated as independent firms; they received little investment from above that they did not actively seek themselves.

[52] Interview, no. B37, August 14, 1998. The primary wholly-owned BAIC enterprise was BAW, the Chinese partner in Beijing Jeep, and even BAW was required during contract negotiations to consult with over 10 separate ministries on a regular basis. Mann (1989: 68).

The problem of institutional fragmentation has not gone unnoticed in these cities, particularly Guangzhou. In 1993, dismayed at the lack of development in the local auto sector, the Guangzhou municipal auto office sent a study group to Shanghai. The report that resulted from this trip (and that was submitted directly to the Guangzhou mayor) made the case for a unified approach to development. Due to the extensive linkages in the auto sector, the report argued, a municipal auto office must have the power to direct development across ministerial boundaries.[53] In 1994, the Guangzhou Auto Office was removed from the Ministry of Machinery and Electronics and placed directly under the mayor's office (as in Shanghai), and plans began to unite the various auto groups within the city.[54] In Beijing, officials also became aware of the problems resulting from institutional fragmentation, but the search for a remedy was eclipsed by an even more serious problem, one of incentives.

B. Fragmented Incentives in Guangzhou

In Shanghai a unified institutional structure was combined with a unified perspective; from the mayor down every official knew that the auto industry was to be given the highest priority. The municipality's traditional position at the core of the central planning system reinforced the focus with which it set out to develop the auto sector. Guangzhou shared Shanghai's desire to develop the auto industry (hence its designation as a pillar industry), but there were competing objectives. Quite simply, in Guangzhou there were too many alternative means of receiving a high return on an investment. Having alternatives is not unusual – Shanghai had them too – but when combined with severely fragmented bureaucratic institutions the result was that the Guangzhou municipal government was not able to direct investment into what it considered promising sectors. The alternatives of the Guangzhou government, and its approach to investment, cannot be understood without first examining the localities relationship with the central government.

---

[53] Guangzhou Municipal Auto Industry Office, "Tan Guangzhou shi ruhe fazhan jiaoche gongye" [Report on Guangzhou Municipality Auto Sector Development], Internal Report, July 21, 1993, p. 3.

[54] Interview, G9, July 7, 1997. Unfortunately, the impact of this change was small because it coincided with the onset of austerity measures and a dramatic decrease in demand. There continued to be calls in the Guangzhou press for further unification of the business groups. Hou Pei Hu, "Guangzhou qiche gongye" [Guangzhou auto industry], *Guangzhou Ribao* [Guangzhou Daily], February 15, 1995.

Relationship with Center. Guangzhou's location has always been ideal for trade, and it has been a regional trading center and port since the Han dynasty in the first century B.C.[55] A primary comparative advantage of the city has always been its location and its international ties. The extent to which these advantages have been exploited, however, has usually depended on the policies of the central government. Sometimes it has been able to ignore edicts from the central government. During the Maoist era, proximity to the capitalist world was a disadvantage – due to strategic concerns industrial projects were concentrated in the interior provinces[56] – but at the dawn of the reform era, this proximity proved to be extremely advantageous. The location and the extensive overseas contacts of Guangdong province were principal reasons it was chosen, along with Fujian province, to be a showcase of experimental policies at the start of the reform period. Foreign capital could be easily attracted and foreign ties exploited. Not of least importance, if things went wrong, the province's position on the periphery would prevent the problems from infecting the center.[57]

The central government struck a bargain with Guangdong: it would be granted the freedom to pursue experimental reform policies without interference, but in exchange it could not turn to the central government for resources. Policy support would open a window of opportunity; it was up to local leaders and enterprises to seize it. In 1979, the central government granted Guangdong the right to retain all revenue above 1.2 billion renminbi, an amount that was fixed for 5 years.[58] This fiscal contract regime (*caizheng dabaogang*) was far more favorable than the contracts that were signed with other provinces in that it was not the ratio of remittances that was fixed, but the actual amount.[59] During the period 1988 to 1991 this system was adjusted so as to increase the amount of remittances to the center, but the new terms continued to be very favorable and Guangdong leaders bargained hard to retain the *dabaogang* system. Following the establishment of the fiscal contract, a series of central documents outlined in greater detail the "special policies, flexible measures" that the province was to receive.[60] Guangdong was to enjoy substantial autonomy

---

[55] Yusuf and Wu (1997: 112).
[56] See Naughton (1988).
[57] Vogel (1989).
[58] The amount was actually reduced in 1980 to 1 billion RMB and again in 1985 to 778 million RMB. Li (1998: 97).
[59] Li (1998: 97).
[60] The three key documents are: Central Document No. 50 (1979), Central Document No. 41 (1980), and Central Document No. 27 (1981). See Hao and Lin (1994: 213–214).

and authority in making economic policy with respect to investment, foreign trade, personnel, the distribution of materials and resources, and the management of commercial activity.[61] Premier Zhao Ziyang, who had served in Guangdong for two decades, believed that Guangdong cadres would be receptive to the opportunities that these experimental policies gave them, and he would not be disappointed.

The dominant attitude among local officials was that "policy windows" provided by the central government had to be exploited fully. The slogan that Ren Zhongyi, the first party secretary in Guangdong, began using to promote reform in 1983 was: "to the outside, more open; to the inside, looser; to those below, more freedom."[62] Decentralization at the provincial level was extended to the subprovincial levels, and cadres were encouraged to take advantage of any potential policy window that allowed them to deepen the reform effort and promote economic production. Just as Guangdong entered into a fixed fiscal relationship with the center, Guangzhou remitted a fixed percentage of its revenue to Guangdong annually, and concomitant to this fiscal relationship was the understanding that the municipality would enjoy greater liberty to promote development as it saw fit.[63] Guangzhou was designated provincial-level economic status (*jihua danlie shi*) in 1984, and the policy environment was designed explicitly to promote official entrepreneurial activity. Changes in the investment policy were central to this effort.[64] Officials were given the responsibility and incentives to mobilize resources in the manner that they thought was most likely to stimulate economic growth, and oversight was loosened. Central government monitoring of investment made at the provincial and municipal level became increasingly tenuous.[65]

In 1987, when the localization drive was making little progress in Shanghai, leaders of the central government's State Economic Commission held a series of meetings in the city to establish what was going

[61] Vogel (1989: 85–86); Hao and Lin (1994: 213).

[62] "*Duiwai, gengjia kaifang; duinei, gengjia fangkuan; duixia, gengjia fangquan.*" Peter T. Y. Cheung, "Guangdong's Advantage: Provincial Leadership and Strategy toward Resource Allocation since 1979," in Cheung, Chung, and Lin (1998: 103).

[63] The amount of remittances changed frequently during the 1980s, but was always high. Guangzhou has always been the cash cow for the province, and provincial authorities had no intention of allowing the municipality to relinquish this role. For details see Cheung, "Guangdong's Advantage," in Cheung, Chung, and Lin (1998: 119).

[64] As one scholar comments, Guangdong could not immediately remove the straitjacket of central planning, but by decentralizing authority to as great a degree as possible – especially with regard to investment decisions – it could stimulate local development within the constraints of the existing policy framework. Cheung, "Guangdong's Advantage," in Cheung, Chung, and Lin (1998: 128).

[65] Cheung, "Guangdong's Advantage," in Cheung, Chung, and Lin (1998: 128).

wrong. Key organizational changes followed. In Guangzhou, despite a similar lack of localization progress, no such meeting was held. While it is possible to point to this incident as a clear indication that the central government was not interested – and unsupportive – of the Guangzhou auto sector, this is more likely a perfect illustration of the contrasting relationship each city had with the central government. At the same time that Shanghai leaders were conferring with the central government, Guangzhou and Guangdong leaders were doing everything in their power to insure that the central government did not revoke the fiscal contracting arrangement that was the basis for their autonomy. In October 1987, local leaders submitted reports to the central government lobbying for still greater autonomy – they hardly wanted to strengthen the hand of Beijing conservatives by calling attentions to problems that were emerging in the local economy.[66]

Considering the history of the relationship between the locality and the center, it is not at all unusual that the State Economic Commission was keeping closer tabs on Shanghai than Guangzhou. As a Guangzhou municipal official explained, the perception of the central government is that Guangzhou has its own money, and it does what it will with it. It needs less attention.[67] This loose, increasingly autonomous relationship between Guangzhou, Guangdong, and the central government did not directly determine auto industry policies in Guangzhou, but the relationship established a context in which certain local policies became both possible and attractive. These policies ultimately led to failed auto sector development.

Alternatives to Auto Sector Investment. Given the autonomy and the history of the municipality it is perhaps not surprising to find that the investment capital in the Guangzhou auto localization fund did not always find its way to automotive supply firms. In the early 1990s, auto-manufacturing firms in Guangzhou seemed unlikely to bring a high return on an investment. The development of a manufacturing base is slow, arduous, and expensive. In Guangzhou there did not seem to be the patience for this time-consuming process – in large part because there was not the need. There were easier methods of earning a quick return on an investment, and officials were instructed to listen to the market, to take advantage of every opportunity. In 1992, even the mayor of Guangzhou, Li Ziliu, was arguing that "speculation" (*touji*) and "profiteering" (*daoba*) were

---

[66] On these lobbying efforts, see Li (1998: 158).
[67] Interview, no. G21, July 20, 1998.

necessary because they were in line with the law of prices. They should be considered legitimate, he was quoted as saying, so long as they were within legal boundaries.[68]

Real Estate. The approach of Guangzhou officials in the late 1980s and early 1990s – the critical time period for the localization drive at GPAC – was to invest where the profits were highest, and investment in real estate or trading companies was far more profitable than investment in manufacturing operations. It is difficult to provide direct evidence that the automobile localization fund was used for purposes other than auto sector development, but the circumstantial evidence is plentiful. Managers in supply firms, the GPAC localization office, and even in the municipal auto office agree that capital collected from the localization fund was invested in real estate projects. According to these managers, the municipal auto office believed that astute investment of this capital outside of the auto sector would over the long run, increase the overall pool of money available for investment in the automotive sector.[69] An official in the auto office confirmed that a certain percentage of capital was invested in the real estate market, some of which went into the development of an Auto Building (*Qiche Daxia*) in downtown Guangzhou, a project that was never completed.[70] Even when capital was invested in auto manufacturing firms, one manager commented, the managers of these firms would take the opportunity to invest in real estate.

The timing of this interest in the local real estate market coincides with the creation of a real estate "bubble" in Guangzhou. Between 1991 and 1995, a period when investment in industry in Guangdong province increased by 27.3% per annum, investment in real estate increased by 76.7%.[71] Real estate prices in Guangzhou increased 30% to US$99 per square foot in 1992. "Many investors were small to medium-sized manufacturers with no experience in property," wrote one reporter. "But they were entranced by one of China's hottest investments."[72] Massive

---

[68] *Nanfang Ribao* [Southern Daily], March 25, 1992, p. 1. Cited in Peter T. Y. Cheung "The Case of Guangdong in Central-Provincial Relations," in Hao and Lin (1994: 225).

[69] Interview, no. G3, July 15, 1997; no. G20, July 2, 1998; no. G16, July 8, 1998.

[70] Interview, no. G21, July 20, 1998.

[71] Cheung, "Guangdong's Advantage," in Cheung, Chung, and Lin (1998: 133). In East Asia, a clear sign of a real estate "bubble" on the verge of bursting seems to be plans to build the tallest building in the world. Guangzhou devised plans for twin 140-story office towers in 1993. They have not been built. "South China plans world's tallest buildings," *The Straits Times*, February 24, 1993, p. 35.

[72] Jeremy Grant, "China Property Market Bursts for Small Firms," *The Reuter European Business Report*, April 30, 1993. Property scams were common. Hong Kong investors were cheated of an estimated HK $5.6 billion in aborted property projects in southern

investment led to oversupply, and beginning in 1993–1994 the soaring prices came crashing down. Investors were left holding unfinished projects – such as the Guangzhou Auto Building – or ones with dramatically decreased value. The auto supply firm that had been promised 8 million renminbi from the localization office in 1992, at the peak of the real estate market, received nothing. The auto office officials simply said there was no money. What was left unsaid, the supply firm manager ruefully commented, was that the real estate market had crashed.[73]

The "Gray" Market. Certainly not all of the money that Guangzhou municipality could potentially have invested in the auto sector was siphoned off into real estate projects. The money that did go into the auto sector prior to 1994, according to an official in the municipal auto office, went primarily to the Junda Auto Group because it was under the control of the same ministry as the municipal auto office.[74] Investment in Junda, however, was not necessarily the same as investment in auto manufacturing. The composition of the Junda Group mirrored that of Guangzhou as a whole – it had manufacturing firms, real estate operations, trading companies, and extensive linkages with Hong Kong – and as in Guangzhou, manufacturing was sometimes neglected. Within Junda the trading companies received a disproportionate amount of attention because many of them were the wholly owned firms from which the Junda head office received 100% of the profits. As one former manager at GPAC commented, "Guangzhou is a trading city and Junda is the same."[75] They were able to import auto parts through Hong Kong at favorable prices, and then resell at a profit.

The Hong Kong connection had a critical influence on developments in the Guangzhou auto sector and the Junda Group. Hong Kong was a key transit point for autos and auto parts into Guangdong. According to some estimates, 80% of all auto parts imported into China in the early 1990s were coming from Hong Kong via Guangdong.[76] Urged on from above to

Guangdong. Linda Yeung, "Ripped off and no place to go," *South China Morning Post*, July 19, 1998, p. 1.

[73] Interview, no. G16, July 8, 1998. Property speculation continued even after the crash. "Like Bangkok, property speculation is dominating business in Guangzhou," one diplomat commented in 1997. "Neither the government in Beijing nor the one in Guangzhou is setting development priorities." Peter Seidlitz and David Murphy, "Guangdong misses its second wave," *South China Morning Post*, May 11, 1997, p. 4.

[74] Interview, no. G21, July 20, 1998. The auto office was under the control of the Ministry of Machinery and Electronics until 1994.

[75] Interview, no. G11b, July 18, 1998.

[76] "The Autoparts Industry in the People's Republic of China" (1996: 75), see fn. 87.

seize every opportunity to promote development, it is hardly surprising that local officials began capitalizing on a key comparative advantage of the region: the porous border with Hong Kong. For small localities on the border smuggling provided the start-up capital for further development. The rationale of local officials is always the same, comments one Chinese author. "In order for the locality to become rich," they say, "the first step is to smuggle. The second step is to produce counterfeit goods of inferior quality. When the economy is going strong, it is then possible to create a spiritual civilization."[77] In effect, it was the natural extension of the "loosening" Ren Zhongyi had been encouraging since the early 1980s and the "profiteering" Mayor Li Ziliu spoke of in the early 1990s – except legal boundaries inevitably began to blur.

The procedure was quite simple.[78] A foreign manufacturer (or its agent/distributor) would establish a relationship with a Hong Kong company that had custom-clearance capability (usually one that had direct connections with a Guangdong counterpart). From the perspective of a foreign manufacturer, minimizing official import duty rates was the only way to compete with low-cost Chinese manufacturers. At the border, a Chinese enterprise – either a private township-village enterprise or a state-owned firm – with excellent personal relationships with the customs officials would serve as the customs clearing agent. Official duties could be decreased by: (1) negotiating a standard rate for a container (regardless of content); (2) paying full duty rates on a portion of a shipment while the rest remains "unnoticed"; (3) basing the tariff on the lowest duty items in the shipment; (4) or using invoices from the Hong Kong company that state a lower-than-actual value of the good being imported.[79] In most cases the duties and taxes can be reduced by 50%, a considerable savings considering that average duties are between 15 and 80% of the value of the shipment (after 1994 an additional 17% VAT tax was added). The shipment than proceeds on to a distributor. At each step of the process, the "handler" takes a percentage based on the total value of the shipment.

---

[77] Li (1997: 160). "Spiritual civilization" (*jingshen wenming*) can have many meanings in Chinese political discourse, but in this context the author seems to mean a law-abiding society.

[78] When I speak of "gray" market auto parts operations in Guangzhou I do so at a high level of generality. I have no direct evidence that the Junda Group – or any other specific auto firm – was involved in such operations.

[79] The last method is considered to be the most reliable. The source of this information is a report written in 1996 by a Chinese consulting company on behalf of a foreign auto parts manufacturer. The author of the report, "The Autoparts Industry in the People's Republic of China," must remain anonymous.

Local distributors in Guangzhou, who receive a mark up on the domestic sale of a shipment, typically achieve gross margins of 120–150% as compared to 10–15% in other major Chinese cities.[80] I am not arguing that GPAC, or even Junda, was directly involved in smuggling operations. It is unlikely that Peugeot CKDs were being smuggled across the border. There clearly was an indirect impact, however. Given the amount of money that was to be made in the importation of auto parts through "gray" market channels there was considerably less incentive to exert the effort necessary to create and nurture a manufacturing operation. Existing auto manufacturers in Guangzhou – even those that did not participate in gray market activity – were handicapped in that they were in effect, operating without the benefit of the tariff walls that protected the rest of the country. GPAC clearly suffered from the resulting international competition. Rampant automobile smuggling during this period (it would be the target of a major central government campaign in the late 1990s) meant that GPAC, in stark contrast to Shanghai, could not even count on a captive local market. Who would buy an expensive, poor-quality Peugeot when cheaper foreign cars were arriving from Hong Kong by boat every night?[81] Similarly, no matter how Junda itself dealt with customs issues, there were clear incentives for other Guangdong firms to focus on trading operations as opposed to manufacturing.

Diversification. The evolution of the Junda business structure gives some indication of the extent to which its operations were intertwined with Hong Kong. In 1993, through a complicated business restructuring, Junda decided to create a publicly traded Hong Kong company, Denway Investment.[82] Junda would hold a 54% share in Denway, and Denway would hold the 46% share in GPAC that was formerly held by Junda. This

---

[80] "The Autoparts Industry in the People's Republic of China," (1996: 87).

[81] In the fall of 1992 alone, 140 smuggling boats were captured off the coast of Guangdong. Among these were ex-service gunboats, torpedo gunboats, escort vessels, and submarine chasers – and these were only the ones that were captured. See David S. G. Goodman and Feng Chongyi, "Guangdong," in Goodman and Segal (1994: 194). General Motors claimed in 1996 that the number of GM cars brought into China by smugglers was twice the number of legal imports. Tom Korski, "GM 'grey market' drives smugglers," *South China Morning Post*, September 25, 1996.

[82] Essentially, Junda utilized Yue Xiu enterprises, the Hong Kong trade and investment arm of the Guangzhou municipal government (and a major player in the Hong Kong property market), as a means of incorporating Denway as a Hong Kong company. After the public offering Junda held 54.26% of the Denway shares, Yue Xiu held 17.74%, Peregrine Investments held 3%, and 25% were publicly owned. Kennis Chu, "Denway's Drive Pays Off," *South China Morning Post*, February 28, 1993, p. 2.

was a time-honored tactic in south China. Channeling money through a "foreign" company was highly advantageous because foreign investment was to a large extent exempt from central government oversight. Yu Fei, a Guangdong vice-governor, was explicit in exhorting his colleagues at a provincial planning and economic meeting to take advantage of this loophole: "We must make every use of the favorable conditions provided by the 'exemptional policy'.... We should try to convert some domestic investment projects and find a foreign linkage for them so they enjoy the 'exemptional' policies."[83] The strategy was particularly advantageous when the central government was attempting to utilize austerity measures as a means of limiting investment, as it began to do in July 1993, six months after the creation of Denway.[84] But according to Xie Gancheng, an executive director at Denway, the intent was simply to utilize foreign capital to expand production capability and manufacturing quality at GPAC. "We would like to produce Mercedes-standard cars," he told the Hong Kong press.[85]

Initially, the plan was a huge success. Investors in Hong Kong were either impressed with the idea of making Mercedes-standard cars in Guangzhou, or knew nothing about the company. Or perhaps both. The public offering of Denway, one of the very first mainland companies to be listed on the Hong Kong stock exchange, was oversubscribed to such an extent – 657 times – that it caused a temporary liquidity crisis in Hong Kong. Applications for shares took HK $240 billion (US $30.7 billion) out of circulation for a week.[86] "Say – this beats the heck out of making cars" read one headline, commenting on the fact that Denway stood to gain more from one week of bank interest (the time period before failed applications were returned) than its entire profits from 1992.[87] Unfortunately, it quickly became apparent to all that the company was not much good at making cars. The company reported a 95% decline in profits in 1994, and an assembly line that was capable of churning out 150,000 cars

---

[83] Cited in Li (1998: 197).

[84] When the central government introduced austerity measures in July 1993, the mayor of Guangzhou, Li Ziliu, said that his government would simply expand the use of foreign capital in its effort to promote continued growth. Li (1998: 197).

[85] Chu, "Denway's Drive Pays Off," p. 2.

[86] "Hong Kong Stock Issue 657 Times Oversubscribed," *The Reuter Library Report*, February 14, 1993. This amount was the equivalent of approximately one third of Hong Kong's GDP.

[87] Beth Selby, "Say – this beats the heck out of making cars," *Institutional Investor*, March 1993, p. 14.

produced only 5,726.[88] With shares trading at half of their issue price, Denway was called "the most spectacular example of investor disillusionment with Chinese stocks. . . . "[89]

Although GPAC remained the core business of Denway, spokespersons began to stress that diversification would allow it to prosper despite declining auto sales. Property sales and storage facilities were said to have contributed to 1994 profits, and a chain of highway service stations were planned for the future.[90] Managers of Junda supply firms claimed that top officials in the Group were far more interested in running the stock company in Hong Kong than in solving the problems of the manufacturing base in Guangzhou. As of 1997, a business description of Denway Limited reported that automobile manufacturing and assembly accounted for 28% of revenue; manufacturing and trading of audio equipment, 18%; trading of motor vehicles, 54%.[91] In Guangzhou, trading was clearly more lucrative than manufacturing.

C. Fragmented Incentives in Beijing

The Beijing municipal government's relationship with the central government was also a key determinant of the city's ability to concentrate investment and resources in the local auto industry; in this case close central ties inhibited auto investment. In order for investment to be focused on a particular economic sector, the municipal government has to be capable both of favoring local interests over national interests while at the same time retaining enough control and discipline to ensure that investment capital flows to its intended target. Beijing could do neither. The municipal government adapted a national rather than local perspective on developmental issues and it perceived itself as a "political and cultural center" rather than a manufacturing base.

Central Ties. "In Beijing," explained one manager, "the supposed goal is to support the nation, not Beijing."[92] The municipal government adapted

---

[88] Simon Fluendy, *South China Morning Post*, May 13, 1995, p. 2; Stephen Vines, "Speculators in China lick their wounds," *The Independent* (London), January 23, 1995, p. 25.

[89] Vines, "Speculators in China lick their wounds," p. 25.

[90] Renee Lai, "Denway bets on diversification," *South China Morning Post*, December 23, 1994, p. 1.

[91] Wright Investors' Service, "Company Summary: Denway Investment Limited," January 17, 1999.

[92] Interview, no. B3, August 6, 1997.

a laissez-faire approach to local auto sector development. "Rather than fight to retain funds as they did in Shanghai," the manager continued, "the officials in Beijing tell the central government to take all of their capital. They wouldn't want to have to deal with the trouble of investing it.[93] This national perspective of the municipal government in Beijing is evident in a wide range of policies affecting the local auto sector. Far from protecting local firms from outside competition – as almost every city in China attempts to do – Beijing actually implemented policies that discriminated against Beijing Jeep. At the beginning of 1996, for instance, the Beijing Public Security Bureau began restricting Jeeps, light buses, and sedans with engines smaller than 1 liter to alternate-day driving rules. In the month following the enforcement of this rule – which did not affect the Santana – sales at Beijing Jeep were down 73% from the same period the previous year.[94] An American manager at BJC asked a municipal official why the Beijing government didn't protect the local auto sector. "[Local] protectionism is something [the central government] is trying to discourage," the city official replied. "Remember, I am the capital. I would love to help you, but the central government won't allow it. I must behave as the capital, not a province."[95] In an article on economic development in Beijing, Yi Xiqun, the assistant to the Beijing mayor writes if not the same words, the same sentiment: "Beijing is China's capital, it is the political and cultural center for the entire nation, and it is this which is its most important function."[96]

Beijing officials take a national perspective because it is in their interest to do so. To a certain extent, organizational and personnel overlaps with the central government limit the Beijing municipal government's potential for autonomous action. Beijing is a provincial-level municipality that is directly subordinate to the central government. The central government controls the appointment of top municipal officials and municipal ministries report directly to counterparts in the national hierarchy.[97] In these two respects Beijing is no different, of course, than the other

[93] Interview, no. B3, August 6, 1997.
[94] Joseph Kahn, "Cross Purposes," *Asian Wall Street Journal*, June 17, 1996; Chang Weimin, "Beijing restriction hurts auto sales," *China Daily*, April 13, 1996. Interestingly, and perhaps an indication of a lesson learned, the municipal government went to great lengths eight years later to insure that local taxi companies purchased Beijing Hyundai automobiles.
[95] Interview, no. B18, August 20, 1997.
[96] Yi (1996: 117).
[97] Hook (1997: 34).

provincial-level cities (Shanghai, Tianjin, and after 1997, Chongqing), or even cities with provincial-level economic status (Guangzhou). Being the seat of the national government, however, means that the municipal government is subject to an unusual degree of central government oversight. As one scholar comments, "the local government [in Beijing] is virtually overwhelmed by the national one, and the two are sometimes hard to distinguish."[98] Career paths of Beijing municipal officials contribute to the blurred lines between local and central hierarchies in Beijing: local officials (and not just top officials as in Shanghai) are frequently promoted to the central government. Not only does this mean that officials are less likely to openly disobey central government directives, but even more importantly, it draws the most talented officials out of the municipal government. Wu Yi, for instance, was very effective as the Beijing vice-mayor charged with overseeing the auto industry, but was quickly promoted to the central government.[99] For talented officials in Beijing, the municipal government is a stepping stone.[100]

Alternatives to the Auto Sector. An additional problem, from the perspective of the Beijing auto industry, derives from the contradictory impulses that result from being a municipality that is also a capital city. The municipal government must promote local development, but seeks to do so without denigrating its position as a political and cultural center. Beijing belongs to the whole country, writes Yi Xiqun, and in the pursuit of economic development it cannot divorce itself from this role.[101] The challenge, he continues, is to exploit the natural advantages and strengthen those industries that do not run counter to its role as the capital city. Automobile manufacturing is not generally viewed as such an industry.

In 1956, when the first "Urban Development Plan" for Beijing was drawn up, the intention was also to emphasize Beijing's role as the political and cultural center of China, but when the rapid industrialization efforts of the Great Leap Forward began two years later these plans

---

[98] Hook (1998: 35). "The central government considers Beijing's money to be its own," one former central government official explained in an interview. Interview, no. B39, June 8, 1998.

[99] Wu Yi was a vice-mayor of Beijing from 1988–1991, and then moved to the central level as vice-minister of Foreign Economic Relations and Trade (MOFERT) in 1991.

[100] Officials who remain in the municipal auto bureaucracy tend to be old-style bureaucrats with little ambition. Managers throughout the Beijing auto sector universally complain about the quality of the city officials.

[101] Yi (1996: 117–118).

were revised in favor of turning Beijing into a "comprehensive industrial base." Municipal officials had lobbied for this shift. "We feel that to be the capital of a great socialist country, Beijing ought to be not merely the political, cultural and scientific center, but should also be made into a fairly modern industrial city," argued the second secretary of Beijing, Liu Ren, at the 8th CCP Congress in 1956.[102] Investment began to be directed toward heavy industry at the expense of urban services and infrastructure. Between 1957 and 1978, investment in heavy industry in the municipality increased by 474% with a particular emphasis on iron and steel, petrochemicals, chemicals, transportation, and machine building.[103] The local auto industry benefited greatly from this emphasis, and until the late 1980s the Beijing automobile sector was considered to be one of the strongest in the country. As late as 1992, the production output value of the local auto industry (8 billion RMB) was the largest of any sector in the city.[104]

There was a cost to promoting heavy industry in Beijing, however. An initial problem was that large industrial complexes occupied prime real estate in the city center. Beijing Jeep, for instance, continued to occupy a huge tract of land on the east side of the city; Beijing Light Automobile had a large complex on the west side. Beginning in 1992, the municipal government began a massive program of industrial relocation so as to make room for service industries in the city center.[105] Depending on the direction of the wind, however, moving heavy industry to the suburbs did little to solve the related problem of air pollution. Beijing, although perhaps the cultural center of China, was a grimy, industrial city – one of the world's most polluted.[106]

Increasingly, Beijing officials began to shift back toward the 1956 conception of municipal development, one that emphasized the city's natural advantages. As in Guangzhou, there were attractive alternatives to manufacturing. Tourism, for instance, became an increasingly lucrative business – what one vice-mayor called "a new powerhouse of our economy" – and one that complemented the role as capital city.[107]

---

[102] Cited in MacFarquhar (1974: 132).
[103] Hook (1998: 137 and 108).
[104] Lao Chang, "Life in the Fast Lane," *China Daily*, January 17, 1993.
[105] Hook (1998: 154).
[106] According to some reports, Beijing was the world's second most polluted city at this point. Hook (1998: 79).
[107] China Daily, August 27, 1998.

In 1986 just under one million foreign tourists visited Beijing; in 1997 2.3 million visited and spent US $2.25 billion in foreign exchange.[108] When combined with 82.2 million domestic visitors, total earnings from the sector were estimated at more than 50 billion RMB (US $6 billion), a figure that represented 12% of the city's total general output.[109] Similarly, service industries, high-tech, and other knowledge-based industries that capitalized on the city's strong educational infrastructure, began to receive the highest priority in municipal development plans.[110] Economic growth was obtainable without the pernicious side effects of heavy industry, and did not necessarily have to come at the expense of the city's position as national political and cultural center.

This is not to say that Beijing succeeded in pursuing a new and enlightened development strategy. There was much hand wringing about pollution and traffic problems in the late 1990s, but very little was done; the policy for dealing with the problems that result from growing auto ownership was notable primarily for its absence.[111] Similarly, the attitude towards auto manufacturing began to shift when the municipal government decided to build a new "auto city" in the suburb of Shunyi.[112] The primary point of consistency is that the Beijing municipal government has been inconsistent in its support for auto sector development.

---

[108] *Beijing Social and Economic Statistical Yearbook 1987* (1987: 556) and *Beijing Social and Economic Statistical Yearbook 1998* (1998: 308).

[109] The figure, 82.7 million domestic visitors, is from *Beijing Social and Economic Statistical Yearbook 1998* (1998: 308). The estimated total earnings from tourism is from "Capital city seeks brighter future for its tourist industry," *China Daily*, August 27, 1998.

[110] Yi (1996: 119). In 1998, Beijing Mayor Jia Qinglin argued in a work report delivered to the municipal people's congress that the city's economic advantages lay in high-tech and related industries such as electronic information, biological engineering, medicine, optical machinery and new materials. By the year 2000, he estimated, 60% of the city's GDP would be from service industries. "Beijing mayor offers economic blueprint," Xinhua News Agency, January 14, 1998.

[111] Unlike Shanghai, which has carefully regulated the number of auto licenses that are issued in the city, Beijing has made little effort to control the growth of private ownership. In 1995, the Minister of Construction in Beijing urged full support for public transportation as an alternative to private car ownership and publicly questioned the wisdom of encouraging private auto ownership, but little was done. New roads were constructed at a furious pace, and they were quickly clogged with more cars. "Traffic problems make private car ownership heated topic," Xinhua News Agency, October 21, 1995.

[112] Beijing Hyundai operates in the new location in Shunyi and a new factory for Beijing Jeep is scheduled to be completed in Shunyi in 2010. "Beijing to construct large-scale motor town," *Asiainfo Daily China News*, June 11, 2002.

D. Limited Developmental Capacity

The laissez-faire approach of the municipal governments in Beijing and Guangzhou cannot be categorically labeled as misguided. For certain industrial sectors, and at certain stages of development, it might have been very effective. The development of the auto sector, however, required a more coherent approach during the very early stages of growth. I have emphasized the manner in which fragmented institutions and incentives prevented the municipal governments in these cities from funneling investment capital into the supply firms. As in the case of the business groups, however, fragmentation also precluded the municipal governments from nurturing supplier development. In Shanghai, the Localization Office of the municipal government complemented the coordinating and nurturing role of the SAIC head office. Supply firms that had manufacturing problems or bureaucratic problems (e.g., obtaining building permits, import licenses, etc.) knew that the Localization Office would either have an answer or know where to find one. In Beijing and Guangzhou, supply firms not only lacked investment capital, but they had nowhere to turn when they encountered problems. The municipal auto offices did very little to compensate for the weaknesses of the business groups. Because the offices did not have separate status within the municipal government they were generally staffed with bureaucrats from the governing ministry rather than auto experts and their political power was slight. Managers of supply firms were very much on their own.

III. CONCLUSION

It is quite reasonable to argue that in Beijing and Guangzhou the failure to develop the local auto sector should be viewed as a success. Capital was not invested in the auto industry in these localities because it was flowing into sectors that were perceived to yield higher returns. In other words, the market did exactly what it is supposed to do. This may very well be true, but it does not lessen the developmental implications of the two cases. Not only did each of these municipalities originally have objectives quite similar to those of Shanghai, it is not clear that their objectives have changed. Undaunted by initial failure, the Guangzhou municipal government sold Peugeot's stake in GPAC to Honda, and in 1998 restarted the whole process of creating a supply network to support a joint venture assembly project; Beijing has done the same with its new joint venture with Hyundai. As I'll explain in Chapter 7, these new projects are more successful, but largely because they are able to completely bypass local auto firms.

Perhaps the most important lesson to be drawn from the cases of Beijing and Guangzhou is a cautionary one: promoting the development of an industrial sector is not simply a matter of choosing the appropriate policies. The range of policies that can be successfully implemented is created by institutional structures, and given the different institutional structures of Beijing and Guangzhou, it was difficult to implement Shanghai-style policies. In the initial stage of development, the structures that organized relations between firms within the sector had to create incentives for investment of both financial and intellectual capital in supplier development. While it was quite easy for a local government to adapt the policies that were deemed necessary – whether it was forming an Auto Office, levying a localization tax, or reshaping business groups – it was clearly difficult to alter the institutional structures upon which implementation depended. Superficial institutional changes more often than not masked fundamental continuity. Policies are changed at the will of the policymakers, but institutions are a product of a locality's history and politics.

This argument forces a degree of modesty on policymakers. It is extremely difficult for a government to pick and choose developmental "models" without carefully considering the capabilities of their institutional infrastructure. In China, this means that the role of the central government again becomes pivotal. Although the institutions of the municipal government played the critical role in auto sector development, it was relations with the central government which to a large degree created the institutional framework within which local institutions evolved. In Shanghai close fiscal ties with the central government led to a tightly controlled planning system which was duplicated at each level, including the auto business groups; in Guangzhou loose fiscal ties with the center and a great deal of investment freedom similarly influenced the institutional structure of the municipality.

The importance of path dependence does not exclude the possibility of change, but such change does require high-level, focused attention. The Shanghai municipal government initially had problems with fragmentation, but was restructured following a series of meetings directed by the State Economic Commission in June 1987. The close supervision of the central government and leading municipal leaders served to overpower any local bureaucratic factionalism that might have existed. In

Guangzhou, by contrast, a similar restructuring was recommended by auto industry experts in 1986, but the advice was ignored. A decade later, however, the changes began to be implemented. The localization efforts of GPAC were acknowledged as a failure, and this failure focused the attention of the municipality and made it possible to overcome bureaucratic opposition to change.

SIX

Changchun and Wuhan

Firm-dominated Localities

The auto joint ventures in Changchun and Wuhan, although more recently created, are also more heavily burdened by history. Changchun has long served as a key industrial base and transportation hub for northeast China. It was the capital city of the Japanese-controlled Manchukuo from 1931 to 1945, and like the rest of Manchuria, it emerged from the Japanese occupation with a relatively well-developed industrial base. The young Communist regime sought to capitalize upon these advantages when it decided to locate the First Auto Works (FAW) in the city in the early 1950s. The "auto city," constructed with the help of Soviet advisors, was the pride of socialist China, producing sturdy blue trucks for the workers and Red Flag limousines for the leaders. By the 1990s, however, the city was at the center of China's rust belt, and the impact of the reform movement was relatively slight. While the municipal auto offices in Guangzhou were moved in the 1990s to a gleaming new skyscraper in the city's rapidly growing business district, the municipal auto offices of Changchun continued to be located in a stolid old building at no. 57 Stalin Street.

Wuhan, located at the intersection of the Yangtze River and the trunk line of the Beijing-Guangzhou railroad, has long served as a transportation link and commercial entrepot for inland China. The bustling port played a key role in foreign trade as early as the mid-19th century, and in the early 20th century the city was second only to Shanghai in domestic trade volume.[1] Ironically, Hubei province, of which Wuhan is the capital,

---

[1] In the 1930s, Wuhan was second in domestic trade volume, fifth in foreign trade volume, and third in overall trade volume. Solinger (1996: 12).

became a center of the Chinese auto industry in the 1960s because of its inaccessibility. Mao, concerned that Chinese industry might be vulnerable to invading armies, sought to re-locate industrial production to the remote interior, and the small town of Shiyan was viewed as ideal. It was surrounded by the forest of Shennongjia (populated by wild men according to local legend) and at the base of Wudang Mountain. "It was considered that not even a guided missile could hit it."[2] In what was quite literally a process of industrial grafting, engineers, equipment, and workers were transferred from Changchun to the mountains of Hubei to create the Second Auto Works (SAW), commonly know as Dongfeng (East Wind). As in Changchun, the auto industry of the region was dominated by the mammoth operations of the centrally-sponsored project. Dongfeng had the benefit of being two decades younger than its counterpart in Manchuria – its product was newer and its methods more innovative – but it was nevertheless built in the image of its predecessor. Both were SOEs on a heroic scale.

The municipalities of Changchun and Wuhan also sought to use joint venture assembly plants to increase the manufacturing capability of domestic firms, but the situation was somewhat different than in other cities. FAW and Dongfeng, the Chinese partners at the joint venture assembly plants, were controlled by the central government rather than the local, and thus it was more difficult for the municipal government to direct them to use municipal supply firms.[3] This created a problem for the local governments because, as in other localities, they had a strong interest in promoting the development of local auto firms. In Changchun, the local economy was completely dominated by the auto industry, with both FAW firms and municipal firms. According to vice-mayor An Li, approximately 52% of the city's industrial output was contributed by the auto industry and future viability of the sector depended on rapid localization.[4] "We are planning to build up a complete car-parts and

[2] Zou Jielan, "China's Detroit' Finds Success," *China Daily*, September 21, 1989, p. 6.
[3] Being "controlled" by the central government simply means they were within the central government's bureaucratic apparatus rather than municipal government's; it is not a commentary on how tightly this control was exercised.
[4] As with the earlier JVs, tariff rates on imported components were to be determined by the domestic content percentage of the vehicle being produced, and the scheduled rate of increases was faster than the previous JVs faced. DCAC, for instance, had a preferential tariff rate of 33% on imported parts for the first three years of production. This rate was set to increase in the fourth year to 37% if a 40% domestic content rate was reached, but if this rate was not reached the import tariff would increase to 50%. In each following year, if the domestic content increased to 60% and then 80%, the tariff rates would drop

component production line for automobiles and establish Changchun as China's major car-parts and finished-car trading center," she explained. "It will be a handicapped industry if we rely on imported parts to assemble cars."[5] Fixed-asset investment in the city between 1996 and 2001 was intended to be RMB 100 billion (approx. US $12.2 billion) and at least half of this would be in the car industry.[6] Wuhan had a more diversified industrial base than Changchun, but it similarly intended to place the new auto joint venture at the center of its industrial development plans. The municipal government began developing the Wuhan Economic and Technological Development Zone for both the assembly joint venture and the parts firms that the city hoped would be developed to support it.

The partnership between FAW and VW was finalized in 1991. From the perspective of FAW, the new joint venture was a clear indication of its interest in moving into the rapidly growing sedan market, and as the largest and oldest auto company in China it was sure to receive strong support from the central government. From the perspective of VW, the new joint venture was an opportunity to tighten their control over the Chinese auto market.[7] Total investment at this stage was RMB 8.9 billion (US $1.1 billion) with FAW holding a 60% share and VW, 40%.[8] The creation of the Wuhan joint venture was similar. The parent company of Citroen, Peugeot Citroen, had an existing joint venture in China (Guangzhou), but was enticed into a second venture by the attraction of working with one of the two largest Chinese automobile companies, also one that would be assured of strong central government support.[9] The talks between Citroen and Dongfeng began in the late 1980s, a Basic Contract was signed in Paris on December 19, 1990, and the final contract on the RMB 4.5 billion (approx. US $550 million) deal was signed on April 8, 1992.[10] The new joint venture was called the Dongfeng-Citroen

to 30% and then 20%. If the required domestic content percentages were not achieved, the import tariff would increase to 50%. Interview, no. W13, May 15, 1997.

[5] Cheung Lai-Kuen, "Changchun car sector focus of expansion plan," *South China Morning Post*, April 18, 1996.

[6] Cheung, "Changchun car sector focus of expansion plan."

[7] "If we didn't invest in FAW, our competitors would have." Martin Posth, VW's president for Asia-Pacific operations later explained. "Part blessed, part stricken," *Business China*, November 11, 1996, p. 2.

[8] "Part blessed, part stricken," *Business China*, November 11, 1996, p. 2.

[9] The central government, in choosing the locations of the JV auto projects, was clearly trying to achieve geographic diversity, and the Wuhan project was the designated auto JV for central and western China.

[10] Citroen continued with the negotiations in the wake of June 4, 1989. In doing so it drew charges that it was violating a European Community ban on investment in China. See Jacques Neher, "Citroen Says France Considers China Project Aid," *International Herald*

Automobile Company (DCAC).[11] Although initially the French stake in the joint venture was smaller than the Chinese share – Dongfeng held 70%, Citroen 25%, and two French banks the remainder – as the joint venture expanded, the French share increased, and by 2002 the two were equal partners.[12]

Neither municipality was as successful as Shanghai in creating a network of local supply firms to support the joint venture assembly project during the 1990s. Although domestic content rates increased rapidly for both joint ventures, as in Beijing and Guangzhou, this was not a result of a strong *local* supply base.[13] The Changchun base is considerably stronger than Wuhan, however. DCAC had difficulty increasing production volumes in the early years, and was quickly forced to rely on the Shanghai supply base. Of the 153 suppliers that DCAC had as of May 1997, only 22 were in Wuhan as compared to 40 in Shanghai.[14] By 2003, as I explain in Chapter 7, over 50% of DCAC components were purchased from Shanghai, and in some cases, Shanghai suppliers were being asked to establish operations in Wuhan.[15] Changchun had similar difficulties in the early years. Although the FAW-VW contract explicitly stated that 28% of the Jetta's components (by value) had to be supplied by FAW firms, in 1997, six years after production began, FAW firms were only supplying 15%.[16]

Tribune, December 21, 1989. The final signing of the contract, however, was delayed by the French sale of Mirage fighter planes to Taiwan.

[11] Dongfeng Company is 100% controlled by the Second Auto Works and is the brand name of the SAW truck. The company chose Aeolus (the Greek god of winds) as its foreign trade name, and the JV was initially known formally as Aeolus-Citroen Automobile Company, but I will use the more common Dongfeng Citroen Automobile Company (DCAC).

[12] At the time of the 2002 capital injection, the name of the joint venture was changed from Dongfeng Citroen Automobile Company (DCAC) to Dongfeng Peugeot Citroen Automobiles (DPCA). For reasons of consistency, I will refer to the joint venture by its original name throughout this chapter. "PSA Peugeot Citroen, China's Dongfeng sign cooperation deal," Agence France Presse, October 25, 2002.

[13] In fact, at this stage even domestic content was unlikely to be true domestic content. According to government regulations any component purchased by the assembly plant in *renminbi* was considered to be domestic content even if the supply firm had imported 100% of this component, hence the most common strategy for artificially inflating domestic content figures (so as to meet local content regulations) was to have the supply firm do the importing rather than the assembly plant. This strategy did not work forever – representatives of the Customs Bureau eventually began imposing the same domestic content standards on suppliers – but it bought the assembly plant some time.

[14] Interview, no. W21, May 13, 1997. The number of suppliers in Wuhan does not fully reflect the number of SAW suppliers that were being utilized in that many of them would be located in Shiyan.

[15] Interview no. W28, January 13, 2003.

[16] An additional 19% was being produced within the FAW-VW factory. Interview, no. C17, July 25, 1997. The majority of the FAW auto supply factories were in Changchun.

Of the joint venture supply firms it purchased from in 1997, 28 were in Shanghai as opposed to only 17 in the home province of Jilin.[17] By 2003, the joint venture assembly plant was doing very well – production volumes rose rapidly at the end of the 1990s – and this helped suppliers considerably, but it still sourced only 20% of its components locally (see Table 2.1), about the same amount that came from Shanghai (Table 2.2). Almost as many suppliers by number were in the greater Shanghai area (44 in Shanghai, 23 in Zhejiang, 28 in Jiangsu) as in the home province of Jilin (104).[18]

While it might be argued that FAW and Dongfeng were content to rely on the stronger Shanghai supply base, and consequently were not as focused on building their own suppliers, this would ignore the strong financial incentives they had to use their own firms, the convenience of a local supply base, and the strong antipathy to giving business to their competitors in Shanghai.

The primary reason local development in Changchun and Wuhan was weak during this early stage was a fragmented bureaucratic structure. Because both FAW and Dongfeng were supervised by the central rather than the local government, the municipal governments in these two cities had limited means of influence over the joint ventures. Unlike in Shanghai, the municipal auto offices in Changchun and Wuhan could neither decrease the risk of local supply firms by guaranteeing them a customer, nor improve their financial situation through the assembly plant pricing policy. Furthermore, because the central government was late in extending preferential policies to these cities, they both had very limited means to independently provide the investment capital that local firm development required. Government inability to direct sectoral development in Guangzhou was the result of the high degree to which the market coordinated economic activity and the independence of economic actors. In Changchun and Wuhan the same outcome was caused by the limited maneuvering ability of local actors and the prevalence of heavily burdened SOEs. Guangzhou was too far from the days of state planning; Changchun and Wuhan were not far enough.

---

[17] Interview, no. C17, July 25, 1997. VW, of course, was not opposed to sourcing parts from Shanghai firms – many were JVs that they had helped establish – but FAW was adamantly opposed. VW managers in Changchun and Shanghai had to be very careful about having contact, for their Chinese partners both viewed the other as being a prime competitor. A VW representative office in Beijing was established to avoid this problem; contact would be through the Beijing office rather than direct.

[18] Interview no. C14, January 17, 2003.

To a certain extent, central control also exacerbated problems within the two business groups. All of the primary Chinese auto firms suffered from the pathologies associated with state ownership; the non-financial interests of the state and weak governance mechanisms made it difficult to monitor managers and discipline inefficient firms. The extent of these problems, however, varied. The identity of the owner (the level of government) and the scale and organizational characteristics of its jurisdiction and industrial base affect the ability of an SOE to overcome the problems associated with state-ownership (i.e., dual dependency and information problems).[19] Andrew Walder uses this argument to explain variations in the performance of small firms owned by county, township, and village governments in China and the large firms owned by higher level government jurisdictions. "[T]he intensity with which financial incentives and budget constraints are felt by these corporations varies systematically with their size and internal diversification, as do the government's non-financial interests in industry, the political constraints that prevent the closure of firms, and the government's ability to monitor enterprise performance and enforce financial discipline."[20] Firms owned by the lower levels of the government hierarchy are monitored more closely, less affected by non-financial objectives, and generally more efficient.

The same logic applies to large business groups: a municipally-controlled business group is more disciplined than a centrally-controlled group. The municipality of Shanghai did have non-financial interests that skewed the incentives of the "owners" of SAIC, but because the internal governance structure of the corporate group provided a mechanism for exercising effective control over the supply firms and nurturing their development, these did not become a major problem until after it had succeeded in creating a manufacturing base (as I will argue in Chapter 8, developing a competitive industrial base requires far more sophisticated monitoring capability than simply developing a manufacturing capability). In contrast to Shanghai, the internal monitoring systems of FAW and Dongfeng were rudimentary, they were controlled by a higher level government jurisdiction (central rather than local), and they were composed of older firms (with consequently larger social burdens) – they were Chinese firms at their largest scale. This complicated the localization process in several respects.

---

[19] Walder (1995: 5).
[20] Walder (1995: 8).

The scale of the two firms and their long histories greatly increased the difficulty of creating successful joint venture supply projects. Foreign linkages, as elsewhere in China, were a key means of increasing technical capability, but the benefits of these linkages were often diluted by the non-financial concerns of the Chinese partner. Foreign supply firms, rather than being allowed to choose the most appropriate Chinese partner, were often forced into partnerships with Chinese firms with large social burdens and inappropriate manufacturing backgrounds. Both FAW and Dongfeng were predominantly truck manufacturers, and while they thought they understood the auto business, few truck manufacturing skills were transferable to the making of a modern sedan, and the internal structures of the groups were not conducive to monitoring and nurturing firm development. Perhaps most importantly, expansion and development of the groups were driven by administrative edicts emanating from the central government. Although mergers with smaller auto firms served to consolidate the industrial structure of the Chinese auto industry – and consequently pleased the central government – when the motivation was other than economic, the mergers often served to dilute rather than strengthen the group.

The first section of this chapter explores the implications of central, rather than local control; the second section analyzes the weaknesses in the governance structures of centrally-controlled business groups.

I. IRRELEVANT MUNICIPAL GOVERNMENTS, CENTRALLY-CONTROLLED FIRMS

In comparing auto sector development in Beijing and Guangzhou to Shanghai, one of the key distinctions was between the bureaucratic structures that governed auto sector development. While a unified bureaucratic structure concentrated resources in a single business group in Shanghai, in Beijing and Guangzhou a fragmented local bureaucratic structure led to dispersed investment. Local ministries in Beijing and Guangzhou had little incentive to promote the development of firms from which they could not control the revenue. Changchun and Wuhan suffered from a similar fragmentation, albeit a fragmentation from a different source: the fragmentation was vertical rather than horizontal. Because FAW and Dongfeng were controlled by the central government, the local governments in Changchun and Wuhan had limited ability to promote the development of local firms.

A. The Municipal Governments: Well Intentioned, but Powerless

Changchun and Wuhan sought to promote the development of local supply firms for the same reasons as the other cities with auto joint ventures: revenue and employment. In Shanghai, the municipal government eased the risk of local supply firms by providing investment capital and by guaranteeing a market. Volumes in Shanghai were low in the late 1980s, and there was no guarantee of eventual success, but the local government helped the supply firms during the initial lean years. Changchun and Wuhan had no such ability: the two cities had neither the ability to influence the actions of the Chinese partner in the joint ventures or the money to independently invest in local supplier development. The former problem was a consequence of the fragmentation caused by central control of the Chinese partners; the latter problem was a consequence of unfavorable fiscal relationships between the municipalities and the central government.

A municipal auto office was created in both cities to oversee the local auto industry. In Changchun, the Municipal Planning Committee originally had responsibility for directing the growth of the auto industry, but in that it had ten different *xitong*s, each of which contained auto related firms, coordination was insufficient. In 1987 a separate office was established for the purpose of coordinating (*xietiao*) relations between firms. The office was placed under the supervision of the Planning Committee – the director of the auto office was a vice-director of the Planning Committee – and was composed of ten people.[21] The Wuhan Auto Office, created in 1994, was composed of three members of the Wuhan Economic Commission (their background was in economic management, not autos) and it reported directly to the mayor's office.[22] It too had the task of coordinating relations between auto firms that were controlled by different ministries and different levels of government (municipal, central, and military). As in the other three cities with auto assembly joint ventures, the auto offices in Changchun and Wuhan were created with the intention of nurturing local development, but without the proper tools, they had very little success.

Lack of Capital and Influence. A prerequisite for successful auto sector development is investment capital. In order to meet the higher technical

---

[21] Interview, no. C5, July 24, 1997.
[22] Interview, no. W1, July 23, 1998.

standards of the joint venture assembly projects, supply firms must invest
in new manufacturing equipment and technology. If loans are used to
meet the cost of large upfront investments, the firms must then have
sufficient revenue to meet their loan payments. The municipal auto offices
in Changchun and Wuhan were intent upon having the assembly plants
source from local firms, but when the managers of the assembly plant
supply division described the sort of investment that would be required to
raise the technical level of a particular supply firm, the auto offices rarely
were able to follow through. The local governments had little money of
their own to invest in the auto industry.

Between 1994 and 1997, according to officials in the Wuhan auto office,
the municipality of Wuhan allocated RMB 140 million to the auto office
as investment capital.[23] This was a paltry sum compared to the RMB
5 billion which Shanghai collected by means of the automobile component tax between 1988 and 1994. The situation in Changchun was even
worse. In 1997, I asked the director of the municipal auto office about
the auto sector investment policy of the municipality. "We talked about
developing a fund to support investment in the auto parts industry for
many years," he replied, "but we still haven't collected any money." Why?
"Everybody needs money and the government simply doesn't have
enough to go around," he explained. The central government provided a
small amount of capital earmarked for the auto industry – money that the
central government took primarily from the Shanghai localization fund –
but it went to FAW rather than the municipal government, and FAW did
not necessarily invest in local firms.[24]

Lack of influence over the assembly joint ventures compounded the
difficulties the municipal governments had supporting supplier development. As an alternative to investing their own money in local supply firms,
the municipal governments might have supported local firms by pressing
the assembly plants to give suppliers favorable prices for the components
they purchased. In Shanghai, municipal control over SAIC allowed the
local government to take a long-range view with regards to auto sector revenue: the auto component tax and the pricing policy of SVW
served as a mechanism for reinvesting revenue in supplier development.
In Changchun and Wuhan, however, the municipal governments did not

---

[23] Interview, no. W1, July 23, 1998. This amount is approximately US $17 million (using the
1997 exchange rate of RMB 8.2 = US $1).
[24] Interview, no. C5, July 24, 1997.

have this type of control over the centrally-run FAW and Dongfeng. Not only were the top officials of the business groups appointed by Beijing, but their presidents were equal (and in Changchun higher) in rank to the local mayor. Although the business groups might decide independently to invest in supplier development, the municipal governments could do little to persuade them. Even when the municipality owned shares in a firm, there was a good deal of ambiguity over whether it could actually exercise control. When FAW began expanding in the late 1980s, joint ventures and mergers between FAW firms and local firms became common. The assets owned by the locality became shares in a new venture that was managed by the business group. Given the trans-regional scope of the auto group, conflicts with the locality were inevitable, and in such cases it was not clear how the locality could exert influence in accordance with its equity stake in the firm.[25]

The descriptions of the local auto offices offered by the supply firm managers in Changchun and Wuhan make it quite evident that these offices did not have the power of their Shanghai counterpart. The offices provided a certain degree of coordination as a liaison between the assembly plant and suppliers, but because the assembly plants were part of the central government bureaucracy, a municipal government office had no authority over them. The municipal auto offices could not prevent the assembly plant from utilizing multiple suppliers for a single component; they could not prevent the assembly plant from putting extreme price pressure on the suppliers.[26] The supply managers at the assembly joint ventures characterize the local auto offices in similar terms. In Wuhan, a French manager said the municipal auto office was well meaning, but without resources or a clear strategy.[27] The Wuhan auto office did provide significant assistance with respect to sales – in order to increase the number of DCAC Fukangs that were used as local taxis, it raised the registration fees on non-local cars and provided preferential financing for local cars – but this was primarily a stopgap measure when austerity policies were pinching volumes; it was not a long-term strategy for developing

---

[25] Xu (1993: 25–26).

[26] In Shanghai, the manager of a Changchun supply firm commented, the municipal government controls everything, but in Changchun the local government has no control over FAW (*guanbuliao*). Interview, no. C4, July 24, 1997. Section two of this chapter explains the assembly plant-supplier relationships more fully.

[27] Interview, no. W13, May 15, 1997.

a supply base.[28] In Changchun, the municipal government did not even provide assistance on the sales end. As in Wuhan, a German manager in Changchun pointed to lack of money as a key reason the local auto office could not play an active role.[29] The office organized numerous meetings, but little was accomplished. The primary manner in which the municipal governments in Changchun and Wuhan could have provided assistance to struggling supply firms would have been to provide investment capital derived from the non-auto related revenue of the city, and in both cities this presented a problem. Neither city was revenue rich.

Central Neglect. Why did these two cities have so little capital of their own? As with other Chinese cities, the financial situation of Changchun and Wuhan must be understood in the context of their fiscal relationship with the central government.

Wuhan, on the one hand, had the considerable advantage of being a key critical commercial center for the Chinese interior prior to the Communist revolution, but became a center of heavy industry after the revolution. In 1949, light industry accounted for 92.5% of gross value of industrial output (GVIO) in the city; in the years that followed light industry never received more than 8% of fixed asset investment.[30] Heavy industry investment went as high as 66.4% in the second five-year plan and Wuhan became the home to many key industrial projects.[31] But the comparative strength of the Wuhan economy consistently declined during the first decade of the reform era. In 1984, at the start of urban reform, the city ranked fourth nationally in terms of GVIO, value of fixed assets, and the amount of taxes and profits it turned over to the central government, but by 1992 – the year the DCAC contract was signed – its GVIO ranked only eleventh, fixed asset investment, ninth, and local in-budget income, seventh.[32] Dorothy Solinger argues persuasively that central government policy has been the primary cause of Wuhan's declining fortunes during

---

[28] In 1996, almost 50% of DCAC's production volume (about 5,000 cars) was sold to local taxi fleets. Interview, no. W25, May 14, 1997. In 1998, taxi companies accounted for 34.7% of national sedan sales, Zhongguo Qiche Jishu Yanjiu Zhongxin (2000: 136).

[29] Interview, no. C7, July 25, 1997. This manager, who had also worked in Shanghai, noted that while he had very little interaction with the Changchun Municipal Auto Office, in Shanghai he met with auto office officials two or three times a week.

[30] Solinger (1996: 7).

[31] Key projects included: Wuhan Iron and Steel Works, Wuhan Heavy-Duty Machine Tool Plant, Wuhan Boiler Plant, and the Yangtze Bridge. Solinger (1996: 7).

[32] Solinger (1996: 3). Furthermore, whereas the average growth rate of gross domestic product nation-wide in China between 1979 and 1991 was 8.7%, in Wuhan it was 8%.

the 1980s.[33] The city actually had fewer SOEs than Guangzhou, and less heavy industry than Dalian, yet both Guangzhou and Dalian were highly successful during this same period. The difference, according to Solinger, was that Wuhan did not have the benefit of preferential policies until 1992. Although city leaders might have liked to try innovative approaches to local development, they had very little capital. Prior to 1984, Wuhan had always been forced to bear a heavy burden for Hubei Province (much like Shanghai did for the country as a whole). In 1981, for instance, it contributed 41.4% of the province's total revenue.[34] When the city was granted provincial status in 1984 (*jihua danlie*), it was freed from its highly conflictual relationship with the province, but was still granted the lowest profit retention rate of any provincial level city (of which there were 22 by 1993).[35]

Not until 1992 and the promotion of the centrally sponsored Yangtze River development plan did Wuhan have the benefit of preferential policies on a par with the coastal areas. The new policies were designed to attract foreign investment to Wuhan, and lower tax rates combined with a conviction that Wuhan was the key to the Chinese interior led to a surge in the city's utilization of foreign capital. In 1992, Wuhan utilized $187 million of foreign capital, an increase of 112% over the previous year.[36] This shift did not necessarily have a great impact on the city's ability to support the development of supply firms, however, and in fact may be indicative of the problem that the city confronted. The dramatic increase of foreign investment in 1992 reflected the creation of DCAC that same year, and the large investments of both Citroen and the suppliers it had persuaded to come to Wuhan. The problem was not attracting initial capital investment, but supporting the projects after large up-front investments had been made. Preferential policies led to a sharp increase in foreign investment in Wuhan, but at least in the short-term they did not increase the local government's ability to help struggling supply firms. Because preferential policies on investment consisted primarily of tax holidays and benefits for new projects, government revenue had not increased, and centrally-initiated austerity measures were just around the corner.

---

[33] The remainder of this paragraph draws from Solinger (1996).
[34] Solinger (1996: 12).
[35] Solinger puts the profit retention rate somewhere between 14 and 20%. Shanghai was also disadvantaged, but as of 1985 even it had a profit retention rate of 23–24%. Solinger (1996: 20).
[36] Solinger (1996: 31).

Capital was still in short supply and the local government still had no control over Dongfeng.

Lack of investment capital in Changchun was also a result of an unfavorable fiscal relationship with the central government. At the start of the reform era, Changchun, and the province of which it is the capital, Jilin, had one of the highest percentages of heavy industry in China,[37] but many of these heavy industry firms were controlled by the central government – the municipality received little revenue from them. Well into the reform period, the region continued to be dominated by enterprises that were controlled by the central government, rather than the locality. In 1995, only 15% of the SOEs in the city of Changchun were centrally-controlled, but these enterprises contributed 75% of the city's gross industrial output. FAW was, of course, by far the largest.[38]

As in Wuhan, the preferential policies that the central government bestowed on coastal regions at the beginning of the reform process had little impact on Changchun. The economic status of the region did not decline markedly during the reform era, but only because it had a relatively low position to begin with: in 1985, the GVIO of Jilin Province ranked sixteenth (out of a total of 29 regions with provincial status); in 1992 it had declined to seventeenth.[39] The ratio of heavy industry to light industry did not change. It was not until 1989 that the city was granted independent planning status (*jihua danlie*), a change that gave it the same degree of expanded authority to approve foreign invested projects that coastal cities enjoyed.[40] As of 1992, however, Changchun was behind even Wuhan in the utilization of foreign capital. Approximately US $100 million in contracts had been signed (in 139 foreign invested enterprises), but only US $15 million had been utilized.[41] By the mid-1990s, rather than being a beacon of reform like Guangzhou or Shanghai, Changchun was

---

[37] In 1985, the percentage of heavy industry relative to light industry in Jilin Province was 63:37. State Statistical Bureau (1986: 53).

[38] In 1995, 88 of the 565 SOEs in Changchun city were centrally-controlled (*zhongyang qiye*), and their total output was valued (in 1995 prices) at RMB 23.2 billion out of a total SOE output of RMB 30.9 billion. *Changchun Economy Statistical Yearbook 1996* (1996: 224, 225). According to the same source, the FAW share of this output was RMB 19.4 billion. *Changchun Economy Statistical Yearbook 1996* (1996: 230). The FAW share of SOE output in Changchun seems far too large, but perhaps it is an indication of the scope of FAW operations beyond truck and car manufacturing.

[39] Jilin Province is used rather than Changchun because the city is not included in earlier statistics since it did not have provincial status. These ranking were determined from State Statistical Bureau (1986: 35) and State Statistical Bureau (1993: 53).

[40] *Changchun Investment Handbook* (1992: 38, 45).

[41] *China Investment Guide* (1995: 614).

a symbol of the obstacles that further reform confronted: a high density of loss-making SOEs burdened with far too many employees. Local leaders were caught between the economic need for massive layoffs and the political need for stability.[42]

B. The Business Groups: Self-contained Societies Tied to the Center

The lack of power and influence of the municipal governments over the joint venture operations in Changchun and Wuhan can also be seen from the perspective of the business groups. The autonomy of FAW and Dongfeng was not a recent phenomenon: both were created as centrally-controlled projects, and they developed independently of the localities in which they were located. In April 1950, the Heavy Industry Ministry in Beijing created the Auto Industry Preparatory Group to oversee the selection of a site for the First Auto Works factory, the selection of a design, and ultimately the construction.[43] Changchun was a natural site because of the industrial base that had been created during the Japanese occupations, and perhaps also because of its proximity to the Soviet Union; FAW was the first key project in China that benefited substantially from the new alliance with the Soviet Union. Despite its location within the municipality of Changchun, the construction of FAW was much like building an entirely new city; engineers were building not only factories, but also power plants, sewer systems, apartment buildings, hospitals, and schools. By the time the first "Liberation" truck came off the assembly line on July 15, 1956, a whole society was well on its way to being created, a society that was quite independent of the municipality of Changchun.

That Dongfeng was also a centrally-sponsored project is not difficult to discern; only strategic reasons could motivate a government to locate a major industrial project in remote and unpopulated mountains. Mao Zedong reportedly first raised the idea of constructing a second major auto producer in 1953 and again in 1958, but the establishment of Dongfeng was not formally approved by the Central Committee of the

---

[42] In 1998, Premier Zhu Rongji traveled to the city to bolster the resolve of local leaders. Adapting administrative measures to protect loss-making firms would only hinder the reform effort and the long-term interests of the workers, he argued. All levels of government had to seek new employment opportunities for laid-off workers. With insufficient resources, however, this was easier said than done. "Zhu Rongji addresses reemployment issues," Xinhua News Agency, March 27, 1998.

[43] Cao Zheng Hou, "Yaolan de Huihuang" [Glory of the Cradle], in Sun (1995: 101).

CCP until 1965.[44] The construction of Dongfeng, which due to the Cultural Revolution did not begin until 1969, was legendary in the Chinese auto industry. Led by Rao Bin, the former director of FAW, the workers (many of whom had also been transferred from Changchun) scattered production facilities across different valleys, often utilizing the many caves of the region. Construction costs were financed by the central government, and in that initially it would be manufacturing military vehicles, it also had close ties with the military command. Regular production of the 2.5-ton military truck did not begin until 1975, the same year that a rail line to Shiyan was finally completed.[45] In the 1980s, as Dongfeng continued its program of reform and development, its remote location became a severe handicap. The sedan joint venture in Wuhan was not only an opportunity to acquire the technology necessary to build a modern car, but also a chance to move from Shiyan to Wuhan.

Both FAW and Dongfeng were classic Chinese SOEs in terms of their scope – manufacturing cars was only a very small part of actual operations. By the 1980s each had between 250,000 and 300,000 workers, pensioners, and dependents.[46] Of the actual work force, a very large percentage were employed in jobs unrelated to the auto industry. There were barbers, sales clerks, teachers, doctors, policemen, etc.[47] Like other Chinese SOEs, the enterprises provided an endless range of benefits and services to its workers: housing, health care, cradle-to-grave welfare, an education for all workers and dependents. At FAW, for example, there are more than 26 schools, as well as 10 kindergartens (for the 20,000 preschoolers) and a technical college. Over the years, the construction department at FAW built 1,000 apartment buildings to house more than 30,000 families. "Each year," explained Geng Zhaojie, the general manager of FAW, "I have to worry about housing for 2,000 couples getting married, nurseries for 2,000 newborn babies, and jobs for 2,500 school-leavers.... I am a mayor as well as factory head."[48] At Dongfeng, the dual nature of the director's role was officially acknowledged: the general manager served simultaneously as the mayor of Shiyan.[49]

---

[44] William A. Byrd, "The Second Motor Vehicle Manufacturing Plant," in Byrd (1992: 377).
[45] Byrd, "The Second Motor Vehicle Manufacturing Plant," in Byrd (1992: 378 and 383).
[46] Hannan (1998: x). SAW officially lists the number of workers at 73,208. *China Auto*, vol. 2, no. 2, April 20, 1992, p. 6.
[47] According to one source, 80% of the FAW workers have jobs which are unrelated to auto manufacturing. Julia Leung, "Snags Beset Ambitious Chinese Car Plan," *Asian Wall Street Journal*, April 5, 1989, p. 1.
[48] Leung, "Snags Beset Ambitious Chinese Car Plan," p. 1 and 7.
[49] This arrangement was changed in 1981. Byrd, "The Second Motor Vehicle Manufacturing Plant," in Byrd (1992: 383).

The institutional arrangements that the central government has used to govern the First and Second Auto Works have undergone numerous changes. Until 1964, FAW was managed out of the First Machinery Building Industry Ministry, control was then transferred to the newly created China National Automotive Industry Corporation (CNAIC).[50] Top leadership were appointed by the central government, output was distributed via the central plan, and all investment capital came from Beijing: the enterprise had very little autonomy. When Dongfeng was under construction it was under the supervision of a field leadership group, and in the 1970s it seemed to be for a time nominally under the leadership of Hubei province, but in 1981 it became unambiguously a centrally run enterprise.[51] Much to the chagrin of the Dongfeng leadership, they were placed under the control of a newly strengthened CNAIC. Rather than helping Dongfeng maximize its competitiveness, CNAIC tried to balance the strength of the firms – at times they forced Dongfeng to relinquish profitable portions of its business to competitors – and maximize the amount of revenue it derived from the firms it supervised.[52] Dongfeng struggled to free itself from what it viewed as a predatory supervisory body, and after three years, succeeded.

In 1984, in a move in keeping with the decentralizing impulse of the reform movement, both FAW and Dongfeng were granted a separate line in the state plan. This was a highly significant change for it increased the autonomy of the enterprises while at the same time gave them considerable power within the central government. Instead of being forced to operate through a bureaucratic intermediary, both firms became directly supervised by the State Planning Commission (SPC). The enterprises were allowed to retain a larger percentage of their profits – if there were any – and each was allowed to create an internal finance company.[53] The result was the enviable position of having significant independence in decision-making, an internally-controlled finance company, and a great deal of leverage at the central level. According to one source, investment decisions were now made through "dialogue" with the SPC (*guojia*

---

[50] See "The History of Administration System & Organization of China Auto Industry," *China Auto*, vol. 2, no. 3, June 20, 1992, p. 6.

[51] Byrd, "The Second Motor Vehicle Manufacturing Plant," in Byrd (1992: 384–5).

[52] Yang (1995: 133). In many cases CNAIC favored rival firms which it also controlled. When assigning mandatory plan targets, for instance, CNAIC would give higher targets to FAW than SAW. For details, see Byrd, "The Second Motor Vehicle Manufacturing Plant," in Byrd (1992: 384–5).

[53] Jiao and Liu (1996: 27). The same privileges were granted to China National Heavy Duty Truck (*Zhongqi*) in Shandong Province.

jiwei duihua) rather than imposed unilaterally from above; FAW and Dongfeng, although enterprises, had the equivalent government status of ministries.[54] The enterprises certainly were not completely independent, the center still appointed top personnel and granted approval on a wide range of issues, but they had many means of influencing the decision-making process, and even central government decisions that were unfavorable could be changed after a barrage of study meetings, fact finding missions, and research reports.[55] During business downturns, of course, such influence could be invaluable. Neither FAW nor Dongfeng had any need to ask for assistance from mere municipal governments when they encountered problems – they could go right to the center.

C. National Enterprise Groups

The degree of independence of FAW and Dongfeng was only increased by the central government auto industrial strategy that began to emerge in the early 1990s. As I explained in Chapter 2, the level of dispersion was a primary structural problem in the Chinese auto industry during this period, and enlarging and strengthening national enterprise groups was seen as means of achieving greater concentration. Although the intent was to imitate the state-led model of Korea, the mechanism for selecting which firms were worthy of state support was problematic. As Chinese policy-makers noted, the Korean government used export contests to determine which firms were worthy of government support; those that proved to be competitive in the international marketplace received the preferences.[56] Not only were there virtually no auto exports from China at this stage, but the government obviously had a non-financial interest in the plight of struggling SOEs.[57] The predictable result was that the central government chose to support the largest existing SOEs in the auto industry, not only because they were already large, but because their many dependents made them politically difficult to abandon.

The stated objective of the 1994 Automobile Industrial Policy was to change "the current situation of dispersion in investment, small production scale and backwardness of auto products...[and to] build China's

---

[54] Jiao and Liu (1996: 30).
[55] Jiao and Liu (1996: 31).
[56] "Yantaohui Zongshu," [Symposium Summary], Ministry of Machinery Industry (1994b: 11).
[57] In 1994, China exported 18,035 vehicles (15,538 of these were trucks) primarily to southeast Asia (Burma, Vietnam, and Bangladesh were the top three). Zhang (1997a: 16).

automobile industry into a pillar industry of the national economy as soon as possible."[58] The central government, according to this policy statement, would support the merging of firms and the development of large enterprise groups that would serve as the backbone of the domestic industry. The intent was to create firms that would have full research and development capacity and be competitive in the international arena. The criterion for choosing which enterprises would receive government support was annual production volumes: those firms that met specified output levels would receive certain tax exemptions, priority in issuing stocks and bonds, preferred access to bank loans and policy loans, and priority in the utilization of foreign capital.[59] In other words, those firms that had previously been at the core of the auto industry – and were consequently the largest producers – would continue to enjoy their privileged position.

FAW, Dongfeng, and SAIC, the enterprises with the highest output levels, would be at the center of the government's consolidation efforts. SAIC, as a locally controlled firm, would not divert its development efforts from the municipality. The president of SAIC, a city official to the core, was well aware that he had to support firms that employed local people and paid taxes to the local government. Development efforts were concentrated and closely monitored. FAW and Dongfeng, however, were not tied to a particular locality, and could expand across the country. Given that official central government policy at the time was to support the largest firms, the top directors at FAW and Dongfeng were not surprisingly in favor of expansion – size determined their bureaucratic importance and level of government support – and lobbied the government to achieve it.[60] A quality product was necessary to increase sales, an important contrast with the era of state planning, but assuming that the competition was relatively weak, expansion was the easiest route to success.[61]

---

[58] "Industrial Policy of China's Automobile Industry," State Planning Commission, February 19, 1994, reprinted in Hu and He (1995: 183).

[59] Degree of support varied by production scale. Those firms that reached annual output of over 300,000 units and sales over 200,000 units by the end of 1995 would qualify for the top level of support. "Industrial Policy of China's Automobile Industry," State Planning Commission, February 19, 1994, reprinted in Hu and He (1995: 186–7).

[60] A retired CNAIC official, explaining why his office in the Machinery Ministry had given the necessary approvals for FAW to import assembly lines based on outdated technology, shrugged his shoulders and said there was no use opposing FAW. If his office did not give the approvals, FAW had the high-level government connections to get the approvals elsewhere. Why step on toes when the decision would ultimately be reversed by some vice-premier?" Interview, no. B29, April 11, 1997.

[61] As Kate Hannan points out in her study of Dongfeng, the production capacity of connected enterprises was counted as part of the group's overall production capacity

In light of the bureaucratic advantages of increased size, it is not surprising that the directors of FAW and Dongfeng were strong supporters of an industrial policy that focused on large enterprise groups, or that they took advantage of the opportunity to expand across the country.[62] Dongfeng began acquiring firms in the late-1980s, and soon had some 300 member firms.[63] FAW implemented a similar strategy of acquisition, and by 1992 the group consisted of 155 automakers, components firms, trading firms, and research organizations.[64] In late 1994, FAW formed a joint venture with the Shunde Automotive Works in Guangdong Province to produce sedans[65]; in 1995, a joint venture between FAW and Jiangsu Mudan Automotive Works (Jiangsu Province) producing truck and bus chassis went into operation[66]; in 1994, it acquired Jinbei Auto (one of the 10 largest auto firms in China); in 1997, it purchased a 51% stake in a joint venture formed with the Yunnan Hongta Group (Yunnan Province; and

and the employees as part of overall employment figure: "the connected enterprises enlarged the SAW/Dongfeng kingdom and so increased the status of the group and the success of the group's management." Hannan (1998: 34).

[62] "As a matter of past experiences worldwide," commented Ma Yu, president of SAW/Dongfeng, "it is truly necessary for a nation to establish strong enterprise groups in upgrading its auto industry." Ma Yue, "Urgent Task Facing the Chinese Auto Industry," *China Auto*, vol. 5, no. 5, September/October 1995, p. 9. The most effective way of developing a self-dependent industry, argued Geng Zhaojie, the president of FAW, was to follow the development path of South Korea. Geng Zhaojie, "Suggestions on Development Strategy of China Auto Industry," *China Auto*, vol. 5, no. 5, September/October 1995, p. 7.

[63] In the 1980s, many of these acquisitions were in the form of lateral equity ties formed in order to secure access to supplies. As mandatory planning began to play a decreasingly important role in allocating materials, Dongfeng sometimes found itself with insufficient inputs for above-plan production, the highly profitable portion of production that came after the firm had fulfilled the requirements of the mandatory state plan. In an attempt to guard against this problem, the firm would either purchase suppliers in their entirety, or purchase enough shares to influence their operations. Because smaller firms were having even more difficulty accessing necessary inputs in the late-1980s they were often eager to form relations with a large enterprise group. As a member of the group they would have secure access to inputs and a degree of insulation from the vagaries of the market. The administrative role of the group replaced, to a certain degree, the administrative role formerly played by the state plan. Hannan (1998: 34).

[64] Tomoo Marukawa, "WTO, Industrial Policy and China's Industrial Development," in Yamazawa and Imai (2001: 36–7).

[65] "Marching towards the coastal areas is an important move in FAW's strategy to become China's biggest auto enterprise," commented Fan Hengguang, executive director of the board of the Shunde company. Liu Weiling, "Nothern car maker drives into the South," *China Daily*, March 12, 1995.

[66] "Bus production lines go into operation in Jiangsu," Xinhua News Agency, August 19, 1995.

in 2002 it acquired Tianjin Auto, a giant in its own right.[67] In China, the biggest got even bigger.

II. SUPPLY SECTOR STRUCTURE

To this point the argument has focused on the manner in which the relationships between the business groups and the central government affected the ability to promote supplier development in Changchun and Wuhan. The ties between the enterprise groups and the central government precluded the municipal governments from actively promoting local firms. FAW and Dongfeng were completely independent of the local governments, and their orientation went far beyond municipal borders. The contrast with the intimate ties between Shanghai and SAIC is a stark one. The scale and scope of their operations, when combined with their relationship with the central government, affected the development of a supply base in three respects: the social burden of the SOEs interfered with the need to utilize joint ventures as a mechanism of modernization, internal monitoring was insufficient, and expansion was not always rational from an economic perspective.

A. The Burden of Age

From the perspective of a joint venture assembly plant, promoting the creation of joint venture supply firms was the most effective way to develop a strong supply base. Auto firms in all settings increasingly rely on supply firms for research and development work, and because large portions of the car are contracted out for subassembly, supply firms must be active participants in the process of knowledge and technology transfer. Given the non-financial interests of Chinese SOEs, however, it was not always easy for them to remain focused on the primary purpose for forming a joint venture; the temptation was to utilize the joint venture as a means of financing the social burden of the SOE. Firms in Shanghai certainly had social burdens – this was simply a fact of life for a Chinese SOE – but it was smaller due to the size and age of the enterprises. In 1995, SVW employed 9,417 workers, while FAW employed 117,281 and Dongfeng employed

---

[67] "The auto industry is an industry that requires a high economy of scale," Zhou Tiejing, Jinbei's deputy general manager commented when taken over by FAW. "Against this background, we decided to transfer the shares and merge with a big (auto) group." Joseph Kahn, "Two Chinese auto makers join forces, reports say," *Asian Wall Street Journal*, February 22, 1995, p. 3.

83,121.[68] Because the automobile industry had not been a major player in the Shanghai industrial scene prior to the reform era, firms did not have large numbers of retired workers to support, or several decades' worth of bad habits to correct – SAIC firms had very little experience in the auto industry. When the supply base was being developed in the late 1980s, joint venture supply firms were a key means of acquiring new skills and the Chinese partners were quite willing to heed the advice of the foreign partner.

In Changchun and Wuhan there certainly was the need to acquire the technology and knowledge that joint venture supply firms had to offer, but it was also quite clear that many of these joint ventures firms were being forced to bear a large portion of the SOE burden. In Wuhan the problems for foreign supply firms often began even before the joint venture contracts were signed. Rather than being able to pick the most appropriate local supplier to partner with, the foreign firms were told that they had to form partnerships with Dongfeng firms from Shiyan. "Usually there is a friendly discussion about whom to partner with," one French manager commented, "but in this case the Dongfeng people simply presented us with a partner."[69] This would not have been a major problem if the chosen partner was the best available, of course, but rarely was this the case: Dongfeng forced foreign suppliers to use Shiyan companies for financial rather than technical reasons.

Utilizing joint ventures as a means of relieving the social burden of the Chinese partner resulted in numerous problems. First, the joint ventures had a very high cost structure. In part this was because the Chinese partners were continually pressing the joint ventures to take more workers than were necessary,[70] but it was also because labor costs were high. Although it was commonly believed that cheap labor was one of China's comparative advantages, this was not the case when the local partner was a cash-strapped SOE. Wages at a Wuhan joint venture were typically twice what would be paid to workers in a wholly-owned Chinese

---

[68] *Zhongguo Qiche Gongye: 1996* (1996: 13). These are comparisons of unlike units in that SVW is the JV sedan project in Shanghai, while FAW and SAW are the whole enterprise group (not the JV), but this is exactly the point. At this time, SVW was the primary employer at SAIC (I do not not have employment figures for the broader group), while FAW-VW and DCAC were dwarfed by the enormity of the broader group. Cars were the primary product in Shanghai; trucks were the primary product in the other two cases.

[69] Interview, no. W17, May 9, 1997.

[70] One JV in Wuhan, for instance, had 50 workers (45 from Shiyan, 5 from Wuhan), but was continually being pressed to take an additional 50. Interview, no. W17, May 9, 1997.

factory,[71] and the joint venture had to provide all the benefits of a traditional SOE. Sixty-five percent of the labor cost, according to one joint venture manager, consisted of contributions to the various funds (insurance, health, housing, pension, etc.) of the Chinese partner. Because the joint venture did not provide these services itself, it had to pay the parent company of the Chinese partner for doing so. While it would not be right for the joint venture simply to siphon off what was useful from the Chinese partner, it was also true that the management of these funds was completely out of the control of the joint ventures – mismanagement only increased the expense.[72] In addition to labor and contribution to the various funds, the joint ventures also provided workers with meals, transportation, and uniforms.[73] According to a foreign general manager who had run comparable manufacturing operations in numerous locations, his total labor costs in China were more than 50% higher than the Philippines, 50% higher than Mexico, and about the equivalent of southern Europe. Given a competitive labor contract, he claimed, the joint venture would be able to export – quality standards were high enough; saddled with a portion of a large SOEs financial burden it was simply not possible.[74] A joint venture in Shanghai that manufactured the same product, by contrast, exported 50% of its output.[75]

In Changchun, foreign joint venture managers found the SOE burden to be creeping up on them; each year FAW placed new demands on them. At one joint venture, for instance, the contract specified that FAW would continue to provide housing and medical care for workers in exchange for a fee. One year after the joint venture was established, however, FAW

---

[71] One factory manager said that monthly wages for workers ranged from 1,000 to 1,800 RMB/month. Interview, no. W17, May 9, 1997.

[72] Stories of mismanaged funds at DCAC were common. According to the JV contract Chinese employees had to receive at least half the salary of foreign employees – an enormous amount by Chinese standards. The actual employee, however only received a small portion of this amount (the former employee who explained this to me, for instance, had a salary of 7,000 RMB/month of which he received 2,000 RMB/month) the rest went to the Dongfeng trade union. In the mid-1990s, one top-level Dongfeng manager ran off with a good portion of this "slush" fund. Interview, no. W26, April 20, 1997.

[73] JVs of a certain size were also required to have a doctor on site. Interview, no. W12, April 3, 1997.

[74] Interview, no. W12, April 3, 1997.

[75] Interview, no. S21, June 18, 1998. Many factors other than the cost of labor will shape the export competitiveness of these two firms, of course, but in that this particular product is labor intensive, the cost of labor is critical. The Shanghai JV was created explicitly for the purpose of employing farmers which had been displaced by the SVW factories (required by law). In addition to their monthly salary the farmers were paid 60 RMB/month compensation.

told the JV manager that "it was getting out of the housing business" and it was now necessary for the JV to construct housing for its workers. The second year after the joint venture was established, FAW told the JV managers that they would have to construct their own medical clinic; FAW was getting out of the medical business.[76] From the perspective of the foreign partner, lack of predictability was a major problem.

The strategy of both FAW and Dongfeng was quite clear. If a firm such as FAW was to continue to be the backbone of the Chinese auto industry (as the central government intended), explained a manager at the FAW joint venture office, it had to separate itself from its social responsibilities and invest more in production units.[77] The challenge was to find somebody able to absorb these responsibilities – the municipal government certainly did not have the money. Joint ventures were an attractive opportunity. A joint venture required a minimum investment on the part of the Chinese partner, often only the land (which usually was a gift from the local government) and machinery (financed by loans), and each new joint venture provided an opportunity to parcel off a small portion of the social burden.[78] Given the low investment, the Chinese partner was putting very little at risk, and the mere existence of the joint venture made life easier for the heavily burdened Chinese partner. "The Chinese say they want technology," observed one disgruntled foreign manager in Wuhan, "but what they really want is cash. They want us to absorb their workers."[79] Unlike the foreign managers, who were under pressure from their home company to start showing a return on the initial investment, the local managers were under pressure to relieve the burden on the Chinese partner. Although joint ventures in China were seldom truly cooperative – the objectives of the partners always vary to an extent – the size and history of FAW and Dongfeng dominated the joint venture projects to a far

---

[76] This example is from an interview with the foreign manager of the JV. Because it was a 50/50 JV, the JV did not completely concede to the FAW demands on either point. Interview, no. C3, July 24, 1997.

[77] Interview, no. C1, July 22, 1997. This is consistent with overall state policy since 1992. As Hannan writes, "Chinese economist and planners have consistently argued that, if state-owned enterprise continue to 'shoulder a heavy social welfare burden,' it will be 'difficult for them to compete on an equal basis [in the market] with enterprises of other types.'" Hannan (1998: 61).

[78] Typically the land, buildings, and existing machinery would be assessed as the equivalent of 50% of the JVs capitalization. The land was often donated by the economic zone in which most JVs were located. Foreign partners rarely had majority control over joint ventures. For assembly JVs, Chinese law forbid the foreign partner from having a majority share.

[79] Interview, no. W12, April 3, 1997.

greater extent than was the case when the Chinese partner was a smaller, younger company.

Personnel issues were an example of how the nature of the Chinese partner could influence the joint venture projects. Because wages were generally twice as high at a JV, employment at the JVs was highly desirable and often claimed by senior workers or the well-connected at the Chinese partner. Rather than placing the most qualified personnel in the JV, personnel decisions were more often made on a patronage basis. At FAW-VW, according to workers, a series of examinations were initially used to determine who would be transferred to the JV, and a great deal of FAW's human capital was transferred to FAW-VW. Eventually, however, the patronage system began to reassert itself: transfers to the JV and promotions within the JV were granted to the well-connected.[80] A German manager at FAW-VW, complaining that VW had no control over the workers that FAW transferred to the JV, was scathingly critical of the Chinese workforce.[81] As in all JVs in China, the foreign partner preferred to have young, well-educated Chinese workers because they were more easily trained.

At DCAC, the patterns of patronage resulted in deep rifts among the Chinese workers. Because the Dongfeng base was in Shiyan, not Wuhan, the top management of the joint venture was from Shiyan. Much to the resentment of the Wuhan workers, the Shiyan "clique" received higher pay, faster promotions, and preferential access to new housing. Workers from Wuhan were initially few in number, but increased to 50% of the workforce within five years. The directors of the eight departments within DCAC were all Dongfeng managers from Shiyan, however. "If you really want a cooperative JV you have to completely cast-off (*baituo*) the old structure," remarked a former Wuhan employee at DCAC. "This is not happening at DCAC. To the contrary, the JV is becoming more and more like Dongfeng."[82] The foreign partners at the JV were not in charge of

---

[80] Interview, no. C10, July 22, 1997.
[81] Interview, no. C6, July 23, 1997. His complaints primarily focused on the lack of initiative of the Chinese workforce, and he attributed it primarily to poor education. In Shanghai, where he had worked at SVW, workers were "better educated and had a different mentality."
[82] Interview, no. W25, April 20, 1997. The factional politics at the enterprise were apparently quite complex: among managers, college alma mater was most important (Qinghua dominated); among workers hometown was most important (Shiyan vs. Wuhan). There was a joke about DCAC circulating in Wuhan: "their parts aren't localized, but their management is."

personnel, were generally unable to replace poor workers, and were only marginally aware of the divisions within the Chinese side.[83]

The sentiments of many foreign JV managers towards their Chinese partners might be best summarized by Chairman Mao. Just as a joint venture sought to remake a Chinese firm, Mao sought to remake Chinese society, and he understood the benefits of starting from scratch. The most beautiful characters and paintings, he said, are written on a blank sheet of paper.[84] Given their long histories, FAW and Dongfeng were far from blank.

B. Hierarchical, But Not Nurturing

In Shanghai, supplier development was facilitated by a dense web of organizational ties. If a supply firm had a problem, it could seek assistance at the head office of the corporate group, the localization office of the municipal government, or utilize the Santana Localization Community to seek the advice of other supply firms. Within this network of organizational ties, supply firms were not only nurtured, but also monitored. SVW carefully tracked the quality record of firms, and there was a continual flow of reports between the head office of SAIC and the supply firms. If a supply firm was having difficulty, it would quickly become apparent at higher levels and the appropriate action would be taken: SVW engineers might visit the firm, SAIC might arrange for a retired German engineer to work at the firm for three months, or the manager might be switched. In Japan, Charles Sabel has argued, auto firms utilize monitoring as a means of facilitating learning. The institutions that link firms together incorporate clear performance standards, and these standards facilitate the identification of problems and a joint search for solutions.[85] Monitoring in Shanghai was rudimentary by comparison, but the close cooperation between the municipality and local firms and the multiple channels of communication was an important reason why Shanghai firms were able to overcome obstacles to development.

---

[83] The foreign manager of a JV supply firm in Wuhan, after complaining that the senior Chinese managers transferred to the JV from SAW had a poor work ethic and were too conservative, said that he could lay off workers, but on doing so had to give the workers one month salary for every year of experience they had in the parent Chinese company. Interview, no. W12, April 3, 1997.

[84] "*Yi zhang bai zhi, meiyou fudan, hao xie zui xin zui mei de wenzi, hao hua zui xin zui mei de tuhua.*" Mao (1969: 33).

[85] Charles F. Sabel, "Learning by Monitoring: The Institutions of Economic Development," in Smelser and Swedberg (1994).

The hierarchical structures of FAW and Dongfeng were similar to Shanghai in that supply divisions were generally wholly-owned branches of the enterprise, but neither enterprise developed the support structure for supply firms in the manner that Shanghai did. In a sense, it is like comparing Ford and General Motors in the 1930s: GM surpassed Ford not because of great product innovations, but because of the organizational changes made by Alfred Sloan. Despite their size, neither FAW nor Dongfeng made a great effort to improve the system by which supply firms were monitored. In contrast to Shanghai, these firms did not have the benefit of the twice annual evaluations of managers and workers, the constant flow of reports, the continual rotation of managers between firms, and the annual training sessions. There also were none of the organizational ties external to the enterprise groups to compensate for the weak oversight within the corporate structures. The local governments in both cities were eager to please, but as I have argued, they had no influence over the centrally-controlled Chinese partners at the JVs. The officials in the municipal auto offices also had little knowledge of the technical side of the automobile industry; they were bureaucrats from the Municipal Economic Commission with backgrounds in economic management. Both cities lacked supplier associations, and there was consequently only limited horizontal contact between firms. As one supply firm manager in Wuhan commented, "it is every enterprise for itself in this group."[86]

A basic problem was that the parent companies were short on capital. The Chinese partners in both joint ventures were virtually bankrupt SOEs, so an increase in shareholder investment was unlikely,[87] and due to weak demand during this period, neither the assemblers nor the supply firms could draw upon revenue from sales for investment capital.[88] Foreign supply firms were originally enticed to form joint ventures in Changchun and Wuhan because the assemblers both planned to raise annual production volumes to 150,000 vehicles within three years. The supply firms made initial investments based on this expectation, and when they did not materialize they had severe difficulties. Wildly fluctuating production volumes made it impossible to devise a production plan;

---

[86] Interview, no. W8, May 9, 1997.
[87] According to a French manager at DCAC, Citroen was willing to increase their investment in the project, but Dongfeng did not have the money to match the increased investment and was unwilling to have its equity stake in the project (70%) decrease. Interview, no. W5, July 23, 1998.
[88] Although both FAW-VW and DCAC were producing volumes similar to SVW at the same stage of development, the price of each car was at least a third lower.

delayed payments complicated finances.[89] Coordinating the development of an auto supply network is challenging under any circumstances, and this was even truer when none of the firms could make accurate production forecasts.

The supply firms also had no security in their relationships with the assembly plants. In order to pressure the supply firms to lower prices, the assembly plants utilized short-term contracts and sought multiple suppliers whenever possible. While SVW made a conscious decision to give supply firms high prices for components so as to facilitate their development, in Changchun this was not possible. A German supplier manager at FAW-VW, who had previously worked at SVW, explained that the situation at the two joint ventures was totally different. Shanghai had always made money, and hence was never concerned about costs; FAW-VW had never made money, and was consequently always pressuring suppliers to lower costs.[90] FAW-VW had to squeeze everything possible out of the supply firms. In Wuhan, the pressure on supply firm managers was similarly unrelenting. In a best case scenario, DCAC would grant a supplier a one year "open" contract (meaning it could be renegotiated at any point) for an unspecified quantity of a particular component. If the supplier did not give the price reduction that the assembly plant requested, it would be given a three or six month contract and be forced to engage in continual negotiations.[91] The assembly plant had all the leverage; the supply firms had made huge up-front investments and had a limited customer base. In one instance, DCAC pressured a joint venture supply firm to reduce its price by 20–30% even after a price had been agreed upon and a contract had been signed. The assembly plant used the qualification process (in which the specifications of the component are examined by the assembly plant) as a bargaining chip. With production levels at only 25% of capacity, the supply firm was in a desperate situation.[92] Supply firms

---

[89] The unreliable nature of production meant that it was extremely difficult for supply firms to order raw materials in advance, difficult to train workers – frenzied production would often be followed by weeks of inactivity – and they were often stuck with excess components when orders were canceled. For the orders that were completed, payments were often behind by 6 months to a year. As one European manager in Changchun related, "I went to the bank to ask for a delay on our interest payments, and they told me I should act like a European general manager and pay on time. I said my customers should act like European customers and pay me on time." Interview, no. C8, July 21, 1998.

[90] Interview, no. C7, July 25, 1997.

[91] Interview, no. W5, July 23, 1998.

[92] Interview, no. W8, May 9, 1997.

hoping to make a profit generally try not to reveal their cost structure during negotiations; in Wuhan, supply managers did just the opposite in the hope that the assembly plant would realize how ill-prepared they were to give further price reductions.

It was not only the shortage of capital that prevented a focus on supplier development, however. In comparison to Shanghai, the size and scope of FAW and Dongfeng operations made them less able and less interested in promoting supplier development. The enterprise groups were less able to help auto supply firms because to a large extent they were in different businesses. While car production was at the very center of SAIC's operations in Shanghai, FAW and Dongfeng remained primarily truck producers. In 1995, for instance, only 3% of Dongfeng's total output was cars, and 20% of FAW's.[93] The core competency of both firms was truck manufacturing, and the primary product was based on technology from the 1960s and 70s. As a German manager at FAW-VW commented, the process technology of the truck operations was ill-suited for a modern auto factory and the equipment could not meet the VW quality standards.[94] Shanghai also had a low technical level in the early stages of development, but in an important sense the local managers were not hindered by previous knowledge. Whereas Shanghai managers knew nothing and were ready to learn, managers in Changchun and Wuhan often had spent their entire lives in the auto industry: *re*training workers often proved to be more difficult than simple training. As Mao knew, it is easiest to work with a blank slate.

Neither FAW-VW nor DCAC was able to lean on the supply firms associated with the Chinese parent company to any great extent. Although the FAW-VW joint venture contract stipulated that 28% of the components for the Jetta were supposed to be sourced from FAW subsidiaries, as of 1997 the joint venture was only managing to source 15% from FAW subsidiaries.[95] The DCAC contract stated that a Dongfeng supplier had to be given preference if it was comparable in quality and price to another supplier, but they rarely were. In 1997, only 20 of the 153 DCAC suppliers

---

[93] In 1995, SAW produced a total of 181,267 vehicles, of which 5,111 were cars. FAW produced 220,525 vehicles that year, of which 43,703 were cars. *Zhongguo Qiche Gongye: 1996* (1996: 24).

[94] VW, the manager commented, spent decades developing its car production techniques in manufacturing operations around the world. FAW was trying to start at the top, rather than making the step-by-step progression that was so important. An example of the inappropriateness of the FAW background was the equipment: the specifications of the parts manufactured by FAW equipment rarely was consistent enough for FAW-VW. Interview, no. C6, July 23, 1997.

[95] Interview, no. C7, July 25, 1997.

were subsidiaries of Dongfeng.[96] "The technical level of the Chinese partner is very low," commented the French manager of one joint venture with a Dongfeng subsidiary, "good enough for trucks perhaps, but not good enough for cars."[97]

The inability of the Chinese partners to actively support supplier development was matched by a distinct lack of interest. FAW or Dongfeng would certainly have been pleased to see the manufacturing capability of local suppliers develop as it had in Shanghai, but given the scope of their operations and obligations this was not their top priority. Again, while SAIC's manufacturing operations were limited primarily to SVW (hence its strong desire to build up supply firms), FAW and Dongfeng had extensive manufacturing operations and a wide range of ties with enterprises throughout China. Even when these enterprises were not officially tied to the enterprise group, they would pay the group's management for the privilege of having preferential ties.[98] Sometimes these pre-existing ties created conflict of interests. In Wuhan, for example, there was one case where a foreign manufacturer was invited by Citroen to establish a JV, but once the factory was built and manufacturing began it had trouble obtaining even 50% of the DCAC business. It turned out that Dongfeng had a well-established relationship with another supplier in Fujian Province and the Chinese supply managers at DCAC were reluctant to break the well-established ties with the old supplier. The new JV was given the "opportunity to contribute" by the Dongfeng managers, but declined.[99] At Dongfeng, old relationships and old habits are not easily changed.

Second, from the perspective of FAW and Dongfeng, if FAW-VW and DCAC were absorbing their workers and lightening their social welfare burden, they were doing an effective job. Profits certainly would have been welcomed, but losses were not necessarily a major problem either.

---

[96] Interview, no. W13, May 15, 1997.

[97] Interview, no. W17, May 9, 1997.

[98] In her study of SAW, Kate Hannan notes that for the priviledge of membership, smaller enterprises "provided funds for the conglomerate's management that were outside the purview and so the direct control of government administrations. These funds were able to be used without tedious explanation and manipulation of government rules and regulations." Hannan (1998: 34).

[99] Sourcing decisions at DCAC are officially by consensus, but according to this supply manager it is the view of the Chinese representatives from SAW which is decisive. Given that Dongfeng held a 70% stake in the JV this is perhaps not surprising. "Side-payments" are, of course, illegal for many foreign companies, but these restrictions are not expected to prevent their Chinese partners from making the necessary payments. Interview, no. W8, May 9, 1997.

In many cases, budget constraints continued to be soft. "If we lose money the government will bail us out depending on the reason for the problem," explained the Chinese manager of a supply firm in Changchun. "If the problem is an economic one they will not help us, but if it is political they will."[100] Fortunately for the firm, almost all problems could be defined as political: the adverse impact of a related firm's financial difficulties (e.g. triangular debt), market difficulties (since political policies shape the market), etc. The incentives of the Chinese partners were further weakened by the fact that they had very little at risk in the supply firms; the capital investment of the Chinese partners in most of these JVs was minimal.

C. Expansion of the Enterprise Groups

From a national perspective, it would appear that FAW and Dongfeng were pursuing the optimal strategy; rather than focusing exclusively on the development of a purely local supply base to support the joint venture projects, the two business groups were national in focus. By acquiring smaller firms across the country, the two firms were expanding beyond their home base and becoming truly national in scope. Expansion of this sort would allow the firms not only to achieve greater economies of scale, but also benefit from specialization between its divisions and the harmonization of product structures. By rationalizing the industrial structure of the auto industry, the national groups countered the regionalism that so often plagued industrial development in China. The beneficial effects of such expansion could only be achieved, however, if it was driven by economic rationales rather than administrative edict, and as I argued in Chapter 2, this was not always the case.

Top government and enterprise leaders had strong incentives to push for consolidation within the industry. From the perspective of the top management of the large enterprise groups, expansion increased their bureaucratic power and the level of government support. From the perspective of government policy makers, mergers and acquisition were an ideal method of disguising the problems of loss-making SOEs. Rather than going bankrupt, smaller firms were simply swallowed up by larger

---

[100] This firm was a SOE controlled by Jilin Province, but it is indicative of many SOEs in Changchun. It is worth noting that the government would not bail out a JV, but the Chinese parent company which was affected by the problems at a JV. Interview, no. C2, July 21, 1997.

firms; bankruptcy and mergers were discussed as alternatives to each other without a clear distinction between when either alternative was most appropriate.

The acquisition of moribund SOEs was a risky business. The primary danger was that the strength of the core firm would be diluted. The problems at a loss-making enterprise did not necessarily disappear just because it merged with a larger firm. Mid-level managers within the auto groups pointed to the dangers of continual expansion: rather than strengthen the acquired company, the new additions often served to weaken the strength of the broader enterprise group. When FAW, acquired a new company, for example, it could resuscitate it by sending new managers to the firm or allowing it to manufacture a product that was more marketable, but FAW was in a rather precarious position itself.[101] The weaker enterprise leaned on the stronger, commented researchers at the FAW Changchun Automobile Research Institute, and although there was little benefit for FAW, the government usually gave them little choice.[102]

The structure of the national groups was in many respects ill-suited for taking on additional burdens. Given the difficulty that FAW and Dongfeng had managing existing members of the group, it was unlikely that their rudimentary organizational structures would be able to smoothly manage newly acquired firms in distant provinces – existing problems with internal monitoring would only be exacerbated by increased size and scope.[103] In Shanghai, the government also directed the expansion of the local auto group, but growth was supported fully by the municipal government, and could be controlled and monitored by the relatively well-developed organizational structure of SAIC. As I will explain in greater detail in the next chapter, a concerted effort was made in the late-1990s to formalize governance structures within Shanghai; each firm had a board of directors

---

[101] Giving products to newly acquired firms also created additional difficulties for local firms in Changchun and Wuhan which were not group members because they were abandoned as suppliers if the group acquired a firm that had (or developed) an overlapping product line. Interview, no. W24, April 4, 1997.

[102] Interview, no. C10, July 22, 1997.

[103] In the early years of expansion, there were also cross-jurisdictional political problems in many cases, as different localities both tried to secure manufacturing operations. For an example of the political problems that emerged in the merger of Jilin City Auto Company and Changchun First Auto Manufacturing Factory, see "Yiqi jituan fahui qunti youshi, youhua chanpin jiegou, cengjiang jingzheng shili," [FAW group brings into play the strengths of a conglomerate, improved product structure, and increased competitive strength] in Industrial Group Division of the National Economic and Trade Commission (1995: 12–13).

that linked it to the asset management structure, and the composition of the board was based on equity shares. At the top of the three-tiered system was the mayor.

At FAW, despite efforts to create a similar system, matters were more complicated. The linkage to the central government remained unchanged: the president reported directly to the central government. It was impossible to clarify ownership and create a board of directors, as was done in Shanghai, because this would force the central government to decide exactly who was in charge of FAW oversight. Within the group, the wide array of arrangements that characterized relationships between firms and the FAW head office during the mid-1990s were replaced by straight forward equity ties.[104] When FAW acquired a new firm, it would choose directors for the board of the firm in accordance with its equity stake. This system did not determine who was responsible for the financial and social burdens of the new firms (debts, pension obligations, etc.), however, and these became critical issues in each new set of negotiations.[105]

III. CONCLUSION

The cases of Changchun and Wuhan reaffirm the importance of the municipal government and the corporate group in nurturing the development of local suppliers, and the difficulty of converting old institutional structures for new uses. First, in both cities the local governments had insufficient capital to invest in supplier development and insufficient influence over the centrally-controlled corporate groups. Supply firms were very much on their own: they could depend on the local government neither for investment capital, nor for smoothing relations with the assembly plant. The municipal governments were eager to promote local development, but because they had little influence over the nationally-controlled business groups, they simply did not have the tools to do so. Second, the structure of the national enterprise groups was inappropriate for promoting local supplier development. The long history of the groups meant that they were heavily burdened with non-financial interests, and their size and scope decreased their ability to monitor the performance of firms.

The comparison of Changchun and Wuhan to Shanghai also helps to clarify the argument about the importance of industrial history. It is not necessarily a large production base that is important – there can be as

---

[104] On the many forms of relationships within FAW during the 1990s, see Marukawa (1999).
[105] Interview, no. C13, January 17, 2003.

many bad habits as good – but the manner in which local institutions structure industrial firms. In contrast to Shanghai, where the local government
and SAIC worked closely together to insure that supply firms were developing appropriate technical capabilities, at both FAW and Dongfeng the
internal monitoring systems were weak, and there was more interest in
absorbing the social burden created by excess workers than in increasing
technical skills. When FAW and Dongfeng were first created they were
both viewed as the pride of the socialist command economy. The weight
of this history made it difficult for them to become the pride of the newly-
created market economy.

Despite the difficulties of local suppliers, FAW-VW has emerged as
a dominant player in the domestic auto industry. The divergence with
DCAC in this respect points to the critical role of the foreign partner
at the level of the assembly plant. VW was successful in Shanghai, and
although it struggled during the early years in Changchun, the reported
profit levels and production volumes of FAW-VW are now comparable
to SVW (see Figures 2.3 and 2.4) – obviously much of the credit must go
to VW. At this later stage, one in which the domestic base of supply firms
was more developed than in the late-1980s and early-1990s, weakness at
home even had its advantages. As a manager at FAW-VW commented
in 2003, while his counterparts at SVW had to struggle to use non-SAIC
suppliers, he was able to use whatever supplier was most qualified.[106]
There was not the presumption that business would stay local.

Would high volumes at the assembly plant translate into a successful
community of supply firms? It is still too soon to know for certain, but it
does seem clear that the composition of this supply base will not be the
same as one which benefited from a decade and a half of nurturing. In
the more competitive domestic market that has emerged since China's
accession to the WTO, assemblers are forced to quickly make the transition to global standards of quality and efficiency, and in Changchun,
only global suppliers can maintain the necessary standards – they are
"local" in terms of geography, but little else. In the next section of the
book I focus on the second stage of auto sector development in China,
the period during which well-established firms, faced with the prospect of
lower tariff barriers, are struggling to increase their competitiveness. The
intent is to understand how the first decade of development prepares a
supply network for the challenge of global competition.

---

[106] Interview no. C14, January 17, 2003.

PART III

DEEPENING GLOBAL INTEGRATION

SEVEN

Global Integration and the Challenge of Upgrading

Shanghai succeeded in the initial stage of auto sector development because the local government took on many of the roles of a developmental state. Firms needed nurturing, and local officials provided it. Even though competition was limited during this period, no other municipality in China did this as well; the institutional infrastructure of Shanghai was particularly well suited for the development of capital- and scale-intensive manufacturing industries. The problem, however, was that Shanghai was succeeding under a very distinct set of circumstances – tariffs were high and products were stable – and just as the municipality was beginning to reap the gains of having mastered this stage of development, the rules of the game began to change. A dramatic rise in FDI and impending accession to the WTO resulted in increasing domestic competition, and cutting costs and increasing technical sophistication replaced the creation of basic manufacturing capability as the primary objective of the local industry.

How effectively would the various municipal auto sectors adjust as the level of global integration increased? None of them were close to being internationally competitive at the end of the 1990s. In 1996, after a decade of development and immediately prior to the dramatic increase in competitiveness, the Development Research Centre of China's State Council commissioned a report on the overall competitiveness of the Chinese auto industry. The authors concluded that the domestic industry was producing cars that were of inferior technology (5–15 years behind), emitted far more pollutants (14.5 times the hydrocarbon, 11.8 times the carbon monoxide, 3.3 times the nitric oxide), and yet were still two to three times the price of comparable foreign cars.[1] The productivity of Chinese auto firms was much lower than global standards, and there were virtually no exports at this stage.[2] This conclusion, of course, should not be surprising – an auto industry cannot be created overnight, and creating basic manufacturing capability was a necessary first step. Unless costs were lowered and technical standards increased, however, even the Shanghai auto sector, the strongest in China, would be wiped out by international competition when tariff barriers were lowered. "If we don't have a period of adjustment before tariffs are lowered," commented Peter Loew, the deputy managing director of SVW in 1997, "we're dead."[3]

A New Era of Competition . . .

The formal transition to the next stage of development in the Chinese auto sector was marked by a signing ceremony in Qatar on November 11, 2001, the day that China was officially voted in to the WTO. The terms of the accession agreement provided an adjustment period for the auto industry, but it was far from generous: tariffs on imported cars were set to decrease from 100% to 25% by 2006, tariffs on auto components would decrease from an average of 24% to 10% by 2006, and quotas on auto imports would be phased out in 2005.[4]

The informal adjustment to these changes began prior to actual accession, however. Although it is difficult to pinpoint exactly when auto firms began to operate under the assumption that WTO accession was imminent, there is good reason to believe that another signing ceremony, this one in Beijing's Great Hall of the People on March 25, 1997, marked a key turning point.[5] Shanghai General Motors (SGM) was the first JV established with the objective of being able to operate competitively in a

---

[1] Long (1996).
[2] Foreign rivals were producing 20–40 cars per worker as compared to the 2–4 cars per worker in China. Liu and Woo (2001: 153). In 1999, China exported 326 sedans. *Zhongguo Qiche Jishu Yanjiu Zhongxin* (2000: 66).
[3] Interview, no. S7, May 22, 1997.
[4] United Nations Conference on Trade and Development (2000: 54).
[5] This signing ceremony attracted attention for many reasons. The headlines say it all: Paul Blustein, "Paying to enter China's shop; economists question Boeing, GM contract concessions," *The Washington Post*, March 26, 1997, p. C11; Douglas Turner, "As Al Gore smiles at Li Peng, our jobs go to China," *The Buffalo News*, March 31, 1997, p. 2b (editorial page); Tom Korski, "Boeing and GM sign China deals amid 'political' grumbles," *South China Morning Post*, p. 1.

post-WTO China; costs were still far too high, but the product was technically equal (if not exactly cutting edge) to those available in international
markets. Rudy Schlais, the president of GM China called his company's
enormous investment an effort to "rewrite the very meaning of competition in the Chinese market," and in some respects it did.[6] But it would
take more than enormous investment to survive the competitive forces
that were quickly unleashed in the Chinese automotive industry.

The combination of impending tariff reductions and increased domestic competition pushed into motion a gradual convergence with international standards. First, the technical level of the products increased. After
the entrance of SGM, and the construction of its state-of-the-art facility
in Pudong, the eastern part of Shanghai that was transformed from farm-
land to an industrial and financial center during the 1990s, it was no longer
possible to ship an old assembly line to China and produce cars that were
two decades behind international standards. The SGM Buick Regal might
not have been particularly appropriate for the Chinese market, but it was
a completely different generation of automobile than the SVW Santana,
and it raised the bar for what would be acceptable in the Chinese marketplace. SVW reached a peak market share in 1996, with a product that was
based on 1970s technology, and then suddenly was confronted by a full
range of modern cars: the Buick was introduced in Shanghai, the Audi A6
and VW Bora in Changchun, and the Honda Accord in Guangzhou.[7] In
2000, SVW finally introduced the Passat; in 2001, after years of minimal
new investment, VW announced that it would invest US$2.2 billion in its
China operations.[8] The Chinese market (and government) was demanding cars at, or at least close to, international standards, and the newly
created joint ventures were delivering the latest models.

Second, the level of competition increased dramatically. After a decade
of rather gentlemanly competition between the five joint ventures in the
passenger vehicle market, the creation of SGM was followed by new
agreements signed by, among others, Honda (1997), Fiat (1999), Toyota

---

[6] Rudy Schlais, as quoted in "Driving In Reverse: China's Car Industry Hoodwinked By
Foreign Auto Giants?" *ChinaOnline*, January 17, 2000 (accessed April 4, 2003).
[7] After rising steadily for a decade, SVW's market share reached a peak of 54% in 1996
(see "Shanghai Volkswagen produces 800,000th Santana," *Xinhua News Agency*, May 30,
1997), and then began a gradual decline as competition intensified. In the first half of
2002, SVW had a market share of 26%, see "China's automotive industry shows signs of
improvement," *Asia Pulse*, October 23, 2002.
[8] "VW to invest another US$2.2 billion in China," ChinaOnline, December 12, 2001
(accessed September 22, 2002).

(2002), Hyundai (2002), Nissan (2002), and Ford (2003).[9] Although tariffs were not lowered until 2005, the central government used an increase in the number of joint ventures to raise the level of domestic competition prior to the onslaught of international competition.[10] The increase in the number of joint ventures was matched at the lower end of the market by an increase in the number of Chinese firms (with no foreign partners) offering less expensive models.[11]

The composition of the Chinese automotive market was also going through a fundamental shift at this time. In 1996, at the end of the first decade of auto sector development, the majority of output continued to be sold to institutions (60%) and taxi companies (22%). The private market had grown considerably, but was still relatively small (18%). By 2002, however, institutional purchases had decreased to 35%, taxi sales were relatively constant at 25%, and private sales, driven by rising incomes and increased access to finance, had increased to 40% (and were expected to rise to 60% by 2007).[12] The growth of the private market created an enormous opportunity for auto manufacturers, but it was also a highly demanding constituency. Individual consumers were more responsive to price than institutional customers, and they were more concerned with quality and style. Perhaps most significantly, many seemed to be willing to delay their purchases until they were convinced that the impact of

[9] In 2002 alone, three foreign automakers invested over US$1 billion each in new 50–50 joint ventures: in August, Toyota committed to US$1.3 billion to a JV with First Auto Works; in September, Hyundai committed US$1.1 billion to a JV with Beijing Auto Industry Corp; in October, Nissan announced plans to invest US$1 billion in a JV with Dongfeng. From January 2002 to June 2003, foreign automakers invested a total of $6.3 billion in China. Automotive News (2004: 3).

[10] Because JVs accounted for less than 6% of domestic automakers in China in 2001, yet accounted for 60% of the profits, analysts increasingly called for more JVs as a way of increasing competitiveness prior to the fall in tariff barriers. Toward this end, Chen Jianguo, an official at the State Development Planning Commission, hinted in 2001 that dozens of new JVs might be approved over the course of the next decade. Gong Zhengzheng, "Auto sector to allow more joint ventures," *FT Asia Intelligence Wire*, June 13, 2001.

[11] These domestic firms (such as Zhejiang-based Geely and Anhui-based Chery) put undeniable pressure on the JVs, but at least initially they occupied a slightly different market niche. Until SGM introduced the Sail sedan at the end of 2001 and SVW introduced the Polo in 2002, no JVs were producing lower-end compact cars. Changan Suzuki, which produced the mini-sedan Alto is a partial exception, but given Suzuki's small stake (4.98% in September 2002) it is not a true JV.

[12] Gao (2003: 10). By 2003, privately owned vehicles made up 51.2% of the cars on the road in China. "China's 2003 Vehicle PARC," *Fourin China Auto Weekly*, January 11, 2004, p. 1.

WTO accession had sufficiently lowered prices. Gone were the days of a reliable institutional market; auto firms that hoped to survive had to provide consumers with a competitive price and an attractive product.

The result of these changes was increased competition and a dramatic decrease in the price of automobiles in China. The price of the basic Santana, for example, which peaked at over 200,000 RMB in the early 1990s had fallen to 89,900 RMB by 2004.[13] In 2002 and 2003 the intensity of the new competition was masked by an unprecedented growth in annual demand – an astounding 55% in 2002 and 75% in 2003 – but this would not last.[14] Much of the boom was driven by private consumers taking advantage of easy access to auto loans, and when the central government pulled the plug on financing in an effort to cool a red hot economy, auto sector demand quickly evaporated. Growth rates remained high by world standards (in the vicinity of 10–12%), but looming overcapacity in the industry and the number of new competitors created an ominous cloud over the industry. Volkswagen, a firm that earned over two-thirds of its global profits in China in 2003 and enjoyed a 50% marketshare not too many years before this, was fighting to remain profitable and retain market share in 2005.[15] Anhui-based Chery, which did not begin producing cars until 1999, had annual sales of over 80,000 cars only four years later and was announcing ambitious (and in the view of many, implausible) export plans.[16] Beijing Hyundai, which did not begin production until the December of 2002, had the top selling car in the first quarter of 2005.[17] As the head of Volkswagen China commented in the spring of 2005, China had suddenly become "the toughest market in the world."[18] The fate of individual firms would inevitably fluctuate over time, but the intensity of the competion would not.

---

[13] In late 2004, the VW Jetta was selling for RMB 100,000, a third cheaper than the price three years before. "Tumbling prices fail to increase car sales," *South China Morning Post*, August, 18, 1995. "Shanghaied; China's car market," *The Economist*, April 23, 2005.

[14] "Shanghaied; China's car market," *The Economist*, April 23, 2005.

[15] According to some reports, the market share of the VW Group had fallen to 10% in the first quarter of 2005. At the same time, Goldman Sachs was forecasting that VW would lose over $500 million in China in 2005. Volkswagen assured the public that this would not be the case. "Shanghaied; China's car market," *The Economist*, April 23, 2005. "Volkswagen remains upbeat about its Chinese business," *Asia Pulse*, April 27, 2005.

[16] Chris Buckley, "Skepticism greets global ambitions of an upstart Chinese carmaker," *International Herald Tribune*, January 7, 2005, p. 13.

[17] Beijing Hyundai sold 56,064 units of its Elantra model in the first quarter of 2005. "Hyundai leads other automakers in car sales," *Xinhua Economic News Service*, April 21, 2005.

[18] Geoff Dyer, "Carmakers feel pain in Chinese market," *Financial Times*, April 23, 2005.

In this highly competitive environment, the challenges for Chinese supply firms are obvious. In the initial stage of auto sector growth, when firms had the benefit of high levels of protection, the joint venture assembly plants had no choice but to use local suppliers. Local content requirements were imposed by the government, imported components were too expensive, and wholly foreign-owned supply firms were difficult to establish. The challenges of supplier development during this stage were not insignificant, but there were also few alternatives for assembly plants that sought to increase their output. In the second stage of development, the new rules of the game created a wider range of possibilities for assembly plants, and supply firms increasingly had to compete on their merits; if a supplier did not meet the quality, price, and service needs of a customer, the assembler could import the necessary components or turn to wholly foreign-owned ventures.

Although the implications of these shifts are far from being fully realized, the signs that assemblers are beginning to rationalize their supply networks are clearly evident. The total value of component exports from China is increasing, but the even more rapid increase of component imports suggests that at least in the near-term trade liberalization is leading to a predictable outcome: sophisticated components (such as automatic transmissions, anti-lock braking systems, and steering systems) are being imported while more labor intensive and low-tech products (such as tires, audio equipment, and wiring) are being exported.[19] The danger – and the likely outcome if the general trend in other Chinese industries is any indication – is that auto part firms will be forced to compete on the basis of cost in relatively low value-added manufacturing while multinational firms dominate the higher value-added portions of the supply chain.[20]

. . . and the Need for Upgrading

Sustained competitiveness requires upgrading, what Amsden and Chu define as "exploiting a different set of competitive assets from previously,

---

[19] According to Fourin, auto component exports from China reached US$5.9 billion in 2003 (an increase of 27% over the previous year); imports for the same year were US$7.2 billion (an increase of 71% over the previous year). "20 billion dollars total, 4.8 billion trade deficit," *Fourin China Auto Weekly*, April 5, 2004, p. 2.

[20] On this general trend see Steinfeld, "Chinese enterprise development and the challenge of global integration," in Yusuf, Altaf, and Nabeshima, eds. (2004: Chapter 6).

using altered organizational and institutional structures to do so, and subjecting these structures to new mechanisms of discipline and control."[21] This chapter analyzes the process of technical upgrading in the Chinese auto sector, and in particular the extent to which supply firms in different localities have been able to meet the higher technical standards that the new models at assembly plants demand.

I argue that incremental development in the Shanghai region over the course of two decades has created a range of possibilities that do not currently exist in other regions. This is not to say that Shanghai is the only location with strong capabilities. An alternative approach is to lean even more heavily on foreign partners.[22] In a more liberal trade and investment environment, foreign direct investment can rapidly transform the auto sector of any region, and it has clearly done so in regions such as Guangzhou; grant an invitation to a strong foreign firm, give it free rein, and production volumes will rise in periods of strong demand. But while the rising tide of production will lift all firms in the supply network (foreign and domestic) there will inevitably be a strong dependence on foreign suppliers, and often these will be wholly foreign-owned. In an intense competitive environment, the pressure to quickly introduce advanced models and increase volumes makes it difficult to integrate local firms into the supply network; if local firms cannot meet the necessary schedule and standards for key components – and they usually cannot – there is no choice but to rely on the foreign suppliers or imports. The transformations of regions such as Guangzhou and Beijing, in short, tell us more about the capabilities of their foreign partners than of local firms, and the

---

[21] Amsden and Chu (2003: 1).

[22] A third alternative, and one that includes cases that were beyond the scope of this study, is to save on development cost by appropriating foreign design and technology without permission. The Geely Merrie closely resembles the Daihatsu Charade, Tongtian's Grow looks much like the VW Polo, and the Chery QQ and Oriental Son are identical to Daewoo's Matiz and Magnus, to name just a few ("China's original passenger cars," *Fourin China Auto Weekly*, August 2, 2004, p. 3). Many of these cases have led to lawsuits and investigations. It remains to be seen whether these companies can make the transition from "borrowed" designs and technology to independent development, but it is much too soon to rule them out. In part this is due to the skill with which they are capitalizing upon the capabilities that the foreign firms have created in China. The leading independent firms are filling their design centers with Chinese engineers that are trained either at JVs or at foreign firms, and astutely utilizing the capabilities of the supply base that the joint ventures have created (particularly in the Shanghai, Jiangsu, and Zhejiang region). The result is a growing ability on the part of firms such as Chery to provide the Chinese consumer with an attractive product at a fraction of the joint venture price.

business groups in these localities are unlikely to emerge with strong and independent manufacturing capabilities.

Shanghai firms continue to depend heavily upon their foreign partners, but the dynamic between foreign and local partners is quite different from the other regions that have joint ventures at the core of local auto development efforts. The contrast is visible in ownership structures, and in the capabilities that are being developed in a given locality. While other localities often attract foreign partners and promote auto sector growth by relinquishing control and ownership over the supply sector, the strength of the Shanghai auto sector allows SAIC and the local government to promote investment and growth while retaining a strong ownership share. Ownership matters because it determines the breadth of future possibilities for a Chinese firm; the skills and technology that it will be able to master and the potential for expansion beyond its home base. Ownership does not guarantee successful growth and expansion, but the lack of ownership (and complete domination by foreign firms) does guarantee that a Chinese firm will never be more than a local agent for its foreign partner. There is a stark contrast between Shanghai supply firms that are becoming systems integrators, building design centers, and expanding outside of the Shanghai region and business groups in other regions that continue to be partners at the assembly plant (as mandated by Chinese law) but are ever more dependant on outside firms for components or imports.

The first section of the chapter describes the nature of the upgrading challenge; the relationship between technology and the current structure of the global auto industry, and the obstacles this creates for developing countries. I use Mexico as an illustration of the difficulty of developing independent capabilities in the global auto industry. The second section considers each of the three different development approaches in China in turn – the local developmental state, the market-driven state, and the firm-dominated locality – with the purpose of establishing how the first stage of development prepared firms for meeting the demands of the second. In the next chapter I analyze the equally important (and difficult) task of upgrading the organizational and institutional structures that govern the allocation of resources within a Chinese business group.

I. THE GLOBALIZATION OF MANUFACTURING

Technology is both the obstacle and the solution for major auto assembly firms that hope to control global production networks. It is an obstacle in the sense that technology generates rapid change, and few companies have the development resources to remain on the cutting edge. Although the rate of change in the high-tech industry is the most celebrated, it is also a primary characteristic of seemingly mundane manufacturing industries such as the automotive. In just the last decade, for instance, the electronic functions in a car (electronic sensors, diagnostic systems, navigational systems, etc.) have approximately doubled, and contribute as much as 35% of the cost of a vehicle.[23] The modern car is as much an electronic product as it is a mechanical one. The competition to introduce the latest features made possible by new technologies (and meet the demands of an increasingly diverse set of consumers) leads to the proliferation of models, and the proliferation of technologically advanced models leads to rising development costs.[24]

Technology is also a solution to rising development costs, however, because it allows for the modularization of the production process and massive outsourcing. Technical advancements in transportation and communications, along with an improved ability to codify complex information through digitization, enables companies to both concentrate design and development of products and disperse the production of components.[25] A core company will focus on the design and marketing of a product, but then outsource modular units of related manufacturing activities to whatever suppliers meet the necessary quality, service, and price qualifications.

Auto companies have taken the lead in this respect.[26] Products are grouped around common underbody platforms and interchangeable modules, and these platforms are launched globally; not only can slight alterations to a model be made as consumer preferences change over time, but slightly different versions of a model (on a single platform) can be created for different parts of the global market. The role of global suppliers

---

[23] Veloso (2000: 6). To give an indication of how Chinese cars lag in this respect, the average electronics content of a vehicle in the global auto industry was 27.5% in 2004 as compared to 5.8% in China. "China's Automotive Electronics Sector: Demand Expected to Soar to 250 Billion RMB by 2010," *Fourin China Auto Weekly*, December 6, 2004, p. 1.

[24] The number of different vehicle models offered for sale in the U.S. alone doubled between 1990 and 1999, a period in which demand was essentially flat, Veloso (2000: 5). On the saturation of markets in developed economies, see Sturgeon and Florida (1999: Table 6-6).

[25] For work on international production networks, see Borrus, Ernst, and Haggard (2000).

[26] Although outsourcing and modularity are general trends in the auto industry, the extent to which they are utilized varies widely by company and region. Timothy J. Sturgeon and Richard K. Lester, "The new global supply base: New challenges for local suppliers in East Asia," in Yusuf, Altaf, and Nabeshima, eds. (2004: 62).

in this process is critical, of course. The first tier suppliers design entire systems, or modules of the car, organize the necessary supply networks for these systems, and then deliver completed modules to the assembly plant.[27] The intent of both the platform strategy and the reliance on global suppliers is to save on development cost. Global platforms spread the costs of development more widely by creating greater economies of scale for each model and the rise of global suppliers passes a large part of the design burden for individual modules on to the supply firms.

There are pros and cons for both sides of this relationship. From the perspective of the assembler, having a global supplier that can integrate an entire subsystem of the car saves it a tremendous amount of trouble and cost, but it means that the first-tier supplier must either follow the assembler to new manufacturing locations, or transfer its technology to a local firm at the new location, because the technical and manufacturing knowledge is increasingly at the level of the global supplier. From the perspective of the global supplier, it is able to capture a valuable piece of the global production chain, but the valuable long-term contracts are awarded only on the condition of continuous improvement in quality (often to higher standards than the assembler's own) and guaranteed annual price reductions. Outsourcing of this sort is perhaps not as dramatic as in the computer industry, but it is not out of the question that the larger of these first-tier suppliers could some day serve as contract manufacturers, producing whole vehicles that are then sold under a particular brand.[28]

Although outsourcing and global platforms are partial solutions to rapid technical change and the rising cost of development, there still are an ever fewer number of firms that have the resources necessary to stay on the cutting edge. The result has been massive consolidation, with the smaller firms being integrated into the global strategies of the larger. Ford

---

[27] Between 1985 and 1997, for example, the value of Peugeot-Citroen cars that was outsourced increased from 45% to 70%. The total number of direct suppliers to Peugeot-Citroen went from 900 in 1986 to 500 in 1996. During the same period, the number of suppliers at Ford decreased from 2400 to 1200 and at Chrysler from 3000 to 1000. Veloso (2000: 10–11). For an excellent diagram of component modularity in the auto industry, see Sturgeon and Lester, in Yusuf, Altaf, and Nabeshima, eds. (2004: 57).

[28] In some locations, this extreme of contract manufacturing has almost been achieved. VW, for instance, has been using a modular consortium approach in its Resende, Brazil plant. It plays a strategic role in design and commercialization, but all of the actual manufacturing and assembly is done by suppliers. See Yannick Lung et al., "Flexibility through Modularity: Experimentation with Fractal Production in Brazil and in Europe," in Lung, Chanaron, Fujimoto, and Raff (1999).

owns Jaguar, Volvo, Land Rover, and Aston Martin; General Motors owns Saab and significant chunks of Suzuki, Isuzu, Subaru, Fiat, and Daewoo; Toyota control Daihatsu; Renault controls Nissan.[29] In 2001, six companies accounted for 59.1% of the word's total automobile production.[30] Given the increase in the responsibilities of first tier suppliers they have also been growing in size, mainly as a result of mergers. In 1992, there were only 28 U.S. suppliers with annual sales between US$1 and 5 billion and 5 companies with sales higher than US$5 billion. In 1998, these numbers were 47 and 13, respectively.[31]

It is here that one can begin to see the implications for developing countries such as China. If well-established automakers in developed economies have difficulty playing an independent role in the global game that the auto industry has become, how is a developing country (even one with huge market potential) supposed to create independent national champions? Given the integral nature of the design process – multiple firms working on distinct parts that come together in a single product – investment in a developing country is now a coordinated process; assemblers must work in conjunction with their major suppliers.[32] The result is a sharply constrained set of possibilities for local firms, because few can compete with the resources and design skills of the global firms. The very real fear of Chinese policymakers is that the opening up of the Chinese market will quickly lead Chinese supply firms to be replaced by global suppliers. This would not be without precedent.

The Threat of Denationalization

For a vision of the fate Chinese policymakers hope to avoid, all one need do is look to Mexico. Like in China, the government invited foreign firms to establish assembly plants within a protected market, but with careful restrictions. According to the 1962 Auto Decree, the foreign ownership of

---

[29] Kenney (1999). Saab, for instance, only recorded an annual profit twice in the 1990s, and was simply too small to fund its own development costs. "Analysts say Saab has suffered from ageing, unchanged body designs at a time when competitors have been bringing out redesigned models at a much faster pace." Nicholas George and Jeremy Grant, "Saab drives GM to launch 'thunderbolt'" *Financial Times*, November 21, 2002, p. 19.

[30] In the same year there were only 13 firms with annual production volumes over one million, and these 13 accounted for 87.4% of global production. Humphrey and Memedovic (2003: 6).

[31] Veloso (2000: 16).

[32] Humphrey and Memedovic (2003). Sturgeon and Lester, in Yusuf, Altaf, and Nabeshima, eds. (2004: 63–65).

supply firms was limited to 40%, and local content regulations were used to promote the development of local firms. The term *Mexicanization* was used to describe the government's desire to utilize foreign investment as a means of promoting the development of firms that were majority Mexican-owned and controlled.[33] The vehicles were not up to modern standards – the core VW model was the old Beetle – but, as in China, in a protected market the assemblers could find local suppliers and make a profit. A 1977 Auto Decree made exports a requirement for foreign assemblers operating in Mexico, and stipulated that 50% of these exports had to consist of parts from Mexican suppliers.[34]

Over the course of the 1980s, however, and in the context of a severe recession, the Mexican economy underwent significant liberalization, a process that culminated in the NAFTA negotiations. By the end of the 1980s this new policy approach was being applied to the auto sector: a limited number of imports were allowed, local content requirements were reduced, and assemblers were given more flexibility in their purchasing operations.[35] Liberalization, combined with the 1994 financial crisis and the subsequent devaluation of the peso and increase in domestic interest rates, led to an export boom from Mexico. Within four years of NAFTA's passage, exports to the United States had doubled, to more than 800,000 vehicles annually, and Mexico had attracted over US$11 billion in new auto sector investment.[36] By the end of the decade, virtually all major U.S. and Japanese auto firms had export-oriented manufacturing bases in Mexico.

The transformation into an export base, although profitable for the assembly firm, fundamentally transformed the nature of Mexican supply networks. When the assembly plants introduced new models for export, they were integrating their Mexican operations with their global operations.[37] A platform was designated for production in Mexico, and because the R&D for the platform had been done in conjunction with global suppliers, these suppliers had to co-locate with the assembly plant. It was

---

[33] Studer-Noguez (2002: 53–5). On the negotiations between the Mexican government and foreign firms over these terms, see Bennett and Sharpe (1985).

[34] Studer-Noguez (2002: 95).

[35] These policies were included in the 1989 Auto Decree. Studer-Noguez (2002: 184).

[36] Joel Millman, "Mexico is becoming hot destination . . . for auto production NAFTA treaty attracting U.S. and foreign car makers," *Toronto Star*, June 25, 1998, p. D6.

[37] See Studer-Noguez (2002: 209) for a detailed account of Ford's switch from a stand-alone approach to Mexican operations to a "global car" strategy in Mexico. By 1995, purchasing, engineering, and computer system functions for Mexican operations had all been switched from Mexico to Ford's U.S. headquarters.

not simply the need for export-level quality, although this was a problem, but the fact that the assembler could not manufacture large modules of the car without the cooperation (or consent) of the global supplier.[38] The result was that the local Mexican supply firms were replaced with large global suppliers.

Prior to 1994, for instance, one of the large American assemblers operating in Mexico had 350 to 400 suppliers in the country, and of these, approximately 40 to 60 were wholly owned Mexican firms.[39] In the six years after the 1994 crisis, the assembler's volumes in Mexico increased by 2 to 3 times, but due to rationalization efforts, the number of suppliers was reduced to 180. Only 3 of these suppliers were wholly Mexican owned, and 95% were U.S.-owned. Although quality may in some cases have been an issue, the more serious problem was a shift in manufacturing philosophy at the assembler, according to which supply firms were part of an "extended enterprise" for a particular platform. The suppliers were chosen based on quote packages tendered prior to design work, the suppliers then designed the components for which they were responsible in conjunction with the assembler.[40] The U.S. assembler would have been willing to work with a Mexican supply firm, but the firm would have to have had design capability, leading technology, and an office in Detroit so as to be able to work in conjunction with the assembler's engineers – a high standard.[41]

The story at Volkswagen de Mexico is much the same. Prior to 1994, the assembler had a strong network of local supply firms, but when new models were introduced after the crisis, the shift was made to global suppliers. For the new Jetta and Beetle, for instance, suppliers were chosen in the design phase,[42] contracts are for the life of a model and have built-in cost reductions, and each supplier must make a commitment to supply for

---

[38] Valdes-Ugalde (2002) argues that "the technological gap between US and Mexican firms is too large, so innovative processes have to be imported.... Thus, we may conclude that, in Mexico, the opportunities provided by NAFTA for access to foreign technology have not been exploited: technology had neither been disseminated, nor spread, nor assimilated by Mexican firms."

[39] The information in this paragraph is from Interview, no. M2, May 12, 2000.

[40] The assembler would measure the performance of long-term suppliers and work with them to achieve cost reductions. These cost savings were then split 50/50.

[41] One Mexican supplier, Macimex (a crankshaft producer), has succeeded in doing all this.

[42] VW has established a design facility in Mexico but it primarily does modifications of existing designs (for example, designing a cup-holder capable of holding the large coffee cups so prevalent in the U.S. market). Major model designs will continue to be done in Germany. Interview, no. M3, May 15, 2000.

the model on a worldwide basis. Between 1996 and 1998, approximately 30 European companies came to Mexico to support the VW assembly plant.[43] The result is a highly sophisticated supply operation in Puebla, Mexico consisting of some 60 firms: the majority of major suppliers are within one industrial park, and logistics are coordinated on a just-in-time basis.[44] The participation of local firms has decreased: only 2 or 3 Mexican suppliers are used for the new platform, and the number of European suppliers is increasing as models change.[45]

Visitors to the Puebla facility in 2000 found a strange juxtaposition of two worlds. In one building was a highly automated manufacturing line, assembling the components of mostly European suppliers into new Beetles. These were bound for world markets – the Puebla facility is the sole manufacturing site for the new Beetle.[46] In the building next door the old Beetle, built for the Mexican market (and now discontinued), was assembled 100% by hand. In comparison to the assembly line for the new Beetle, it was "like the Flintstones," commented one VW manager.[47]

In making the dramatic shift from the stone age of manufacturing to a state-of-the-industry facility, the contribution of the VW operations to the Mexican economy is considerable, and not just simply as a source of tax revenue. VW salaries are among the highest manufacturing salaries in the country, and its workers are able to hone their skills in a training facility modeled on the German apprenticeship program.[48] A third of these workers leave the VW plant after their training is complete, and their skills enrich the broader supply base. But for policymakers interested in

---

[43] The decision is not always one of choice. As the Mexican commercial director of Benteler, a maker of structural metal components and a VW supplier, explained, "We had to move to Mexico to keep the [VW] business." Elisabeth Malkin and Jonathan Wheatley, "Parts shops are tailgating carmakers in Latin America," *Business Week*, October 23, 2000, p. 56.

[44] VW has outsourced logistics to Exel, a Spanish company. When a particular car is 80 minutes from final assembly, an electronic signal is sent to Exel with the sequencing information and the bill of materials. Exel sends this on to suppliers (some of whom will only then manufacture the component) and then coordinates the collection of the components, and delivers them to the assembly line. Interview, no. M4, May 15, 2000.

[45] Interview, no. M3, May 15, 2000.

[46] Shipping a completed car from Mexico to Europe costs US$300, according to VW managers, only $50 more than the shipping costs to the U.S.

[47] Interview, no. M3, May 15, 2000. Robots are used in the assembly of the new Beetle because the levels of precision required by the design of the car are too high to achieve by hand.

[48] VW has had, at times, contentious relations with its unions in Mexico, but the union is quite powerful, and has been successful in achieving many demands. Labor strife is more severe in the supply firms.

developing locally owned firms, it is undeniable that VW de Mexico works with very few Mexican-owned firms. Although denationalization of this sort is hardly unusual – it has happened in Brazil, Thailand, and even to a certain extent, Korea – it is exactly the result that Chinese policymakers hope to avoid.[49]

II. TECHNICAL UPGRADING IN THE CHINESE AUTO INDUSTRY

Measuring the technical capabilities of local firms – the ability to competently perform certain activities in the value chain – and their ability to adjust and upgrade as the competitive environment changes is not without its challenges, and it is particularly difficult when the evolutionary process is far from complete.

The most persuasive evidence of technical upgrading would be export performance; it is a standard "control" mechanism for governments that seek to assess the relative performance of domestic firms.[50] Data on exports provides us with limited evidence thus far, however. Although auto part exports from China have been growing rapidly – the value of auto part exports increased 75.7% in 2004 to US$10.4 billion – they are still a relatively recent phenomena.[51] Even more importantly, there is limited data on the geographic breakdown of these exports.[52] There are only two component firms listed among the top ten automotive exporters in 2003. The number three exporter is a SAIC firm that manufactures interiors, Shanghai Yanfeng Johnson Controls (US$94 million in exports), and the number five firm is Kunshan Liufeng Machinery, a Taiwanese-Japanese wheel manufacturer located outside of Shanghai

---

[49] "In 1995," according to Humphrey and Memedovic (2003: 30), "ten of the 20 largest component manufacturers in Brazil (by value of sales) were wholly or majority locally owned. By 1998, seven of these ten firms had been taken over by transnational companies." In Thailand, virtually all of the 250 first tier suppliers are subsidiaries or affiliates of foreign firms. Doner, Noble, and Ravenhill, "Production Networks in East Asia's Automobile Parts Industry," in Yusuf, Altaf, and Nabeshima, eds. (2004: 172). In Korea, more than 100 component firms are estimated to have transferred 50% of more of their equity to foreign firms since the financial crisis. John Ravenhill, "From National Champions to Global Partners: Crisis, Globalization, and the Korean Auto Industry," in Keller and Samuels (2003: 133).

[50] See Amsden (2001: 8).

[51] "China's automotive import/export: automobile related trade deficit halved in 2004," *Fourin China Auto Weekly*, April 4, 2005, p. 5.

[52] The *China Automotive Industry Yearbook* does not include data on export volumes by region.

(US\$67.9 million in exports).[53] The remaining component firms among the top 50 exporters produce a range of products – tires, car audio, aluminum wheels, brake discs, universal joints, bearings, and glass – and are scattered throughout China. The most obvious trend is the prominence of independent (and often private) Chinese firms such as Wanxiang (based in Zhejiang Province) and Torch Automotive Group (based in Hunan Province) that have had rapid success in penetrating foreign aftermarket and replacement parts markets.[54] Fewer firms have broken into global OEM networks, but many of those that have are Shanghai firms. Shanghai Koito, a JV between SAIC (50%), Koito Manufacturing (45%), and Toyota Tsusho (5%), began exporting auto lights to General Motors in 2003, and signed contracts to supply Ford and Daimler-Chrysler in 2004.[55] Delphi, which has seven joint ventures in the Shanghai region, sourced US\$250 million from China in 2003 and intends to increase this amount to US\$1 billion by 2007.[56] Japanese manufacturers have just begun to export components from the growing base in Guangzhou.[57]

Within the domestic market, which continues to be the primary focus of most Chinese automotive firms, the overall strength of the Shanghai supply sector has proven to be durable as competition has increased. Not only was the value of Shanghai's output three times greater than any other locality in 2003, it has also helped transform the neighboring

[53] The list of top 50 automotive exporters (by firm) published by Fourin is dominated by motorcycle firms (15), manufacturers of light and heavy commercial vehicles (9), and tire companies (8). "20 billion dollars total, 4.8 billion trade deficit," *Fourin China Auto Weekly*, April 5, 2004, p. 6.

[54] See "Local supplier focus: Wanxiang looks to expand beyond China," *Fourin China Auto Weekly*, June 7, 2004 and "Torch Automobile Group: Parent company's financial troubles curtail business," *Fourin China Auto Weekly*, January 11, 2005.

[55] Shanghai Koito has the largest share of the China's auto lighting market. By November 2003 it had exported US\$5 million to General Motors. "Automotive Lighting System Manufacturing in China," *Fourin China Auto Weekly*, June 21, 2004, p. 1. Shanghai Koito opened a US\$8.3 million automobile headlight technology center with 120 engineers in 2003.

[56] Currently, Delphi exports are largely labor-intensive products such as wire harness. Half of the revenue for Delphi Electric Shanghai Systems, for instance, is from exports. This firm has been designated a GM "Best Supplier" (200 out of 30,000 companies) for three years in a row. "Global Suppliers in China: Bosch Pushes Technology, Delphi Expands Exports," *Fourin China Auto Weekly*, June 14, 2004, p. 5.

[57] Interview, no. T8, October 13, 2004. The investments of Japanese firms tend to be more recent than those of European and U.S. firms: 39% of Japanese projects began between 2001 and 2003 (as compared to 23% for European and U.S. firms). *"Seikai saiteki seisan jitsugen muke juushisareru nichibeiou buhin meegaa no chuugoku shinshutsu"* [Japanese, U.S., and European component makers advance in China to realize the most appropriate way of manufacturing in the world] *Fourin*, no. 91, October 2003, p. 1.

Output of Automotive Parts by Region in 2003 (in million RMB)

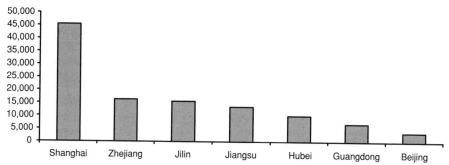

Figure 7.1: Output of automotive parts by region in 2003 (in million RMB). *Note*: Production of FAW and Dongfeng firms from *all* regions is counted under the location of their head offices (Jilin and Hubei, respectively). This is not a complete list; also in the top ten are Shandong (10,900), Chongqing (8,300), Liaoning (8,000), and Hunan (6,200). *Source*: "Auto Industry Development by Region," *Fourin China Auto Weekly*, January 24, 2005, p. 2.

provinces of Zhejiang and Jiangsu into major bases of component production (see Figure 7.1).[58] Unable and unqualified to assess the actual technical capabilities of firms in the manner of an engineer, I again focus on the sourcing patterns of each assembly plant. The assembly plants in Shanghai are most able to rely on local supply firms and other regions are also increasingly dependent on Shanghai firms (Tables 2.1 and 2.2).[59] As the joint venture assembly plants introduce models with higher technical demands throughout the country, they are forced to purchase components from technically superior supply firms, and these are often (although certainly not exclusively) in Shanghai. In many respects, this trend simply reflects the fact that technically superior supply firms generally require foreign investment, and the early success of the Shanghai auto industry (in addition to its overall appeal) has made it the dominant location for automotive foreign direct investment in China: 38% of European and U.S. automotive investments and 15% of Japanese investments were located

---

[58] On the relationship between Shanghai state-owned firms and supplier firms in Jiangsu and Zhejiang, see Buck (2002).

[59] This trend is confirmed by the statistical analysis of Tomoo Marukawa (2003: 143). Using the *Directory of Spare Parts Suppliers for Chinese Automobiles*, Marukawa codes the likelihood of an assembler using the suppliers of different regions (excluding aftermarket suppliers), and although he finds that overall most Chinese suppliers continue to serve primarily local customers, Shanghai is the one region that is heavily utilized by outside assemblers.

Location of Foreign Automotive Component Firms in 2003 (by project)

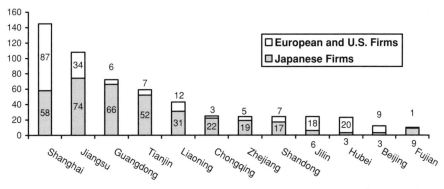

Figure 7.2: Location of foreign automotive component firms in 2003 (by project). *Note*: This chart only includes the twelve provinces with the highest number of foreign projects. Changchun (FAW-VW) is in Jilin Province; Wuhan (Dongfeng-Citroen) is in Hubei Province. *Source*: "*Seikai saiteki seisan jitsugen muke juushisareru nichibeiou buhin meegaa no chuugoku shinshutsu*" [Japanese, U.S., and European component makers advance in China to realize the most appropriate way of manufacturing in the world] *Fourin*, no. 91, October 2003, p. 2.

in Shanghai in 2003, and the percentages are even higher if neighboring Zhejiang and Jiangsu are included (see Figure 7.2).[60] In 2002, Bosch Shanghai provided 58% of China's engine management systems; Shanghai Delphi controlled 45% of the market for automotive air conditioners.[61]

Although the relative strength of Shanghai supply firms is clear, because of the prevalence of joint venture firms, it is extremely difficult to distinguish between the respective contributions of the Chinese and foreign partners. In an attempt to parse out the contribution of each, managers at supply firms were asked about the source of their technology, how new capabilities are developed as models change, and the roles of both the Chinese and the foreign partner in this process. SAIC firms

---

[60] "*Seikai saiteki seisan jitsugen muke juushisareru nichibeiou buhin meegaa no chuugoku shinshutsu*" [Japanese, U.S., and European component makers advance in China to realize the most appropriate way of manufacturing in the world], *Fourin*, no. 91, October 2003, p. 2.

[61] Bosch has invested 152 million RMB in a Shanghai engine management research center; Delphi has invested US$50 million in a Shanghai development center. "Global Suppliers in China: Bosch Pushes Technology, Delphi Expands Exports," *Fourin China Auto Weekly*, June 14, 2004.

continue to be heavily dependent on foreign partners for design and technology, but they play an important role in these partnerships. Firms within the market-driven localities, by contrast, have been largely abandoned in favor of outsiders. Beijing has dropped all pretences of creating a strong automotive business group: Beijing Jeep sources more components from Shanghai than it does from Beijing, Hyundai uses primarily Korean component firms and imports, and BAIC has essentially become a holding company that provides real estate and government connections to foreign partners that want a manufacturing base in China. Guangzhou is rapidly becoming a production base for Japanese firms. There is somewhat of a divergence between the centrally controlled SOEs: while supply firms in Wuhan continue to be weak, and DCAC supplies more than half of its component from Shanghai, the supply base in Changchun is small, but growing. Its suppliers have benefited from VW's success at the assembly JV.

The Local Developmental State

Local firms in Shanghai have not been replaced by global suppliers. Local suppliers have benefited from a process of incremental improvement driven by the foreign JV partners; technical capabilities have been gradually upgraded, and the level of integration with global suppliers has increased. The capabilities that have been developed are not independent, yet they are also not wholly foreign. The first stage of development provided the foundation upon which the second could be built.

The supplier standards demanded by Shanghai General Motors, beginning in 1997, were fundamentally different than those of Shanghai Volkswagen. The joint venture was producing a model that was technically more advanced, and the intention was to do so at export-level quality standards. It was acknowledged that costs would be far above international levels, but given the large price cushion created by tariff barriers, this was acceptable for the time being. The first step was to assess the capabilities of existing suppliers in China.[62] In 1996, after GM and SAIC had signed a MOU, a GM team spent 30,000 person-hours conducting two-day assessments of 1,000 suppliers throughout China. Only forty of these firms were deemed technically capable of meeting GM technical specifications: 35%

---

[62] The description of this process is based on two interviews. Interview, no. S34, June 30, 2000 and Interview, no. S43, August 6, 2002. The two accounts were the same.

were JVs, 65% were SOEs, and 5% were private Chinese firms.[63] Well over 50% of those firms that qualified as capable nationwide were within Shanghai, and about 70% of these were SAIC firms. Being capable did not mean that these firms were without problems – 100% of the SOEs would require further help – but they "*did* qualify" and usually it was because of the experience of supplying SVW. Without SVW and the financial support of the Shanghai municipal government, "GM would have had to start from zero" and the local suppliers would be "just another Chinese company...just like those outside Shanghai."[64] In the second stage of the process the "acceptable" firms were invited to submit bids for particular components, and product engineers from North America evaluated whether the suppliers had the capabilities to fulfill the bids (both technically and in terms of price), and then the bids were taken to the purchasing committee at SGM. Increasingly there was no escape for recalcitrant supply firms; the competitive pressure from SGM led SVW to launch the Passat in Shanghai, and thus SVW also was forced to begin pressuring supply firms to upgrade their capabilities.

In order to meet the new level of expectations of their customers, the common response of Shanghai supply firms between 1997 (formation of SGM) and 2000 (launch of Passat at SVW) was to increase their level of foreign cooperation. Foreign partners were needed not for financial capital – after a decade of highly profitable Santana business both SAIC and the supply firms could finance much of the upgrading internally – but for the technical and managerial skills.[65] In 1997, just under 30% of SVW suppliers were joint ventures (see Figure 7.3). By 2002, virtually every major firm within the SAIC group – approximately 90% of the total – was a joint venture.[66]

---

[63] This ownership breakdown corresponds well with the breakdown by ownership of SVW suppliers in 1997: 28% JVs, 12% SOEs with licensed technology, and 60% SOEs. See Figure 7.3.

[64] A problem in many cases was that technology was underutilized. With the support of the local government, supply firms had been able to purchase advanced technology, but because SVW was producing an old model they had never been pushed to fully utilize it. Interview, no. S34, June 30, 2000.

[65] One manager used blueprints as an example of the technical shortcomings of local firms. VW did all of its design work in Germany, and then simplified the blueprints before giving them to Chinese supply firms. When GM came to Shanghai they found that supply firms were simply not capable of handling the complexity of the designs that they were given. Interview, S34, June 30, 2000.

[66] Interview, no. S44, August 7, 2002. The firms that remained 100% SOE manufactured relatively minor parts such as springs.

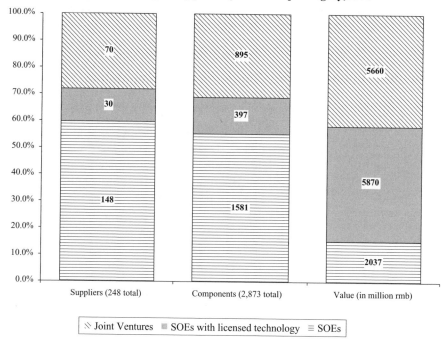

Figure 7.3: SVW suppliers by ownership category in 1997. *Source*: Shanghai Volkswagen.

The evolution of capabilities is particularly evident in firms that must compete on the basic of technology and design capabilities as opposed to labor. Firm A, one of the largest suppliers in the SAIC group, formed a joint venture with a U.S. global supply firm in 1994, but then had to undergo a major upgrading process in the late 1990s in order to obtain the business for the new models at SVW and SGM.[67] The objective of the firm was to integrate an entire system of tightly coupled components for the assembler, and have the capacity to cooperate on design functions. As was usually the case with new models, VW requested that the supplier in China use the exact same processes as the original supplier in Germany, and the Shanghai firm had to license the technology and buy the equipment from the European firm. In total, the joint venture spent US$60 million on this upgrading effort.[68]

---

[67] Interview, no. S52, January 21, 2003.
[68] As I mentioned, this firm, like many within the SAIC group, had large cash reserves from a decade of highly profitable SVW business, and could have financed this upgrading

Firm B had used the same technology for a key engine part – licensed from a German firm – for a decade as a supplier for the Santana, but a licensing arrangement was inadequate (it "is only a business relationship") when it sought to become a supplier for the new models at SGM and SVW.[69] Labor was only one-third of the total cost for the product it produced, and the technology that was required was relatively advanced. It sought a partner that would provide technology, managerial skills, and good relationships with customers. The German firm that it had a licensing agreement with fulfilled all three requirements, a joint venture was formed in 1998, and it was able to develop new components for SGM, SVW, and FAW-VW. Foreign exchange for new equipment came from the foreign partner's capital contribution to the new joint venture.

Firm C also produced key engine parts, and was moving towards an ability to provide the assembler with modular units, rather than individual components. It used a combination of low-interest loans and internal financing in the early 1990s to license technology from a foreign firm, and increased its annual production volumes from 30,000 units to 820,000.[70] When SVW introduced the Passat, the central government initially resisted allowing Firm C to form a JV – the firm had been very successful developing independent capabilities – but as competition intensified, and the global VW supplier resisted licensing technology due to concerns with respect to intellectual property rights, a new joint venture was formed.

In Shanghai, technology from foreign firms has been supplemented with design and development support. The 50/50 joint venture between General Motors and SAIC, the Pan Asia Technical Automotive Center (PATAC), plays a central role in strengthening local design skills, and is a very conscious effort on the part of GM to demonstrate their willingness to aid SAIC in its effort to cultivate design and development skills in China. "For China to have a globally competitive automotive industry, it must have its own vehicle development capacity," commented Phil Murtaugh, the head of General Motors in China.[71] In the short term, the

---

internally. Because the nature of the investment qualified as high-tech the JV was able to receive no-interest loans from the national government. The JV took the loans, banked its own money, and paid off the loans as soon as they were due.

[69] Interview, no. S42, July 13, 2000.

[70] For details on the financing arrangements during this period, see Chapter 4. This account is based on three interviews at the firm over the course of 5 years. Interview, no. S14, May 20, 1997; Interview, no. S41, July 13, 2000; Interview, no. S48, August 16, 2002.

[71] Xiao Gong, "PATAC Develops Models," *China Daily*, August 19, 2002. Given the public relations benefits of such a statement, of course, it should be taken with a grain of salt.

primary activities of PATAC have been the redesign of GM products for the Chinese market, but it intends to create the capability for complete vehicle design by 2010.[72] Although PATAC is a joint venture, SAIC has been careful to supplement the role of PATAC with independent efforts, and this creates the opportunity for cross-fertilization as SAIC employees move between PATAC and independent SAIC operations. In August 2002, the group combined its previous R&D efforts into the Shanghai Automotive Engineering Academy, a technology center of 450 technicians, and intends this institute to eventually have full design capabilities for engines and bodies.[73]

In the characteristic style of a local developmental state, the local government has also worked to provide institutional support for technical upgrading at the firm-level. Because it was not possible to create strong development departments in every Shanghai firm, the municipal government funded and promoted the Advanced Manufacturing Technical Center at Jiaotong University.[74] The intent was to concentrate resources in one technical center, and create capabilities that individual firms could then draw on for technical work. The emphasis was not on design so much as the process and manufacturing technologies that were required by the higher technical standards that suppliers were increasingly expected to have. Firms confirmed the role of the technical institute, particularly with respect to increasing manufacturing capabilities. Firm B (above) cooperated with the Jiaotong technical center on custom machine design and model design, and now has these capabilities in-house.[75] Firm C (above) used the technical center both to provide designs for new equipment (welding equipment for producing torque converters), and in cases when it needed to purchase foreign equipment, the technical center provided

---

The foreign acquisition strategy of SAIC is strongly motivated by its inability to gain key technological know-how from its JV partners – GM included.

[72] The initial investment in PATAC was US$50 million, and the JV was designed to be independent of SGM to enable it to work for other clients in China. In 2004, the two partners announced they would invest US$250 million in new facilities over 3 to 4 years (including the most advanced prototype laboratory in China, a virtual reality design studio that will be the first of its kind in China, a noise, vibration and harshness test lab, and a kinematics and compliance lab). PATAC had 670 employees in 2004; this is expected to increase to 900 by 2005, and 1,200 by 2010. Martin Young, "GM relocates Asia-Pacific headquarters to China," *Asia Times Online*, June 25, 2004.

[73] For details on the Shanghai Automotive Engineering Academy (SAEA), go to www.saicgroup.com. Its long-term objectives are described in "China's original passenger cars," *Fourin China Auto Weekly*, August 2, 2004, p. 7.

[74] Interview, no. S40, July 12, 2000.

[75] Interview, no. S42, July 13, 2000.

technical assistance in installing and utilizing the equipment.[76] By supporting the technical center, the municipality was providing a resource that enabled local firms to maximize the advantages of foreign linkages.[77]

It is the political dynamic, of course, that led most global suppliers to establish joint ventures in China rather than wholly foreign owned firms, as they did in Mexico. Quite simply, all of the assembly plants in China must be 50/50 joint ventures, and thus the Chinese partners at the assembly plants continue to have a strong voice in purchasing decisions. A joint venture supply firm, as opposed to a wholly owned foreign firm, has the advantage of being on the inside of this purchasing system. This said, local firms in Shanghai have not been completely dominated by their foreign partners, but have been working with them to rationalize the structure of the SAIC business group (see Table 7.1). The trend is toward a tiered structure with the larger supply joint ventures serving as system integrators.

Firm A (above), for instance, has become a small business group itself. Since the formation of the joint venture in 1994, the average annual return on the original investment has been 43%, and it has used the profits from the Santana business to expand and gain new capabilities.[78] Five subsidiary joint ventures have been created, and a technical center is being built in Shanghai at a cost of US$18–20 million.[79] The firm has the capability to design and manufacture complete modules for its customers.[80] The JV is still reliant on the foreign partner for technology – it would not

---

[76] Interview, no. S41, July 13, 2000.

[77] Doner (1994: 109) points to the lack of such public goods provisions in SE Asia as a primary reason that there is weak local capacity to absorb technology from Japanese firms.

[78] The firm generated 700 million RMB in consolidated revenue in 2002. Beginning in 2000, despite rapid re-investment of profits, the JV began to pay out dividends to its two shareholders (SAIC and the foreign firm). For the first two years each partner received 50 million RMB, in 2002 the dividend was 150 million RMB each, and it was expected be higher in 2003. In that the original investment of the foreign partner (US$25 million) has been returned at this point, the firm is a pure profit center. Interview, no. S52, January 21, 2003.

[79] In 2001, the design center at the firm consisted of 11 people; this increased to 44 the next year, 70–75 the next, and was expected to reach 150 by 2005. Interestingly, due to the subsidiary JVs that have been created, the Shanghai firm has a broader range of capabilities than the global supplier with which it is partnered.

[80] It is this sort of capability that is making possible the rapid rise of Chinese auto firms with no foreign linkages (such as Chery and Geely) – they draw heavily on the skills of the strong supply base in Shanghai. The firm, just described, for instance, has done critical design work for Chery. The demand for this sort of sophisticated design work from domestic firms, in turn, provides suppliers with experience that is vital to their upgrading efforts.

Table 7.1: *Ownership and Profiles of SAIC Group Suppliers*

Firm	Investment Share	Major Products	Major Customers
Shanghai Sanden Behr Air Conditioner	Shanghai Automotive (Stock) 38.5%; Shanghai Longhua 9%; Sanden (Japan) 35%; Behr (Germany) 17.5%	A/C compressors and A/C systems	SVW, SGM, FAW-VW, DPCA, Beijing Jeep
Yanfeng Visteon (Y-V owns or controls manufacturing plants in Shanghai, Beijing, Chongqing, Wuhan, and Guangzhou)	SAIC 50%; Visteon (US) 50%	Cockpit systems, interior and exterior systems	SVW, SGM, FAW-VW, DPCA, Beijing Jeep and Hyundai
Shanghai Koito	SAIC 50%; Koito (Japan) 45%; Toyota Tsusho 5%	Auto lamps	32 companies (21% of domestic market in 2002)
United Automotive Electronic Systems	UAES (a Chinese consortium) 50%; Bosch (Germany) 50%	Engine management systems	SVW, SGM, FAW-VW, DPCA and others (58% market share in 2002)
Shanghai Valeo Automotive Electrical Systems	SAIC 50%; Valeo (France) 50%	Starters and alternators	SVW, SGM, FAW and others
Shanghai Sachs Powertrain Components	SAIC 50%; ZF Sachs AG (Germany) 50%	Clutch and torque converter	SVW, SGM, FAW, FAW-VW, DPCA, Beijing Jeep, and other local manufacturers
ZF Shanghai Steering	SAIC 49%; ZF Lenksysteme (Germany) 51%	Designs and manufacturers steering systems	SVW, SGM, FAW-VW, Changan Ford, Brilliance Auto
Shanghai Automotive Braking Systems	SAIC 50%; Continental AG (Germany) 50%	Anti-lock brake systems	SVW, SGM, FAW-VW, FAW
Shanghai GKN	SAIC (35%); GKN Driveline (Germany) 50%; State Development & Inv Co. 10%; Bank of Communication 5%	Drive shaft	SVW, SGM, FAW-VW Changan Ford, FAW, GM, DPCA, Beijing Jeep
Shanghai Kolbenschmidt Piston	SAIC 50%; Kolbenschmidt-Pierburg Group (Germany) 50%	Aluminum alloy pistons	SVW, SGM, FAW-VW, FAW-Toyota, Changan Ford, and others
SIIC Transportation (An SAIC sub-group with 4 wholly owned firms and 6 JVs)	50/50 JVs with Valeo, Brose, ArvinMeritor; SIIC minority JVs with Delphi (40/60) and Lear (45/55)	Electrical parts, door modules, sunroof systems, and door locks	SVW, SGM, FAW-VW, FAW, Chang-an Ford and Suzuki, Jinbei GM
Volkswagen Transmission	VW 60%; FAW 20%; SAIC 20%	Transmissions	SVW, FAW-VW
Hua Dong Teksid	SAIC/Nanjing Auto 50%; Teksid (Italy) 50%	Foundry manufacturer of cylinder blocks	SVW, SGM

Source: SAIC Group website (SAICgroup.com) and various news reports. This is not a complete list.

231

have sustainable R&D without the foreign partner[81] – but the relationship as a whole is a partnership rather than complete dependence: when the global supplier expands within China, it does so through the Shanghai joint venture, rather than from its home base, so as to draw upon the JVs growing technical and financial strength.[82] Early success has allowed it to expand rapidly and establish a dominant position throughout the country.

The challenge now is for SAIC to create independent development capabilities. Despite the group's heavy dependence on its foreign partners, and its very successful utilization of these partnerships, it would be a mistake to assume that SAIC is content to be solely a local partner for foreign multinationals that are seeking access to the Chinese marketplace. A first step toward independence was the creation of SAIC Yizheng Automobile Company in 2003. It is a small company located in Jiangsu Province, but it is significant because it is the first wholly owned SAIC subsidiary to produce passenger vehicles, however modest they may be.[83] The second step is to acquire technology that is free of the constraints imposed by a joint venture partnership. Although two decades of cooperation with foreign firms has created substantial production capability within the SAIC group and significant financial resources, there are limits to how much the foreign partners will share. SAIC is now seeking to buy technology with fewer strings attached. It purchased a 48.92% stake in Ssangyong Motors, Korea's fourth largest automaker, in October of 2004, and entered into talks with MG Rover before deciding against purchasing the British car maker. The intent in both cases was the same: to combine the financial strength of SAIC with the engineering and development skills of a foreign firm to create a new SAIC branded model.[84] Shortly after SAIC backed away from purchasing a controlling stake in MG Rover – perhaps a wise move given the troubled state of the British company – it announced that it would begin manufacturing an SAIC-branded vehicle based on Rover

---

[81] The JV has skilled engineers, commented a foreign manager, but foreign participation is still necessary for any sophisticated design work. Interview, no. S45, August, 8, 2002.

[82] Delphi, with seven production firms in Shanghai, its China headquarters, and a new R&D center, has a similar strategy – Shanghai is becoming the hub of its Asian operations.

[83] The objective is to produce 50,000 Shanghai Auto-branded vehicles by 2007. "Shanghai Auto to make home-grown cars," *AFX News*, March 12, 2004.

[84] Interview no. S54, July 15, 2004. See also "China's original passenger cars," *Fourin Auto China Weekly*, August 2, 2004, p. 7. The financial demands of foreign acquisitions are a primary motivation behind the planned IPO in New York and Hong Kong.

technology in 2007.[85] The proposed vehicle, of course, would be in direct competition with the cars rolling out of its joint venture factories.

While these plans are certainly subject to change, they are an indication of SAIC's ambitions, and these are not small: the company hopes to achieve a manufacturing capacity of 4 million vehicles and 800 billion RMB in sales by 2020. This would make SAIC the top automaker in China and place the group among the top six of global auto firms.[86] As I explain in the next chapter, the ability of SAIC to efficiently manage its resources will be as important as technical capabilities.

The Firm-Dominated Localities

During the initial stage of development, supply firms in Changchun and Wuhan were handicapped by the fragmented focus of the Chinese partners. Because the First Auto Works and Dongfeng were controlled by the central government, they had little incentive to focus their developmental efforts on a particular locality, or heed the parochial concerns of local governments. This trend has continued in more recent years. Just as automotive firms in the United States are often eager to invest outside the rust belt of the mid-West that is the industry's traditional core, the centrally-controlled auto groups in China have not hesitated to invest in regions that do not have historical burdens of their original bases. This national orientation is in the interest of the group as a whole, but it causes problems for local firms in Changchun and Wuhan: fortunes improve during periods when demand is high, but underlying weaknesses in the supply base emerge when competition increases.[87]

In the passenger vehicle segment, the First Auto Works is in the stronger position of the two groups. It has strong interests outside of

---

[85] SAIC purchased the rights to manufacture the Rover 75 and Rover 25 in November 2004. According to industry sources, the vehicle that SAIC proposes to produce in Yizheng will be based on the Rover 75 chassis with a new exterior. The Rover 75 was introduced in Britain in 1999, and was the company's best-known model. Mark O'Neill, "Shanghai Auto wants to build own brand," *South China Morning Post*, May 2, 2005, p. 1.

[86] These goals were listed in the long-term business plan that SAIC released in August 2004. "Shanghai Automotive Industry Corporation," *Fourin Auto China Weekly*, January 31, 2004, p. 1.

[87] After a brief resurgence during the high demand period of 2002 and 2003, the woes of DCAC returned in 2004. The firm reported losses of US$65 million, and attributed them to falling sales and high costs. "Sino-French JV vows to turn tide," *Business Daily Update*, January 18, 2005.

Changchun – since acquiring a controlling share in Tianjin Auto, a major focus of its passenger car operations has been the joint venture with Toyota in Tianjin – but the FAW-VW joint venture has also been doing well. Sales and profit levels are roughly the same as at Shanghai VW (see Figures 2.3 and 2.4), and the expectation at Volkswagen is that the production volumes of FAW-VW will eventually eclipse those of SVW. At the end of 2004 the opening of a second production facility in Changchun doubled the production capacity of the joint venture.[88] This success is evidence of the positive impact a foreign partner can have in an assembly joint venture.

Although many of the newer models (the Audi A6 and the Bora) have relatively low rates of domestic content, success at the assembly firm has created new potential for the supply base and attracted global suppliers.[89] It is too soon to determine how much of an impact these new foreign partners will have on their local partners. One new supply joint venture, formed in 2001 to support the new models, is completely dependent on the foreign partner for design and technology. Purchasing for the joint venture will be controlled out of the Shanghai purchasing center of the foreign partner.[90] A second joint venture, also formed in 2001, has plans to create a design center in Changchun, but for design changes to the current models it has relied on its Shanghai joint venture. In this case, the motivation for creating design capabilities in Changchun come from a global supplier that is doing everything possible to capitalize on the less expensive engineering capability that is available outside of its North American base. In addition to the design capabilities in Shanghai, this firm has 300 engineers in a design center in India supporting its European and North American operations.[91]

Overall, FAW-VW's reliance on Changchun suppliers remains relatively low – it was able to source 20% of its components (by value) from within Changchun in 2003 – and its reliance on Shanghai suppliers remains uncomfortably high. Although FAW would only approve the use of SAIC suppliers when it had no other choice, this was still quite often: 20% of FAW-VW components (by value) were being sourced from Shanghai in

---

[88] The new plant was an investment US$1.5 billion. "VW opens new auto venture in northeast," *China Daily*, December 8, 2004.
[89] The rapid change of models (and in particular, a pending platform change) can also cause problems for local supply firms because there is little incentive for the assembly plant to localize the production of components for models that will soon be phased out.
[90] Interview, no. C11, January 16, 2003.
[91] Interview, no. C12, January 17, 2003.

2003.[92] At this time there were 16 European and U.S. firms operating in the municipality of Changchun compared with 87 in Shanghai.[93] But FAW clearly has great ambition, it has the strong support of the central government, and if the rising fortunes of FAW-VW can be matched with resources at the supply level it should be able to increase its technical capabilities. The more critical problem, as I explain in the next chapter, will be improving the governance of FAW.

Wuhan continues to aspire to be a major base of automotive production, but it faces daunting challenges at every level. The assembly plant continues to struggle. Sales dropped 13.6% in 2004 and the joint venture recorded losses of US$65 million. "Our minimum target this year is to get back in the black," one official woefully commented at the beginning of 2005.[94] The local supply base was in no better shape, and increasingly the joint venture has had to turn to outsiders for support. Dongfeng Peugeot Citroen had 230 suppliers in 2003, and only 10% of these were within 100 km of the assembly plant.[95] There were only 11 European and U.S. component firms operating in Wuhan at this point.[96] As is the case with Beijing, one solution is to purchase in Shanghai – in excess of 50% of DCAC suppliers were in Shanghai in 2003 and higher by value. Another approach is to persuade firms from outside, particularly Shanghai, to establish operations in Wuhan. A Shanghai firm that is leading the trend toward becoming a systems integrator, for instance, is establishing a three-partner joint venture in Wuhan: Dongfeng (40%), the Shanghai joint venture (30%), and the global supplier (30%).[97] Originally, Dongfeng had hoped to use an existing supplier and license technology from a European supplier,

---

[92] By contrast, SVW was only sourcing 2–3% of its components (by value) from Changchun. Interview, no. C14, January 17, 2003.

[93] *"Seikai saiteki seisan jitsugen muke juushisareru nichibeiou buhin meegaa no chuugoku shinshutsu"* [Japanese, U.S., and European component makers advance in China to realize the most appropriate way of manufacturing in the world], *Fourin*, no. 91, October 2003, p. 2.

[94] "Sino-French JV vows to turn tide," *Business Daily Update*, January 18, 2005.

[95] By contrast, 90% of SVW suppliers were within 100 km of the assembly plant. The distance of DCAC suppliers was partly because the machining factory for DCAC was located in Xiangfan (400 km away).

[96] *"Seikai saiteki seisan jitsugen muke juushisareru nichibeiou buhin meegaa no chuugoku shinshutsu"* [Japanese, U.S., and European component makers advance in China to realize the most appropriate way of manufacturing in the world], *Fourin*, no. 91, October 2003, p. 2.

[97] The global supplier is the same one that is the partner in the Shanghai JV. As previously explained, it chooses to expand via the Shanghai JV, rather than independently, because it seeks to leverage the capabilities of the Shanghai JV. It also has a separate equity stake in the new Wuhan JV so that its equity share is not diluted. This account is based on

but the licensing arrangement did not provide adequate commitment from the foreign firm. The Shanghai joint venture, by contrast, would be able to support the new joint venture with a base of 4,000 people a few hours away, a design center of over 100 people, and strong financial resources. Although cooperating with competitors is quite common in the global automotive industry, this deal was reportedly quite humbling for Dongfeng; reliance on foreign firms was one thing, but reliance on upstarts from Shanghai was quite another.[98]

Dongfeng has also changed its approach to foreign partnerships. During the 1990s, the firm was reluctant to fully tie its fate to a foreign partner; it thought of itself as the premier auto manufacturer in China and it preferred to utilize its pre-existing capabilities.[99] As the level of competition intensified in the late 1990s, however, it realized that this approach was no longer viable. In July 2001, the CEO of Nissan, Carlos Ghosn, visited Beijing with the intent of gaining approval for an assembly joint venture in China, one that was much like all those that had come before, but the Chinese leadership had other ideas for the legendary turn-around artist. "We have many SOEs in China," commented Vice-Premier Wu Bang-guo, "and in light of China's accession to the WTO there is urgent talk in the government about the need to improve SOE management."[100] In the case of the typical assembly auto joint venture, he continued, a high profit is made at the JV, but there is little improvement in the Chinese parent company. Wu wanted to see what Ghosn could do with a Chinese SOE in its entirety.

The result of this meeting was the creation of the Dongfeng Motor Company in July 2003, a 50/50 joint venture between Nissan and the Dongfeng Motor Corporation.[101] Unlike most joint ventures, the new JV incorporated the bulk of the Chinese partner's operations – it would employ 70,000 of the 117,000 employees of the Chinese partner – and

---

interviews in both Wuhan and Shanghai. Interview, no. W28, January 13, 2003; Interview, no. S52, January 21, 2003.

[98] Interview, no. W28, January 13, 2003.

[99] This is in contrast to Shanghai, which essentially did not have a pre-existing auto industry when SVW was created. The attitude of Dongfeng, remarked one foreign manager in Wuhan, is that "they can make anything on 4 wheels with an engine." Interview, no. W28, January 13, 2003.

[100] This account is from a Nissan representative who was present in the meeting. Interview, no. T9, October 14, 2004.

[101] The Japanese partner contributed US$1.01 billion and the Chinese partner contributed 80% of its existing assets to form the US$2 billion joint venture. The names of the Chinese parent and the new JV, it should be noted, are easily confused.

a full product range: commercial trucks would be produced in the old Dongfeng base of Shiyan, sedans and sports utility vehicles in Xiangfan, and passenger vehicles in the Huadu District of Guangzhou. The Huadu plant, which was launched in May 2004, is probably the most telling. Rather than struggle to build upon its existing base for passenger vehicles in Wuhan, Dongfeng will be a Wuhan-registered JV that produces the majority of its passenger vehicles in a greenfield location in a distant province.[102] The new plant will have ready access to both a growing base of Japanese suppliers in Guangzhou and Taiwanese suppliers that have technical agreements with Nissan.[103]

The Laissez-Faire Local States

The Dongfeng move to Guangzhou could prove to be a wise one. In a period in which the dominant concern is lowering costs, a supply network that is organized by market relations has a critical advantage; the competition that is built into the network (in the form of multiple suppliers for each component) can be used by the assembly plant as leverage to lower prices. This is particularly true if market relations are supplemented by Japanese-style networks, and it becomes possible to create a competitive impulse within a cooperative framework. The laissez-faire local states might yet thrive.

The early failures in Beijing and Guangzhou had both a positive and negative effect on the future prospects of the localities. On the one hand, there was a willingness on the part of local officials to try a new approach – it was very clear in both cases that the old approaches had not worked. On the other hand, there was a very weak supplier base to build upon. Again, the reliance on arms-length market relationships in the early stages of growth meant that assemblers turned away from suppliers that failed to meet expectations rather than work with them to improve, and in an industry characterized by complex and frequent transactions, this approach proved to be fatal – the assembler's bargaining power vis-à-vis the supply

---

[102] The Huadu plant will have an initial production capacity of 240,000 vehicles; the Xiangfan plant will have a capacity of 60,000 vehicles. "Dongfeng's multibrand strategy sees 6 global partnerships," *Fourin China Auto Weekly*, March 22, 2004, p. 3.

[103] Nissan is increasingly utilizing Yulon suppliers in China. Yulon (25% of which is owned by Nissan) was the original Dongfeng partner in Guangzhou (Aeolus Motor). The Yulon-Dongfeng JV was absorbed by the Nissan-Dongfeng partnership. Interview, no. T9, October 14, 2004; "Production ventures and investment in China," *Fourin China Auto Weekly*, May 17, 2004, p. 8.

firms was achieved at the cost of establishing a collaborative relationship that would be able to promote shared technical progress. Firms with weak technical capabilities fell by the wayside as competition increased.[104] The new approaches that were adapted leaned heavily upon foreign firms.

The supply network in Beijing, never particularly strong, has crumbled in the face of increased competition. "The competition has passed us by," commented a manager at Beijing Jeep in 2002, "and we are now in a rebuilding phase." The strategy is to introduce new models – the Grand Cherokee, the Mitsubishi Pratero Sport – and "benefit from our competition by switching from our old suppliers to our competitors."[105] For the new Grand Cherokee, BJC began to rely completely on this new base of suppliers, and it is gradually making the transition for older models as well. In 2002, approximately 50% of BJC suppliers by number (and far higher by value) were located in Shanghai, and 10% or less in Beijing.[106] In 2003, Beijing firms manufactured 3.7 billion RMB of auto parts; Shanghai firms manufactured 45.5 billion (Figure 7.1).[107]

Hyundai has been a primary beneficiary of early failure in Beijing, and the consequent willingness on the part of BAIC to adapt new approaches. One of the primary reasons that Beijing Hyundai has been able to rapidly increase production volumes (see Figure 2.4) is because Mobis, the auto parts affiliate of Hyundai, established wholly owned ventures for engine and transmission production. According to one former employee of the Beijing Hyundai purchasing department, 80% of domestic sourced of components in 2004 were purchased from Korean-invested firms, and 60% of these firms were wholly Korean-owned.[108] Wholly owned parts ventures are able to rapidly establish themselves in China and deliver complete modules to the joint venture assembly

---

[104] This was as true in the United States (see Helper 1991) as it was in Beijing and Guangzhou.

[105] Interview, no. B42, July 30, 2002. In December 2004, Beijing Jeep was renamed Beijing Benz-DaimlerChrysler. In the summer of 2005 a new production facility will begin producing Mercedes-Benz sedans. "JV renamed Beijing Benz-DaimlerChrysler," *Business Daily Update*, December 7, 2004.

[106] Interview, no. B42, July 30, 2002.

[107] "Auto industry development by region," *Fourin China Auto Weekly*, January 25, 2005, p. 2. At this time there were only nine European and U.S. component firms operating in Beijing. "*Seikai saiteki seisan jitsugen muke juushisareru nichibeiou buhin meegaa no chuugoku shinshutsu*" [Japanese, U.S., and European component makers advance in China to realize the most appropriate way of manufacturing in the world], *Fourin*, no. 91, October 2003, p. 2.

[108] Interview, no. B45, July 19, 2004 and Interview, no. B49, July 22, 2005.

plant.[109] A large percentage of components also continue to be imported, and the JV also does not hesitate to utilize suppliers located in other regions of China. Hyundai established a purchasing office in Shanghai in 1999, and purchases widely from Zhejiang and Jiangsu.

BAIC is perfectly willing to utilize non-BAIC suppliers at this point, explained a manager in the head office of the business group. This flexibility may stem in part from structural factors – because BAIC had so little success in the first stage of development, it is only a partial investor on the the Chinese side of the joint venture – but it is primarily a reflection of the sad state of the Beijing supply network.[110] "Our suppliers are very poor," the BAIC manager commented, "but we are very open, so we won't say [to the assembly plants] you have to use this or that."[111] This new strategy may effectively increase the automotive output of the municipality, but it is creating a very different type of automotive industry and enterprise group in Beijing: BAIC is essentially becoming a real estate company that sells its access to the government to foreign auto firms. It has officially changed its name from an enterprise group (*jituan gongsi*) to a holding company (*konggu gongsi*), and the head office readily acknowledges that it does not try to coordinate development – it is simply a shareholder. "Our strategy is as an investor," explained a top manager. "We are no longer a manufacturing company, and if we are not realistic about this, we will take the wrong road."[112]

A supply firm just north of Beijing's city center perfectly illustrates the new strategy. After struggling for years, the U.S. partner at the joint venture sold its share in the firm back to BAIC for 10 RMB – even though the real estate alone was valued at RMB $10–15 million – and formed a new joint venture with BAIC and a Shanghai firm.[113] In the new joint venture there was a clear division of labor: the foreign partner would provide the technology, the Beijing partner would provide real estate

---

[109] One Hyundai Mobis plant has the capability to deliver chassis modules that include the engine, transmission, brakes, struts, and steering wheels. It is the first plant in China with this capability, according to Hyundai Mobis officials. "Hyundai Mobis completes plant in China," *The Korea Herald*, November 1, 2003.

[110] The Chinese partner at the JV is the Chinese Automotive Investment Company. BAIC is the largest shareholder and the Shougang Group, one of China's largest steel producers, is the second largest. "Steel giant eyes auto industry," Xinhua Economic News Service, January 28, 2003. Interview, no. B45, July 19, 2004.

[111] Interview, no. B44, January 10, 2003.

[112] Interview, no. B44, January 10, 2003.

[113] Interview, no. C12, January 17, 2003.

and connections with the customer, and the Shanghai partner provided manufacturing and design capabilities within China.

Guangzhou has had an even more profound transformation than Beijing. After the collapse of the joint venture with Peugeot, the municipal government persuaded Honda to invest, and there was a sense of determination not to repeat past mistakes. According to an auto office official, the Guangzhou mayor explicitly directed local firms to subvert narrow development objectives for the good of the joint venture, even if this meant abandoning firms that the local government had spent a decade attempting to cultivate. "Our purpose is not to support Guangzhou suppliers," the mayor explained at the establishment of the JV, "but to insure that Guangzhou Honda succeeds."[114]

Essentially, Honda was able to start from scratch. Like General Motors in Shanghai, the Japanese performed a careful evaluation of supply firms throughout China, and found 83 suppliers that conformed to Honda standards. Only 4 of these were firms that had been part of the Guangzhou Peugeot supply base.[115] Local firms were mainly for relatively simple components, and they compete on the basis of costs – none have development capability.[116] In some cases Honda utilized the Japanese suppliers that were established earlier in the decade to support the Honda Wuyang motorcycle JV. A primary solution for key components, however, was to persuade Honda suppliers from Japan to co-locate in China. Honda has about 60 key suppliers in Japan, and approximately 20 of these established operations in China.[117] In 2003, the domestic content for the Accord was 70%, and 60% of this amount was out-sourced. Of the amount that was outsourced, 90% was to Japanese-invested firms.[118] The Accord has been

---

[114] Interview, no. G24, August 22, 2003.

[115] Interview, no. G22, July 1, 2002.

[116] Interview, no. G23, July 2, 2002.

[117] Many of the new Honda suppliers are in Shanghai rather than Guangdong: 32% of domestic suppliers are in Shanghai as compared to 45% in Guangdong. By value, however, 72.45% of components come from Guangdong. Interview, no. T3, June 4, 2003.

[118] Interview, no. T3, June 4, 2003. It is worth noting that Southeast Motors, a JV between a Taiwanese auto company and a local company in Fujian Province has taken the same strategy. The Taiwanese firm "persuaded" its Taiwanese supplies to co-locate with it in Fuzhou, primarily by making future contracts in Taiwan contingent upon the supplier investing in a plant in the industrial park alongside the new China assembly plant. Headquarters believed that it was necessary to bring their own suppliers to China not only to assure quality, but also because it would allow them to launch production of other models more quickly and easily. Between 1997 and 1998, 30 Taiwanese component firms built wholly owned factories in an industrial park next to the assembly plant. By 2000 these firms were supplying the JV with 80% of its parts (by value), while the remaining

enormously popular, and the joint venture project has been extremely successful (see Figures 2.3 and 2.4).

Honda provided the Guangzhou beachhead for Japanese firms. Nissan followed a few years later in its partnership with Dongfeng, and soon it will be the only city in the world producing cars for the three largest Japanese auto firms: Honda, Nissan, and Toyota. Toyota's original base for passenger vehicle production in China was in Tianjin, a partnership with FAW, but this will soon be eclipsed by a new production facility in the Nansha District of Guangzhou. The joint venture between Guangzhou Auto and Toyota, approved by the central government in July 2004, will produce the Camry in a greenfield plant, and will have an initial capacity of 300,000.[119] Although the world's most efficient and profitable auto firm was late to enter China, it is wasting no time in establishing its network in Guangzhou. "Bringing in the Toyota production system" is necessary to "increase localization and reduce costs," explained Akio Toyoda, the director in charge of China operations, and a full range of Toyota suppliers is in the process of establishing production facilities.[120] Virtually all of the key firms that were established in 2004 were wholly Japanese owned (Table 7.2).

The benefits of locating in Guangzhou are clear for the Japanese firms. First, there will be the obvious benefits of concentration and greater economies of scale once the Honda, Nissan, and Toyota supply networks are complete.[121] As one Guangzhou auto official commented, even though the firms may belong to different *keiretsu* networks, the concentration of auto firms will reduce costs for base materials and standard parts and increase local firms' familiarity with Japanese production techniques.[122]

20% came from 56 Chinese firms, 30 of which are Shanghai Volkswagen suppliers in Shanghai. Interviews in Fuzhou, January 2000.

[119] "Toyota suppliers advance in Guangzhou," *Fourin China Auto Weekly*, December 27, 2004, p. 1. Even before the assembly JV was approved the two partners had created an engine JV that will have a production capacity of 300,000. Two-thirds of this output will be exported to Japan.

[120] Mark O'Neill, "Toyota juggernaut drives into China," *South China Morning Post*, October 4, 2004. Although Toyota supports its suppliers, it is also famous for the pressure it places on them; its executives have spoken of how the "China benchmark" will provide a new standard for component prices. See Chester Dawson with Karen Nickel Anhalt, "A 'China Price' for Toyota," *Business Week*, February 21, 2005.

[121] In 2003, Guangdong Province already had 66 Japanese components firms with investments, a number that was second only to Tianjin (see Figure 7.2).

[122] Interview with Zheng Qinghong, Assistant Manager of Guangzhou Auto, "Guangzhou Auto Industry Group: Taking on major players through Japanese investment," *Fourin*

Table 7.2: *Ownership of Toyota Group Suppliers Established in Guangzhou in 2004*

Firm	Investment Share	Major Products	Major Customers
Fengai Guangzhou Automotive Seat Parts	Toyota Boshoku 51%; Aisin Seiki 49%	Seat backs, cushions, tracks, etc.	Guangzhou Intex Parts
Guangzhou Intex Auto Parts	Toyota Boshoku 50%; Takanichi 25%; GAIC Auto Parts 25%	Seats, door trim, headliners, etc.	Fengai Automotive Seat Parts
Toyota (Foshan) Gosei Auto Parts	Toyota Gosei 65%; Taiwan subsidiary 30%; Toyota Tsusho 5%	Interior and exterior parts	Toyota and other Japanese automakers
Toyo Automotive Parts (Guangzhou)	Toyo Tire & Rubber 100%	Rubber NVH products	Japanese automakers
Aisan (Foshan) Autoparts	Aisan Industry 95%; Yoyoda Tsusho 5%	Fuel injectors, related engine parts	Toyota and other Japanese automakers
Foshan Tokai Rika Automotive Parts	Tokai Rika 100%	Key-lock sets, seat belts	Toyota and other Japanese automakers
Aisin Seiki Foshan Automotive Parts	Aisin Seikie 100%	Engine parts	Toyota and other Japanese automakers
Huizhou Zhucheng Wiring Systems	Sumitomo Wiring 20.4%, Shenzhen Dongf. 25%, Shenzhen Sumitomo Equipment 24%	Automotive wire harness	Japanese automakers
Guangzhou Hayashi Telempu	Hayashi Telempu 51%, GAIC 49%	Interior Parts	Japanese automakers
Mitsui Chemicals Plastic Compounds (Zhongshan)	Mitsui Chemicals 100%	Poly propylene compounds	Japanese automakers

Source: "Toyota suppliers advance in Guangzhou," *Fourin China Auto Weekly*, December 27, 2004, p. 2.

Production volumes will also be heightened by exports. The most innovative part of the Honda strategy in Guangzhou, is an export factory; innovative because all firms – Honda included – agree that production costs in China are currently higher than the United States or Japan, primarily because of the high costs of components and materials.[123] The Honda intent, however, is to use the export factory to both raise the production volumes of its suppliers in China, and thereby lower their costs, and use the new factory to establish an export-level quality of production for local suppliers.[124] Much like GM used its worldwide purchasing prices to establish an objective benchmark for domestic firms, Honda intends to use the export factory as a global standard for suppliers within China. Because the export factory will share a supply base with Guangzhou Honda, the higher volumes will benefit all local suppliers, and the improvements in the supply base will benefit both assembly plants.

Second, early and complete failure in Guangzhou created a receptive environment to the Japanese approach. The problem in the initial stage of development in Guangzhou was that municipal officials were attempting to transform the locality into something that it was not – a local developmental state.[125] The result was the worst possible combination for local firms; the local government pressured the assembly plant to support local firms, but it was completely ineffective in nurturing and channeling resources to local suppliers. After the failure of Guangzhou Peugeot, the municipal government has returned to a more traditional approach for the locality. It creates the incentives for growth and is receptive to any approach that a firm might decide to pursue, so long as an inordinate degree of government support is not required. When combined with the obvious technical and management strengths of a Japanese auto firm, the approach has great promise. In a development stage when cutting costs is of paramount importance the hands-off approach is fine, but only if firms have access to the technology necessary to compete in the marketplace.

It is the ideal opportunity for Japanese firms because they are allowed to transplant their production system to China with a minimum degree of

---

China Auto Weekly, August 23, 2004, p. 2. As of 2004, Honda managers said they were able to implement very few just-in-time delivery techniques. Interview, no. T8, October 13, 2004.

[123] The export factory is a JV between Honda (65%), Guangzhou Auto (10%), and Dongfeng (25%). The factory began producing cars for European and Asian markets in April 2005. Neil Gough, "Honda plant rolls out made-for-export cars," *South China Morning Post*, May 16, 2005, p. 3.

[124] Interview, no. T3, June 4, 2003.

[125] On the challenge of institutional change in Guangzhou, see Thun (2004).

interference (relative to the rest of China). In general, studies of Japanese multinationals have tended to find a strong reliance on Japanese suppliers, in the form of both imports and Japanese firms that have co-located with an assembler abroad.[126] Honda and Toyota, for instance, are pointed to by Noble as examples of Japanese firms that have "zealously protected their independence" despite pressures to alter organizational strategies in the face of global challenges.[127] In contrast to Japanese auto companies that are now partially controlled by Western firms, such as Nissan, Honda and Toyota have strengthened their relationships with parts companies and maintained employment levels. Noble uses the example of Toyota's aggressive investments in Southeast Asia and China to illustrate how this strategy shapes supplier development abroad: "Toyota accepts the move toward greater modules, but it wants those modules to be built by first-tier Japanese affiliates under its control rather than by independent global suppliers."[128] No effort has been spared in the effort to support affiliated supply firms.[129] Guangzhou will probably be an excellent Chinese base for implementing the Toyota, or any other Japanese system.

Whether the new Japanese production base will translate into strong local firms is less certain. The municipal government has ambitious plans for the local auto base, an annual output of 1.3 million vehicles by 2010 is the stated objective,[130] but at least thus far, there is little indication that it will seek independent capabilities for local firms. The Mexican path is the more likely outcome: a vibrant hub of foreign firms. Although Guangzhou

---

[126] One study of Japanese firms in Malaysia from 1987 to 1989, for instance, found that even when the number of locally owned firms increased, their share of overall procurement remained constant. The share of locally based Japanese firms increased during the same period. For a good summary of research on the local sourcing of Japanese firms, see Ravenhill (1999: 267). Honda representatives in Tokyo, however, insist that they do not prefer Japanese firms in their Guangzhou operations. All decisions are based on the quality, cost, and delivery provided by the supply firm. Interview, no. T8, October 13, 2004.

[127] The alternative model is that of Nissan, where Renault forced the company to slash employment, close outdated factories, and severe ties with traditional suppliers. Noble (2002: 148).

[128] Noble (2002: 145–147). In Tianjin a similar model seems to be in place. After not investing in the 1980s, the Chinese government forced Toyota to establish a supply network prior to approving a JV assembly plant. When the new assembly plant began production in 2002, only 16 out of 62 suppliers were Chinese firms. Interview, no. T7, June 6, 2003.

[129] In Thailand, for example, Toyota suppliers were operating at 20–30% of capacity after the financial crisis, but there was not one bankruptcy among the 120 subcontractors in the Toyota Motor Thailand Group. Noble (2002: 147).

[130] "Guangzhou Automobile Industry Group," *Fourin China Auto Weekly*, August 23, 2004, p. 3.

was never well-suited for taking on the role of a local developmental state, it has always been ideally suited to an outward trade-oriented approach to development, and so long as they continue to bring technology and manufacturing capabilities from home, this approach will suit the Japanese firms perfectly.

III. CONCLUSION

There can be little doubt that auto firms located in China will rise to the challenge of global integration; firms are already manufacturing cars that have the technical standards of any available outside of China. The only question that remains is whether there will be much that is Chinese about these firms and their broader supply networks.

What determines the technical strength of a regional automotive network in China and the upgrading capacity of local firms? The role of a foreign partner is clearly critical within the walls of an assembly plant. Honda is a success in the same factory building where Peugeot failed miserably; Hyundai has been rapidly increasing production volumes in Beijing; Volkswagen has managed to make a success of a very difficult partnership in Changchun. As the foreign partners readily concede, however, they play a less prominent role in the development of the broader supply network. They grade suppliers, they advise them, and they recommend foreign partners for them. But there are limits to what they can do for local firms; when a local supply firm has no financial resources, little technical capability, and poor human capital, it is much easier for an assembler to look elsewhere for its components.

The success of an assembly plant, of course, creates fertile ground for a supply network. When there are fewer restrictions on imports, an assembly plant can raise volumes prior to carrying out a localization drive. Given time, the inherent advantages of co-location in the auto sector will create an incentive for the assembler to begin seeking out local suppliers, and the high volumes will eliminate the risk and collective action problems that plagued early supplier development. The vibrant network of supply firms that emerges will not necessarily realize Chinese government's objective of developing strong Chinese auto firms that are capable of competing on world markets, however.

In regions where the base of local firms is weak, the danger is that the initial response will be to rely more heavily on the foreign partners and their home-country suppliers. Local supply firms are relegated to the lower tiers, and although they are extremely competitive at producing commodity-like components, upward mobility is not easy. The assembly plants must immediately introduce their latest model, a model that has been designed in cooperation with suppliers in the home country, and there is little time for the laborious process of putting a local firm through a time-consuming apprenticeship. To varying extents this can be seen in both the laissez-faire local states (Beijing and Guangzhou) and the firm-dominated localities (Changchun and Wuhan), although at least the latter have the advantage of large national business groups that have independent capabilities and traditions (although primarily in commercial vehicles).

When a locality has benefited from an incremental process of development, as in Shanghai (and neighboring Jiangsu and Zhejiang), local firms have a higher likelihood of becoming system integrators and capturing larger portions of the value chain. The evidence of this can be seen in the patterns of expansion outside of the home base. Foreign firms in China often choose partners for political reasons; either they are forced by Chinese regulation to find a partner, or they believe a partner will provide an inside track to their customer base. When a global supplier expands in China in partnership with a Shanghai joint venture rather than independently, however, it is not doing so for political reasons – and in fact it may be a disadvantage given regional rivalries – it is doing so because the Shanghai firm (or joint venture) has a broader range of capabilities than its competitors. A nuanced state role widens the set of opportunities for local firms as global integration increases.[131]

This is not to say that Shanghai firms do not face significant challenges. Competitive pressures will be unrelenting as assemblers take advantage of lower tariff rates on components to rationalize their supply networks. Perhaps even more important will be the structural pressure: as assemblers introduce global platforms, they must choose between bringing a new global supplier to China and paying a (sometimes exorbitant) licensing fee to transfer the technology to the pre-existing supplier in China. It is a two-level game for multinational firms; there is the China strategy and the global strategy. A global supplier that does not have a presence in China, but is a key supplier for a new model that is being introduced by an assembler in China, is often reluctant to license its technology to a Chinese

---

[131] This hypothesis can be easily falsified by future developments. If in ten years there is little difference in the roles played by Chinese suppliers in Shanghai and Guangzhou, for instance, this would be strong evidence that a successful assembly plant (and foreign partner) is more important that the role of a local developmental state.

supplier, because the Chinese supplier is already in a joint venture with a global firm that is its prime competitor in other markets. As the rate of model changes increases, this is a problem that is very much on the minds of both the purchasing managers at the assembly joint ventures and the suppliers that are afraid of losing their business immediately after having made expensive upgrades.[132] The dilemma is hardly unique to Shanghai supply firms, of course. Given a general trend toward modular production in the global industry, all but the very largest of global suppliers face the danger of being relegated to lower tiers of the value chain.

The Chinese central government, ever eager to promote the development of independent national champions, is aware of the challenges and seems to have grudgingly accepted the need for foreign partnerships. During the year prior to the issuing of the 2004 industrial policy statement for the auto industry, the National Development and Reform Commission circulated drafts of the policy that indicated that the government would demand that half of the intellectual property of cars built in China should be of Chinese origin by 2010 (although how intellectual property or its origin would be defined was not clear), but this demand was dropped from the final draft.[133] Although the new policy continues to restrict the activities of foreign firms within the domestic marketplace, it encourages the domestic firms to team up with foreign partners. Rather than forge an entirely independent path, the globalization of the industry seems to be accepted in the short run at least, and the challenge is to maximize the benefits for Chinese firms. As I discuss in the next chapter, the hurdles facing these firms will relate as much to the classic problems of a state-owned enterprise as technology.

---

[132] For obvious reasons, the conflict was often between the home technical department of the foreign partner at the assembly plant (which wanted to work with only one global supplier for a particular platform) and the China operations (which wanted to support the local supply JVs). Interview, no. C14, January 17, 2003.

[133] James Mackintosh and Richard McGregor, "A leap over the cliff," *The Financial Times*, August 25, 2003, p. 15; Gong Zhengzheng, "Release of new auto policy 'within days'" *China Daily*, May 28, 2004; State Development and Reform Commission (2004).

EIGHT

Growth, Change, and the Challenge of Governance

When the primary concern of Chinese auto firms was increasing manufacturing capability, Shanghai firms had a critical advantage: the municipal government and SAIC were able to ease the risk of individual firms and nurture the development of an entire sector. The Shanghai municipal government, to use Lindblom's memorable characterization of authority systems, was all thumbs at this stage, and that was fine.[1] With the comfort of high tariff barriers, even relatively crude means of channeling resources into the sector would be rewarded with increased sales.[2] Shanghai firms were able to rapidly achieve economies of scale and capture market share. The considerable profits were plowed back into the supply network, and this created the strong foundation that later allowed them to upgrade their technical capabilities.

The challenge as competition and global integration increased, however, was matching technical progress with the ability to cut costs. Cultivating a supply network of efficient firms – as opposed to merely capable – was a task that imposed far greater demands on municipal institutions for two reasons. First, the governance structures within the local business group had to be improved, so as to create mechanisms of discipline and control. Rather than simply channeling resources to all firms within the network, resources had to be allocated according to the effectiveness with which they were utilized; those firms that were operating efficiently had

---

[1] Lindblom (1977: Chapter 5).

[2] Paul Krugman might refer to this as the "myth" of the Shanghai miracle in the same manner that he argued (1994) that the Asian "miracle" was simply the result of high investment rates, and would need productivity gains if it were to prove durable.

to receive further investment, those that were not, had to be cut off. Second, the municipal government had to allow market forces to distinguish between those firms that were competitive and those that were not.[3] The process of technical upgrading is not particularly easy, but because the distributional consequences are minor, it is not politically difficult. Distinguishing between winners and losers involves an entirely different set of calculations, and elites within the municipal government, in contrast to economic actors, have incentive structures that mix financial, political, and social objectives. In short, well-established patterns had to be altered if the local auto sector was going to continue to grow and prosper.

Thus far I have argued that institutional structures vary across space, and these differences are durable. The development approach of each locality was heavily influenced by history. This chapter explores the implications of institutional durability within a single locality over time.[4] There are three primary points. First, the "fit" between the development needs of an industrial sector and a particular policy approach (and consequently, institutional structure) is not permanent. In the initial stage of growth an activist state was beneficial to auto sector development, and some institutional structures were better suited to this approach than others. As firms within the sector developed, however, it became increasingly important to increase efficiency; this required institutional arrangements of a very different sort, and the speed with which the needs of the sector changed outstripped the capacity for organizational change.[5] Success over the long term required a certain degree of institutional flexibility.

Second, the style of reform in China, and in particular the policy of fiscal decentralization, provides insufficient impetus for change in many cases. If the incentives to shift from one policy approach to another – usually specified as a consequence of competition between localities competing in a common national market – are greater than the force of institutional inertia, the problem of institutional change would not be that great. A local government might find it difficult to shift away from a suboptimal development strategy, but it would be forced to do so. At the very least it would be limited in its ability to pursue unsuccessful strategies indefinitely.

---

[3] As noted in Chapter 1, this would correspond with a shift from the upper-left quadrant of Table 1.1 toward the lower-left quadrant.

[4] See Thun (2004) for a comparison of the process of institutional change in Guangzhou and Shanghai.

[5] In democratic states, this is an often-heard argument against infant industry policies: no matter how deserving an industry is for protection, once it receives it, it is very difficult politically to remove it.

In China, however, this is too often not the case; not only do regions resort to local protectionism, but the close ties between local governments and enterprises dilute the ability of market competition to wean local governments from suboptimal policies.

Third, although political organizations in China are resistant to change, linkages to the global economy (through both trade and investment) are important forces for change. The prospect of trade liberalization provides the ultimate impetus, but prior to the decrease in tariff barriers, massive amounts of foreign investment serve as a Trojan horse of sorts (albeit of a positive nature). Foreign firms bring the expectations and standards of global competition within the protectionist barriers, they expect to do business in the same manner as they do elsewhere in the world because they realize that tariff protection is temporary, and they are not subject to the same degree of political control as local firms.[6] It is often argued that "openness" is a critical driver of innovation and competitiveness at the firm level, but the impact on institutional frameworks is equally important.[7] Although the needs of sectors change more rapidly than the ability of institutions to evolve and meet these needs, external pressure helps to prevent the gap from growing too wide.

I. SHANGHAI REVISITED: ALL THUMBS AND NO FINGERS

Economic development, when it is successful, is inherently a process of change, and as a result, can create its own problems. If, as I have argued, there is a certain "fit" between the development needs of an industrial sector and local institutional structures, it follows that the changing needs of a sector may threaten this fit. It is what Richard Doner and Ansil Ramsay call "growing into trouble," a situation in which the "institutions favorable for one stage of economic growth are less suitable for a subsequent stage."[8] To a certain extent the problem is pervasive, given the broad differences between the policies that are needed to ignite economic growth and those that are required to sustain it.[9] As Rodrik argues, the former

---

[6] In cases where trade liberalization is not predetermined, it should be noted, foreign firms will often lobby for continued protection.

[7] On the relationship between liberalization, increased foreign competition and the improved productivity of domestic firms, see for example, Hallward-Driemeier (2001). On the impact that openness to trade will have on institutional structures, see Rodrik (1999: 31). On alternative "host" country FDI policy approaches, see Moran (1998).

[8] Doner and Ramsay (2004: 97).

[9] Rodrik (2003: 19).

involves an investment strategy that will allow an economy to breakout of a low-activity equilibrium; the latter requires the construction of "high-quality" institutions that will induce socially desirable behavior on the part of economic agents over the long term. This latter challenge takes far more time and effort.[10]

The development of the Shanghai auto sector provides a perfect example of "growing into trouble." In the short-run, the primary challenge was overcoming a coordination problem: the success of any individual supply firm depended on the simultaneous development of every other firm in the network, and a local developmental state provided a very blunt answer to this problem. By the late 1990s, however, the coordination of scarce investment capital was no longer an obstacle – SAIC actually began looking for opportunities to export capital at this point[11] – but there was great difficulty lowering costs. Bernard Leissner, the president of Volkswagen Asia-Pacific, estimated in 2003 that it cost VW 18% more to produce a car in China than in Germany, primarily due to the high cost of components.[12] This problem of relatively low productivity was not unique to Shanghai, of course, but was characteristic of Chinese SOEs in general. SAIC had a far stronger base than other regions, and as I explained in the last chapter, the solid foundation of the local auto industry continued to serve it well, but it was not internationally competitive and it faced strong, new domestic challengers.

Although China is missing more than one "high-quality" institution, from the perspective of industrial development, none is more important than effective corporate governance. Developing powerful business groups requires not only large amounts of capital, but also governance mechanisms to ensure that the capital is effectively utilized. Although in transitional economies it is often believed that transferring the ownership of assets from the state to private actors is the key element of reform, an examination of large-scale industrial firms in capitalist systems makes it

---

[10] These may include meritocratic public bureaucracies, independent judiciaries and effective legal systems, antitrust and regulation, financial supervision, social insurance, and/or political democracy. Rodrik (2003: 26).

[11] The first overseas move came in 2002, when SAIC bought a 10% stake in the General Motors-Daewoo JV in Korea at a cost of US$59.7 million. "Chinese automaker invests in GM-Daewoo joint venture," *Asia Pulse*, October 14, 2002.

[12] Keith Bradsher, "China's factories aim to fill the world's garages," *The New York Times*, November 2, 2003. This was undoubtedly a conservative estimate. Paul Alcala, president and CEO of Beijing Jeep, estimated that in the case of his company, costs were 20–30% higher than in the U.S. or Japan. John Ridding, "Turning the corner on route to profits," *Financial Times*, December 16, 2003.

clear that the identity of the owner is not the only, or even the most important, problem.[13] In massive industrial firms, there are many actors pulling the strings – managers, creditors, and shareholders to name a few – and preferences vary. The separation of ownership and management requires the development of a system of internal incentives that will ensure that managers follow the preferences of owners, and external incentives that will serve as a final arbiter of performance.[14]

While state ownership in China does not preclude good corporate governance, it does create severe challenges. The Chinese state, as shareholder, is indistinct. It is bureaucrats – often spread across numerous ministries – that represent the state, and they rarely have the incentive to act as effective monitors; they are neither rewarded for effective governance, nor penalized when ineffective.[15] In theory, state bureaucrats are supposed to manage enterprises on behalf of the people, much like a fund manager controls a fund owned by shareholders, but in practice this is not the case. Because there is no contract specifying the obligations of the state with respect to the financial return to the assets owned by the people, state officials have been able to ignore the cost of state capital and pursue objectives that have little to do with maximizing the return on the state's investment.[16] In many cases, the non-financial objectives are driven by the social services that continue to be tied to the firm; in some cases, officials simply are not paying adequate attention.

The driving – if, as yet, unrealized – purpose of enterprise reform has been to separate the ownership function of the state from its political and social functions. This effort began with the promulgation of the Company Law in 1993.[17] By clarifying the rights and obligations of a firm as an

---

[13] Steinfeld (1998: 40). It should also be noted that state-owned firms can be quite efficient when properly governed. See Mako and Zhang (2002).

[14] An effective system is complex and multi-faceted: an independent board of directors monitor and supervise managers; managerial labor markets align the interests of management and shareholders through the use of bonuses and/or stock options; capital markets force management to be concerned with the terms on which capital will be provided to the firm; high levels of transparency and auditing standards provide the information necessary to evaluate firm performance; and competitive markets serve as the ultimate constraint on poor performance. There is also no single best system of corporate governance. The United States approach is a classic example of outsider control; the Japanese and German systems are classic examples of insider control. Prowse (1995: 6–11).

[15] Mar and Young (2001: 282).

[16] Mako and Zhang (2002: 7).

[17] This discussion draws from World Bank (1997), Lin and Zhu (2001), and Broadman (2001).

autonomous legal entity, the intent of the Company Law was to isolate the commercial purposes of the firm from the political purposes of the state, as owner. In contrast to the SOE of old, which was essentially the production unit of a government ministry or bureau, the Company Law provided the legislative basis for the state to be a shareholder in a firm, and specified the structures through which it would govern the conduct of managers.[18] Mechanisms were included that both protected and preserved the dominant role of state ownership and paved the way for the eventual sale of state shares and broadening of ownership structures.

But identifying the part of the state that was the actual "owner" was rarely straightforward. There were often competing claims among government departments and agencies, and the process was often complicated by the large liabilities of SOEs. Everybody wanted the valuable assets, nobody wanted the liabilities, and there was neither a formal and transparent mechanism for sorting out the claims, nor a uniform policy approach to the problem.[19] In 1997, larger enterprises became the central focus of government efforts, while smaller SOEs were "released" through bankruptcy, debt write-offs, mergers, and sale.[20] This reduced the number of state-owned firms, but did little to solve the difficulties of the "priority" firms that the state hoped to "grasp" and reinvigorate.[21] Ownership continued to be vague, non-financial interests were still important, and transparent financial information on firm performance was rare. Large industrial enterprises operating in such a context, no matter how great the level of state support, will have more in common with the SOE of old, than the modern capitalist firms that they aspire to be.

Problems with Internal Governance

The weakness of governance structures is a critical problem for enterprise groups that developed rapidly with the benefit of state support, but now face pressure to rapidly cut costs in order to survive. SAIC, during the

---

[18] The reform turns SOEs from public sole proprietorships into four alternative organizational forms: limited liability stock company, limited liability company, employee shareholding co-operative and private enterprise. Generally, the latter two are for small-scale enterprises. Lin and Zhu (2001: 310).

[19] Broadman (2001: 863).

[20] For a careful account of policy refinements during this period, see Broadman (2001).

[21] According to Lin and Zhu (2001: 340), some 24,000, or 10% of SOEs had been given corporate forms by 1998. The percentage varied widely by region.

1990s was a prime example. It dominated the domestic auto market during the 1990s and was immensely profitable, but the internal governance of the group was a shambles.

The root of the governance problem during this early period was the non-financial interests of the state. Although not officially part of the local government bureaucracy, SAIC was very much a part of the local government. The primary linkage between the business group and the government was at the level of top management. Until 1995, the SAIC president served concurrently as the director of the Municipal Localization Office, a role that not only gave him control over the massive Localization Fund (and obviously simplified the process by which SAIC firms applied for funds), but also in charge of the government bureaucracy that oversaw the auto industry.[22] SAIC managers were appointed by the municipal government – until 1997 they reported to the Shanghai Economic Commission – and the rotation of leaders between SAIC and high-level municipal posts ensured that there was no divergence of views within the leadership of Shanghai's auto industry.[23]

Political control created a strong interest in balanced growth within the business group: the municipal government was developing the auto sector because it provided a large number of people with employment and social welfare benefits. Personnel policy was the most obvious manifestation of this objective.[24] As was almost universally the case in Chinese SOEs until the late-1990s, SAIC firms had excess workers, and given political realities, they were difficult to shed.[25] Not only was there the

---

[22] Interview, no. S16, May 27, 1997. In 1995, as part of an effort to make SAIC appear to be independent of government influence, this linkage was eliminated.

[23] The career path of the chairman of the SAIC group in 2005, Chen Xianglin, is a good example of how the leaders of the industry were shuffled through high-level positions in the municipal government. He was president of SAIC from 1983 to 1986; director of the Shanghai Planning Commission from 1987 to 1993, vice-secretary of the Shanghai branch of the Chinese Communist Party (CCP) from 1993 to 1994, and finally director of the Shanghai foreign trade office from 1994 to 1995. In 1995, Chen again became SAIC president (replacing Lu Jian, who in turn, returned to the Shanghai Municipal Economic Committee as vice-director) and then chairman of the board in 1999. Interview, no. S16, May 27, 1997 and Interview S26, June 11, 1998.

[24] As Andrew Walder observed in the mid-1990s, the nonfinancial interest in full employment "comprises one of the most difficult remaining political barriers to the further reform of state industry, as reformers who threaten sacrosanct guaranteed employment make themselves vulnerable to the mobilization of the worker and trade union support by officials opposed to rapid reform." Walder (1995: 19).

[25] This was the case even in JVs because the Chinese partner was usually in charge of personnel. The number of workers a JV was responsible for was always a point of contention when the JV contract was being negotiated. From the Chinese perspective, there was a strong desire to force the JV to absorb as large a portion of its labor burden as possible.

financial burden of these workers – in addition to being paid, they had to be housed, and provided with social services that in western countries would typically be provided by the government – they also made it difficult to reform management techniques in an enterprise,[26] they forced the group to expand in ways that would soak up excess workers,[27] and at times they precluded the use of technologies that would improve competitiveness, but reduce the need for workers.[28] In stark contrast to a western firm that is trying to cut costs, SAIC did everything possible to *avoid* downsizing.

The political objective of balanced growth, and the unquestioning embrace of the local government, made it extremely difficult to create effective governance mechanisms within the business group. Although on the surface SAIC looked much like a corporate group in a capitalist system, it functioned in a very different way.

The key flaw was the lack of an objective means of evaluating supplier performance. Beginning with the use of over-priced imported components (in the form of complete knocked-down kits) in 1985, the assembly JV purchased components at prices far above market value. A top manager explained the unwritten agreement that VW had with Shanghai: "I, VW, will keep quiet about paying inflated prices for components because I can get my customer – the state – to pay high prices [for the cars we produce], but the understanding is that the 70%–80% mark-up that Shanghai gains will be used to invest and create a competitive supply industry."[29] As the JV began to localize production, the willingness to pay inflated prices for components was an indication of its commitment to building a strong auto supply base in Shanghai; it was an investment that was necessary to develop a capable supply base.[30] Given the low

[26] As one foreign manager remarked, it was extremely difficult to push some employees to work hard and efficiently when others were sitting around reading the paper and drinking tea. The discrepancy created internal tension. Interview, no. S1, May 28, 1997. Usually, the excess workers that were particularly undesirable were elderly workers with uncompetitive skills.

[27] Expansion efforts were often motivated not by a desire to capture economies of scale or scope, but by a desire to soak up excess labor. Within the SAIC group, there were restaurants, hotels, taxi fleets, even a bottled-water company, that had no economic rational other than relieving the labor pressure.

[28] Interview, no. S21, June 18, 1998.

[29] Interview, no. S25, June 17, 1998.

[30] Component prices were determined by establishing the costs of the supply firm, and then negotiating an acceptable profit for them. "It was a bit like having big brother look after you," commented the manager of one firm. Interview, no. S19, June 16, 1998. Firms within the SAIC group did not even negotiate directly with SVW. The price was decided by the finance department of the SAIC head office and then sent down to the firm.

volumes of SVW at this stage, price support was necessary to fund supplier development. But the managers of Shanghai supply firms reiterated that there was a contract that was unwritten, but completely understood: SVW would help out the supply firms by paying higher prices in the early years with the understanding that the supply firm would help them out within five years by giving them lower prices.[31] The problem, of course, was that even after five years had passed it was very difficult to force supply firms to lower prices.

There were two aspects to this problem. First, there was no competitive pressure on supply firms. During the first stage of development, the Shanghai Municipal Localization Office had taken care to ensure that there was no duplication of manufacturing capability within the supply network so as to maximize economies of scale. Consequently, in the vast majority of cases the assembly plant had a single supplier for each component, they were all firms within the group, and the suppliers knew that the local government would ensure that they supplied the assembly plant no matter how high their costs.[32] From the perspective of the SAIC head office it did not matter if profits were concentrated at the level of the supply firm or the assembly plant. As one German manager at SVW explained, "We do not have commercial relations with our suppliers. Pricing has nothing to do with costs; it is moving money from the right pocket of SAIC to the left."[33]

Second, it was difficult for a head office to determine exactly who was responsible for poor performance in a particular supply firm. The weakness of market forces within the Shanghai auto sector did not necessarily preclude efforts to cut costs and increase competitiveness; the concept of the modern corporation is premised on the belief that in some instances it is efficient to replace markets with a hierarchy. The head office of a

---

[31] Interview, no. S27, June 22, 1998; Interview, no. S19, June 16, 1998.

[32] The importance of relationships was clearly evident in a 1997 effort to lower prices. Firms within the SAIC group were asked to reduce prices by 5%; firms within the municipality of Shanghai but not members of the SAIC group were asked to reduce prices by 10%; firms outside of Shanghai were asked to reduce prices by a minimum of 15%. One manager of a non-SAIC firm reported that they were beginning to make queries about the possibility of joining the SAIC group because "it is simply too competitive if you are not in SAIC. You can have the best quality and the lowest price, and still not survive. You need protection." Interview, no. S21, June 18, 1998.

[33] Theoretically, he continued, component prices might be lowered by sourcing a certain percentage of each part from secondary suppliers, but in practice his Chinese colleagues – SAIC employees – would not cooperate. They would be completely uncooperative with outside suppliers they would not give them the necessary drawings, would not even talk with them. Interview, no. S25, June 17, 1998.

multidivisional corporation, divorced from actual operations, manages strategic planning, and reallocates capital to those divisions where it believes yields will be highest.[34] Successful reallocation, however, depends on the ability of the head office to audit and monitor the performance of individual divisions. The form of auditing varies – in many cases figures are developed measuring divisional cost, revenue, profit, and investment performance – but it is the key to success.[35] Within SAIC, however, it was difficult to isolate the performance of one firm from the performance of the rest of the group. This was partly a consequence of the head office's refusal to divorce itself from operations at the firm level (as is commonly done in Western corporations). Because planning was always in conjunction with the head office, responsibility for poor performance could never be completely divorced from the head office.

Even more important, however, was that efforts to balance the performance of various firms within the SAIC group hopelessly obscured individual performance, and made it impossible to select between firms that were efficient and those that were not. If a firm within SAIC was a consistently strong performer, for instance, it would quite likely be given a lower price for the component it supplied to SVW (decreasing the strength of its balance sheet), and quite possibly would have workers transferred over from struggling firms (adding to the labor burden). If, on the other hand, a firm was having difficulties, it would receive a higher price for its components (artificially strengthening the balance sheet), and perhaps have its labor burden reduced. The result was a blurring of distinctions between firms. Although in a Western corporation divisional managers would be infuriated by such a policy, in Shanghai it was seen as quite natural. Financial relationships were loose, with supply firm managers consistently commenting that it was not important whether profit was reported in their firm, another firm (due to pricing policy), or at the head office; it was all in the SAIC family, and within the family there was a strong desire for balanced growth.

"In the past," explained the manager of a Shanghai components firm, "the [Shanghai] government was more interested in development than the economics of a particular enterprise. The attitude was the bigger the better." Top officials of SAIC confirmed this view – the emphasis was on

---

[34] Williamson (1981: 1556).

[35] When products move between divisions, transfer prices are often used, and the level they are set at can be a critical determinant of whether a manager appears to be a success or failure. Milgrom and Roberts (1992: 80).

development, not competitiveness.[36] "We have always had a parent/child relationship with our enterprises," a vice-president of SAIC commented in 1998, "the problem now is that the enterprises have the attitude that mom and pop always have money, and this is a very dangerous tendency."[37] The external environment was changing rapidly at this point, but old habits died hard.

II. INCOMPLETE DECENTRALIZATION, INSUFFICIENT EXTERNAL PRESSURE

Weak managerial incentives to cut costs and push competitiveness, and a head office unable to select those divisions that do so effectively, are hardly characteristics unique to state-owned firms in China. General Motors, for instance, suffered from much the same problems in the 1970s and 1980s. Although GM made every effort to monitor the performance of in-house divisions, the prices of components from these divisions were invariably higher than the same component purchased from an outside supplier.[38] In the case of GM, however, the impetus for change came not from within, but from the onslaught of Japanese competition in the 1980s; the shortcomings of internal governance were exposed by external pressure. In the heavily protected Chinese marketplace, external pressure clearly was not going to come from international competition, but what about domestic competition? Japanese firms were protected from international competition during their high-growth stage, but at least in some industries, glaring inefficiencies were kept in check by fierce competition within the domestic marketplace.

In theory, economic decentralization should have provided just this sort of competition within China, and indeed this was an often heard prediction. As I noted in Chapter 1, the theory of market-preserving federalism predicts that competition between regions in China will lead to policy imitation. When regions are given the autonomy and the incentives to pursue economic growth it is natural that their different interests, expectations, and capabilities will lead to a diversity of policy choices initially, but the expectation is that among regions with similar policy

---

[36] Interviews, no. S27, June 22, 1998; no. S23, June 25, 1998.

[37] Interview, no. S23, June 25, 1998.

[38] A mid-1980s General Motors survey of subsidiary suppliers found that parts sourced from GM suppliers were as much as 50% more expensive than similar parts sourced from outside the company. Lamming (1993: 20).

objectives, competition will lead to gradual policy convergence.[39] As I explained in Chapter 2, decentralization in China was considerably more complex. While decentralization may lead to positive economic outcomes when local governments are forced by the central government to adhere to hard budget constraints – meaning the localities will not be bailed out when they continue to support and/or subsidize inefficient and unproductive enterprises – if the central government does not have the ability to impose such budget constraints, local governments have little incentive to constrain spending, and economic outcomes are likely to be worse.[40] In China during the early to mid-1990s, this latter situation was more the norm. Decentralization was, in many respects, a result of central government weakness, and this made it difficult to impose discipline on local governments.

Shanghai demonstrated all of the weaknesses of decentralization in China. The municipal government did not want to subject local supply firms to market competition for the simple reason that local politics precluded the withdrawal of support from a municipal firm. It had non-budgetary funds to support local firms – the approximate 5 billion RMB in the localization fund – and it did not hesitate to play dirty with respect to the competition. In 1996, for instance, the municipality banned cars that had an engine capacity of below 1.6 liters from municipal streets, a move that conveniently ruled out cars from rival auto manufacturers in Tianjin.[41] It also ensured that local taxi companies, all owned by the local government, purchased only locally manufactured cars. Whether competitive or not, Shanghai municipal officials protected their own, and as a result there was little pressure, prior to WTO accession and the rise of the private market in China, to fundamentally correct the weaknesses in the internal governance of the local business group.

III. IMPROVING GOVERNANCE

The Chinese central government was well aware of the need to separate commercial and political objectives in the management of state assets – efforts to develop more effective corporate structures at the level of the firm would be pointless if these firms were not isolated from political

---

[39] Montinola, Qian, and Weingast (1995: 59).
[40] See Rodden (2001).
[41] Geoffrey Crothall, "Tianjin alleges car industry bias" *South China Morning Post*, March 7, 1996.

pressures of the owner – and by the late 1990s it began to reform the organizational structure of state asset management.

Top-Down Reorganization: Limited Success

Under the old system a government ministry or agency was in direct control of a particular firm, and for this supervising authority the firm was a source of both power and revenue. The intent of the restructuring efforts has been to separate the commercial and governmental role of the state, by placing firms under the control of independent asset management offices. The result is a three-tiered structure: at the top is an asset management office (that reports to the government), in the middle are holding companies and enterprise groups (many of which were formerly line ministries), and at the bottom are the manufacturing firms.[42]

The top tier at the national level is the State-owned Assets Supervision and Administration Commission (SASAC), and it is still quite new. This powerful central government agency was created in 2003 with the intent of clarifying the ownership and improving the oversight over the core state assets – no small task. The First Auto Works clearly illustrates the nature of the problem. A complex array of ties between the second (the business group) and third (the manufacturing firms) tiers were replaced with a relatively consistent system based on equity shares in an early restructuring effort in the late 1990s.[43] Each firm within the group was given a board of directors, and representatives on the board were determined by the equity share of each investor. In an effort to isolate the operating units from their social responsibilities, the social burden of firms (pensions, hospitals, schools, etc.) was transferred to the head office of FAW, and while this did not solve the problem, it did increase the level of transparency within the group.[44] The critical remaining problem was between the first and second tiers of management. In contrast to SAIC, which was clearly governed by the municipality of Shanghai, FAW suffered from the ambigous nature of central government control over the group.[45] SASAC was the proposed solution to this problem.

---

[42] The best depiction of this structure is in World Bank (1997: Chapter 3).

[43] For an account of the old system, see Marukawa (1999). The new system of equity shares seems to be common to all business groups – BAIC now has this system too.

[44] When FAW acquires new firms it is often extremely difficult to determine what share of the social burden of the new firm it will be responsible for. There seems to be no fixed approach to this problem; it is a matter of negotiation each time.

[45] This problem was exacerbated by the frequent organizational changes in Beijing. Interview, no. C13, January 17, 2003.

The center was perfectly willing to release hundreds of thousands of smaller firms to local governments, many of which would be privatized by one means or another, but SASAC was to provide a means of consolidating its control over the key firms in each sector. Although the degree to which SASAC will improve the governance of the largest SOEs is still not clear, it has emerged as a powerful player in Beijing. In the words of one observer, it has become "a highly powerful and centralized 'nanny' over state-owned enterprises."[46]

As is so often the case in China, restructuring efforts at the local level began much earlier than at the national level, and Shanghai has been at the fore of these efforts.[47] The first of the three-tiered structure in Shanghai consists of the Shanghai Municipal Asset Management Committee (*Shanghai shi guoyou zichan guanli weiyuanhui*), of which the Mayor is head, and the Shanghai Municipal Asset Management Office (*guoyou zichan guanli bangongshi*), which is the actual operating office.[48] This office does not manage firms, but it must approve new investment projects and make sure that they conform to government regulations.[49] The creation of this office enables the business groups in the city to gradually begin acquiring the trappings of modern corporations. The second tier of the overall structure – the head offices of the business groups – is linked to the Municipal Asset Management Office by a board of directors. The board for SAIC, created in 1999, is composed of four people from within SAIC and three from other government ministries.[50] Relations between the second tier and the third (the firms) are now completely characterized by the equity share that SAIC owns in any respective firm, much as if it is a holding company with a stake in different companies. The head office of SAIC receives dividends from the firms based on its equity share, and is taxed by the city.

Although a municipality certainly has an advantage over the central government with respect to the ease with which it can clarify and consolidate the ownership control of local firms, the impact of the changes in Shanghai should not be exaggerated. As Shanghai officials readily acknowledge, the changes are in many respects mere window

---

[46] Chris Buckley, "In China, power to the center: State firms' agency still calls the shots," *International Herald Tribune*, June 1, 2005.

[47] Shenzhen has also been leading these efforts. Tenev and Zhang with Brefort (2002: 26).

[48] Interview, S46, August 13, 2002.

[49] As one official in the office explained, an office of approximately 100 people could not possibly have the expertise to manage all the firms under its control. It acts as the owner, but gives firm managers autonomy. Interview, no. S47, August 14, 2002.

[50] The chairman in 2005 was Chen Xianglin, the former president of SAIC.

dressing – the "outsiders" on the board of directors are government officials who do not have a detailed knowledge of the auto industry (and consequently cannot challenge the views of SAIC board members), the party committees within holding companies continue to heavily influence appointments, salaries are not linked to performance, and perhaps most importantly, the sole shareholder is still a local government with political interests.[51] The intent seems to be to create the structures of formal corporate governance, even if they are initially less than effective, so as to create the possibility of a public listing and the eventual participation of more effective minority shareholders.[52] Such changes are a necessary first step, in short, but their impact at the firm level is not necessarily large. What SAIC needed in the short-term was an objective mechanism for evaluating supplier performance, and the resolve to make sourcing decisions based on performance rather than politics.

Bottom-up Change: FDI as a Positive Influence

When the president of GM China predicted that his company would rewrite the meaning of competition in China, he might have been closer to the truth than he realized. Foreign firms, to an extent, are doing from the bottom-up what the Chinese state has been unable to do (as of yet) from the top-down: improving the governance of Chinese firms.[53] In a very direct sense, foreign partners will push for proper accounting and financial management within a JV for the simple reason that it would be impossible to divide profits and losses according to equity shares without effective accounting. As I have explained, SAIC is overwhelmingly a business group composed of JVs – of the close to 50 firms within the SAIC

---

[51] In an excellent analysis of Shanghai holding companies and reforms of the asset management system, Christopher McNally points to the continued influence of party committees as being the critical problem. Given the party's control over personnel, he argues, the primary concern of managers is " . . . presenting the right political image. . . . Effectively managing state assets is secondary, especially since there are few negative consequences of economic mismanagement." McNally (2002: 109).

[52] In December 2004, SAIC announced the creation of a shareholding company, the Shanghai Automotive Group Company Limited. This new company would be the vehicle for an expected public offering in New York and Hong Kong. "Shanghai Automotive to launch shareholding company," *Xinhua Financial Network News*, December 31, 2004.

[53] Some argue that Chinese acquisitions of foreign companies – the Lenovo Group's acquisition of IBM's personal computer division being the notable example – are motivated as much by the Chinese firm's desire to understand the corporate governance and management of the Western firm as they are motivated by a desire for technology. Reg Birchfield, "China's Governance Buy-up," *New Zealand Management*, June 2005, p. 70.

group, only 7 continue to be 100% SAIC owned – and as a vice-director of the Shanghai Asset Management Office commented: "if 90% of your people are in JVs their thinking begins to change; all those people are working in a Western system."[54]

FDI, and GM in particular, also improved interfirm relations within the SAIC group. The primary problem within the Shanghai business group during the period of rapid growth was the weakness of internal incentives. Supply firms within the group had little incentive to cut cost not only because the head office of SAIC forced SVW to use SAIC suppliers, regardless of prices, but also because efforts to balance resources within the group obscured the performance of individual firms. VW did not complain in the early years of the JV because the protected market provided such a generous margin, vast inefficiencies could be overlooked. When the level of competition increased and VW wanted to pressure suppliers to lower prices, it was stuck with the old purchasing system. GM, by contrast, started its JVs with the expectation that China would be joining the WTO, and it would have to face international competition in a relatively short amount of time. Given this expectation, GM sought to establish a purchasing system that would be able to operate in a post-WTO environment.

The relationships that GM established with local suppliers were fundamentally different than those that SVW had with the same suppliers.[55] The American firm was able to pressure its supply firms because it introduced a purchasing process that was based on objective global benchmarks. In operations worldwide, GM makes purchasing decision based on a standard process of supplier evaluation, and a budget for every component based on the worldwide purchasing price for the part. The golden rule of GM purchasing is not to pay more than the price listed in the "cost book."[56] This approach, of course, led to much conflict during the purchasing meetings at SGM because SAIC would advocate purchasing local components that were far above the GM worldwide purchasing price. SAIC managers would invariably claim that the best and only domestic option was a SAIC firm, and in many instances this was indeed true. After all, Shanghai firms were the beneficiaries of

---

[54] Interview no. S47, August 14, 2002.
[55] This account of SGM purchasing is based primarily on Interview, no. S29, 2000; Interview, no. S43, August 6, 2002; and Interview, no. S53, August 14, 2002. It was corroborated at supply firms throughout the SAIC group.
[56] The GM supplier evaluations are based on the QTSP process (quality, technology, service, price).

15 years of strong growth. But after the initial survey of 1,000 supply firms throughout China, GM had the information necessary to evaluate these claims independently, and point to competing firms in China, or perhaps argue that it was worth importing a particular component.[57] Benchmarks from abroad decreased the market distortions created by Chinese tariffs; benchmarks from other provinces decreased the power of local politics.

Armed with objective evidence of the differential between local and global prices, GM used the prospects of falling tariffs after WTO accession as leverage. GM purchasing managers were well aware that SAIC was under enormous short-term pressure to increase the capacity utilization of SAIC firms – the foreign partners certainly would not win every disagreement over purchasing – but they were also keenly aware of SAIC's long-term desire to become a world-class company.[58] They presented the GM purchasing system as a model to be emulated. When GM owned its own group of supply firms, Delphi, it was in a situation exactly analogous to SAIC: competitiveness suffered because business was allocated to firms within the group without using benchmarks. The key to Delphi's eventual strength, GM managers continually told their Chinese counterparts, was the use of strict benchmarks based on quality, service, technology, and price. If a Delphi firm did not measure up, purchasing outside the group was not abandonment, but a means of providing the competition that would strengthen the entire group. To reinforce the point, GM made a point of taking top SAIC and Shanghai municipal government officials on trips to GM operations around the world, and to seminars on the worldwide purchasing techniques of GM.

The results of the more systematic purchasing process at SGM, although inconsistent, were undeniable. Increasingly there were two purchasing systems within the Shanghai supply network: the old SVW system and the new SGM system. The former was all about relationships; the

---

[57] This is the survey described in the previous chapter. In the case of power trains, for instance, 138 firms in 12 provinces were evaluated. Forty firms were ultimately given contracts, of which roughly half were Shanghai firms. Interview, S34, June 30, 2000. Liberalization of access to foreign exchange made imports increasingly possible.

[58] GM managers consistently spoke of SAIC's ambitions as a means of motivating the group. As one GM manager commented, "SAIC understands the need for competitive prices, and they are motivated by the desire to be a world class company." Interview, no. B45, July 26, 2002. This ambition was fueled by both the local and central government. By the late-1990s, the central government industrial policy was focusing on three core firms in the auto industry: SAIC, FAW, and Dongfeng. Although the style and approach of the three business groups differed, their ambition was similar.

latter was above-board negotiations, competition, and hard bargaining.[59] In many cases, firms sold similar components to SVW for one price, and then another (lower) price for SGM. In one case, a supply firm was selling a component to SGM at a loss because it was forced to meet the GM worldwide purchasing price, but was unable to achieve the economies of scale that would make it profitable to do so. It was willing to do this in the short-term, in order to secure the contract.[60] In another case, a Taiwanese-Japanese JV in Shanghai, that had never been able to obtain SVW business because it was not part of SAIC, was finding that SGM was becoming an important customer.[61] Overall, SGM acknowledged that component prices for the W-car (Buick) were consistently above world purchasing prices – and varied by component – but prices for the S-car (Sail), introduced several years later, were much closer to the targets.[62] SGM, commented the Chinese manager of one supply firm, was bringing a "new mentality" to SAIC.[63]

SVW had no choice but to respond, and after introducing a new model of its own in 2000, it began to duplicate the SGM purchasing system. While component prices for the Santana continued to be procured by the old purchasing methods, VW began to use global purchasing prices as the benchmark for Passat and Polo components.[64] The target for the Polo, for instance, was to have the average price for components sourced within China to not exceed the purchasing price in Germany by more than 15–18%. Although it came close, SVW did not achieve this goal.[65] In addition to the problem of having pre-existing relationships with suppliers, an additional problem was that VW was itself quite new to the type of systematic purchasing process that was being implemented in Shanghai. In Germany,

[59] Firms closely guard the purchasing prices for components, but in interviews would speak generally about relative prices. This assessment is based on interviews with 4 purchasing managers at the Shanghai assembly plants and interviews at 9 Shanghai supply firms between 2000 and 2003.

[60] Interview, no. S42, July 13, 2000. When this firm was interviewed in 2000, managers pointed to 100,000 units at SGM as the volume at which they would break even. Total SGM volumes in 2002 were 100,000, but only 45,000 of these were Buicks.

[61] Interview, no. S36, July 11, 2000.

[62] Interview, no. S43, August 6, 2002. GM managers acknowledged that they had to pay well above their targets for many components.

[63] Interview, no. S41, July 13, 2000.

[64] Interview, S44, August 7, 2002. As one supply manager explained, the Passat had been launched in Europe only a few years before, and when negotiations took place in Shanghai, VW (much like GM), increasingly, said "hey look, this is the way we do it in Europe – here are the prices we expect." Interview, S45, August 8, 2002.

[65] Interview, no. S51, January 20, 2003.

according to managers at SVW, these approaches had been quite foreign to VW until the arrival of Jose Ignacio Lopez de Arriortua in 1993. Lopez, of course, had previously been the vice-president for worldwide purchasing at GM, where he had achieved fame for his ability to cut costs and streamline production – exactly what was needed at SAIC.[66]

In short, there are important differences between foreign partners, and different partners bring different aspects of a modern firm to the table. VW might have been an excellent choice during the first stage of development, when the emphasis was on manufacturing skills, but GM was a better choice when it came time to implement a more systematic approach to management.

IV. CONCLUSION

That a state-owned enterprise in China finds it difficult to drive down costs is hardly a surprise. But it does point to the challenge that the Chinese central government faces in its desire to support large-scale internationally competitive business groups. The starting point of the government's industrial policy is to support the largest of the SOEs; although they are not competitive, they are at least large. In the absence of effective governance, these efforts are unlikely to succeed. The institutional changes that are required are complex, and there is little consensus on the way forward.[67]

The continuing efforts to improve governance structures will most likely have to be complemented by a reduction in the state's equity share of the business groups. In addition to increasing the distance between the political and financial interests of the ownership, a further benefit

---

[66] There is much evidence to support those who point to the importance of Lopez's influence on VW purchasing, and indeed this evidence became central to a celebrated case of industrial espionage when Lopez was accused by GM of illegally taking "trade secrets" with him to VW. The legal case centered on whether Lopez stole the GM "cost book," which would have revealed what the company paid for its components worldwide, and given VW a considerable advantage in negotiations with suppliers. In the end, VW settled (and paid GM US$100 million), but admitted no wrongdoing. See Keith Bradsher, "Former G.M. Executive Indicted On Charges of Taking Secrets," *The New York Times*, May 23, 2000, p. C1.

[67] Steinfeld (1998), for example, emphasizes the absence of effective governance mechanisms, and argues that massive privatization would be counterproductive. The only solution is to cut SOE access to cheap credit, and only the state can effectively do so. McNally (2002), on the other hand, argues that party interference in SOE governance is so pervasive it is unlikely that the state will be able to effectively harden budget constraints.

would be an enhanced ability to explore new organizational forms within the auto sector. GM, for instance, has pushed SAIC away from a rigid hierarchy – where a supply firm assumed it had a guaranteed market – and toward an approach that introduces elements of competition, but there are limits on how far this trend can progress. Currently, an SAIC supply firm has to worry about the outside benchmarks that GM contributes, but it still has the inside track at the assembly plant purchasing office. If the ownership ties between the SAIC assembly plant and supply firms are severed, however, and the equity share of the local government is reduced, it becomes possible to move even further away from the strict hierarchical approach that has limited the ability of SAIC firms to increase competitiveness.[68] Over the long run, only further institutional change will create a framework that will support the long-term development of competitive firms.

Yasheng Huang, in his book *Selling China*, also argues that institutional weakness has inhibited the growth of Chinese firms, but his view of the interaction between Chinese and foreign firms is very different from my own.[69] Huang argues that the massive inflow of FDI in China is caused by the systemic discrimination against China's most efficient firms – those in the private sector. Chinese financial institutions limited the access of private firms to investment capital, Chinese political and legal institutions refused to give private firms the same rights and recognitions as state-owned firms, and economic fragmentation within China made it difficult for Chinese firms to expand and purchase the assets of firms in other jurisdictions. Because foreign firms did not suffer the same disadvantages, they were able to fill a void that otherwise would have been filled by dynamic and efficient Chinese firms – FDI is a second best solution.

While Huang's argument concerning the problems that stem from the "political pecking order" of firms in China and the fragmentation of the economy is certainly correct, his argument concerning the value of a foreign firm's contribution in China is problematic, primarily because it is too general. His argument has great merit for labor-intensive activities and what he calls "quintessentially" Chinese activities – private Chinese firms might very well thrive in these areas if it were not for the discrimination

---

[68] If there is a public offering of SAIC shares, and this seems to be a goal, the group would be able to sell off the supply firms in the manner that GM and Ford both sold Delphi and Visteon.

[69] Huang (2003).

they faced – but it is less persuasive for economic activities in which foreign firms have an advantage in either hard or soft technologies. Because FDI dominates across the boards, Huang largely abandons such distinctions.[70] The problem with this lack of specification, is that readers can easily come away with the conclusion that FDI is preventing Chinese firms from dominating critical aspects of the Chinese economy (e.g., the "pillar" industries such as autos) when a more modest version of the argument is probably more accurate: private firms in labor-intensive and traditional Chinese industries would be able to more effectively compete with foreign firms if it were not for the institutional discrimination against private firms in China.

The case of autos highlights this weakness. Huang uses SAIC as a central example of how economic fragmentation artificially increases the need for FDI: the regionally based strategy of SAIC led it to abandon capable suppliers in other provinces in favor of local suppliers, and due to the enormous amount of capital required by this strategy, SAIC was forced to rely on FDI to a greater extent than its competitors because it needed the capital.[71] "An FDI demand of this sort is driven more by an institutional imperative and less by actual business needs to source price-competitive and quality components," Huang argues.[72] But this was not the case. While there were certainly capable suppliers outside of Shanghai that SAIC ignored for institutional reasons, the local bias of Shanghai did not lead to a shortage of capital (and thus artificially inflate the demand for FDI). Much to the contrary, SAIC was capital rich in the 1990s (due to the enormously profitable Santana) and as I have explained, it actually began to look for opportunities to *export* capital at the same time that it continued to form new joint ventures in the supply sector.[73]

Why did SAIC continue to form new JVs in the latter half of the 1990s despite its abundance of capital? First, a new assembly partner provided the latest technology and a systematic approach to purchasing that made it possible to improve governance within the supply network. Second,

---

[70] He also argues that FDI in technology- and capital-intensive sectors is a relatively small portion of the overall total. Huang (2003: 1–2).

[71] Huang (2003: p. 282–4).

[72] Huang (2003: 281).

[73] The offshore investments began in 2002. As I pointed out in the previous chapter the number of SVW suppliers that were JVs in 1997 was just under 30% (see Figure 7.1). By 2002, virtually every major firm within the SAIC group was a JV. It was only in 2004 that the strategy of overseas acquisitions created the need for public offering to raise capital.

the more advanced models that were introduced at the assembly JVs necessitated an upgrading of the technical capabilities of the supply firms. In some cases licensing arrangements were viewed by the Chinese partner as being inadequate for their needs[74]; in other cases foreign firms were unwilling to license technology due to concerns about intellectual property rights.[75] Foreign firms provided skills and technology that would not have been present in their absence.

In many respects, what is surprising is not that these supply firms were JVs rather than Chinese-owned firms, but that they were not wholly foreign-owned (an option that was open to supply firms but not assemblers). Although foreign firms increasingly preferred wholly owned ventures, auto supply firms needed the Chinese partner because the partner controlled purchasing at the assembly plant. The high presence of JVs, in other words, was an indication of continued Chinese leverage, not weakness. By 2002, virtually every major firm within the SAIC group was a JV.

If the major auto groups in China are hampered by weak governance and the problems associated with state-ownership, would private auto firms have been able to develop independently of FDI had they not faced systematic discrimination? Firms such as Geely (in Zhejiang) and Great Wall (in Hebei) have great potential at the low end of the market, and have been very successful in capitalizing on the capabilities of the supply networks that have been developed by the JV projects. The shortcomings of intellectual property rights protection in China have also worked in the favor of such firms (to the dismay of the MNCs). But while these firms are highly skilled at copying and undercutting on the basis of price, they are likely to find it difficult to compete with the resources and design skills of the global firms in more advanced models.[76] Far from being a disgrace, this is the trend for auto firms in all countries. As I explained in

---

[74] This is "Firm B" from the previous chapter.

[75] The top Chinese manufacturer of a key engine component wanted to license technology from VW for a new model – the central government wanted it to remain independent – but VW refused. As competition increased, however, the central government realized that the Chinese firm would be unable to remain independent, and it was granted approval for a JV. Interview, no. S48, August 16, 2002.

[76] On the prospects for these independent firms, see footnote 22 in Chapter 7. Geely, which produced China's cheapest passenger car in 2003, increased its output from 20,000 in 2001 to 86,000 in 2004. Mark O'Neill, "Investors rush into car industry," *South China Morning Post*, April 23, 2003; "2004 Domestic passenger car sales," *Fourin China Auto Weekly*, May 9, 2005, p. 2.

the previous chapter, very few firms in any country have the resources to independently design and launch a full range of models.[77]

In an ideal world, the development of national champions in China would not be hindered by poor governance mechanisms. In an ideal world, local governments in China would not burden firms with political and social responsibilities. In the very real world of a developing country, however, institutional capabilities fall short of the demands that are placed on them, and governments lack the political will to make painful choices. These problems cannot simply be wished away. In the short term at least, the increase of FDI in Shanghai began to provide the competition that was needed to push firms and local bureaucrats to increase efficiency and prepare for post-WTO China.

---

[77] Even in Beijing, this is hardly an unusual viewpoint. At an industry forum in 2003, Bai Jinfu, the vice director of the research center attached to the SASAC, explained that the objective of independent auto technology could not work counter to the trend of globalization. The objective, he argued, should be to cooperate with foreign firms so as complement each other's strengths, share risks, and form new innovations. "China's auto industry seeks to forge own brands," *Xinhua Economic News Service*, April 19, 2004.

PART IV

CONCLUSION

NINE

Local Institutions in a Global Economy

The rise of China as a manufacturing power has corresponded to profound shifts in the global economy. In the early 1980s, when a consensus began to emerge among policymakers in Beijing that the automotive industry should be the target of industrial development efforts, the
environment was a familiar one for a developing country in East Asia,
and it was one that centered around the nation-state: the domestic market was heavily protected, linkages to foreign markets and technology
were critical, but tightly controlled, and the state was receptive to playing
an active role in the development process. As the development process
gathered steam in China, the integration of national economies picked
up speed and intensity. World export volumes continued to increase, but
it was international production that was becoming the primary driver
of the global economy and economic development.[1] Whereas in 1980,
foreign direct investment inflows formed 11.7% of gross domestic capital formation in manufacturing in developing countries, this number had
increased to 36.7% by 1998.[2] There was a slight decline in total FDI flows
to the developing world after 2000, largely as a result of declining flows to
middle-income Latin American countries, but the flows to China continued to increase, and in 2003 it became the top destination for FDI in the

---

[1] In terms of delivering goods and services to foreign markets, foreign investment became
more important than international trade during the 1990s. Foreign affiliate sales (of goods
and services) in domestic and international markets were approximately $11 trillion in
1998, for example, compared with approximately $7 trillion in world trade the same year.
UNCTAD (1999: xix).
[2] UNCTAD (2000: 5).

world.[3] The global economy was increasingly becoming a single market for goods, services, capital, and labor, and China was its poster child. Tariff barriers were falling, FDI inflows were the highest in the world, and Chinese firms were playing key roles in global production networks.

If firms are increasingly operating in a single global economy, why focus on local institutions? As many scholars have recognized, the nation-state has been pressured not only from above, but also from below. Central governments, swept up in a wave of neoliberal sentiment, have been devolving power to local governments at the same time that manufacturing firms, motivated by post-Fordist manufacturing techniques, have increasingly been seeking to draw upon the advantages of local industrial clusters. "There is, in other words, a double movement of globalisation on the one hand and devolution, decentralization or localization on the other," writes Eric Swyngedouw – what he calls "glocalisation."[4] The state continues to be a key determinant of the local institutions that are central to development, but as Doner and Hershberg argue, the appropriate policies are likely to be less uniform than in the past, and highly contextual in nature – both place- and industry-specific.[5]

China, of course, has been an important example of this process. Economic decentralization has been a primary characteristic of Chinese economic reform. By the early 1990s, the weakening of central power was so pronounced, some feared the state itself would collapse.[6] The limited ability of the central government to direct industrial development efforts in China was a starting point of this book. The center was not without important levers of power – it selected the major players (through the JV approval process), set the rules (domestic content regulations), and controlled interaction with the global economy – but it was far from the bureaucratic ideal that lies at the core of the developmental state model. It was left to local governments and their foreign partners to experiment with alternative approaches to development. Approaches varied, as did outcomes – an ideal opportunity to examine exactly how local institutions affect development outcomes. Why did outcomes between localities vary so widely? How durable were institutional arrangements, and how did the degree of durability affect outcomes over time? What can the experience

---

[3] The World Bank (2004: 79) points in particular to declining flows to Brazil and Argentina. Because of this decline, Asia's share of FDI to the developing world increased from 38% in 2002 to 42% in 2003. 94% of this latter figure went to China (World Bank 2004: 80).

[4] Swyngedouw (1992: 40).

[5] Doner and Hershberg (1999: 51).

[6] Wang and Hu (2001).

of the Chinese auto sector tell us about the challenges of development in the new global economy? In this conclusion I consider each of these questions in turn.

I. COMPARATIVE INSTITUTIONAL ADVANTAGE AT THE LOCAL LEVEL

Despite decades of central planning in China, there is no single approach to development. The nation is a mosaic of local patterns. In this book I have characterized the institutional patterns of different localities according to the internal structure of local bureaucracies and business groups. When Shanghai sought to develop the local auto industry it became a *local developmental state*. The municipality developed a unified bureaucratic structure that, in partnership with a large business group that coordinated interfirm relations by means of a hierarchical structure, directed a process of industrial transformation. Beijing and Guangzhou were examples of a *laissez-faire local state*. The investment efforts of the local state were dispersed, and because firms were owned by different ministries, each with its own set of incentives, they competed with each other for business and investment capital. Firms were left to their own devices. Changchun and Wuhan were both examples of *firm-dominated local states*. The business groups were hierarchically organized, but the local governments had little capacity to support firm development (see Figure 1.1).

In the first stage of auto sector development in China, an initial problem was the need for coordinated investment. Assembly plants were forced by local content regulations to develop domestic suppliers, but no single supplier wanted to risk investing heavily to upgrade production facilities until it was clear that all firms would do so, because only then would the assembly plant be able to raise volumes and allow suppliers to achieve economies of scale. This problem was exacerbated by a high degree of asset specificity: it was common at this stage for a supply firm to be supplying only assembly plants within the home locality. Finally, the pace of technical change during this stage was not rapid. It was a heavily protected market, and the products were far behind international standards – there was little need for innovation.

The institutional pattern that was most appropriate for a sector with these characteristics was the local developmental state. The Shanghai municipal government collected the necessary investment capital and coordinated the process of investment; the hierarchically organized business group provided security for small firms (by guaranteeing a market for their products) and nurtured firm development. Knowledge was critical to firm development – knowledge about markets, knowledge about management, knowledge about technology – and the structure of the business group effectively disseminated this knowledge.[7] The laissez-faire approach of Beijing and Guangzhou did not do this effectively. Fragmented bureaucracies failed to coordinate the investment process, and the business groups used market competition to drive down the prices of fledgling suppliers. Few had the resources to develop. The firm-dominated localities of Changchun and Wuhan had hierarchical business groups, but because they were controlled at the central level, their focus was fragmented. The local governments were completely out of the loop: they did not have any influence over the assembly plants and had few resources of their own.

If this argument about sectors and local institutions is correct, the localities that were not appropriate for auto sector development should have attributes that are beneficial for sectors with a different set of characteristics. Portions of the information technology (IT) industry, for instance, are in many respects the opposite of the auto industry: the technological pioneers are often small firms, capital requirements are limited (when compared to auto assembly plants), and innovation is extremely rapid.[8] Whereas the auto industry requires an organizational structure that will monitor the learning process in each supply firm and insure that there are no deviations from a prescribed set of standards, firms involved in the production of computer hardware, software, components, and peripherals require a flexible structure that will cultivate innovation and change. IT firms benefit from dense interpersonal linkages and the exchange of ideas between firms and research institutes, but these tend to be informal and horizontal rather than imposed from above. Start-up capital is necessary, but because the fate of an individual firm is not linked through a supply chain to a network of firms over which it has no control, there is not the same need for coordination as in the auto industry. While the state can play a productive role in the development process, it is a less intrusive role.

Adam Segal, in his research on the development of high-tech firms in China, found that Shanghai, the city that was most successful in developing the manufacturing capability of auto firms, was least effective in

---

[7] Pyke (1992: 11) discusses the importance of knowledge in small firm development.

[8] This section on the IT sector is based on Segal (2003) and Segal and Thun (2001). In a challenge to the conventional characterization of the IT industry (and in particular Taiwan's) as being populated primarily by SMEs, Amsden and Chu (2003) argue that it is large firms that play the central role in the upgrading process.

fostering the growth of innovative and competitive firms in the IT sector. Why? In large part because the municipality's approach to high-tech development was little different from its approach to auto sector development, despite the critical differences between the sectors. When the central government placed the Shanghai electronics firms under municipal control in 1985, the local bureaucracy did what it did best – organized firms into large industrial groups. "In Shanghai," a central government official explained to Segal, "the local government dominates and it knows how to take advantage of the old planning system. Even branches of central state ministries must first answer to the local government."[9] Rather than grant science and technology personnel the independence to direct research and development, bureaucrats attempted to coordinate the development of high-tech firms so as to complement broader development efforts in the locality. Smaller and more flexible nongovernmental firms (*minying qiye*) were discriminated against with respect to funding, regulations, and supervisory policies. As one manager at a high-technology enterprise explained, "state-owned enterprises are so big in Shanghai there is room for nothing else – they are like trees blocking out the sun."[10] Not surprisingly, Shanghai firms did well in the technology areas that were conducive to coordination and planning, such as integrated circuits and other areas of IT hardware.[11]

In Beijing, by contrast, a fragmented local government gave IT firms a degree of autonomy that stimulated informal ties within the sector, entrepreneurship, and experimentation. Without the planning capacity of Shanghai, the approach of the municipal government was to promote development policies that did not require extensive government intervention or large corporate groups; officials clarified and refined the property rights of the small nongovernmental firms, provided the space for them to develop, and let individual scientists and entrepreneurs take the lead in the development of the sector. This approach served to tighten the links between the university-based scientific community and small firms because scientists, rather than being pushed under the umbrella of a large business group, were encouraged to join (or create) small firms.[12] The role of the local government in fostering "innovation networks" was subtle, but important. Beijing led the country in terms of high-tech

---

[9] Segal (2003: 92).
[10] Segal and Thun (2001: 572).
[11] Segal (2003: 87).
[12] Segal (2003: Chapter 3); Segal and Thun (2001: 577–580).

innovation, receiving 32.5% of all awards given to National Technology Entrepreneurs between 1988 and 1994, and by 1999, it had 4,000 IT firms that registered $5.4 billion in annual volume of business.[13]

The approach of the Guangzhou municipal government to the IT sector was hands-off, in the style of a laissez-faire local state, but with an important difference to Beijing. Just as the ability to import components distracted from the task of nurturing manufacturing capability in local auto firms, the municipal government, eager to attract foreign investment and foreign exchange provided generous tax breaks to foreign firms that invested in the Tianhe Science Park. By 1995 the Park had received over $100 million in investment, but critics were increasingly pointing out that these were assembly operations and relatively low-tech.[14] As Segal argues, "scientific planning was often side-tracked from the more difficult path of fostering innovation by more short-term, profit-oriented goals."[15]

This is not to argue, of course, that local institutional structures are destiny, completely determining the economic outcomes of a locality. Automobiles and computers are products that are made in factories and the management and resources within those factory walls will obviously be important. The identity of foreign partners, in particular, can be a critical ingredient. GM had a far more systematic approach to purchasing operations than VW; Honda was quite willing to rely almost exclusively on its Japanese suppliers. When discussing the development of entire economic sectors, however, the institutional patterns within a locality will have important economic consequences. As Peter Evans comments, "sectoral characteristics define what roles are likely to work; the nature of the state determines whether a role can be carried out."[16] Brazil, Korea, and India all adapted a highly interventionist approach to the steel sector development, but only Korea succeeded. The Korean state could effectively intervene, Evans argues, because its bureaucratic structures fit the needs of the sector. It was a sector in which the product technology was stable and the process technology was diffused. The developmental state could provide the financial support and nurture the development of a

---

[13] By the late 1990s, Shanghai also had 7,000 minying firms, but they continued to play a relatively minor role – 87% of Shanghai's total high-tech output in 2000 was from 6 large SOEs. Segal (2003: 87–88). The number of Beijing firms in 1999 is from Segal (2003: 52).

[14] The Guangzhou Science and Technology Commission, for instance, declared that in 1992 only 5% of HK invested enterprises were involved in high-tech processes or products. Segal (2003: 133).

[15] Segal (2003: 125).

[16] Evans (1995: 94).

large Korean SOE. The argument here is similar, but the variation is in local institutions. The institutional pattern of Shanghai is similar to Korea; Beijing is perhaps closest to the Taiwanese model, with its combination of flexible SMEs and government-sponsored research institutes; Guangzhou might be closest to the *maquiladora* pattern of Mexico.

Does the size of the localities in China make them exceptional cases? Cities such as Shanghai (population over 12 million) and Beijing (population over 10 million) have the populations of many small countries: larger than Belgium and Switzerland, and half of Taiwan. Is this only an argument for very large countries? The argument is certainly more powerful in a large state with numerous and diverse localities than it would be in a small, relatively homogenous country, but in a world increasingly characterized by regional integration and trade liberalization, the trend is toward larger economic units. When the nation-state is the basic unit of the world economy, there are incentives for states to duplicate each other's economic capabilities. Although in theory, free trade should create incentives for states to concentrate on their comparative advantage, in reality, barriers to trade, politics, and the desire to control what are perceived to be highly profitable industries often leads realist nation-states to duplicate capabilities. Free-trade zones, however, begin the process of breaking down these barriers and starting a process of regional integration. When these efforts succeed, the playing field is transformed from one consisting of numerous small players to one consisting of a few big players. The European Community, for instance, might be looked at as a unit very similar to China: internally it is a free trade zone with a single currency and a central policymaking organization, but it is composed of localities that have different customs, languages, institutional strengths, and interests. It makes just as much sense to speak of Frankfurt or Milan in such an environment, if that is the internal unit with the most pronounced institutional variation, as it does to speak of Germany or Italy. Paradoxically, as the units of the world economy increase in size, the importance of localities may also increase.

II. THE CHALLENGE OF INSTITUTIONAL CHANGE

The importance of local institutions creates an obvious interest in their origins: is the secret to development success simply adapting the institutional structures that match the developmental objectives of a state? Within the social sciences there is sometimes the assumption that, although imperfect, the policymaking process is at some level characterized by a process of rational imitation; government officials consider a variety of policy alternatives that have been proven successful elsewhere and choose the "blueprint" that is most appropriate for their own circumstances. In many instances, the view of institutional development and change is functional; as policies change and evolve, new institutions will be created to serve new purposes.[17]

As I have noted, the expectation of rational imitation is explicit in the theory of market-preserving federalism.[18] It is also often implicit. When scholars advocate a particular policy approach as being the most effective path to rapid development, there is seldom an investigation into the historical roots of particular policies, or the degree of transferability.[19] In Eastern Europe and Russia, after the fall of the Soviet Union, Western advisors advocated the rapid and wholesale adoption of market institutions; scholars of East Asia, at much the same time, drew the conclusion that the institutions of a developmental state were the solution to the challenges of economic development.[20] In both cases it was generally assumed that knowledge of the correct policies was the key, and that successful implementation would easily follow. The case studies in this book demonstrate the difficulty of dramatic and rapid change across both space and time.

Policy Imitation: Rational, But Not Easy

With respect to the former, the single national context, common objective, and clear understanding of the variety of policy approaches that were being used, created a perfect opportunity for different localities to imitate those policies that proved to be successful elsewhere. But policy approaches were deeply rooted in the institutional histories of the different localities. Shanghai's history as the core of the central planning system meant that bureaucratic planning was second nature within the municipality: the government bureaucracies were organized in a manner

---

[17] For a discussion of functionalist arguments about institutions, see Pierson (2000a: 476). As Pierson comments, much of this tendency is a result of building on the new institutional economics, which sees particular organizational forms as emerging because rational actors seek to reduce transaction costs.

[18] Montinola, Qian, and Weingast (1995).

[19] This is a point that Atul Kohli has made as well. See Atul Kohli, "Where do high-growth political economies come from? The Japanese lineage of the Korea's 'developmental state'" in Woo-Cumings (1999: 94 and 97).

[20] On the former, see Stark (1992) and Blanchard (1991); on the latter, see Johnson (1982); Amsden (1989); Wade (1990).

conducive to industrial planning, career paths rotated officials between top government and industry jobs so that there was a unified municipal perspective, ownership ties created a sense of common purpose among firms, and firm managers were accustomed to working in close cooperation with a head office. Shanghai did not take a bureaucratic, large corporate group approach to auto sector development because Shanghai policymakers thought this would be the most effective approach; they took this approach because it was what they always did. Proof of this lies in the fact that they adopted the same development approach both when it was appropriate to do so, as in the case of the auto sector, and when it was *not* appropriate to do so, as in the case of the IT sector. The political and industrial history of Beijing, on the other hand, lent itself to a more hands-off governmental role. The municipality took the same approach in both the IT and auto sectors, and succeeded in the one case in which that approach was appropriate: the IT sector. Guangzhou tried to imitate the Shanghai "model." It actually sent a study team to Shanghai in 1993, and this team recommended unifying control within the local auto sector so as to better nurture firm development.[21] The prescription was accurate, but change was slight. Although the development literature often makes the assumption that a state can effortlessly adapt the policies of a more successful competitor, this is easier said than done.

Evolving Sectors, Lagging Institutions

The evolution of an industrial sector over time creates challenges of its own. Industrial sectors are in a constant state of flux, responding to advances in technology, changes in regulatory institutions and consumer demand, and cyclical patterns within a sector.[22] The rate of change and the competitive dynamic may vary between sectors, but none is static. IBM had to face the emergence of the nimble manufacturers of IBM-compatible computers; Ford and General Motors had to face a resurrected Chrysler and competition from Japan. Change is the heart of Schumpeter's "creative destruction."[23]

---

[21] Guangzhou Municipal Auto Industry Office, "Tan Guangzhou shi ruhe fazhan jiaoche gongye" [Report on Guangzhou Municipality Auto Sector Development], Internal Report, July 21, 1993, p. 3.

[22] For examples of each, see Kitschelt (1991); Piore and Sabel (1984); Fine (1998).

[23] "Capitalism, then, is by nature a form or method of economic change. . . . The opening up of new markets, foreign or domestic, and the organizational development from the craft shop and factory to such concerns as U.S. Steel illustrate the same process of industrial

The rate of change in the context of late development can be particularly dramatic. In the initial stages of growth, firms are coddled in a developmental cocoon, enjoying tariff protection and state subsidies, and the primary challenge is borrowing technology from abroad and mastering (and hopefully improving) the required manufacturing techniques; in subsequent stages, if they aspire to be globally competitive, they must meet their global competitors on an equal footing. The institutional requirements of a particular sector will vary at each stage. The local developmental state approach of Shanghai worked extremely well when the local auto firms were concerned with basić manufacturing capability rather than efficiency, I have argued, but this same approach made it difficult to increase efficiency as growth occurred.

This phenomenon of "growing into trouble," to use the phrase of Doner and Ramsay, is hardly unique to Shanghai.[24] The political and economic institutions of the Japanese developmental state (a strong bureaucracy that focused on promotion rather than regulations, a centralized financial system, *keiretsu* groups, and close state-business ties) worked well during the catch-up phase of development, but ran into problems as the economy matured. When technology could be borrowed or reverse-engineered, the rate of technical change was relatively slow, and the international environment was positive (open foreign markets, protected domestic markets, and ready access to foreign technology), Japanese firms prospered in sectors with high barriers to entry, long product cycles, and slow profit turnaround.[25] As the environment changed – due to appreciation of the currency, increasing costs at home, and trade tensions – Japanese firms had to move into the higher value-added sectors where technical change was rapid and discontinuous. Both corporate structures and systems of innovation were ill suited for these new challenges, and the sources of strength in the past, argues Marie Anchordoguy, became critical liabilities. "The lack of an objective umpire and mechanism for 'creative destruction' of industries, the tendency toward cooperative, risk-sharing competition, and the unwillingness to promote efficiency and economic growth if the cost is sharply increased social instability have locked Japan into a set

---

mutation – if I may use that biological term – that incessantly revolutionizes the economic structure *from within*, incessantly destroying the old one, incessantly creating a new one. This process of creative destruction is the essential fact about capitalism. It is what capitalism consists in and what every capitalist concern has got to live in. . . ." Schumpeter (1950: 82–83).

[24] Doner and Ramsay (2004).

[25] This paragraph draws from Anchordoguy (2001).

of outdated policies and institutions."[26] Although "locked" might be too strong a word, few would argue with the idea that Japan, after experiencing tremendous growth, ran into trouble.

What determines the capacity of an institutional context to evolve and change in accordance with the needs of an industrial sector and the external environment? Neither economic nor political organizations have the capacity for seamless change, and in fact, many scholars have argued that there are similar dynamics of change in both forms of organization. The study of technology and its social context, for instance, has clarified how set-up costs, learning effects, coordination effects, and adaptive expectations will shape the creation and evolution of organizations and institutions, and the implications are important in a wide range of economic, political, and social contexts.[27] Path-dependent arguments of this sort focus on the "supply" side of institutional change.

The "demand" for change – or the pressure which is exerted on actors or felt by actors – will vary in economic and political contexts. Economic actors operating in competitive markets may differ in preferences (perhaps as a result of the identity of the owner), but the demand for change will be similar for all firms: at some level they must be able to survive in the marketplace in which they compete, the price mechanism provides a common metric, and this competitive dynamic shapes organizational change. This is a simplistic view, of course, but it provides a large part of the foundation of economic theory. It is also this unified incentive structure for an economic actor that allows Charles Fine to point to a common dynamic of organizational change across sectors. As a particular firm within a manufacturing chain becomes more powerful, Fine argues, it uses its market power to bundle together discrete parts of the chain so as to add value and increase its control over the final product. The result is increased vertical integration, in the manner of an IBM or GM. As one firm becomes increasingly dominant, however, it becomes difficult both to avoid the organizational rigidities that are endemic to large companies

---

[26] Anchordoguy (2001: 7–8). Richard Katz (1998: 4) makes a similar argument: "The root of the problem is that Japan is still mired in the structures and policies that prevailed in the 1950s–60s. What we have come to think of as the 'Japanese economic system' was a marvelous system to help a backward Japan catch up to the West. But it turned into a terrible system once Japan had indeed caught up. Korea's problems after the Asian financial crisis were a more tumultuous example of the same phenomenon." On the Asian financial crisis, see Pempel (1999) and Haggard (2000).

[27] Pierson (2000: 254) provides the best review of these issues; Thelen (1999) places the work on path dependence in the broader perspective of historical institutionalism.

and to advance on many technological fronts and markets simultaneously. Gradually, niche competitors with lower costs break the strangle hold of the dominant firm, and the structure of the sector becomes more horizontal.[28] Firms will vary in their ability to meet the demands of the market, and in theory, a freely operating market will ruthlessly and single-mindedly select the firms that do so most effectively.[29]

The political world is far more complex: there is no measuring rod of price, political actors pursue a range of goals, it is difficult to measure performance, and even when it is possible to gauge performance, it is difficult to assign responsibility for the outcomes and pressure the responsible actors for change.[30] When a firm faces the increased competition resulting from a reduction in a tariff barrier, the stimulus is concentrated and clear. A local government bureaucracy in this situation will not have the benefit of the same clarity. The impact of a tariff reduction may be unclear, because there will be both winners and losers within the locality; the goals of different ministries within the government will vary according to their responsibilities; a political leader may be tempted not to deal with a problem of which the consequences will not emerge until after the leader's term in office has ended.[31] Change is certainly not impossible in such a context, but it is likely to be halting and inconsistent from the perspective of economic actors that have a single purpose and a clear perspective.[32]

The problem in China is that the political and economic structures are closely intertwined. Auto policy in Shanghai, as in the other regions of China, was always as much about local politics as about building a better car factory, but during the first decade there was no conflict in objectives. In a highly protected market, local firms could gradually improve their manufacturing capability while providing employment and social welfare

---

[28] Fine (1998: Chapter 4).

[29] The business literature often extols managers to embrace "discontinuity" as a means of staying close to the ever-changing market. Richard Foster and Sarah Kaplan (2001), for example, draw on a McKinsey dataset of 1,000 companies in 15 industries in order to make the case that the most successful companies in the current economic environment are those that make change the basis of corporate decision-making and organization and "make themselves more like the market."

[30] Pierson (2000: 260).

[31] Pierson refers to the short time horizons of political leaders. Pierson (2000: 261).

[32] As Douglass North (1990: 99) argues, "the increasing returns characteristic of an initial set of institutions that provide disincentives to productive activity will create organizations and interest groups with a stake in the existing constraints. They will shape the polity in their interests."

benefits to the local population. When competitive pressure increased dramatically at the end of the 1990s, however, the political and economic objectives began to diverge. At the level of the top leadership, where SAIC continued to be welded firmly to the municipal bureaucracy, incentives were mixed: municipal leaders wanted to develop competitive firms, but they also did not want there to be any failures. The emphasis was on balanced growth, and the local government continued to seek to mute the competitive pressure on local firms. At the level of the firm, however, the combination of pending trade liberalization and the presence of a foreign partner in virtually every major firm in the SAIC group created strong pressure for change. Because the foreign partners did not have the institutional ties to the political establishment, they responded to competitive pressures as economic actors and made demands that local firms could not. This process was a struggle, and the foreign partners clearly did not win every battle. Would it not have been preferable for the local government to sever the linkages between economic and political organizations, and thus allow the local firms to grow and prosper independent of foreign ownership? Perhaps, but wishing for rapid institutional change would not have made it any more feasible.

China, although extreme in the extent to which political and economic actors are fused at the top level, is certainly not alone in finding it difficult to reform an economic system in which political and economic incentives are closely intertwined. In coordinated market economies, relationships between firms and labor, firms and banks, and between different firms, tend to be long term and cooperative, and the state and intermediary associations play a key role in creating the framework for this cooperation.[33] Firms consequently do not respond to competitive pressure in the same way that they might in a liberal market economy.[34] Steven Vogel, for example, points to the linkages that tie together the German and Japanese economies to explain the difficulty of reform in these countries. In the face of profound crisis, neither country has moved quickly to reform their economic systems. In part, this is because the competitive sectors, which would presumably benefit from liberal reform, are closely bound to the less competitive parts of the economy through the labor and financial

---

[33] Vogel (2001: 1105).

[34] On varied capacity for regulatory reform, see Vogel (1996). The "varieties of capitalism" approach distinguishes between liberal market economies and coordinated market economies according to the clusters of institutions that bind an economic system into a cohesive whole: governance and finance, industrial relations, education and training systems, interfirm relations, and labor relations. Hall and Soskice (2001: 8).

systems. In part, it is because the industry associations and political parties that would have to push for change represent both advocates and opponents of reform.[35] As a result of these mixed preferences, the rate of reform is slow, and foreign investment can provide much needed bottom-up pressure for change. Carlos Ghosn and Renault, unconstrained by the same breadth of political and economic linkages as a Japanese firm, have been able to transform Nissan because they could severe ties to uncompetitive *keiretsu* partners and abandon lifetime employment. Ghosn (and his ability to enact radical change) has become something of a folk hero in Japan largely because he is able to act in a very *un*-Japanese fashion.[36]

The difficulty of institutional change leads to several conclusions. First, and perhaps most importantly, there is the need for a certain amount of modesty on the part of policymakers. Institutional structures are a critical determinant of development capacity and some will be better suited to particular economic objectives than others. But this does not mean that policymakers can choose from a menu of potential institutional configurations and form them at will. Not only is rational imitation unlikely, it is probably not advisable in many cases: the needs of an economic sector change far more rapidly than institutional structures, hence going to great lengths to alter organizations for the purpose of promoting growth in a targeted sector is a losing battle. In this respect, the belated decision of localities such as Beijing and Guangzhou to give more autonomy to their foreign partners makes a great deal of sense: rather than struggle to develop local capabilities that are not well suited to local institutions, it is much easier to draw on strengths that have been developed outside of the home locality.

This is not to say that policy change is impossible and policy imitation is always ill-advised, but it is important to specify when each is more or less likely to succeed. An industrial policy for heavy industry requires particularly strong state institutions because the state is deliberately "getting prices wrong" so as to direct investment capital to targeted sectors. In the absence of strong existing institutions, and given the difficulty of rapidly

---

[35] Vogel (2001: 1108 and 1110). According to Vogel, the powerful industry federations in Germany and Japan "have been stymied by internal dissension, preventing them from putting forth a unified voice." Vogel (2001: 1112).

[36] As Keio University professor Masayuki Tadoko comments: "Ghosn is genuinely respected in Japan. People admire what he has done at Nissan. He was able to do it because he did not have the same ties, network or background that a Japanese CEO might have had, which would have constrained him." Warren Fernandez, "Is Japan back for good?" *The Straits Times*, June 28, 2004, p. A2.

creating such institutions, intervention of this sort is unlikely to succeed. Policies that are less dependent on surrounding institutions – incentive programs for foreign investment, policies focused on light industry, and so on – can be adapted and discarded more easily, and hence rational imitation might be the norm. Failing to understand this relationship, and attempting remake the state so as to imitate policy approaches that have succeeded in very different institutional settings, is a recipe for frustration. It makes far more sense to understand the capabilities and strengths of local institutions so as to fully exploit them.

Second, it is as important to impose negative incentives on local states as it is to have positive incentives. Given the constantly changing demands of economic development, and the inability of political institutions and organizations to match this rate of change, there must be restraints on state action. In circumstances where a local government has the means to bail out, protect, or subsidize local firms, it is likely that effort and investment will continue to flow toward activities that are characterized by low productivity. For there to be change, mistakes must be costly.[37] Openness to foreign trade and investment prevents government officials from pursuing policy approaches that are no longer appropriate because it limits their ability to mute the cost of mistakes; the outside pressure serves as a counter to the institutional incentives that favor doing things as they always have been done.[38] In some cases even the *threat* of increased openness can be beneficial. The approach of the Shanghai municipal government to auto sector development was fundamentally altered when it became apparent that local firms would soon face global competition.

Many developing countries, of course, are reluctant to expose themselves too rapidly to the rigors of international competition, and as I argued in Chapter 8, FDI can serve as something of a Trojan horse in such cases; assuming the foreign firms are expecting to compete on international markets, they provide international pressure behind the protection of still existing tariff barriers, exposing domestic actors, both economic and political, to the demands and expectations of the global economy.[39]

---

[37] This is a point made by Montinola, Qian, Weingast (1995: 54), I differ from them in the extent to which I see this condition being fulfilled in China.

[38] There are, of course, many arguments in favor of openness: the benefits for firms (see, for example, Hallward-Driemeier: 2001); the need to counter special interests (Olson: 1982); the importation of ideas (Rodrik: 1999).

[39] The expectation of global competition is a critical assumption. A multinational that is collecting rents in a protected market will be as resistant to change as any state-owned enterprise if it has a reasonable expectation that this is possible.

Foreign investors expect a stable legal environment, they expect to be able to use competitive markets to source inputs, and they have the built-in comparative reference point of their operations elsewhere in the world. Because foreign firms have neither the pre-existing institutional ties nor the social burdens (i.e., excess workers) of local firms, they are in a position to make demands that local firms are not. Rather than being co-opted by local politics and long-standing institutional arrangements, as many local firms are, foreign firms are sometimes in a position to force the institutional changes that a successful transition to a market economy require, but that are often so difficult to achieve. Pressure from external actors can, in some respects, save local governments from themselves. If local firms are to prosper in the face of this pressure, however, they must receive the proper support.

III. LOCAL DEVELOPMENT IN A GLOBAL ECONOMY

At the core of the developmental state concept in East Asia was the idea that the state could help firms overcome the obstacles of late development. Tariff protection could provide local firms with a domestic market; subsidized credit and preferential policies, judiciously allocated by competitive means, would help them rapidly achieve economies of scale and scope; carefully controlled interaction with global production networks would provide opportunities for learning. Industrial upgrading in countries such as Korea and Taiwan was a system of apprenticeship: the firms within a developmental state *borrowed* technologies and *learned* from firms in more advanced economies, often in the context of a supply network.[40] A foreign firm would identify a potential local supplier, transfer the skills and technology necessary to manufacture a certain product, and provide the market for the output.[41] The industrial newcomer challenged the incumbents on the basis of cost rather than innovation, and given an effective state role, the benefits would ripple throughout the economy. The backward linkages that were a primary benefit of development in a sector such as autos were assumed to be natural and inevitable.[42]

---

[40] See, for instance, Amsden (1989).

[41] This process is described by Sturgeon and Lester and labeled "supplier-oriented industrial upgrading." Timothy J. Sturgeon and Richard K. Lester, "The new global supply base: New challenges for local suppliers in East Asia," in Yusuf, Altaf, and Nabeshima, eds. (2004: 36).

[42] Hirschman (1958: 99) provides one example of these assumptions. A critical development stimuli, he argues, results "from the fact that the setting up of an industry brings with it

In the contemporary global economy there are obvious difficulties with the more muscular examples of state intervention – the WTO has changed the rules of the game – but less obvious are the ways in which changes in the structure of global production networks create obstacles to apprenticeship.[43] In sectors with rapidly changing and integral technology, the creation of backward linkages can no longer be assumed. The increasing sophistication and complexity of a product, and the consequent high cost of developing new models, drive consolidation and lead core assembly firms to outsource design work to global suppliers. The assemblers introduce common platforms around the world so as to maximize economies of scale, and because much of the design work belongs to the suppliers, they must bring these suppliers with them.[44] This need for co-location fundamentally changes the range of opportunities for local firms. Unless a firm is cooperating with the assembler from the inception of a new model, it is automatically relegated to a lower tier of the value chain. Moving out of the low value-added position is not easy; the expectations are higher and the opportunities for apprenticeships are fewer. Local institutions can play a critical role in filling the resulting gap.

In a world in which national governments are constrained by the rules of the global trading regime, and multinationals choose to source high-value added components from global rather than local suppliers, firms must rely more on local resources. It is very difficult for a national government to promote the creation of large and powerful firms that can immediately go head-to-head with the global giants, but it is possible for a local government to create a nuanced policy approach that will give smaller firms the resources that they need to become valuable pieces of these global production networks. The role of government is less that of a director than it is coordinator, providing information, financing, training,

---

the availability of a new, expanding market for its inputs whether or not these inputs are supplied initially from abroad." He describes (1958: 113) the process as a natural one, assuming that a "backward linkage unfailingly triggers additional net capital formation whenever the imports of some commodity pass the 'threshold' of minimum economic size." He does modify this assumption at a later point (1958: 118), and explains why an industrialist might be reluctant to localize inputs in some cases.

[43] On this theme, see Yusuf, Altaf, and Nabeshima, eds. (2004) and Humphrey and Memedovic (2003).

[44] If the global supplier does not create a manufacturing operation the technology must be licensed. On "follow sourcing" and its implications for development, see Humphrey and Memedovic (2003). On the rise of global suppliers and the problem this creates for "supplier-oriented industrial upgrading," see Timothy J. Sturgeon and Richard K. Lester, "The new global supply base: New challenges for local suppliers in East Asia," in Yusuf, Altaf, and Nabeshima, eds. (2004: 36).

and organization. Given time and support, of course, the hope is that local firms will grow and prosper, and this will only be possible if they have a source of competitive advantage other than cost. The challenge is to achieve the benefits of integration with global production networks while maintaining firms with enough autonomy to pursue independent development strategies.

The local developmental state in Shanghai demonstrates both the constraints and the opportunities of this new global economy. Local firms in Shanghai are not yet the independent national champions that Chinese leaders dream of creating and they are still far from this goal. The dependence on foreign partners is heavy, and this dependence is significant because China is in many respects a best case scenario for local development: local firms have had a highly protected market for two decades, domestic content restrictions and foreign exchange restrictions forced multinationals to localize production, and assembly projects still cannot be majority foreign owned.[45] But Shanghai does demonstrate the importance of local institutions and the potential for incremental upgrading. The local government and business group fostered ties between firms and local university research institutes; they supported a supplier community that provided a forum for firm managers to discuss problems involving process technology and firm management; they provided small-and medium-sized firms with market intelligence. The local firms that benefited from this support are strong and capable partners in their joint venture projects, they dominate the domestic market, and they are carving out a role for themselves in the global production chains of which they are part. SAIC, in other words, is not simply selling its government connections to foreign firms, like many of its domestic competitors; it is using foreign partnerships to incrementally increase the capacity of local firms. The success of SAIC's independent endeavors and foreign acquisitions will depend as much on its ability to improve governance as its technical capabilities, but it is clear that heavy investment and support for local firms in the initial stages of growth created a foundation that could be built upon as integration with the global economy increased.

The absence of local support does not preclude the growth of vibrant networks of automotive firms, but it does have important implications for

---

[45] Even after tariff levels decline, the size of the Chinese marketplace and the rate of growth create incentives for multinationals to locate activities in China that they would not place in smaller markets, and create leverage for the Chinese government to force them to do so.

the role that local firms will occupy within these networks. When local suppliers in China did not receive support in the first stage of development, increasing *local* capabilities in the second stage has proven to be difficult. In the cases where feeble local support was combined with weak foreign partners, the prospects for local supply firms are weak. Beijing Jeep has abandoned the effort to create a local supply base; Dongfeng, although based in Wuhan, is building its new base for sedan production in Guangzhou. Both Beijing Jeep and Dongfeng Peugeot Citroen purchase over half of their components (by value) from Shanghai. In cases where weak local support was compensated for by a strong foreign partner at the assembly joint venture, there can still be considerable success at the assembly plant, but the rising volumes and profitability are in large part a result of the assembler being able to by-pass local supply firms, at least initially. FAW-VW was sourcing less than a quarter of its components locally in 2003; Beijing Hyundai relies primarily on Korean suppliers; Japanese-owned supply firms have moved rapidly into Guangzhou. Continued success at the assembly plants in these locations will probably translate into healthy local supply bases, but it is less certain whether local firms will play key roles in these networks. Quite possibly, a resemblance to the Mexican auto industry is more likely; clusters of global suppliers will support the assembly projects for sedans and local firms will be relegated to the lower tiers. This story, of course, is far from complete.

The future of automotive manufacturing in China has never been in doubt. When the central government in China decided to open the doors to foreign investment, the creation of a domestic auto industry was assured so long as continued economic growth increased the size of the market and barriers to imports created an incentive for investment. But market size and openness to investment did not guarantee that there would be anything that was "Chinese" about this industry; that local firms would be involved, even if only in partnership with foreign firms. State policy, appropriate institutions, and effective governance were the key to developing capable local firms. The central government created the policy framework, and local political and economic institutions shaped the ability of local firms to thrive within this framework. Although this approach was very different from the industrial policy ideas that were circulated in Beijing during the early 1990s, this more circumscribed role of the central state was probably more appropriate for the new global economy.

State policy may be less obvious in an era of globalization, but it is no less important or necessary. In a global context in which it is more difficult for a central government to raise high tariff barriers and direct the process of industrial development from the center, the institutional characteristics of local economies become more important. Rather than re-make the state in order to achieve grand industrial policy objectives, local governments should exploit the institutional comparative advantages of their locality and seek a more nuanced version of industrial policy. Rather than smooth out local institutional differences, in an effort to imitate the most recent policy fad, local governments should view these differences as a source of strength and seek to exploit them. The resulting development strategies might not lead to the development of proud national champions, or have a one-size-fits-all appeal, but they are likely to be more viable over the long term.

Appendix on Research Methods

In writing this book, I have relied heavily on primary sources. The most important source was extensive interview data from local governments and firms over an eight-year period (September 1996 to August 1997, June–August 1998, July 2000, June–July 2002, January 2003, and July–August 2004). In each municipality, interviews were conducted with officials in the auto office of the municipal government, the general managers (in some cases) and the purchasing managers (in all cases) of the JV assembly project (both Chinese and foreign), managers in the head office of the Chinese partner, the general managers of individual supply firms (at both JVs and Chinese SOEs), and in some cases the managers in charge of manufacturing.

Interviews were structured (according to the category of interviewee), but were open ended. Questions would start off with general background, proceed to the nuts and bolts of operations, and then finally move on to broader questions (biggest challenges, prospects for the future). To give a flavor of the types of questions that were asked, local government officials were asked general background questions about the structure of the local auto sector (number of firms, ownership of firms), the organization of the corporate group, and its bureaucratic, financial and personnel relationships with local government, reasons for supporting auto sector development, specific means of support (investment figures), and so on. Managers at the assembly plant were asked about their relationships with the local government, relationships between the JV partners, and about the process of localization: the geographic distribution of suppliers, number of suppliers, the percentage that are JVs, how they support supplier development, how pricing decisions are made, distribution of profits, who they pay taxes to and how much, labor burden, and so on. Managers of supply firms, in addition to the questions that would be in common with the assembly plant, would be asked about the sources of financial capital, how decisions were made about importing technology, and the content of their relationships with the assembly plant and the local government, and so on. Interviews with Chinese managers were conducted in Mandarin Chinese; interviews with foreign managers were conducted in English. The length of an interview was generally around one hour.

I was able to confirm and reconfirm the data collected in interviews by meeting with people involved in all aspects of the development effort, often I met with over half of the firms in a regional network, and in many cases I returned to firms over a period of several years. In total, 187 interviews were conducted in China. The breakdown by municipality was: Beijing, 48 interviews, 18 different firms; Changchun, 17 interviews, 7 different firms; Guangzhou, 26 interviews, 15 different firms; Shanghai, 57 interviews, 19 different firms; Wuhan, 32 interviews, 12 different firms; Fuzhou, 7 interviews, 7 different firms. Firm level interviews were supplemented with local academics, lawyers, and consultants involved with the auto industry. In Beijing, interviews were also conducted with central government officials in the State Planning Commission's Industrial Policy Bureau and the China National Automotive Corporation. Additional interviews were conducted in Mexico in 2000 and Japan in 2003 and 2004.

The interviews are coded to preserve confidentiality. I give the date of the interview, and indicate the location by the letter in the interview number (i.e., B for Beijing, C for Changchun, etc.). The number given to the interview is not necessarily chronological. In some cases contacts were utilized to gain access to supply firms, in other cases I simply chose from the list of local firms, and independently arranged interviews. Local government officials or host units were not used to arrange firm interviews.

Data from interviews was supplemented with information from statistical yearbooks, planning documents, newspaper reports, academic journals, and commercial sources. As the Chinese automotive market has grown, press and commercial coverage has become more widespread and I have used these published sources whenever possible.

Bibliography

Amsden, Alice. 1989. *Asia's Next Giant: South Korea and Late Industrialization.* New York: Oxford University Press.

Amsden, Alice. 2001. *The Rise of 'The Rest': Challenges to the West from Late-Industrializing Economies.* New York: Oxford University Press.

Amsden, Alice, Jacek Kochanowicz, and Lance Taylor. 1994. *The Market Meets Its Match: Restructuring the Economies of Eastern Europe.* Cambridge: Harvard University Press.

Amsden, Alice, and Takashi Hikino. 1994. "Project Execution Capability, Organizational Know-how and Conglomerate Corporate Growth in Late Industrialization." *Industrial and Corporate Change* 3(1): 111–47.

Amsden, Alice and Wan-wen Chu. 2003. *Beyond Late Development: Taiwan's Upgrading Policies.* Cambridge: MIT Press.

Anchordoguy, Marie. 2001. "Whatever Happened to the Japanese Miracle?" Japan Policy Research Institute, Working Paper no. 80 (September).

Asanuma, Banri. 1989. "Manufacturer-Supplier Relationships in Japan and the Concept of Relation-Specific Skill." *Journal of the Japanese and International Economies* 3(1)(March): 1–30.

Automotive News. 2004. "2004 Guide to Automakers in China." Beijing: Automotive Resources Asia.

Beijing Social and Economic Statistical Yearbook. Multiple Years. Beijing: Zhongguo Tongji Chubanshi.

Bennet, Douglas and Kenneth E. Sharpe. 1985. *Transnational Corporations versus the State: The Political Economy of the Mexican Auto Industry.* Princeton: Princeton University Press.

Berger, Suzanne (ed.). 1981. *Organizing interests in Western Europe: pluralism, corporatism, and the transformation of politics.* New York: Cambridge University Press.

Berger, Suzanne. 2000. "Globalization and Politics." *Annual Review of Political Science* 2: 43–62.

295

Berger, Suzanne and Ronald Dore (eds.). 1996. *National Diversity and Global Capitalism.* Ithaca: Cornell University Press.

Berger, Suzanne and Richard K. Lester (eds.). 1997. *Made by Hong Kong.* Hong Kong: Oxford University Press.

Berman, Sheri and Kathleen R. McNamara. 1999. "Bank on Democracy: Why Central Banks Need Public Oversight." *Foreign Affairs,* 78(2) (March/April 1999): 2–8.

Blanchard, Olivier, Rudiger Dornbusch, Paul Krugman, Richard Layard, and Lawrence Summers. 1991. *Reform in Eastern Europe.* Cambridge: MIT Press.

Blecher, Marc, and Vivienne Shue. 1996. *Tethered deer: government and economy in a Chinese county.* Stanford: Stanford University Press.

Borrus, Michael, Dieter Ernst, and Stephan Haggard. 2000. *International Production Networks in Asia: Rivalry or Riches?* London and New York: Routledge.

Brada, Josef C., Inderjit Singh, and Adam Torok. 1994. *Firms Afloat and Firms Adrift: Hungarian Industry and the Economic Transition.* Armonk: M.E. Sharpe.

Broadman, Harry. 2001. "The Business(es) of the Chinese State," *The World Economy* 24(7) (July): 849–875.

Buck, Daniel Patrick. 2002. *Constructing China's Capitalism, Connecting Shanghai's Urban and Rural Industries.* Berkeley: University of California, Berkeley. Ph.D. Dissertation.

Burki, Shahid Javed, Guillermo E. Perry, and William R. Dillinger. 1999. *Beyond the Center: Decentralizing the State.* Washington, D.C.: The World Bank.

Burns, John P. 1994. "Strengthening central CCP control of leadership selection: The 1990 *Nomenklatura.*" *China Quarterly* 138 (June 1994): 458–491.

Byrd, William A. 1991. *The Market Mechanism and Economic Reforms in China.* Armonk, NY: M.E. Sharpe, Inc.

Byrd, William A. (ed.). 1992. *Chinese Industrial Firms Under Reform.* Oxford: Oxford University Press.

Calder, Kent E. 1993. *Strategic Capitalism: Private Business and Public Purpose in Japanese Industrial Finance.* Princeton: Princeton University Press.

Campbell, John L., and J. Rogers Hollingsworth and Leon N. Lindberg. 1991. *Governance of the American Economy.* Cambridge: Cambridge University Press.

Carlson, Allen. 2000. *The Lock on China's Door: Chinese Foreign Policy and the Norm of State Sovereignty.* New Haven: Yale University. Ph.D. dissertation.

Cassidy, John F. 2002. *Japanese Direct Investment in China: Locational Determinants and Characteristics.* New York and London: Routledge.

Chandler, Alfred D. 1962. *Strategy and Structure: Chapters in the History of the Industrial Enterprise.* Cambridge: MIT Press.

Chandler, Alfred D. (ed.). 1964. *Giant Enterprise: Ford, General Motors, and the Automobile Industry.* New York: Harcourt, Brace & World, Inc.

Chandler, Alfred D. 1977. *The Visible Hand: The Managerial Revolution in American Business.* Cambridge: Belknap Press.

Chandler, Alfred D. 1990. *Scale and Scope: The Dynamics of Industrial Capitalism.* Cambridge: Belknap Press.

Chandler, Alfred D., Franco Amatori, and Takashi Hikino (eds.). 1997. *Big Business and the Wealth of Nations.* Cambridge: Cambridge University Press.

Chang, Gordon G. 2001. *The Coming Collapse of China*. New York: Random House.

Chang, Ha-Joon and Peter Nolan. 1995. *The Transformation of the Communist Economies: Against the Mainstream*. New York: St. Martin's Press.

Changchun Economy Statistical Yearbook 1996. 1996. Beijing: Zhongguo Tongji Chubanshi.

Changchun Investment Handbook. 1992. Changchun: Changchun Shiwei Yanjiushi.

Cheung, Peter T. Y., Jae Ho Chung, and Zhimin Lin (eds.). 1998. *Provincial Strategies of Economic Reform in Post-Mao China: Leadership, Politics, and Implementation*. Armonk, NY: M.E. Sharpe.

Chen, Bingcai. 1996. "Hanguo da qiye jituan de tezheng ji zhengyi" [The characteristics and debates over Korean large corporate groups]. *Jingji Yanjiu Cankao* [Economic Research Reference] 58(858) (April 12): 34–38.

Chen, Xiao Hong. 1996. "Zhongguo qiche gongye fazhandong yin ji qi qianjing" [Motivations and prospects for the development of the Chinese automotive industry] *Jingji Gongzuozhe Xuexi Ziliao* [Economic Worker Study Materials] 28 (May): 12–16.

China Automotive Technology Center. 1999, 2000, 2001, 2002, 2003, 2004. *Zhongguo Qiche Gongye Nianjian* [Chinese Automotive Industry Yearbook]. Tianjin: Zhongguo Qiche Jishu Yanjiu Zhongxin.

China Investment Guide. 1995. Hong Kong: Longman.

Chung, Chin. 1997. "Division of Labor Across the Taiwan Strait: Macro Overview and Analysis of the Electronics Industry," in Barry Naughton (ed.), *The China Circle*. Washington, D.C.: Brookings Institution Press.

Coble, Parks M., Jr. 1980. *The Shanghai Capitalists and the Nationalist Government, 1927–1937*. Cambridge: Harvard University Press.

Cusumano, Michael A. 1985. *The Japanese Automobile Industry: Technology and Management at Nissan and Toyota*. Cambridge: The Council on East Asian Studies, Harvard University.

de Melo, Marth, Cevdet Denizer, and Alan Gelb. 1996. *From Plan to Market: Patterns of Transition*. Policy Research Working Paper no. 1564. Washington: The World Bank.

Deyo, Frederic C. 1996. *Social Reconstructions of the World Automobile Industry: Competition, Power and Industrial Flexibility*. New York: St. Martins Press.

Doner, Richard F. 1991. *Driving a Bargain: Automobile Industrialization and Japanese Firms in Southeast Asia*. Berkeley: University of California Press.

Doner, Richard F. 1994. "Japanese Automotive Production Networks in Asia," in Eileen Doherty, ed., *Japanese Investment in Asia*. San Francisco: The Asia Foundation and BRIE.

Doner, Richard F. and Eric Hershberg. 1999. "Flexible production and political decentralization in the developing world: elective affinities in the pursuit of competitiveness." *Studies in Comparative International Development* 34(1) (Spring): 45–82.

Doner, Richard F. 2004. "Growing into Trouble: Institutions and Politics in the Thai Sugar Industry." *Journal of East Asian Studies* 4(1) (January–April): 97–138.

Donnithorne, Audrey. 1972. "China's Cellular Economy: Some Economic Trends Since the Cultural Revolution." *China Quarterly* 52 (October–December): 605–619.

Duckett, Jane. 1998. *The Entrepreneurial State in China*. London: Routledge.

Evans, Peter. 1979. *Dependent Development: The Alliance of Multinational, State, and Local Capital in Brazil*. Princeton: Princeton University Press.

Evans, Peter. 1995. *Embedded Autonomy: States and Industrial Transformation*. Princeton: Princeton University Press.

Fewsmith, Joseph. 1994. *Dilemmas of Reform in China: Political Conflict and Economic Debate*. Armonk, NY: M.E. Sharpe.

Fewsmith, Joseph. 2000. "The Politics of China's Accession to the WTO." *Current History* (September): 268–273.

Fewsmith, Joseph. 2001. *China Since Tiananmen*. Cambridge: Cambridge University Press.

Fine, Charles. 1998. *Clockspeed: Winning Industry Control in the Age of Temporary Advantage*. Reading, MA: Perseus Books.

Foster, Richard and Sarah Kaplan. 2001. *Creative Destruction: Why Companies That Are Built to Last Underperform the Market – And How to Successfully Transform Them*. New York: Doubleday.

Frieden, Jeffry A. 1991. *Debt, Development, and Democracy: Modern Political Economy and Latin America, 1965–1985*. Princeton, NJ: Princeton University Press.

Frieden, Jeffry A. and Ronald Rogowski. 1996. "Actors and preferences in international relations." In Helen Milner and Robert Keohane (eds.), *Internationalization and domestic politics* (pp. 25–47). Cambridge, UK: Cambridge University Press.

Friedman, Thomas. 1999. *The Lexus and the Olive Tree*.

Fu, Feng-cheng. 1992. "The Decentralization of Peking's Economic Management and Its Impact on Foreign Investment," *Issues and Studies* (February).

Gao, Paul. 2002. "A tune-up for China's auto industry," *The McKinsey Quarterly*, no. 1.

Gao, Paul. 2003. "Capturing the Growth Opportunities in China's Automotive Market," McKinsey Automotive & Assembly Extranet, https://autoassembly.mckinsey.com.

Gao, Shangquan and Chi Fulin (eds.). 1997. *Reforming China's State-Owned Enterprises*. Beijing: Foreign Language Press.

Garrett, Geoffrey. 1998. "Global Markets and National Politics: Collision Course or Virtuous Circle?" *International Organization*, 52(4) (Autumn): 787–824.

Gates, Susan, Paul Migrom, and John Roberts. 1996. "Complementarities in the Transition from Socialism: A Firm-Level Analysis," in John McMillan and Barry Naughton, eds., *Reforming Asian Socialism: The Growth of Market Institutions*. Ann Arbor: The University of Michigan Press.

Gerring, John. 2004. "What is a case study and what is it good for?" *American Political Science Review* 98(2) (May): 341–354.

Gerschenkron, Alexander. 1962. *Economic Backwardness in Historical Perspective*. Cambridge: Belknap.

Gilpin, Robert. 2000. *The Challenge of Global Capitalism: The World Economy in the 21st Century*. Princeton: Princeton University Press.

Goldman Sachs. 2003. "Global Automobiles: The Chinese Auto Industry." Accessed October 21, 2004 at http://www.gs.com/hkchina/insight/research/pdf/chinese_auto_industry.pdf

Goodman, David S. G. and Gerald Segal. 1994. *China Deconstructs: Politics, trade and regionalism*. London: Routledge.

Granovetter, Mark. 1985. "Economic Action and Social Structure: The Problem of Embeddedness." *American Journal of Sociology* 91(3) (November): 481–510.

Grub, Phillip Donald and Jian Hai Lin. 1991. *Foreign Direct Investment in China*. New York: Quorum Books.

Guojia Qiche Gongye Zhengce Xinbian (1993–1994) [A new volume of national automotive industry policies (1993–1994]. 1994. Beijing: Guonei Maoyibu Guojia Xinwen Fazhan Gongsi.

Guojia Qiche Gongye Zhengce Xinbian (1994–1995) [A new volume of national automotive industry policies (1994–1995]. 1995. Beijing: Beijing Haitehua Jidian Jishu Kaifa Gongsi.

Guojia Xinxi Zhongxin [National Information Center]. 1997. *Zhongguo Qiche Shichang Zhanwang 1998* [Forecast of the Chinese Auto Market 1998]. Beijing: Zhongguo Jihua Chubanshi.

Guojia Xinxi Zhongxin [National Information Center]. (ed). 1999. *Zhongguo Qiche Shichang Zhanwang* [Forecast of the Chinese Auto Market]. Beijing: Zhongguo Tongji Chubanshe.

Guthrie, Doug. 1999. *Dragon in a Three-Piece Suit: The Emergence of Capitalism in China*. Princeton: Princeton University Press.

Haggard, Stephan. 1990. *Pathways from the Periphery: The Politics of Growth in the Newly Industrializing Countries*. Ithaca: Cornell University Press.

Haggard, Stephan. 2000. *The Political Economy of the Asian Financial Crisis*. Washington, DC: Institute for International Economics.

Halberstam, David. 1986. *The Reckoning*. New York: Morrow.

Hall, Peter A. and Rosemary C. R. Taylor. 1996. "Political Science and the Three New Institutionalisms," *Political Studies* XLIV.

Hall, Peter A. and David Soskice, (eds.). 2001. *Varieties of Capitalism: The Institutional Foundations of Comparative Advantage*. Oxford: Oxford University Press.

Hallward-Driemeier, Mary. 2001. "Openness, Firms, and Competition." Unpublished paper prepared for "Globalization, Growth and Poverty Policy Research Report," World Bank (June). Available at: http://rru.worldbank.org/Documents/PapersLinks/1248.pdf

Hannan, Kate. 1998. *Industrial Change in China: Economic restructuring and conflicting interests*. London: Routledge.

Hao, Jia and Zhimin Lin. 1994. *Changing Central-Local Relations in China: Reform and State Capacity*. Boulder: Westview Press.

Hao, Yen-P'ing. 1970. *The Comprador in Nineteenth Century China: Bridge between East and West*. Cambridge: Harvard University Press.

Harwit, Eric. 1995. *China's Automobile Industry: Policies, Problems, and Prospects*. Armonk, NY: M.E. Sharpe.

Harwit, Eric. 2001. "The Impact of WTO Membership on the Automobile Industry in China." *The China Quarterly*(September): 655–667.

Helper, Susan. 1991. "Strategy and Irreversibility in Supplier Relations: The Case of the U. S. Automobile Industry." *Business History Review* 65 (Winter): 781–824.

Helper, Susan and Mari Saki. 1995. "Supplier Relations in Japan and the United States: Are They Converging?" *Sloan Management Review*, 36(3), (Spring 1995): 77–84.

Herrigel, Gary. 1996. *Industrial Constructions: The Source of German Industrial Power*. Cambridge: Cambridge University Press.

Hiraoka, L. S. 2001. "Foreign Development of the China's Motor Vehicle Industry," *International Journal of Technology and Management*, 21(5/6): 496–512.

Hirschman, Albert. 1958. *The Strategy of Economic Development*. New Haven: Yale University Press.

Hirst, Paul and Grahame Thompson. 1996. *Globalization in Question*. Cambridge, MA: Blackwell.

Hollingsworth, J. Rogers, and Philippe C. Schmitter, and Wolfgang Streeck. 1994. *Governing Capitalist Economies: Performance and Control of Economic Sectors*. New York: Oxford University Press.

Hook, Brian (ed.). 1997. *Guangdong: China's Promised Land*. Oxford: Oxford University Press.

Hounshell, David A. *From the American System to Mass Production, 1800–1932*. Baltimore: Johns Hopkins University.

Howell, Jude. 1993. *China Opens Its Doors: The Politics of Economic Transition*. Boulder: Lynne Rienner.

Howson, Nicholas C. 1997. "China's Company Law: One Step Forward, Two Steps Back? A Modest Complaint," *Columbia Journal of Asian Law* 11(1): 127–173.

Hu, Zhuangjun, and Xuesheng He. 1995. *China: Developments of the Automobile Industry (1985–1994)*. Beijing: DRC Institute of the Development Research Center of the State Council.

Huang, Jianping. 1990. "U.S. Direct Investment in China: A Motivational Analysis," *Research in Asian Economic Studies*, 2.

Huang Yasheng, 1998. *FDI in China: An Asian Perspective*. Hong Kong: The Chinese University Press.

Huang, Yasheng. 2002. "Between Two Coordination Failures: Automotive Industrial Policy in China with a Comparison to Korea." *Review of International Political Economy*, 9(3) (September).

Huang, Yasheng. 2003. *Selling China: Foreign Direct Investment During the Reform Era*. New York: Cambridge University Press.

Huan, Guoyu. 1996. "Han, re liang guo jingji gaosu cengzhang shiqi hongguan jingji guanli de jingyan qishi" [The macroeconomic management experience from the high growth economies of Korea and Japan]. *Jingji Gongzuozhe Xuexi Ziliao* [Economic Worker Study Materials] 30–31 (April): 65–78.

Huchet, Jean-Francois. 1999. "Concentration and the Emergence of Corporate Groups in Chinese Industry," *China Perspectives* (May–June).

Humphrey, John and Olga Memedovic. 2003. "The Global Automotive Value Chain." Vienna: United Nations Industrial Development Organization.

Industrial Group Division of the National Economic and Trade Commission. 1995. "Guojia daxing shidian qiye jituan gaige zhuanji" [Collection of articles on trial reform of national large-scale enterprise groups]. *Jingji Yanjiu Cankao* [Economic Reseach Reference] 83 (May): 11–16.

Inoue, Ryuichiro, Hirohisa Kohama, and Shujiro Urata (eds.). 1993. *Industrial Policy in East Asia*. Tokyo: JETRO.

Iwagaki, Makoto. 1986. "The State of China's Automobile Industry," JETRO. *China Newsletter*. no. 63" 9–16.

Jefferson, Gary H., and Thomas G. Rawski. 1994. "Enterprise in Chinese Industry." *Journal of Economic Perspectives* 8(2) (Spring): 47–70.

Jefferson, Gary H., Thomas G. Rawski, and Yuxin Zheng. 1992. "Growth, Efficiency, and Convergence in China's State and Collective Sector." *Economic Development and Cultural Change* 40(2): 239–266.

Jia, Li. 1998. "Yinjin Jishu: Hanguo biaoshi dui Zhongguo de jiejian yiyi" [Importing Technology: Lessons of the Korean experience for China]. *Qiye Jingji* [Enterprise Economics], no. 4.

Jia, Hao and Zhimin Lin. 1994. *Changing Central-Local Relations in China: Reform and State Capacity*. Boulder: Westview Press.

Johnson, Chalmers. 1982. *MITI and the Japanese Miracle: The Growth of Industrial Policy, 1925–1975*. Stanford: Stanford University Press.

Jiao, Ying and Shi Jin Liu. 1996. "Woguo qiche gongye shengchan jizhong tujin de shizheng yanjiu" [Empirical research on means of focusing production in the Chinese automotive industry]. *Jingji Gongzuozhe Xuexi Ziliao* [Economic Worker Study Materials] 84 (November): 23–43.

Kang, Myung Hun. 1996. *The Korean Business Conglomerate: Chaebol Then and Now*. Berkeley: Institute of East Asian Studies.

Katz, Richard. 1998. *Japan, The System that Soured: The Rise and Fall of the Japanese Economic Miracle*. Armonk, NY: M. E. Sharpe.

Katzenstein, Peter J. (ed.), 1978. *Between Power and Plenty: Foreign Economic Policies of Advanced Industrial States*. Madison: University of Wisconsin Press.

Katzenstein, Peter J. 1985. *Small States in World Markets*. Ithaca: Cornell University Press.

Keister, Lisa A. 2000. *Chinese Business Groups: The Structure and Impact of Interfirm Relations During Economic Development*. Hong Kong: Oxford University Press.

Keller, William W. and Richard J. Samuels. 2003. *Crisis and Innovation in Asian Technology*. Cambridge: Cambridge University Press.

Kenney, Martin. 1999. "Merger Activity in the Global Economy: Implications for Korea." Paper prepared for "Conference on Industrial Globalization: East Asia's Strategic Importance and the Role of Korea." Honolulu, Hawaii, August 1999.

King, Gary, Robert O. Keohane, and Sidney Verba. 1994. *Designing Social Inquiry: Scientific Inference in Qualitative Research*. Princeton: Princeton University Press.

Kitschelt, Herbert. 1991. "Industrial governance structures, innovation strategies, and the case of Japan: sectoral or cross-national comparative analysis?" *International Organization* 44(4) (Autumn).

Kleinberg, Robert. 1990. *China's 'Opening' to the Outside World: The Experiment with Foreign Capitalism*. Boulder: Westview Press.

Kornai, Janos. 1980. *Economics of Shortage*. 2 vols. Amsterdam: North Holland.

Kornai, Janos. 1990. *Vision and Reality, Market and State: Contradictions and Dilemmas Revisited*. New York: Harvester Wheatsheaf.

Krugman, Paul R. and Maurice Obstfeld. 1991. *International Economics: Theory and Policy, Second Edition*. New York: HarperCollins.

Krugman, Paul R. 1994. "The Myth of Asia's Miracle." *Foreign Affairs* (November/December).

Lamming, Richard. 1993. *Beyond Partnership: Strategies for Innovation and Lean Supply*. New York: Prentice Hall.

Lardy, Nicholas R. 1998. *China's Unfinished Economic Revolution*. Washington: Brookings Institute Press.

Lardy, Nicholas R. 2002. *Integrating China into the Global Economy*. Washington: Brookings Institute Press.

Li, An Ding. 1997. *Jiating Jiaoche Youhuo Zhongguo* [The Family Sedan Seduces China]. Beijing: Zuojia Chubanshe.

Li, Feng and Jing Li. 1999. *Foreign Investment in China*. New York: St. Martin's Press.

Li, Hong. 1988. *Zhongguo Qiche Gongye Jingji Fenxi*. [An Economic Analysis of the Chinese Auto Industry]. Beijing: Zhongguo Renmin Daxue Chubanshe.

Li, Linda Chelan. 1998. *Centre and Provinces: China 1978–1993*. Oxford: Clarendon Press, 1998.

Li, Youping. 1993. "Current Regional Blockades and Suggested Solution." *Chinese Economic Studies* 26(5) (Fall 1993).

Lieberthal, Kenneth and Michel Oksenberg. 1988. *Policy Making in China: Leaders, Structures, and Processes*. Princeton: Princeton University Press.

Lieberthal, Kenneth and David M. Lampton, eds. 1992. *Bureaucracy, Politics and Decision Making in Post-Mao China*. Berkeley and Los Angeles: University of California Press.

Lijphart, Arend. 1975. "The Comparable Case Strategy in Comparative Research." *Comparative Political Studies* 8: 158–177.

Lin, Shao-jung. 1990. "Aspects of Technology Transfer: China's Experiences." *Research in Asian Economic Studies*, 2.

Lin Yi-Min and Tian Zhu. 2001. "Ownership Restructuring in Chinese State Industry: An Analysis of Evidence on Initial Organizational Changes." *China Quarterly* 166: 305–341.

Lincoln, Edward J. 2001. *Arthritic Japan: The Slow Pace of Economic Reform*. Washington, DC: Brookings Institution Press.

Lindblom, Charles E. 1977. *Politics and Markets: The World's Political-Economic Systems*. New York: Basic Books.

Liu, Guy Shaojia and Wing Thye Woo. 2001. "How will ownership in China's industrial sector evolve with WTO accession." *China Economic Review* 12: 137–161.

Locke, Richard M. 1995. *Remaking the Italian Economy*. Ithaca: Cornell University Press.

Long, Guoqiang. 1996. "Zhongguo jiaoche gongye guoji jingzhengli fenxi" [Analysis of the international competitiveness of the Chinese auto sedan industry]. Development Research Centre of the State Council, PRC. Research Report no. 92, August 9, 1996. Internal circulation.

Long, Guoqiang. 1996b. "Jinkou guanshui dui zhongguo jiaoche gongye de yingxiang" [The impact of import tariffs on the Chinese auto sedan industry]. Development Research Centre of the State Council, PRC. Research Report no. 93, August 9, 1996. Internal circulation.

Lung, Yannick, Jean-Jacques Chanaron, Takahiro Fujimoto, and Daniel Raff (eds.). 1999. *Coping with Variety: Flexible Productive Systems for Product Variety in the Auto Industry*. Aldershot, England: Ashgate.

MacFarquhar, Roderick. 1974. *The Origins of the Cultural Revolution 1: Contradictions Among the People 1957–1957*. New York: Columbia University Press.

Mako, William and Chunlin Zhang. 2002. "Exercising Ownership Rights in State Owned Enterprise Groups: What China Can Learn from International Experience." World Bank Note. Available at http://www.worldbank.org.cn.

Mann, Jim. 1989. *Beijing Jeep: How Western Business Stalled in China*. New York: Simon and Schuster.

Mao, Zedong. 1969. *Mao Zhuxi Yulu* [The Quotations of Chairman Mao]. Beijing: Renmin Chubanshi.

Mar, Pamela and Michael N. Young. 2001. "Corporate Governance in Transition Economies: A Case Study of Two Chinese Airlines." *Journal of World Business* 36(3) (Fall 2001): 280–302.

Martin, Ron, and Peter Sunley. 1996. "Paul Krugman's Geographical Economics and Its Implications for Regional Development Theory: A Critical Assessment." *Economic Geography*, 72(3) (July 1996): 259–292.

Marukawa, Tomoo. 1995. "Industrial Groups and Division of Labor in China's Automobile Industry." *The Developing Economies*, XXXIII-3 (September 1995): 330–355.

Marukawa, Tomoo. 1999. "The Contradictions of Industrial Groups: A Case Study of the First Automobile Works Group." *China Perspectives* 23 (May–June): 18–26.

Marukawa, Tomoo. 2003. "The Supplier Network of the Chinese Auto Industry." *The Journal of Social Science* (University of Tokyo), 54(3), March 2003.

Matsuyama, Kiminori. 1997. "Economic Development as Coordination Problems." In Masahiko Aoki, Hyung-ki Kim, and Masahiro Okuno-Fujiwara, eds., *The Role of Government in East Asian Development*. Oxford: Clarendon Press.

Maxfield, Sylvia and Ben Ross Schneider (eds.). 1997. *Business and State in Developing Countries*. Ithaca: Cornell University Press.

Maynard, Micheline. 1995. *Collision Course: Inside the Battle for General Motors*. New York: Birch Lane Press.

McMillan, John and Barry Naughton. 1992. "How to Reform a Planned Economy: Lessons from China." *Oxford Review of Economic Policy* 8(1) (Spring): 130–143.

McNally, Christopher A. 2002. "Strange Bedfellows: Communist Party Institutions and New Governance Mechanisms in Chinese State Holding Corporations." *Business and Politics* 4(1): 91–115.

Milgrom, Paul and John Roberts. 1992. *Economics, Organization and Management.* Englewood Cliffs, NJ: Prentice Hall.

Milner, Helen V. 1988. *Resisting Protectionism.* Princeton: Princeton University Press.

Ministry of Machinery Industry. 1993 through 1997. *Zhongguo Qiche Gongye Nianjian* [Chinese Automotive Industry Yearbook]. Beijing: Ministry of Machinery Ministry.

Ministry of Machinery Industry. 1994b. *Dangdai Zhongguo Guoji Jiaoche Gongye Fazhan yu Zhongguo Jiaoche Gongye Fazhan Zhanlue* [The development of the contemporary Chinese international auto sedan industry and the Chinese auto sedan development strategy]. Beijing: Ministry of Machinery Ministry.

Monteverde, K. and D. J. Teece. 1982. "Supplier Switching Costs and Vertical Integration in the Automobile Industry." *Bell Journal of Economic* 13: 206–213.

Montinola, Gabriella, Yingyi Qian, and Barry R. Weingast. 1995. "Federalism, Chinese Style: The Political Basis for Economic Success in China." *World Politics* 48 (October): 50–81.

Moran, Theodore H. 1998. *Foreign Direct Investment and Development.* Washington, DC: Institute for International Economics.

Murphey, Rhoads. 1953. *Shanghai: Key to Modern China.* Cambridge: Harvard University Press.

Nadvi, Khalid and Hubert Schmitz. 1998. "Industrial Clusters in Less Developed Countries: Review of Experiences and Research Agenda," In Philippe Cadene and Mark Holstrom, *Decentralized Production in India: Industrial Districts, Flexible Specialization, and Employment.* Thousand Oaks, Ca: Sage Publications.

National Bureau of Statistics of China. 2001. *China Statistical Yearbook 2001.* Beijing: China Statistics Press.

Naughton, Barry. 1988. "The Third Front: Defense Industrialization in the Chinese Interior." *China Quarterly* 115: 351–386.

Naughton, Barry. 1990. "China's Experience with Guidance Planning." *Journal of Comparative Economics* 14: 743–767.

Naughton, Barry. 1992. "Implications of the State Monopoly Over Industry and Its Relaxation." *Modern China* 18(1) (January): 14–41.

Naughton, Barry. 1995. *Growing Out of the Plan.* New York: Cambridge University Press.

Naughton, Barry. 2003. "The State Asset Commission: A Powerful New Government Body." *China Leadership Monitor* 8 (Fall): 1–10.

Nee, Victor. 1992. "Organizational Dynamics of Market Transition: Hybrid Forms, Property Rights, and Mixed Economy in China." *Administrative Science Quarterly* 37 (March): 1–27.

Nevins, Allan, and Frank Ernest Hill. 1957. *Ford: Expansion and Challenge, 1915–1933.* New York: Charles Scribner's Sons.

Nishiguchi, Toshihiro and Masayoshi Ikeda. 1996. "Suppliers' Process Innovation: Understated Aspects of Japanese Industrial Sourcing," in Toshihiro Nishiguchi (ed.), *Managing Product Development*. New York: Oxford University Press.

Nishiguchi, Toshihiro. 1994. *Strategic Industrial Sourcing: The Japanese Advantage*. New York: Oxford University Press.

Noble, Gregory W. 1998. *Collective Action in East Asia: How Ruling Parties Shape Industrial Policy*. Ithaca: Cornell University Press.

Noble, Gregory W. 2002. "Japanese Automakers in ASEAN," in Vinod K. Aggarwal and Shujiro Urata, *Winning in Asia, Japanese Style: Market and Nonmarket Strategies for Success*. New York: Palgrave Macmillan.

Nolan, Peter. 1995. *Large Firms and Industrial Reform in Former Planned Economies: The Case of China*. DAE Working Paper No. 9516.

Nolan, Peter. 2001. *China and the Global Economy: National Champions, Industrial Policy, and the Big Business Revolution*. New York: Palgrave.

North, Douglass C., and Robert Paul Thomas. 1973. *The Rise of the Western World: A New Economic History*. Cambridge: Cambridge University Press.

North, Douglass C. 1990. *Institutions, Institutional Change and Economic Performance*. Cambridge: Cambridge University Press.

Ohmae, Kenichi. 1990. *The Borderless World*. New York: Harper Collins.

Organization for Economic Co-operation and Development. 2000. *Reforming China's Enterprises*. Paris: OECD Publications.

Oi, Jean C. 1989. *State and Peasant in Contemporary China: The Political Economy of Village Government*. Berkeley: University of California Press.

Oi, Jean C. 1992. "Fiscal Reform and the Economic Foundations of Local State Corporatism in China." *World Politics* 45 (October): 99–126.

Oi, Jean C. 1995. "The Role of the Local State in China's Transitional Economy." *China Quarterly* 144 (December): 1132–1149.

Oi, Jean C. 1999. *Rural China Takes Off: Institutional Foundations of Economic Reform*. Berkeley: University of California Press.

Oksenberg, Michel and James Tong. 1991. "The Evolution of Central-Provincial Fiscal Relations in China, 1971–1984: The Formal System." *China Quarterly* 125 (March).

Olson, Mancur. 1965. *The Logic of Collective Action: Public Goods and the Theory of Groups*. Cambridge: Harvard University Press.

Olson, Mancur. 1982. *The Rise and Decline of Nations*. New Haven: Yale University Press.

Ostrom, Elinor, L. Schroeder, and S. Wynne. 1993. *Institutional Incentives and Sustainable Development*. Boulder: Westview Press.

Pearson, Margaret M. 1991. *Joint Ventures in the People's Republic of China*. Princeton: Princeton University Press.

Pearson, Margaret M. "Mapping the Rise of China's Regulatory State: Economic Regulation and Network and Insurance Industries," paper prepared for the Annual Meeting of the Association of Asian Studies, New York, March 27, 2003.

Pempel, T. J. ed. 1999. *The Politics of the Asian Economic Crisis*. Ithaca: Cornell University Press.

Perkins, Dwight. 1988. "Reforming China's Economic System." *Journal of Economic Literature* 26 (June): 601–645.

Perkins, Dwight. 1994. "Completing China's Move to the Market." *Journal of Economic Perspectives* 8(2) (Spring): 23–46.

Perry, Elizabeth J. 1993. *Shanghai on Strike: The Politics of Chinese Labor.* Stanford: Stanford University Press.

Pierson, Paul. 2000. "Increasing Returns, Path Dependence, and the Study of Politics." *American Political Science* Review 94(2) (June): 251–267.

Pierson, Paul. 2000a. "The Limits of Design: Explaining Institutional Origins and Change." *Governance: An International Journal of Policy and Administration,* 13(4): 475–547.

Piore, Michael J. and Charles F. Sabel. 1984. *The Second Industrial Divide: Possibilities for Prosperity.* New York: Basic Books.

Polanyi, Karl. 1944. The Great Transformation. Boston: Beacon Press.

Porter, Michael E. 1992. *Capital Choices: Changing the Way America Invests in Industry.* Washington, D. C.: Council on Competitiveness.

Prakash, Aseem and Jeffrey A. Hart (eds.). 2000. *Responding to Globalization.* London and New York: Routledge.

Prowse, Stephen. 1995. "Corporate Governance in International Perspective: A Survey of Corporate Control Mechanisms Among Large Firms in the U.S., U.K., Japan and Germany." *Financial Markets, Institutions & Instruments,* vol. 4(1) (February): 1–63.

Pyke, Frank. 1992. *Industrial Development Through Small-Firm Cooperation: Theory and Practice.* Geneva: International Labor Office.

Qiche Gongye Guihua Cankao Ziliao [Auto Industry Programme Reference Materials]. 1997. Tianjin: Zhongguo Qiche Jishu Yanjiu Zhongxin.

Ravenhill, John. 1999. "Japanese and U. S. Subsidiaries in East Asia: Host-Country Effects," in Dennis J. Encarnation, *Japanese Multinationals in Asia,* New York and Oxford: Oxford University Press.

Rawski, Thomas. 2002. "Recent Developments in China's Labor Economy." Report prepared for the International Policy Group, International Labor Office, Geneva. Available at: http://www.pitt.edu/~tgrawski/

Remick, Elizabeth. 2002. "The Significance of Variation in Local States: The Case of Twentieth-Century China." *Comparative Politics,* 34(4) (July 2002): 399–418.

Rodden, Jonathan A. 2001. "Decentralization and the Challenge of Hard Budget Constraints." *PREM Note 41.* Washington D.C.: The World Bank.

Rodden, Jonathan and Erik Wibbels. 2002. "Beyond the Fiction of Federalism: Macroeconomic Management in Multitiered Systems." *World Politics* 54 (July 2002): 494–531.

Rodrik, Dani. 1999. *The New Global Economy and Developing Countries: Making Openness Work.* Washington, DC: The Overseas Developmental Council.

Rodrik, Dani. 2003. "Growth Strategies." Unpublished paper (September). Available at: http://www.ksg.harvard.edu/rodrik/

Roe, Mark J. 1994. *Strong Managers, Weak Owners: The Political Roots of American Corporate Finance.* Princeton: Princeton University Press.

Rokkan, Stein. 1970. *Citizens, Elections, Parties: Approaches to the Comparative Study of the Process of Development*. New York: David McKay Company.

Rosen, Daniel H. 1999. *Behind the Open Door: Foreign Enterprises in the Chinese Marketplace*. Washington: Institute for International Economics.

Sachs, Jeffrey D. and Wing Thye Woo. 1997. *Understanding China's Economic Performance*. Working Paper 5935. Cambridge: National Bureau of Economic Research.

Sako, Mari. 1992. *Prices, Quality and Trust*. Cambridge: Cambridge University Press.

Saxonhouse, Gary. 1983. "What is All This About Industrial Targeting in Japan?" *World Development* 6(3): 253–273.

Schmitter, Philippe and Gerhard Lehbruch, (eds.). 1979. *Trends Towards Corporatist Intermediation*. Beverly Hills: Sage.

Schumpeter, Joseph A. 1950. *Capitalism, Socialism, and Democracy, Third Edition*. New York: Harper & Brothers Publishers.

Segal, Adam M. 2003. *Digital Dragon: National Technology Policy, Local Governments, and Enterprises in China*. Ithaca: Cornell University Press.

Segal, Adam and Eric Thun. 2001. "Thinking Globally, Acting Locally: Local Governments, Industrial Sectors, and Development in China," *Politics & Society*, 29(4): 557–588.

Shafer, Michael D. 1994. *Winners and Losers: How Sectors Shape the Developmental Prospects of States*. Ithaca: Cornell University Press.

Shah, Anwar and Theresa Thompson. 2002. "Implementing Decentralized Local Governance: A Treacherous Road with Potholes, Detours, and Road Closures," presented at "Can Decentralization Help Rebuild Indonesia?" Andrew Young School of Policy Studies, Georgia State University, Atlanta, GA, May 1–3, 2002.

Shanghai Auto Industry History Editorial Committee. 1992. *Shanghai Qiche Gongye Shi* [History of the Shanghai Auto Industry] Shanghai: Shanghai Renmin Chubanshe.

Shapiro, Helen. 1994. *Engine of Growth: The State and Transnational Auto Companies in Brazil*. Cambridge: Cambridge University Press.

Shimokawa, Koichi. 1985. "Japan's Keiretsu System: The Case of the Automobile Industry." *Japanese Economic Studies* 13(4) (Summer): 3–31.

Shirk, Susan L. 1993. *The Political Logic of Economic Reform in China*. Berkeley: University of California Press.

Shonfield, Andrew. 1965. *Modern Capitalism: The Changing Balance of Public and Private Power*. New York: Oxford University Press.

Sloan, Alfred P. Jr. 1964. *My Years With General Motors*. Garden City, NY: Doubleday and Company, Inc.

Smelser, Neil J. and Richard Sewdberg (eds.). 1994. *The Handbook of Economic Sociology*. Princeton: Princeton University Press.

Smitka, Michael J. 1991. *Competitive Ties: Subcontracting in the Japanese Automotive Industry*. New York: Columbia University Press.

Snyder Richard. 2001. "Scaling Down: The Subnational Comparative Method." *Studies in Comparative International Development*, 36(1) (Spring 2001): 93–110.

Solinger, Dorothy J. 1993. *China's Transition from Socialism: Statist Legacies and Market Reforms, 1980–1990*. Armonk: M.E. Sharpe.

Solinger, Dorothy J. 1996. "Despite Decentralization: Disadvantages, Dependence and Ongoing Central Power in the Inland – The Case of Wuhan." *China Quarterly*, no. 145 (March): 1–34.

Soskice, David. 1997. "Divergent Production Regimes: Coordinated and Uncoordinated Market Economies in the 1980s and 1990s." Forthcoming in Herbert Kitschelt *et al.* (eds.), *Continuity and Change in Contemporary Capitalism*. Cambridge: Cambridge University Press.

Stark, David. 1992. "Path Dependence and Privatization Strategies in East Central Europe." *East European Politics and Societies*, 6(1) (Winter): 17–54.

State Development and Reform Commission. 2004. "Qiche gongye fazhan zhengce." [Auto Industry Development Policy]. May 21, 2004.

State Statistical Bureau. 1986. *China Statistical Yearbook, 1986*. Hong Kong: Economic Information Agency.

State Statistical Bureau. 1993. *China Statistical Yearbook, 1993*. Beijing: State Statistical Publishing House.

State Statistical Bureau. 1996. *China Statistical Yearbook, 1996*. Beijing: State Statistical Publishing House.

Steinfeld, Edward S. 1996. *Property Rights and Performance in the Chinese State-Owned Enterprise*. Ph.D. Dissertation, Department of Government. Harvard University.

Steinfeld, Edward S. 1998. *Forging Reform in China: The Fate of State-Owned Enterprises*. Cambridge: Cambridge University Press.

Stiglitz, Joseph E. and Shahid Yusuf, eds. 2001. *Rethinking the East Asia Miracle*. Oxford: Oxford University Press.

Stoner-Weiss, Kathryn. 1997. *Local Heroes: The Political Economy of Russian Regional Governance*. Princeton: Princeton University Press.

Studer-Noquez. 2002. *Ford and the Global Strategy of Multinationals: The North American Auto Industry*. London and New York: Routledge.

Studwell, Joe. 2002. *The China Dream: The Elusive Quest for the Greatest Untapped Market on Earth*. London: Profile Books.

Sturgeon, Timothy and Richard Florida. 1999. "The World that Changed the Machine: Globalization and Jobs in the Automotive Industry." Final Report to the Alfred P. Sloan Foundation.

Sun, Haishun. 1998. *Foreign Investment and Economic Development in China: 1979–1996*. Aldershot, UK: Ashgate.

Sun, Nian Yi. 1995. *Zhongguo Qiche Jixing* [Notes on the Chinese Auto Industry]. Beijing: Zhongguo Tongji Chubanshe.

Swyngedouw, Erik A. 1992. "The Mammon Quest. 'Glocalisation,' Interspatial Competition and the Monetary Order: the Construction of New Scales," in Mick Dunford and Grigoris Kafkalas, *Cities and regions in the new Europe*. London: Belhaven Press.

Takayama, Yuichi. 1991. "The Chinese Automobile Industry." JETRO. *China Newsletter*, no. 94 (September–October): 16–21.

Tenev, Stoyan, and Chunlin Zhang with Loup Brefort. 2002. *Corporate Governance and Enterprise Reform in China: Building the Institutions of*

Modern Markets. Washington, D.C. World Bank and International Finance Corporation.

Thelen, Kathleen. 1999. "Historical Institutionalism in Comparative Politics," *Annual Review of Political Science*, 2 (1999).

Thompson, Dennis F. 1999. Democratic Theory and Global Society. *The Journal of Political Philosophy*, 7(2): 111–125.

Thun, Eric. 2004. "Keeping Up with the Jones': Decentralization, Policy Imitation, and Industrial Development in China." *World Development*, 32(8): 1289–1308.

Thun, Eric. 2004b. "Industrial Policy, Chinese-Style: FDI, Regulation, and Dreams of National Champions in the Auto Sector." *Journal of East Asian Studies* 4 (2004): 453–489.

Tian, Gang. 1996. *Shanghai's Role in the Economic Development of China*. Westport: Praeger.

Tong, James. 1989. "Fiscal Reform, Elite Turnover and Central-Provincial Relations in Post-Mao China." *Australian Journal of Chinese Affairs* 22 (July).

Treisman, Daniel. 1996. "The Politics of Intergovernmental Transfers in Post-Soviet Russia." *British Journal of Political Science*, 26(3) (July 1996): 299–335.

Tsai, Kellee S. 2000. "Off Balance: Fiscal Federalism and the Rise of Extra-Budgetary and Informal Finance in China." Paper delivered at the 2000 Annual Meeting of the American Political Science Association.

Tsai, Kellee S. 2002. *Back-Alley Banking: Private Entrepreneurs in China*. Ithaca: Cornell University Press.

United Nations Conference on Trade and Development. 2000. *World Investment Report 2000: Cross-border Mergers and Acquisitions and Development*. New York and Geneva: United Nations.

Upton, David and Richard Seet. 1995. "Shanghai Volkswagen." Harvard Business School case no. 1-695-080. Boston: Harvard Business School.

U.S-China Automotive Industry Cooperation Project: Final Report. 1989. Ann Arbor: The University of Michigan.

Valdes-Ugalde, Jose Luis. 2002. "NAFTA and Mexico: A Sectoral Analysis," in Edward J. Chambers and Peter H. Smith, *NAFTA in the new millennium*. La Jolla, CA: Denter for U.S.-Mexican Studies, UCSD; Edmonton: University of Alberta Press.

Van Wolferen, Karel G. 1986/7. "The Japan Problem." *Foreign Affairs* 65(2) (Winter).

Veloso, Francisco. 2000. "The Automotive Supply Chain Organization: Global Trends and Perspectives." Cambridge: Massachusetts Institute of Technology. Working Paper.

Vernon, Raymond. 1998. *In the Hurricane's Eye: The Troubled Prospects of Multinational Enterprises*. Cambridge: Harvard University Press.

Vogel, Ezra F. 1989. *One Step Ahead in China: Guangdong Under Reform*. Cambridge: Harvard University Press.

Vogel, Steven K. 1996. *Freer Markets, More Rules: Regulatory Reform in Advanced Industrial Countries*. Ithaca and London: Cornell University Press.

Vogel, Steven K. 2001. "The Crisis of German and Japanese Capitalism: Stalled on the Road to the Liberal Model?" *Comparative Political Studies* 34(10) (December): 1103–1133.

Wade, Robert. 1990. *Governing the Market: Economic Theory and the Role of Government in East Asian Industrialization*. Princeton: Princeton University Press.

Walder, Andrew G. 1994. "Corporate Organization and Local Government Property Rights in China," in Vedat Milor (ed.), *Changing Political Economies: Privatization in Post-Communist and Reforming Communist States*. Boulder: Lynne Reinner.

Walder, Andrew G. 1986. *Communist Neo-Traditionalism: Work and Authority in Chinese Industry*. Berkeley: University of California Press.

Walder, Andrew G. 1995. "Local Governments as Industrial Firms: An Organizational Analysis of China's Transitional Economy." *American Journal of Sociology* 101(2): 263–301.

Wang, Hong and Wang Shu Ye. 1999. "Guoyou qiye gaige de ji liangyao: heli liyong waizi shishi gaizao" [The right medicine for restructuring SOEs: rational utilization of foreign investment]. *Shuiwu yu Jingji* [Taxation and Economy], no. 1 (January 15).

Wang, Shaoguang and Angang Hu. 2001. *The Chinese Economy in Crisis: State Capacity and Tax Reform*. Armonk, NY: M.E. Sharpe.

Wang, Yong. 2000. "China's Domestic WTO Debate." *The China Business Review*, (January–February).

Wedeman, Andrew. 1999. "Agency and Fiscal Dependence in Central-Provincial Relations in China." *Journal of Contemporary China* 8(20): 103–122.

Wedeman, Andrew. 2003. *From Mao to Market: Local Protectionism, Rent-Seeking, and the Marketization of China, 1984–1992*. New York: Cambridge University Press.

Wei, Xiu Jian. 1999. "Woguo liyong waizi zhong de wenti yu duice" [Problems and solution in utilizing foreign investment]. *Lilun yu Shijian* [Theory and Practice], (June 25).

Weber, Max. 1968. *Economy and Society*. Guenter Roth and Claus Wittich (eds.). New York: Bedminster Press.

Weil, Martin. 1986. "Overhauling the Automotive Industry." *The China Business Review* (July/August): 28–33.

Williamson, Oliver E. 1975. *Markets and Hierarchies*. New York: Free Press.

Williamson, Oliver E. 1981. "The Modern Corporation." *Journal of Economic Literature* 19 (December): 1537–1568.

Williamson, Oliver E. 1985. *The Economic Institutions of Capitalism*. New York: Free Press.

Williamson, Oliver E. 2000. "The New Institutional Economics: Taking Stock, Looking Ahead." *Journal of Economic Literature* 28 (September): 595–613.

Willis, Eliza, Christopher Garman and Stephen Haggard. 1999. "Decentralization in Latin America." *Latin American Research Review* 34 (1): 7–56.

White, Lynn T. 1989. *Shanghai Shanghaied? Uneven Taxes in Reform China*. Hong Kong: University of Hong Kong.

White, Lynn T. 1998a. *Unstately Power Volume I: Local Causes of China's Economic Reforms.* Armonk: M.E. Sharpe.

White, Lynn T. 1998b. *Unstately Power Volume II: Local Causes of China's Intellectual, Legal and Governmental Relations.* Armonk: M.E. Sharpe.

Whiting, Susan H. 2001. *Power and Wealth in Rural China.* Cambridge: Cambridge University Press.

Who's Who in China: Current Leaders. 1994 (revised edition). Beijing: Foreign Language Press.

Wolf, Charles Jr., and K. C. Yeh, Benjamin Zycher, Nicholas Eberstadt, Sung-Ho Lee. 2003. *Fault Lines in China's Economic Terrain.* Santa Monica: Rand.

Womack, James P., Daniel T. Jones, and Daniel Roos. 1990. *The Machine That Changed the World.* New York: HarperPerennial.

Wong, Christine P. W. 1987. "Between Plan and Market: The Role of the Local Sector in Post-Mao China." *Journal of Comparative Economics* 11(3) (September): 385–398.

Wong, Christine P. W. 1992. "Fiscal Reform and Local Industrialization: The Problematic Sequencing of Refrom in Post-Mao China." *Modern China* 14: 3–30.

Woo-Cumings, Meredith (ed.). 1999. *The Developmental State.* Ithaca: Cornell University Press.

World Bank. 1993. *The East Asian Miracle: Economic Growth and Public Policy.* Oxford: Oxford University Press.

World Bank. 1997. *China's Management of Enterprise Assets: The State as Shareholder.* Washington: World Bank.

World Bank. 2004. *Global Development Finance: Harnessing Cyclical Gains for Development.* Washington: World Bank.

Xu, Tie Quan. 1993. "Gufenzhi qiye jituan de zujian yu gaizao" [Formation and transformation of shareholder enterprise groups]. *Jingji Zong Heng* [Economic Review] 4: 25–27.

Yamazawa, Ippei and Ken-ichi Imai. 2001. *China Enter the WTO: Pursuing Symbiosis with the Global Economy.* Tokyo: Institute of Developing Economies.

Yang, Xiaohua. 1995. *Globalization of the Automobile Industry.* Westport: Praeger.

Yeung, Y. M. and Yun-Wing Sung (eds.). 1996. *Shanghai: Transformation and Modernization under China's Open Policy.* Hong Kong: The Chinese University Press.

Yi, Xiqun. 1996. "Beijing fazhan kaifangxing jingji de zhanlue sikao" [Strategy of economic development and opening in Beijing]. *Zhanlue yu Guanli* [Strategy and Management] 3: 117–120.

Yusuf, Shahid and Weiping Wu. 1997. *The Dynamics of Urban Growth in Three Chinese Cities.* Oxford: Oxford University Press.

Yusuf, Shahid and M. Anjum Altaf, and Kaoru Nabeshima. 2004. *Global Production Networking and Technological Change in East Asia.* Washington: The World Bank.

Zhang, Feng. 1994. "Hanguo, reben, deguo de gongye fazhan zhengce ji shijie jingji jiegou bianhua qushi" [The industrial development policies of Korea, Japan, and Germany and the changing trends of the world economic structure].

Jingji Yanjiu Cankao [Economic Reseach Reference] 148(548) (September 27): 32–40.

Zhang, Le-Yin. 1999. "Chinese Central-Provincial Fiscal Relationships, Budgetary Decline and the Impact of the 1994 Fiscal Reform: An Evaluation," *The China Quarterly* 157 (March 1999).

Zhang, Wei and Robert Taylor 2001. "EU Technology Transfer to China: The Automotive Industry as a Case Study," *Journal of the Asia-Pacific Economy*, 6(2): 261–274.

Zhang, Xiaoji and Zhao Jinping, Long Guoqiang, Zhang Qi, Hu Jiangyun, Zhang Liping, and Xu Hongqiang. 2005. "China in the Global Economy." *China in the Global Economy*. Beijing: China Development Forum.

Zhang, Xiaoyu (ed). 1997a. *Zhongguo Qiche Gongye 1997* [The Chinese Automotive Industry 1997]. Beijing: Beijing Institute of Technology Press.

Zhang, Zhen Yu. 1997b. "Dui 1996–1997 nian Guangdong jingji de jidian kanfa he jianyi" ["Several perspectives on the Guangdong economy in 1996–1997], *Nanfang Jingji [Guangzhou Economy]* 3 (May 25): 7.

Zhongguo Qiche Gongye: 1996 [The Chinese Automotive Industry: 1996]. 1996. Beijing: Beijing Institute of Technology Press.

Zongguo Qiche Jishu Yanjiu Zhongxin [The China Automotive Technology Research Center]. 2000. *2000 Nian Zhongguo Qiche Shichang Zhanlan* [The Year 2000 Chinese Automotive Industry Market Exhibition]. Beijing.

Zweig, David. 2002. *Internationalizing China: Domestic Interests and Global Linkages*. Ithaca: Cornell University Press.

Zysman, John. 1984. *Governments, Markets and Growth: Financial Systems and the Politics of Industrial Change*. Ithaca: Cornell University Press.

Index

Eric Thun is the Peter Moores University Lecturer in Chinese Business Studies at the Saïd Business School and a Fellow of Brasenose College at Oxford University. He formerly served as Assistant Professor of Politics and International Affairs at Princeton University's Woodrow Wilson School. Dr. Thun has held grants from the International Motor Vehicle Program, the Social Science Research Council, and the Mellon Foundation. He holds a Ph.D. from Harvard University and was a post-doctoral Fellow at the M.I.T. Industrial Performance Center.

JACKET DESIGN BY JAMES F. BRISSON

Printed in the United States of America